I Believe in The Church

By the same author:

TOWARDS TOMORROW'S CHURCH

MY GOD IS REAL

GOD'S FREEDOM FIGHTERS

ONE IN THE SPIRIT

IN SEARCH OF GOD

LIVE A NEW LIFE

I BELIEVE IN EVANGELISM

I Believe in The Church

by

DAVID WATSON

HODDER AND STOUGHTON
LONDON SYDNEY AUCKLAND TORONTO

Acknowledgments

THIS HAS BEEN the most difficult book I have yet written! To
begin with, where do you start or stop on a subject as vast as
'the church'? The more I have worked on the revisions of the
original manuscript the more clearly I have seen glaring
omissions, scanty references to huge themes, and much
personal ignorance on some of the crucial issues of the day.
My own sense of inadequacy for the task has grown continually. Yet I have felt from the start a strong burden to share
with others what we humbly believe God is teaching us in
York – however slow and failing we are as his children.

Added to that, the constant pressure of attempting to lead
a sizeable church in York, and to be available for the missions
of the church on a wider scale for three months each year, has
caused the writing of this book to be in fits and starts. 'When
do you find time to write?' I'm often asked. The unsatisfac-
tory answer is half a day here; then two or three weeks later
half a day there; and so the book has limped along.

For this reason, I owe a special debt of gratitude to more
helpers than usual – which perhaps is no bad thing when
talking about the church enriched by the variety of gifts of its
members!

I cannot sufficiently express my thanks to Canon Michael
Green for his constant encouragement alongside his illumin-
ating suggestions; and also to Professor G.W.H. Lampe for his
frank and detailed criticisms of the first manuscript. Both
spurred me into more extensive revisions than I had antici-
pated! To Thomas Dye I owe reference to early church
documents which illustrated the stages of development of the

church's ministry. I am most grateful also to Edward England, of Hodder and Stoughton, whose steady enthusiasm I have constantly valued.

To Judy Frampton and Bridget Coates I owe the painstaking work of typing and re-typing. To David and Jan Ord I am deeply grateful for their advice and work during the final revisions of the book. And to several others, especially various members of my own church, I wish to express my thanks for their comments on a variety of themes, and for their persistent and loving prayer throughout.

Editor's Preface

A DISTINGUISHED AUTHOR recently said to me, 'It seems to me that in the last century such leadership in thought as was to be found in the Church derived from Anglo-Catholic sources. Today the fresh thinking is coming from the Evangelicals.' There is, I suppose, some truth in this observation. For a very long time it has been a justifiable criticism of Evangelicals that they were very interested in the gospel of Jesus, but very disinterested in the church Jesus left behind. Church architecture, music, art, was largely neglected by them. Church ministry and sacraments were on the whole lightly esteemed by them. Church organisation, its synods and committees were largely eschewed by them. Nowadays, it is very different. By far the largest proportion of ordinands come from Evangelical sources: writings on the sacraments have been more adventurous and imaginative in Evangelical publications than in any other during the past twenty-five years. New forms of worship, new experiments in communal living, new structures of lay ministry, new understandings of the nature of the church have been flowering in Evangelical circles. And nowhere more than in York, where David Watson exercises a ministry which spreads far wider than the city and neighbourhood. He is well known as a missioner and preacher. What may well prove to be a far more significant contribution to Christianity in the twentieth century is the fact that he has rediscovered the dying art of church building: not in bricks and mortar, but in lives. He has seen a remarkable work grow under his hand during the past twelve years or so. It is a church where the leadership is shared, where prayer is central, where the sacraments are dynamic, where art and drama and dance adorn the worship. A church where the gifts of the Spirit mingle with His graces of character – and also, no doubt, with many failures! But it is a church which does not depend on its minister. Indeed, it tends to grow when he is away. It is a church which has learnt the pastoral value of the small group, the renewing power of the Holy Spirit, the mutual caring of members for one another. Bishops from many parts of the world go to see something of this church when they are visiting York, and what they find surprises them. For it is not a church based on personality cult or middle-class culture, or a succession of bright ideas. It seeks to go back to the New Testament. And herein lies the paradox both of the church in York and of this book. Both are in one sense very radical, full of fresh ideas, arresting, vital. But both are in another sense very ordinary. There is nothing new here. Merely the rediscovery of biblical precedents and principles which are often enough forgotten. And so in one sense as you read this book, and reflect on the biblical pictures of the bride, the army, the building and so forth, you will rightly be able to say 'We have heard all this before'. In another sense you will be staggered at the revolutionary impact of a Christianity which is radical enough to get back to the New Testament, and courageous enough to apply it in practice.

This is not a major theological treatise: its author is not an academic theologian, and in any case, most theological libraries positively groan with the weight of heavy tomes on the nature of the church. But it is that much rarer contribution to the Christian reading public: a thoughtful, intelligent and above all 'earthed' presentation of what, according to the Bible, God intends his church to be like. 'Earthed' is an inadequate word. The reader will find this book more like a bridge than an earth wire. For one end is firmly rooted in faith in the presence and vitality of God's Holy Spirit in the midst of his people, while the other end is rooted in the practical and effective expression of these principles at ground level. It is a book that could point the way to renewal for many a church that has lost confidence and even credibility, and its irenic and penitent tone in handling long-standing differences between Rome and other communions will astonish the hard-liners, and breathe hope into many hearts.

Michael Green
Oxford 1977

Contents

Page

PART I: A LOOK AT THE CHURCH

1   Who Believes in the Church?   13
2   The Last Two Thousand Years   20
3   'I Will Build My Church'   39

PART II: THE NATURE OF THE CHURCH

4   The Kingdom of God   51
5   The Church of God   64
6   The People of God   75
7   The Body of Christ   96
8   The Building of God   115
9   The Bride of God   129
10 The Army of God   140
11 The Spirit in the Church   165

PART III: THE LIFE OF THE CHURCH

12 Worship   179
13 Preaching   199
14 Sacraments   225
15 Ministry and Leadership I   245
16 Ministry and Leadership II   269
17 The Mission of the Church   298
18 The Unity of the Church   331
19 The Mark of the Church   356

To the members of St. Michael-le-Belfrey, York,
whose love, support, encouragement, patience and
forgiveness have made both the title and content
of this book true for me.

PART I

A LOOK AT THE CHURCH

CHAPTER ONE

Who Believes in the Church?

'JESUS — YES! CHURCH — NO!' So read a placard carried by a student. In this spiritually hungry age, the interest in the person of Jesus is unmistakable, as evidenced by Jesus Festivals, Jesus Movements, musicals such as *Godspell* and *Jesus Christ Superstar*, films such as Zeffirelli's *Jesus of Nazareth*, not to mention a spate of Christian books that have flooded the market. At the same time the popular image of the church is that of empty and decaying buildings, aged and female congregations, and depressed and irrelevant clergy. Thus the growing enthusiasm for Jesus seems tragically offset by the almost total disenchantment with the church.

'Nothing in the contemporary scene is more striking than the general regard which is felt for Jesus Christ and the general dislike of the organised church which bears his name.'[1] And in the words of Soren Kierkegaard, 'Whereas Christ turned water into wine, the church has succeeded in doing something more difficult; it has turned wine into water.'

Today there is no shortage of critics who take delight in caricaturing and knocking the church. Television and radio have firmly established the image of the ecclesiastical eccentric, of insipid little men surviving in a fantasy world of their own, the quaint relics of some bygone age, answering incomprehensibly the questions that no one is asking.

The 'God-slot' on Sunday's viewing, if it still exists at all on some television channels, has largely capitulated to academic

[1] S.C. Neill, *Christian Faith Today*, Penguin Books, 1955.

theologians who all too often appear to be undermining the crumbling foundations of the faith of ordinary folk. Today, apparently, we cannot believe in anything, or at least be sure of anything, concerning the existence of God or the divinity of Jesus — for instance *The Myth of God Incarnate*,[2] as seven professional university theologians chose to discuss the person of Jesus, patronisingly describing him as 'one of the most and possibly the most wonderful human being who ever lived'.

The vicar of a well-known abbey, in a nationwide televised service on Easter Day, must have encouraged the atheist (in his own daring position of faith) when he said in his sermon: 'God was, but not is. Today God does nothing, God says nothing, God means nothing.' We can understand why Goethe, a self-confessed agnostic, once urged a preacher: 'Tell me of your certainties. I've enough doubts of my own.'

It is for reasons such as these that no one bothers to attack the churches or the clergy of today; they seem to be destroying themselves very effectively on their own. In the eyes of many, the church has lost any credibility worth having.

'Not many years ago, a plausible case could still be made for the survival of the Christian churches,' wrote Bill McSweeney of the University of York in *The Times*.[3] 'But things have got worse... Who wants to belong to a church that has nothing to offer but a secular version of the gospels, that has lost its nerve to evangelise and takes refuge in the smug alleluias of pentecostalism?'

It is the irrelevance of so much of the church that troubles those who are genuinely looking for something solid to believe in. How effectively is the church beginning to communicate with the man in the street, especially in the industrial areas? A Christian may not be able to change his middle-class background and common education, for these are facts of the past; but when the church seems to identify middle-class values and western culture with the radical teaching of Jesus concerning the kingdom of God, it is scarcely surprising that

[2] Edited by John Hick,   [3] April 16, 1977.
S.C.M. Press.

those from a very different culture remain totally unimpressed.

In an article entitled *Why the Church is remote*,[4] T.E. Utley expressed the view that 'when the Archbishop of Canterbury proposed that the people, faithful and unfaithful alike, should get together of an evening in little groups to discuss with each other what kind of society they wanted and what sort of people they must become in order to get it, he was displaying not spiritual other-worldliness but the other-worldliness of the intelligentsia. Nobody but a professional intellectual could suppose that so academic and pretentious a pursuit would have any appeal for a working man, that it could indeed have any function in English life other than as a pretext for some congenial, middle-class social occasion.' In fairness, this section of society needs the love and forgiveness of Jesus as much as any other; but it is not the whole story, and certainly does not bridge the increasing gap between the church and the world in the eyes of the majority of the public.

Malcolm Muggeridge, an outspoken critic of the established church, particularly on this matter of relevance, once put it in his own characteristic style:

In an average English village today Anglican worship has become little more than a dying bourgeois cult. A small cluster of motor-cars may be seen outside the parish church when a service is in progress; the bells still ring joyously across the fields and meadows on Sunday mornings and evenings, but fewer and fewer heed them, and those few predominantly middle-class, female and elderly... It must be desperately disheartening, and the incumbent often gives the impression of being dispirited and forlorn. Whatever zeal he may have had as an ordinand soon gets dissipated in an atmosphere of domestic care and indifference on the part of his flock. Small wonder, then, that in the pulpit he has little to say except to repeat the old traditional clerical banalities, as invariable as jokes in *Punch*; sometimes, in deference to the 20th century, lacing the sad brew with references to the United Nations, *apartheid* and the birth pill. He doubtless feels himself to be

[4] *Daily Telegraph*

redundant. The villagers stoically die without his minis-
trations; they would resent any interruption of their evening telly if he ventured to make a call, and have for
long accustomed themselves to cope without benefit
of clergy with minor misfortunes like pregnancy and
delinquency. In the large cities the situation is not dissimilar.[5]

Criticisms and quotes such as these could be multiplied *ad
nauseam.* It is for this reason that the church of today is faced
with an identity crisis. What is its place and role in modern
society, rural or industrial? In May 1977, the Church of
Scotland, to take just one example, debated in their General
Assembly the dual crisis of declining congregations and
shortage of funds. More than 1,500 people were leaving the
church *each month.* Offerings averaged a pitiful 35p a week for
each member. Other denominations, in Western Europe at
least, have similar tales of woe.

Why is the church in such a parlous state? Why could
William Temple speak, even in his day, of 'the vast chaos
which for us represents the church, with its hateful cleavages,
its slow-moving machinery, its pedantic antiquarianism...its
indifference to much that is fundamental, its age-long ineffectiveness, its abundant capacity for taking the wrong side in
moral issues...'? It is not only that the wheat and tares must
grow together until the harvest; the church is at best only
a fellowship of sinners who have humbly acknowledged
their need of a Saviour. The church is Christ's hospital;
and if we go to a hospital which claims to heal sick people,
and find it full of sick people, we do not conclude that
it is a useless hospital; it is simply in touch with the right
people.

When I moved to York in 1965 I went to one of twelve
potentially redundant churches in the city. The congregation
had been reduced to a loyal but tiny handful, the total
offerings averaged £2 a Sunday, and the outlook was bleak.
On my first official day in the parish I had to escort the
Redundant Churches Uses Committee round the building as
they were considering alternative uses of the property

[5]Article in the *Weekend Telegraph.*

when it was finally closed down as a place of worship. We had been given one year's grace.

The Chairman of the Committee took me on one side. 'Do you honestly think that this church has any future?' he asked.

I replied in what may have seemed a pious comment by a young and still enthusiastic clergyman: 'I believe that if anyone really preaches the simple gospel of Christ, trusts in the power of prayer, and opens his life to the renewal of the Spirit, this church will be full in no time!'

By the grace of God those words became true. However, at the time the Chairman's questions posed for me a much more fundamental question that many are asking today: Has the church as a *whole* any future? Who can believe in the church today? Can these dry bones live again?

Some would see the answer to these criticisms in a fresh call to evangelism. In England we have already seen a Call to the North, and there have been long discussions concerning a mission to the nation. Certainly there is a need for fresh zeal and energy in personal evangelism, local church missions, town and city crusades, diocesan and united church campaigns. Since about one third of each year for me is spent in leading such evangelistic enterprises, I have no doubt as to the urgent imperative to obey the Great Commission of Christ in reaching those outside the church with the gospel of Christ. For many years now, I have felt this to be God's primary calling as far as my own ministry is concerned.

Others would see more clearly the urgent need for the church to become much more involved in the social and political issues that face us today, and to give a strong lead over questions about abortion, divorce, euthanasia, women's rights, prison reform, mental health, and justice for immigrant and minority groups. Certainly all these, and many more, are areas of increasing concern, and the church should be in the forefront when it comes to justice and righteousness within the very structures of our society, as it has often been in the past. God forbid that we should retreat into religious ghettoes, piously content with hymn-singing and prayer-meetings to comfort our own Christian hearts.

However, I have come to believe that there is one prior necessity which must precede both evangelism and social action, and that is the *renewal of the church*. Both the proclamation and demonstration of the good news of Jesus Christ must be done not just by the individual, but by the church. 'The church that preaches the gospel must embody the gospel'. The good news must be seen in our corporate relationships, worship, joy and life. With the steady erosion of relationships in today's world, the church needs urgently to become a visible community marked by love, God's new society in Christ. Unless renewal precedes evangelism, the credibility gap between what the church *preaches* and what the church *is*, will be too wide to be bridged. It is only when the world sees the living body of Christ on earth that it will be in any way convinced of the reality and relevance of Christ himself. Dr. Ramsey once made this shrewd comment:

> When therefore we say that we believe in the church, we do so only and always in terms of our belief in the God who judges and raises up. The mistake of ecclesiasticism through the ages has been to believe in the Church as a kind of thing-in-itself. The apostles never regarded the Church as a thing-in-itself. Their faith was in God, who had raised Jesus from the dead, and they knew the power of his resurrection to be at work in them and their fellow-believers despite the unworthiness of them all.[6]

How, then, can renewal come to the church today? Although ultimately the answer lies with the Spirit of God, who alone can bring new life to his people, the first step is to try to understand the nature of the church as God intended it to be, as it was in the days of the early church, and as it has been at various times when God has brought fresh spiritual life into the dry bones of the institutional structures. Further, since many of our ideas about the church have been deeply embedded into our thought-patterns since birth (if raised in church-going families), it is no easy task trying to think again, perhaps with new and fresh understanding, some of the most basic principles concerning the church.

It is for this reason that I have devoted Chapters 4 to 11 to

[6]A.M. Ramsey and Leon-Joseph Suenens, *The Future of the Christian Church*, S.C.M., 1971.

a study of the biblical phrases and metaphors for the church, which may help us to look carefully again at the nature of the society that Christ came to build. I have deliberately left the technical discussion of the mission and ministry of the church until Part II — not that these issues are less important, but they need to come from a clear and maybe fresh understanding of the biblical foundations of the church.

Moreover, since the renewal of the church *must* begin with the local church, and not with an ever-increasing proliferation of para-church structures, I have concentrated primarily on those issues that affect the church where it will most of all be seen and experienced, at the local level. If there is a failure here, there can be no significant renewal at all. In some respects, therefore, this book will be more conspicuous by what it does *not* say than by what it does. If you are looking for the detailed historical dimensions of the church over 2,000 years, you will be disappointed. If you want a wide canvas of what the church is doing today in different parts of the world, you will find here little information. If you hope to find an academic critique on the question of Papacy, on the creeds and formularies of the church, on contemporary fashions in theology, you will have to look elsewhere. If you need original proposals concerning the church's role in racial conflicts, or the church's attitudes towards liberation armies, the balance of nuclear powers, the political issues in capitalist and communist societies, you will have to turn to other sources. The theme of the church is so vast that any writer must be selective, depending on his own understanding, experience and aim. If in any measure this book helps ministers and leaders of local churches in particular towards renewal, then its primary purpose will not have been in vain.

My intention is therefore to look at the church as it was designed to be, and as it can become when we have a living faith, not in the church, but in God — Father, Son and Holy Spirit.

CHAPTER TWO

The Last Two Thousand Years

THE MAIN THRUST of this book may give the impression that the church was very much alive and doing remarkably well in the first century, but that now in the twentieth it is battling to survive. In between are the misty and murky centuries best forgotten, due to the distortions and corruptions of the simple revolutionary teaching of Jesus of Nazareth.

The aim of this chapter is to glimpse at two millennia of church history! This will I fear be depressingly superficial for any true historian, but it may reveal the constant ebb and flow of spiritual life within the church all down the years. When the tide has seemed at its furthest distance, it has always found the capacity under God for turning and coming back again, sometimes with staggering strength. No situation is beyond hope, no decadence has been incapable of renewal. Those who have recently declared that God is dead, that the church is redundant or that the spiritual darkness of this gloomy age may now finally engulf us, must know little of the God of history, the God who raised Jesus back to life, and the God who is able to work through human suffering and sin to reveal his reality to the world. Indeed many of the present tensions and divisions within the church might well have been avoided had our knowledge of church history been greater.

Nevertheless, Christians down the centuries have not always inspired confidence or convinced the observer of the reality of their God.

Something of a caricature of the church has recently been given in the fascinating television series and handsome volume by Bamber Gascoigne, *The Christians*.[1] Not that I am accusing Bamber Gascoigne or others like him of error and inaccuracy. I am sure that he — and they — have been most painstaking in their research. However he found the messages of the Bible 'so varied and self-contradictory' that he was

> able to recognise the sources of all the different Christiani-
> ties which twenty centuries have produced. Christ the
> King for the imperial churches; suffering for the Middle
> Ages; quietness and humility for those who find that path
> to God; a note of radical protest for the revolutionaries; the
> Apocalypse for the apocalyptic. In recent years, when the
> western world has made almost an alternative religion of
> personal relationships, we have emphasised...that the
> message of the gospels is Love. If our countries move
> gradually into a Socialist form of society, we shall hear
> rather more...that the central theme of Christianity is
> sharing. This is not a cynical point, nor would such a
> development be cynicism on the part of Christians. To be
> able to adapt is strength in a religion as much as in a
> species. It is something which two thousand years of
> Christianity have amply proved.[2]

So much is fair. Nevertheless Gascoigne was perhaps a little too preoccupied with the eccentricities and inconsistencies of the church down the centuries, and there is another side of the coin to be seen. The Christianity of today is far from dying or dead. Approximately one thousand million, or one-third of the world's population, profess to follow Jesus Christ — more than double any other of the great religions. Some of the statistics, from the best known available sources, would surprise many an unbeliever.

In 1900 $7\frac{1}{2}$ per cent of the population of Africa were Christians; today the percentage is 33 per cent, expected to rise to 50 percent by AD 2000. In Latin America the current growth of population is 3 per cent; yet amongst evangelical Christians alone the growth rate in recent years has been 10 per cent. There are some 70 million Christians in Asia. In Indonesia, there have been over 50,000 baptisms in five years.

[1] Jonathan Cape, London, 1977.   [2] Op. cit., p. 291.

Far from Christianity being the last-ditch stand of middle-class culture in the west, in the last few years more than 200 missionary societies have been founded in the Third World, with 3,000 missionaries sent out.

While there is no room for complacency, the Christian church is far from a relic of the past. This is even more significant in view of the numerous attacks down the years, varying from the vicious persecutions of the first century to the present day, to the scathing intellectual assaults at the various 'ages of reason' which have shaken but never destroyed the faith of Christ's people. The church has therefore continued to expand, and seemingly no power on earth has been able to prevent this.

Reasons for growth

The capacity for constant reform and renewal has been one of the remarkable features of the Christian church since its conception on that Day of Pentecost. Although the spiritual blackness of certain times has threatened to extinguish the light of Christ, John's words have continued to remain true: 'The light shines in the darkness, and the darkness has not overcome it.'[3] There are few clearer evidences of the reality of the risen Christ and the power of the Holy Spirit at work in the church than this constant ability to bring life out of death and light out of darkness.

Added to this, the missionary zeal of the church, although waxing and waning at various seasons, has never vanished. Fresh evangelistic thrusts and social concerns have not only re-emerged as surely as spring has followed winter, but these have often been most marked under times of extreme pressure and persecution. The blood of martyrs has repeatedly been the seed of the church, and the attacks and corruptions have sooner or later led to a purifying of the faith and a return to the New Testament message. Every significant renewal by the Spirit of God has brought back to the church something lost since the days of the early church. Yet these renewals have often been preceded by times of particular crisis, causing an urgent return to the essentials of the faith or to some particular aspects which have long been neglected.

[3] John 1:5

Laying the foundations

Clearly the New Testament church became the basis for all future developments. From 'the foundation of the apostles and prophets, Christ Jesus himself being the chief corner-stone', everything else emerged. For the Roman Catholic and Eastern Orthodox communities, questions concerning catholicity, authority and priesthood became foremost in their minds. For Protestant churches, the matter of biblical authority was the all-important issue. Nevertheless, all look back to the first century for the basis of belief and pattern of growth.

Unquestionably one of the great appeals of the early church was the simplicity of life-style marked by the disciples. They were known for their love, even towards those who bitterly persecuted them. They were characterised by their infectious joy and praise. They displayed peace in the midst of untold pressures. They never ceased to show generosity towards the poor and afflicted. They exhibited a high moral standard which gave integrity to their message. They were loyal citizens, apart from refusing to call Caesar Lord. Of course there were blots and blemishes. But in general the simple and moral beauty of this new society, so utterly different to the pagan standards of the Roman world around them, earned them the title of 'the third race'.

In Christ all the barriers were down: Jew and Gentile, slave and free, male and female — all were one in God's family. The appeal of this to the numerous lonely and outcast, orphans and widows, racial and other minority groups, is obvious. Theirs was a fellowship marked by love, worship, prayer, study of the Scriptures, teaching of the apostles, preaching of Christ, and sacrificial service for the benefit of others. The practical outworking of *agape* — a quality of love unknown to the ancient world — was the most tangible proof that God was surely among them.

With the nature of man as it is, such an ideal state was soon to be mixed with impurities. With the 'superior enlightenment' of the Gnostics, the Christological deviations of the Docetists, and the spiritual arrogance of the Montanists, the Christian fathers from the second to the fifth centuries were forced to enshrine the fundamentals of the apostolic faith in the various creeds of the church. At the same time, some definition was necessary concerning which writings were truly apostolic, and in this way the 'canon' of the New Testament was generally accepted in the church by the late fourth century, although certain books have been challenged at various times (Luther called the Epistle of James an *epistle full of straw!*).

As a further attempt to protect the continuity of the church from the days of the apostles, attempts were made to trace some unbroken connection from the first leaders through a line of bishops and priests. This 'apostolic succession' was intended to guarantee the pure transmission of the faith from one generation to the next, and it is for this reason episcopal ordination, coming through the claimed unbroken line from the days of the apostles, is still thought in certain parts of Christendom as indispensable to the future of the church.

The rise and fall of the Roman Empire — and of the church?
To begin with the church went through incredible tribulation. Tacitus once described the horrific persecution of Christians under the Emperor Nero (AD 54-68): 'In their deaths they were made a mockery. They were covered in the skins of wild animals, torn to death by dogs, crucified or set on fire — so that when darkness fell they burned like torches in the night. Nero opened up his own gardens for this spectacle and gave a show in the arena.' Later emperors, such as Domitian, Trajan, Pliny, Marcus Aurelius, Decius and Diocletian followed suit, with varying degrees of ferocity. Since this continued up to AD 305, it is something of a miracle that the Christian church survived at all.

The turning point came in 312 when the Emperor Constantine was converted to Christ; and although he died in 337, by 395 Christianity had become the only official state religion. From the tiniest beginnings in the upper room when the Holy Spirit fell on the 120 disciples, on through one of the bloodiest periods in the history of the church, the mighty Roman Empire had now fallen to the Christian faith.

Paradoxically it was a mixed blessing. Certainly the heat of persecution was off, but with it the evangelistic fires died down. It is a sobering fact that the rapid expansion of the church during those first three centuries, in spite of the appalling suffering, has never been equalled. Moreover with the comforts of an accepted faith the corruptions began to develop. Although the fourth century still produced a few shining lights, such as Ambrose (339-97) and Augustine (354-430), east and west began to split, the hierarchical structure of bishops and priests intensified, the split between clergy and laity widened, the emphasis on formal liturgical worship grew, and the presence and power of the Spirit steadily decreased.

So did the power of the Roman Empire. Eaten from within by moral decay and invaded from without by the marauding barbarians, the glories of the Empire disappeared over the next few centuries. In place of the political power of the state, the institutional church based on Rome grew in financial wealth and structural strength, and became the dominant force of the Middle Ages. The eastern churches gathered under the leadership of the Patriarch of Constantinople. North Africa was lost to Islam, and the fiery spread of the Muslim faith was checked only in France in 732.

By this time two centres had been firmly established for the Christian church — Rome under the leadership of the Pope, and Constantinople under the guidance of the Patriarch. Soon the powerful emperors of the east increasingly controlled both church and state. However, successive Popes in Rome grew immeasurably in both religious and political power, although five centuries of struggle with princes and rulers meant the virtual spiritual stagnation of the church during this period. The true vitality of the Christian faith inevitably suffered, and by the tenth century the corruption of the Papacy reached an all-time low. Pope John XII (955-64), for instance, came into office at the age of eighteen, was later deposed for numerous sordid crimes, and in his place a layman was chosen who received all his ecclesiastical orders in one day to become Pope Leo VIII.

Monastic renewal of the church
Benedict of Nursia in the sixth century, sickened by the moral climate of Rome where he was studying, fled to a hermit's life in a cave. He then began to establish a number of small communities, leading eventually to his famous Rule of

Benedict which became the basis for all western monasteries and many other communities ever since.

In 910 the monastery of Cluny was founded in central France in an attempt to revive the Benedictine Rule, although integrating monastic life with the society surrounding it. Further spiritual and moral reforms followed, encouraged by Pope Gregory VII (1077-1088). The Cistercians of the twelfth century, together with the Franciscans and Dominicans of the thirteenth, were foremost in this growth of spiritual renewal and church reform, which also led (as any genuine renewal seems to have done) to fresh missionary zeal. The Franciscans in particular brought about a revival of preaching. Francis of Assisi went to the Muslims. The Eastern Orthodox Church went to the Slavs and on into Russia. This led to the start of the Russian Orthodox Church, which later claimed to be the true successor of Rome and Constantinople.

Lay challenges to the church
With the centuries of clerical domination stifling much of the church's activities new movements of anti-clerical feeling emerged in the twelfth century, the most powerful being the Waldensians and the Albigensians — understandably branded and persecuted as heretics by the institutional church. Of these two main movements, the Waldensians were thoroughly apostolic and orthodox in their beliefs, and challenged the worldliness of the church — a challenge which was so hotly opposed that they were obliged to flee to the Alps for refuge, where they have largely remained to this day.

However the challenge had been noted by many spiritually-minded Christians who were increasingly disenchanted by the temporal power and riches of the instituional church. This led to a search for true spirituality in both monasticism and mysticism, and later to much creative and formative theological thinking as seen by Peter Abelard (1079-1142) and Thomas Aquinas (1224-1274).

Unfortunately this was comparatively short-lived. The fourteenth and fifteenth centuries saw a decline in spiritual life and missionary concern, which led in turn to barren scholasticism, endless internal strifes (mostly over the question of authority), and a diversion from the true goal of the church to the artistic pursuits of the early Renaissance.

The Reformation

Such turmoil and unrest within the ranks of the church, coupled with the unscrupulous means of raising funds for the rebuilding of St. Peter's in Rome, gave all the seeds needed for reform. In 1517, when the citizens of Wittenberg travelled to the nearby town of Jüterbog to hear the devious preaching of Johann Tetzel, it was time for action. Tetzel was skilfully selling indulgences (the profits for St. Peter's, of course) by offering instant relief for the souls of the dead. In his famous jingle:

> As soon as the coin in the coffer rings,
> The soul from Purgatory springs.

At the same time, the local prince of Wittenberg, Frederick the Wise, offered a glimpse of his many thousands of holy relics (on payment of the required sums of money) in order to escape two million years in purgatory. The combination of these unholy practices forced the leading theologian of Wittenberg University to make his famous protest on the eve of All Saints' Day. Martin Luther nailed his ninety-five theses to the door of the castle church, but certainly Luther himself could have had no idea of the eventual consequences of this action. Mainly due to the invention of printing some sixty years before, his protest spread like a forest fire throughout Europe, and led to the greatest rupture of the Christian church which has, more often than not, been bitterly pursued ever since.

This break from Rome, although probably inevitable due to the corruption of the time, unfortunately led to split after split within the body of Christ, with the result that the mission of the church is today seriously handicapped by the bewildering plethora of endless denominations. Some of these divisions may have speeded up the spread of the gospel throughout the world, but a torn and divided Christianity is nevertheless a scandal for which all Christians need deeply to repent.

Luther and John Calvin (1509-1564) were the main architects of the Protestant Reformation, and these gave rise respectively to the worldwide Lutheran Church, and to the Presbyterian and Reformed Churches, as well as to the

Puritans in England. It was not only a traumatic time in the history of the church; there was also much violence.

The peasant unrest due to intolerable feudal conditions was somehow linked with the protest of Luther, who to begin with was tolerant of their demands. But as the violence grew, he hastily penned a tract *Against the Murderous and Thieving Hordes of Peasants*, in which he wrote: 'Let everyone who can, smite, slay and stab, remembering that nothing can be more devilish than a rebel. It is just as when one must kill a mad dog.' Luther believed all rebellion to be essentially evil and deserving punishment. Perhaps partly as a result of his tract the aristocratic reprisal, when the peasants had been defeated, meant the butchering of 100,000 of them. Luther's forceful words were not forgotten nor easily forgiven. The Reformers had much to learn.

In 1536 Geneva welcomed a Reformation refugee from France, John Calvin. Through his massive thinking and application of reformed principles, Geneva aimed at becoming a perfect model of a godly city. Justice certainly ruled, even if mercy was sometimes lacking. Adultery was punishable by death, in accordance with Leviticus 20:10; and on one occasion a young man was beheaded for striking his parents (Exodus 21:15). Worldly pursuits were banned, discipline was strict. John Knox nevertheless described Geneva as 'the most perfect school of Christ that ever was in the earth since the days of the Apostles'.

Not all was perfect, however. Both in the Reformation and Counter-Reformation which followed, intense suffering and numerous martyrdoms became horrifyingly common. The existing violence in Ulster today is, 400 years later, one of the legacies of that monumental break with Rome. On the positive side, the renewal of spiritual life, the reform of the church, and the rediscovery of biblical doctrines were all the benefits of the Reformation — and for that we can thank God. But the price has been staggeringly high in terms of human suffering. Whenever the body of Christ is divided, for whatever reason, the results will always be painful.

Further, many felt that neither Luther nor Calvin had gone far enough. There was a strong desire to go back to the primitive model of the New Testament church in matters other than doctrines of salvation. The Anabaptists in particular rejected any idea of a national or territorial church, and taught the concept of the 'gathered fellowship' of baptised believers only. Protestant Zürich reacted sharply against this independent action of adult baptism outside the organised church. Anyone even attending an Anabaptist ceremony was to be drowned — if they want water they shall have it! Almost unbelievably, proportionately more Anabaptists were martyred for their faith than any other Christian group in history. Many of them found refuge in America, and today the Mennonites of Pennsylvania and Ohio are their direct descendants. In England the seventeenth-century offspring from the same movement were the Baptists, who are now the largest Christian group in the world, apart from Roman Catholics.

The Reformation in England

The Church of England was a direct product of the Reformation. For political and marital reasons, Henry VIII made England's break with Rome in 1532, enabling the biblical reform of the church in England to make rapid progress, while retaining the best of the liturgical worship of the medieval church. A new middle-way (*via media*) between the extremes of Romanism and Puritanism was developed, but despite the attempts by Queen Elizabeth I to prevent any deviation from this, the Puritan movement, although failing to influence the Anglican church in the way it had hoped, grew in strength.

Some years after the comparatively peaceful reign of Elizabeth, the Puritans joined in the revolution (1642-1649) to overthrow the Crown. For a time, a Puritan Republic was established, but with the death of Oliver Cromwell in 1658 the monarchy was soon restored. During these years many Puritans had sailed to America, where their influence can still be strongly felt in the reformed churches in that continent.

Roman Catholic Counter-Reformation

It was not only Luther who was repelled by the Roman church of the early sixteenth century. Several Popes and hundreds of priests were also deeply concerned about the renewal of the decadent church to which they belonged. Although the doctrinal and Protestant split with Rome hardened with the Council of Trent (1542-1563), this Council revitalized much of the ecclesiastical life of the church, re-defined Roman doctrines, and corrected Roman abuses. In particular a spiritual 'commando' unit was formed, the Society of Jesus, or Jesuits, founded by Ignatius of Loyola (1491-1556). These were well trained both to counter the rapidly increasing Protestant threat and to engage in missionary expansion. The Jesuits launched themselves with astonishing zeal into America, Africa and Asia, and many millions were added to the Roman Church.

At the same time the persecuted Protestants, especially the Puritans, Independents, Quakers and Baptists, also fled to America, which resulted in the growth of Protestantism. Later they were joined by Lutherans and other Reformers who were still seeking refuge from the atrocities they experienced in Europe.

The age of revival
One outstanding consequence of the Reformation, which had been in the first instance concerned with the great issues of personal salvation, was the spread of evangelical faith. This was marked by a strong appeal to the authority of the Bible, and by calling men and women to put their faith in Jesus Christ as their Lord and Saviour. For too long Protestantism had lapsed into an ineffective moralism. It was the Pietists in Europe, under the notable leadership of men like Count Ludwig von Zinzendorf (1700-1760), who stressed again the need for a personal experience of Christ. Zinzendorf also founded the famous Moravian church, whose missionary zeal became second to none. Evangelism returned to the forefront of Protestant life.

The Anglican church in England during the first part of the eighteenth century had become depressingly formal, crippled by the establishment, and sapped by a worldly comfort which was hardly conducive to spiritual health. However, several earnest young clergymen were searching for a quality of life that was much more fitted to the calling of their Master. One of these, John Wesley (1703-1791), even travelled as a missionary to America as a part of his own personal pursuit after holiness. On board ship he met up with some Moravian missionaries, whose radiant faith and joyful praise even in the midst of violent storms shook Wesley to the core. Back in London he recorded, 'I went very unwillingly to a society in Aldersgate Street, where one was reading Luther's preface to the Epistle to the Romans. About a quarter before nine, while he was describing the change which God works in the heart through faith in Christ, I felt my heart strangely warmed. I felt I did trust in Christ, Christ alone, for salvation; and an assurance was given me, that He had taken away my sins, even mine, and saved me from the law of sin and death.'

In the main, Wesley's experience of the new birth and consequent enthusiasm was rejected by the Anglican church, and Wesley was forced to turn to the unevangelised working population of England, often using market places and fields for his preaching of the gospel. Hundreds of thousands turned to Christ. And although many stayed within the Church of England, bringing fresh life into its ranks, others were forced into new denominations such as the Baptists and the Congregationalists, while Wesley himself gathered his young converts into an efficient and methodical class system, each with its own leader. Thus the Methodist Church was born.

A major influence in the spread of this new evangelicalism lay in the immensely popular hymns written by the Wesley brothers, especially Charles. The straightforward and personal preaching for salvation coupled with fervent hymn-singing developed not only through the whole of the British Isles, and to some extent Europe; it also spread rapidly into America, and has become a major force in the Protestant tradition ever since. The Wesleys realised that to sing the great doctrines of the faith in rousing tunes was just as important as to preach them. Fervent singing has always been a mark of spiritual revival.

Although Wesley was perhaps the architect for this revival in England, the prince of preachers was undoubtedly his colleague George Whitefield (1714-1770). Influenced by Howell Harris and the Welsh revival, he developed a more pronounced Calvinistic form of Methodism in contrast to the Arminianism of the Wesleys, and the tension between them on this issue was never healed. Like John Wesley (who averaged 5,000 miles a year on horseback!), Whitefield travelled prodigious distances, moving all over England and

Wales, paying fourteen visits to Scotland and seven to America.

America, meanwhile, had experienced its first Great Awakening under the revivalist influence of Jonathan Edwards (1703-1758). Once again following the decay and deadness of the existing church, the dry timbers caught fire, initially in New England. Then the revival swept up and down the east coast of America bringing hundreds of thousands to Christ, renewing the life of the church, purging the corruptions of society, and developing a new sense of social responsibility.

It also split almost every denomination into those who were for it and those who were against it. It was only the American Revolution of 1776 that, to a large extent, halted the spiritual fire and diverted energies into other directions. Due largely to the influence of the Baptists and other dissenters, the new constitution of the United States, in its Bill of Rights (largely the work of Thomas Jefferson), brought about the separation of church and state — an altogether new concept since the conversion of Constantine fourteen centuries before.

The spirit of revolution was meanwhile growing in France, erupting in 1789. This too led to a sharp and bitter conflict over the connections between church and state. The revolutionaries attempted to banish the church from French life altogether. And while the Catholic hierarchy predictably sided with the monarchy, many of the priests (as often is the case today) joined in with the calls of justice by the revolutionaries. This led to a fierce struggle well into the nineteenth century, resulting in strict laws limiting the powers of the church in France.

The age of reason

The revolutionary turmoils of those times were sparked off, in part, by what was known as the Enlightenment, an intellectual attack on the Christian faith by men such as Voltaire (1694-1778) whose biting satire was aimed at the French aristocratic church, and Thomas Paine (1737-1809). It was an age in which human reason was brought to bear on many aspects of the church's beliefs. But it had the healthy result of fresh theological thinking, a renewed examination of the reality and credibility of Christian claims, and also a further surge of missionary movements throughout the world.

It was yet another example of the way in which the church, under the guidance of the Spirit of God, has been able to survive — and indeed move forward — under attack. The very house in which Voltaire predicted that the Bible would be no more than a museum piece within a hundred years, later became one of the many printing houses for the Bible Societies. Today the worldwide hunger for the Scriptures is greater than it has ever been.

The age of missions

The great revivals of the eighteenth century led to a promulgation of the faith as never before, except (proportionately) during the first century. William Carey founded the Baptist Missionary Society and sailed to India in 1793, where he devoted his life to the translation of the Scriptures into several languages. In 1795 the London Missionary Society was born; in 1797 the Netherlands Missionary Society; and in 1799 the Church Missionary Society (as it was later called) — the largest missionary society of the Church of England. 1804 saw the start of the British and Foreign Bible Society (now amalgamated with others into The Bible Societies); in 1810 several societies were launched from the United States. Thus the Great Commission of Christ was taken seriously by Protestant Christians in many parts of the world.

The Roman Catholic Church in Europe meanwhile was being shaken by the violent revolutions of 1830 and 1848, forcing Pope Pius IX (1846-1878) to react strongly against any threat to the church or papacy. In his *Syllabus of Errors* (1864) he attacked virtually all modern religious movements as heretical, and condemned many political, social and intellectual reforms that had been undermining the structural rock on which Rome was built. Vatican I was called in 1869, during which the much contested doctrine of papal infallibility in matters of faith and doctrine came into being. The result of these new initiatives from Rome led to the widespread revival of the Catholic faith in Europe, and influenced the Tractarian (High Church) movement in England.

The Tractarian Revival, or the Oxford Movement, sought to redress the evangelical emphasis on the Bible by appealing again to the traditions of the catholic, apostolic church and its apostolic ministry. John Keble, John Henry Newman, and Edward Pusey were all notable leaders and strong sacramentalists. They could not accept the validity of ordination of the dissenters, and they were aware of the corruptions of the Church of Rome. Their answer was to press for a true church based on the episcopally ordained Anglican clergy, who were therefore within the all-important apostolic succession. With the growing strength of evangelicals in England the Tractarians tried hard, with Newman's *Tract 90*, to keep their own group within the Anglican communion. But this tract caused such protest that in 1845 Newman himself was received into the Roman Catholic Church. Nevertheless the Tractarians restored a sense of dignity in worship and discipline in prayer and communion, that has been of considerable influence in the Anglican tradition ever since.

Evangelical reformers
While the missionary movements were sending recruits to all corners of the world, several leading evangelicals in England were pressing for urgent social reforms. The activities of William Wilberforce and the Clapham Sect led to the abolition of slavery in the British Empire. Lord Shaftesbury was able to improve the appalling factory conditions for the working classes, and regulate child and female labour. The tracts written by Hannah Moore were read widely at court and by the upper classes, restoring a sensitive conscience concerning the irresponsible frivolities of those times. All this was good. Yet as has so often occurred within the church, when the motivating love of Christ under the inspiration of the Spirit waned, the residue became the hypocritical and repressive Victorian morality, to which there is still a sharp reaction.

It was also a time of spiritual confusion as British and American missionaries supported the imperialist policies of their respective governments, who 'opened up doors' for the gospel into numerous areas. The result was culturally a highly western version of the Christian faith, with imperialist attitudes often influencing missionary work. It was an unfortunate mixture of the church riding in on the crest of worldly principles, causing patterns of church development in other countries which sometimes led to disastrous consequences. Native Christian communities were required to adopt a western style of the Christian faith, creating inevitable tensions with the majority of the unconverted in that land, and often active and bloody persecution. Further, when European missionaries suffered, this often led to European military intervention in the internal affairs of foreign powers. To give only one example, this sparked off the terrible Boxer Rebellion in China in 1900 when many thousands of Christians were slaughtered.

The twentieth century

The nature of this century has been explosive in every way. We are now faced with a population explosion, with approximately 1,000 million in the world in 1850, 2,000 million in 1930, and almost double that figure at this present time. Christian missions are thus challenged by the vast problems of hunger, and also double the number of non-Christians today than there were in 1900.

We have also experienced a knowledge explosion, with the speed of technological and scientific progress almost beyond belief. Parallel with this there have naturally been further intellectual attacks on the Christian faith. Starting from the end of the last century, the clash between Darwinism and Christianity emerged, and grew into a bitter conflict as some of the foundational beliefs in God seemed to be crumbling. The crisis was eased as serious attempts were made to bring the biblical and scientific views closer together.

Then came World War I, which shattered the utopian dreams of the millennialists. Later the superficiality of much of the twenties was crushed by the depression of the early thirties as it eroded its way into the spiritual as well as the economic life of the western world. Biblical criticism questioned the validity of many Christian beliefs, liberal theology stripped away the divine and supernatural elements of the gospel, denominational and ecumenical debates ground slowly on, and evangelism sagged. Extremists in both camps were quickly polarised. The obscurantists and fundamentalists dogmatically dug in their heels against any scientific encroachment by the modernist liberals, and those who preached a 'spiritual gospel' fiercely attacked those who propounded the 'social gospel'. Often these quarrels were marked by much bigotry and ignorance, and they led to a virtual withdrawal of most evangelicals from the social and political scene until the 1960s.

Two major movements

Earlier in the century two movements were born which were to have worldwide significance in a remarkably short space of time. Towards the end of the nineteenth century there had been a renewed belief in certain parts of America in the 'baptism in the Holy Ghost' and in certain spiritual gifts, notably healing. Then in 1906 a revival broke out in Azusa Street, Los Angeles — a revival marked inwardly by this 'baptism in the Spirit' and outwardly by speaking in tongues, taken as the initial evidence of the baptism.

From this the fires of Pentecostalism spread, and it has since become a fourth major strand in Christendom alongside Orthodoxy, Roman Catholicism and Protestantism. During this century it has developed into a powerful movement throughout the world, with enormous influence in Latin America and Africa. In many Latin American countries, Pentecostalism is the largest non-Catholic Christian move-ment. With the present rate of Pentecostal growth, there may well be by AD 2000 more Christians in Latin America and Africa than in the rest of the world put together.

In more recent years this movement has spawned the 'charismatic renewal', which is being increasingly embraced by large numbers of both Roman Catholics and Protestants, and which has been described by more than one church leader as one of the greatest causes for Christ this century. Certainly, as it grows in maturity, as it draws together Christians from widely differing traditions, as it renews and revives many Christians and churches that have been prepar-ing for spiritual burial, it is perhaps the best hope for the church at this present stage of its history.

The second major movement, that has since captured one third of the world this century, is of course communism, which burst into the world with the Russian Revolution in 1917. Its roots lay much further back, with the *Manifesto of the Communist Party* in 1848 by Marx and Engels and *Das Capital* by Marx in 1867; but for many years it seemed little more than political theory discussed between intellectuals, until the time was ripe for revolution. Since then it has not only been the fastest growing movement of modern history, it has produced in Stalin the greatest mass-murderer of all time, and has been the constant scourge and persecutor of the Christian church, not to mention the atrocities committed against Jews and political opponents. The methods of oppression may have changed over the years, from crude physical torture to more sophisticated forms of psychological pressure (although certainly both exist together all too frequently in many countries), but opposition to any vital and organised religion still remains in most communist countries.

Towards tomorrow's church
Once again, we see the remarkable fact of the resilience of the church, sustained by the ever-promised presence of the Spirit of God. Always able under his direction to change and adapt, the church has not only survived, but positively flourished in some communist countries, with a number of astonishing signs of present-day revival springing up through the concrete paths of atheism. It is part of the nature of God and his work in the world that a root is able to rise out of dry ground, and the desert is able to blossom as a rose. In many respects, Christians in Eastern Europe reveal the vigour of New Testament Christianity that the 'free' west has not known for many years.

What seems to be clear is that we are entering into the last quarter of this twentieth century with both a profound consciousness of the utter futility of life without God, and at the same time an altogether new hunger and thirst for spiritual reality. What is equally clear is that the old order of the established and organised church, relying on its structures and traditions instead of the renewing of the Spirit of God, will not do. The formularies and creeds of the church, devoid of evident spiritual life, will never satisfy those who in their own different ways are searching for the living God.

If, however, the church is able to rediscover its identity, as originally given by God in the Scriptures and made alive and relevant by the Spirit of God for every generation, we could

CHAPTER THREE

'I Will Build My Church'

CHRIST CAME TO establish a new society on earth. It was not enough for him to call individual sinners to God. He promised that he would build his church. It would be the most powerful force on earth providing it could be created, inspired and sustained with his life and love. Nothing could stop — or ever has stopped — the revolution of love which he began two thousand years ago.

Someone once commented: 'I am far within the mark when I say that all the armies that ever marched, and all the navies that ever sailed, and all the parliaments that ever sat, and all the kings that ever reigned, *put together* have not affected the life of man upon earth as has that one solitary life.'

It is worth looking first, then, at the longing in the heart of Jesus when he prayed for his disciples shortly before his sufferings and death. In John 17 we have a glorious picture of the purpose of God's church on earth, as Jesus prayed that it should be marked by four main things: the glory of God, the word of God, the joy of God, and united in the love of God.

Revealing the glory of God
This is clearly the main burden of Christ's prayer from the fact that the words 'glory' and 'glorify' come no less than seven times: 'Glorify thy Son that the Son may glorify thee... I am glorified in them.' The chief end of man is to 'glorify God and to enjoy him for ever'. This word 'glory' (*doxa*) means basically the visible manifestation of the splendour and power and radiance of God. It is God revealing himself so that, as far as possible, we can see the beauty and majesty of

his living presence with us. For example, after Solomon's prayer of dedication, the temple was filled with the glory of God;[1] God was manifestly and powerfully in their midst.

In New Testament days, of course, God revealed himself supremely in the person of his Son, when 'the Word became flesh and dwelt among us, full of grace and truth,' wrote John; 'we have beheld his glory, glory as of the only Son from the Father.'[2] Not everyone recognised the glory of God in Jesus, and even those who did were not always sure what to do about it, as happened on the Mount of Transfiguration, when Peter and the others 'saw his glory'.

However, today the glory of God is clearly meant to be seen in the church. Paul wrote about the 'glorious liberty of the children of God',[3] or, literally translated, 'the liberty of glory of the children of God', referring to the freedom that God's children experience when his glory is revealed in our midst. Spiritually speaking, when God comes down, we go up! We are caught up into his presence, and lost in wonder, love and praise. That should certainly be the experience of God's people, at least from time to time. Not everyone will re-cognise it when it happens, and others who do may not always be sure of what to do about it. Established church-men, in particular, may feel uncomfortable with the outward signs of spiritual renewal, let alone revival. Never-theless, it is worth noticing three points about this word 'glory'.

First, in secular Greek the word means 'reputation' or 'opinion'. And it is a sobering truth that God's reputation in the world, or the world's opinion of God, will depend, to a large extent, on how far his glory is seen in the church. Tragically, so often people do not see the reality of the living God in the institutional church, and this fact understandably becomes a major hindrance to personal faith. The psalmist sometimes longed that God should do something new to stop the taunts of the unbelievers who were saying, 'Where is your God?' What evidence is there today of his reality that is clearly seen among his people? That is why Paul prayed that the Ephesian church, according to the riches of God's glory,

[1] 2 Chronicles 7:1-13.   [3] Romans 8:21.
[2] John 1:14.

might be strengthened by God's Spirit and rooted and grounded in God's love: that there might be 'glory in the church' as well as in Christ Jesus.[4] Interestingly, the Jerusalem Bible translation of this prayer is that God might 'give you power through his Spirit for your *hidden* self...' As with Jesus, God's glory is not self-evident for everyone; but it can and will be seen by those who have the eyes to see and who are searching for the truth.

Secondly, the almost shocking and unthinkable message of the incarnation was that the glory of God should be manifested in human form. Many Greek thinkers believed that the human body was intrinsically evil; it was like a filthy prison from which one day we would thankfully escape. Therefore they saw true spirituality in terms of severely disciplining the body (or, the exact opposite, ignoring it altogether), and cultivating the mind and spirit instead. Although there are few within the Christian church who would hold any such dualistic view of life nowadays, western Christianity has been, especially since the Reformation, strongly cerebral and activist. Providing we think the right thoughts, believe the right doctrines, and do the right deeds (evangelism and/or social action), our bodies, emotions and relationships have seemed largely irrelevant. However, God's glory is to be *seen* in the church; and it may be for that reason that the Spirit of God is both bringing Christians together into the living body of Christ where deep relationships with one another, based upon a serious, costly and practical commitment, are of immense importance; and, at the same time, is creating colour and movement in worship once again, with dance, mime, drama, visual arts and spiritual gifts being rediscovered, all of which can communicate very powerfully to what is often called a 'feelings generation'. People today need to feel God's presence and sense his reality before they are able to listen to his words. His words are still very important, and the mind still needs to grasp the wonder of God's salvation. But, in the first instance, communication often best occurs when the glory of God is seen in Christians, as it was in Christ. It is the lives of Christians together, their worship and work together, their

[4]Ephesians 3:14-21.

service and love towards one another that will most clearly reveal the glory of God, providing the Spirit is at work in his power.

Thirdly, 'glory', especially in John's Gospel, has a particular reference to the death of Jesus, leading on to his resurrection and ascension.[5] If, therefore, the glory of God is to be seen in the church, there must likewise be a very real experience of crucifixion and death as far as our self-life is concerned. Only in this way can the risen life of Christ be seen and the glory of God revealed. There are no short cuts! The baptism of Jesus was a wonderful experience, when the heavens were opened, the Spirit poured out, and numerous signs and wonders followed afterwards throughout his powerful ministry. However, there was a straight line from Jordan to Calvary — via the temptations in the desert! And so there will be for every Christian, and for every church, that is concerned about spiritual renewal. If God's glory is once more to be seen in his church, old patterns of living and thinking may have to die. Our whole life-style may have to undergo a radical change. Attitudes, values, prejudices, ambitions — all these, and many more, may have to go through the exceedingly painful process of crucifixion. We shall be thinking much more about this in the rest of this book.

Paul once wrote that 'we have this treasure in earthen vessels, to show that the transcendent power belongs to God and not to us'. To make his meaning perfectly plain, Paul went on to say how they were afflicted, perplexed, persecuted and struck down, 'so that the life of Jesus may be manifested in our bodies.'[6] That is the price of glory in the church.

Guided by the word of God
In John 17 Jesus prayed much about the word of God. 'I have given them thy word... They have kept thy word... Sanctify them in the truth; thy word is truth...' The word for 'keep' (*tereo*) means to keep safe, to watch over, to hold fast, to guard. God's word is a sacred deposit that has been entrusted to the church for safe keeping; and although we are to understand the historical, cultural and religious setting in which that word was first given (in order to relate it accurately for today), we are not to tamper with God's word,

---

[5] For example, John 12:23f, 27f.   [6] 2 Corinthians 4:7-12.

not to alter it, add to it, or subtract from it in any measure. We must be concerned with the truth, the whole truth, and nothing but the truth.

Paul once made the same point emphatically to Timothy, who was called to lead one of the most influential churches of the first century: 'Follow the pattern of the sound words which you have heard from me, in the faith and love which are in Christ Jesus; *guard the truth* that has been entrusted to you by the Holy Spirit who dwells within us.'[7]

Many of the great revivals of the past have begun with deep repentance, great joy, fresh love and spontaneous praise; but have withered away due to the neglect of God's word. The roots have not gone deep enough. Perhaps even worse, the movement, which began with the Spirit, went off on a tangent and later proved disastrous. This was certainly true of the Montanist movement in the second century, which began as a genuine work of God, but which became unscriptural and the leaders further refused to have their teaching tested by the Scriptures. In other words, they did not 'keep God's word', and from that moment onwards the whole thing went sour on them. Christ once had to rebuke his opponents by saying that they did not know the Scriptures nor the power of God. It is the church which bases its life upon obedience to God's word, especially the written word in the Scriptures, that is likely to see the power of God at work, providing that church is also dependent on the power of the Spirit.

However, there is also the need for the church to listen very carefully to God, in whatever way he may speak. When Peter, James and John were in danger of missing the whole significance of what was happening on the Mount of Transfiguration, God spoke directly from heaven, 'This is my Son, my Chosen; *listen to him!*' The church that is alive and relevant for today's generation must always be a prophetic church. We must therefore listen very carefully in order to discern what God is saying to us *today*. It will always be in accordance with the teaching of Scripture, and there is no such thing as new revelation or new doctrine — but the Spirit of God will always be wanting to pin-point certain aspects of the total truth of God's word that are especially relevant for

[7] 2 Timothy 1:13f.

today — and that will almost certainly be different from what was especially relevant for yesterday. It is sadly possible for a church to remain thoroughly orthodox in doctrine and yet entirely without the power of God's prophetic word — a word which should come like a hammer to hit the nail very firmly on the head, or like a sword which cuts through the apathy and disobedience of God's people to expose the hidden thoughts and intentions of the heart. The church that is alive for God will let the word of Christ dwell richly in the minds and hearts of its members, and be alert to what God is saying now.

I realise, of course, that I am adopting a particular theological position concerning the authority of Scripture, and also the validity of at least some prophetic utterances, which many in the church may not share. There is no space in this single volume on the nature, life, ministry, mission and unity of the church to go into the complex questions surrounding the whole matter of revelation as well. However, taking the Gospel records as at least substantially accurate historical documents, it seems clear that Jesus upheld the Scriptures as the supreme authority concerning our beliefs and behaviour as the people of God. He sometimes had to correct the false interpretation of the Scriptures; but time and again he referred back to what God had said through the law and the prophets.

The rationalists of his day, the Sadducees, were rebuked when they looked to reason for their final court of appeal concerning certain doctrines which they found hard to accept, for example the resurrection. 'You are wrong,' said Jesus to them firmly, 'because you know neither the scriptures nor the power of God'; and he went on to remind them of God's own revelation of himself through Abraham, Isaac and Jacob.[8] The traditionalists of his day, the Pharisees, likewise were told that they had 'a fine way of rejecting the commandment of God, in order to keep your tradition!'[9] Again, Jesus brought them back emphatically to the touchstone of Scripture. He also repeatedly claimed equal authority for his own words and teaching, which had been given to him by his Father. Moreover, Paul, Peter and John later

---

[8] Matthew 22:29-33.   [9] Mark 7:1-13.

certainly claimed that what they were writing to the churches had come through the inspiration of the Spirit of God.[10] These claims by themselves do not demand that they were right; but there is a remarkable consistency of doctrine and thought throughout the Scriptures, in spite of the fact that they were compiled by numerous authors from a variety of backgrounds over hundreds of years. These are some of the reasons (albeit in note form, and of necessity ignoring the intricate questions that some would raise) that lie behind my presupposition throughout this book that the Scriptures are the Spirit-inspired word of God.

It is worth noting in the Anglican/Roman Catholic *Agreed Statement on Authority* that the Scriptures are termed 'the inspired documents...accepted by the Church as a normative record of the authentic foundation of the faith. To these the Church has recourse for the inspiration of its life and mission; to these the Church refers its teaching and practice. Through these written words the authority of the Word of God is conveyed.' There is nothing in the Statement which adds to these words anything about the authority of tradition which, in the past, has effectively changed or undermined some of the real authority of the Scriptures. In many sections of the church, not least among Roman Catholics, there has recently been a return to the sufficiency of Holy Scripture for the details of the Christian faith.

Filled with the joy of God
Christ longed that his joy might be 'fulfilled' in his disciples. Often he referred to this: 'These things I have spoken to you, that my joy may be in you and that your joy may be full.'[11] The New Testament church was filled with this remarkable quality of joy, even in the midst of the fiercest trials, and this in itself was a powerful witness of the life of God's Spirit within that church. Paul, writing from prison and awaiting his likely death, wrote constantly about joy in his letter to the Philippian church: 'Rejoice in the Lord always; again I will say, Rejoice.' Peter, writing to a persecuted church, told them

[10]For example, 1 Corinthians 14:37f; Galatians 1:11f; 2 Timothy 3:16; Peter 3:15; Revelation 1:1f; et.al. [11]John 15:11; 16:24.

that, in the midst of considerable suffering, as they believed in Jesus they would 'rejoice with unutterable and exalted joy'.

Richard Wurmbrand, tortured for his faith in Christ, and for fourteen years in communist prisons, said that 'alone in my cell, cold, hungry and in rags, I danced for joy every night... Sometimes I was so filled with joy that I felt I would burst if I did not give it expression.'[12] All down the ages, in every conceivable situation, Christians have known something of that joy which, said Jesus, no man could take from them.

In a world marked by hopelessness, gloom and despair, the radiant joy of Christ in the lives of Spirit-filled Christians is of special significance. After a televised *Songs of Praise* from our church on Easter Sunday we received numerous letters, many of which referred to this fact of joy. One man, who described himself as an 'ex-convict', said that he could not get the service out of his mind. He wrote about the faces of those who were singing. They revealed joy and happiness; they were alive; they obviously believed in what they were singing; it was all so *real*. 'I've been disturbed by it,' he wrote. 'I've thought constantly about you all. Can you tell me more? Can I write to you?' After a short correspondence that man had committed himself clearly to Christ. Earlier today, before I typed these words, I had a long talk with a young man, with no previous contact with the Christian church, who had been deeply impressed by the joy so clearly expressed by a group of Christians singing and dancing praises to God outside our church in York. It was the most striking feature that had got right through to him.

Christians, too, need the constant encouragement that joyful praise can bring. Christ never promised that following him would be easy — just the reverse. In John 17 he told his Father that his disciples would be hated by the world and tempted by the evil one. That was why he wanted them to be filled with his joy so that they might overcome the testings that they would soon experience. A few years later we see Paul and Silas in prison, their backs smarting from a severe beating, singing praises to God at midnight! What a way to encourage one another! And in that particular case it had the most striking consequences.

[12]*In God's Underground*, W.H. Allen, p. 54.

In Isaiah 60 we have a beautiful picture of the restoration of God's people. It would come in a time of great darkness for other people: 'Behold, darkness shall cover the earth, and thick darkness the peoples; but the Lord will arise upon you, and his glory will be seen upon you. And nations shall come to your light, and kings to the brightness of your rising. Lift up your eyes round about and see; they all gather together, they come to you... You shall see and be radiant, your heart shall thrill and rejoice...'

A national newspaper once had an article entitled 'Why must Christians be so miserable?' That is certainly the general impression. But God wants his people to be bathed in the beauty of his glory and filled with the radiance of his joy. And when, in some measure, that happens, the church will become a magnet for the lonely and distressed, the hungry and confused, the strong and the weak. They will increasingly emerge from the gathering gloom of the world into the light of Christ in the midst of his church.

United in the love of God

In John 17, Jesus prayed four times that his disciples might be perfectly united in love: 'that they may be one, even as we are one...that they may all be one, even as thou, Father, art in me, and I in thee...that they may be one, even as we are one...that they may become perfectly one, and that the love with which thou has loved me may be in them.' The reason for his tremendous burden is also clear: it is that the world might believe and know the truth about God and about his Son Jesus Christ.

A Latin American theologian wrote that 'the proclamation of the gospel apart from the unity of the church is a theological absurdity'. The heart of the gospel is that, through the death of Jesus Christ, all the barriers are down. We have access into God's presence; and we are all one in Christ Jesus. There are no more walls of hostility — except those of our own making. How, then, can we preach a message of love, forgiveness and reconciliation — between man and God, and between man and man — unless the reality of that can be seen by our unity and love as Christians? This should be the distinguishing mark of all true disciples of Christ: that we love one another as he loved us.

Any denial of that love is a denial of the gospel, however eloquently the message may be preached.

When the Spirit was poured out upon the disciples at Pentecost, they were all filled with the love of God. They were all together, and had all things in common. They worshipped together, prayed together, studied together, shared together; and, not surprisingly, 'the Lord added to the number day by day those who were being saved.'

'As a further testimony to the absolute necessity of this love, the apostles never ceased to urge the the Christian churches to get their relationships sorted out. Any tension or conflict, any bitterness or anger, would at once grieve the Spirit, and God would be quite unable to work in the way he wished until his people had come back to the cross and experienced his love once again. 'Above all these things,' wrote Paul to the Christians at Colossae, 'put on love, which binds everything together in perfect harmony.' Whenever God's people dwell in such love and unity, it is there that he commands his blessing.

Such, then, is the character of the Christian church for which Christ prayed so fervently before he went to his death. Later, after he had risen from the dead and ascended into heaven, the Spirit was poured out upon the disciples, and Christ's prayer was answered. When they were filled with God's glory, his word, his joy, united in his love, nothing could stop them. On and on they went, against all human odds and terrible persecution, as they began the greatest spiritual revolution that the world has ever known.

God has never changed, and his Spirit is still available for all those whose lives are open to him. What we need to grasp clearly is a vision of the church as God has revealed it to us in the Scriptures. If we then act upon that vision, with patient and persistent prayer and with plenty of hard work, we — and others — will see the reality and glory of God once again in our midst.

God is doing a new thing in his church. Just at the time when the forecast is bleak, and there seems little hope on the horizon, God is proving again that what is impossible with men is possible with God. If our faith is in him and in the power of the risen Christ, we can certainly believe in the church which *he* will build, against which the powers of hell itself cannot prevail.

PART II

THE NATURE OF THE CHURCH

CHAPTER FOUR

The Kingdom of God

IN AN AGE when the future of the church is being seriously questioned and when the role of the church in a secular, technological society is uncertain, it is important to ask again the basic question, what *is* the church?

Interestingly, Jesus himself said almost nothing about the church. The word 'church' (*ekklesia*) comes only twice in the Gospels: the first in the highly controversial passage where Jesus said that he would build his church 'on this rock',[1] and the second in a passage about discipline when he said that the sin of an unrepentant brother should be told to the church.[2]

However, the phrase 'the kingdom of God' (*basileia tou theou*) comes about a hundred times in the Synoptic Gospels, and it is therefore here that we should expect to find some underlying principles which later emerged in the apostles' doctrine of the church. As Alfred Loisy once commented, 'Jesus proclaimed the kingdom of God, and what came was the Church.'[3]

It would be wrong to *identify* the kingdom of God with the church, or even to talk of the church as 'the present form of the kingdom of God.' The full power and glory of God's kingdom are yet to come, and the church must continually press towards this ideal. Indeed the striking and humbling differences between the existing church and the coming kingdom need constantly and painfully to be brought into the light; and the renewing and re-shaping of the church as a

---

[1]Matthew 16:18.
[2]Matthew 18:17.

[3]A. Loisy, *L'Evangile et l'Eglise*, Paris 1902, p. 111.

result of this exposure should always be a matter of prime importance. Only then can God's glory be seen in the church, and through the church to the world.

What new society had Jesus in mind? What did he mean when he said, 'The time is fulfilled, and the kingdom of God is at hand; repent, and believe in the gospel'?[4] Often he taught about the kingdom. He spoke about entering the kingdom,[5] he urged his disciples to pray for the coming of the kingdom,[6] he told them to preach the kingdom,[7] he demonstrated the kingdom in power,[8] he illustrated the kingdom in parables,[9] and he promised the future blessings of the kingdom.[10]

What, then, is the kingdom? The disciples themselves were confused about this even after Jesus had spent forty days speaking to them about the kingdom of God.[11] They were looking for political power to overthrow the Roman oppression, and for a new religio-social order in their country. When they asked when Christ would 'restore the kingdom to Israel' they were still looking backwards to the political theocracy of the Old Testament. Christ, however, had something quite different in mind, as his answer revealed.

In contemporary usage, the word 'kingdom' means either a realm over which a sovereign exercises authority (such as the United Kingdom of Great Britain), or a people belonging to that realm. In the Bible, 'kingdom' means in the first instance *the authority and rule of a king*. 'His kingdom rules over all,' sang the psalmist.[12] Following on from this we see a number of truths concerning the kingdom of God.

It is the sovereign act of God
God's kingdom is not brought into being by the efforts of man or by the discussions of the church. It is God who 'gives' the kingdom,[13] who 'appoints' it,[14] and who declares for whom it shall be.[15] It is God who issues the invitations, who calls men

[4] Mark 1:15.
[5] Matthew 5:20; 7:21; 18:3.
[6] Matthew 6:10.
[7] Matthew 9:35; 10:7f.
[8] Matthew 12:15, 22, 28.
[9] Matthew 13.
[10] Matthew 25:31, 34.
[11] Acts 1:3, 6.
[12] Psalm 103: 19.
[13] Luke 12:32.
[14] Luke 22:29f.
[15] Matthew 5:3; Mark 10:14.

to 'come, for all is now ready', who compels people to enter, and who refuses and rejects those who have spurned his offer of grace.[16] Man can only receive the kingdom like a child, and, unless he does so, he has no place within it.[17] Certainly he is to pray for God's kingdom to come,[18] to seek it first in his life,[19] and to be watchful and ready for the return of Christ in reigning power.[20] But in himself and by himself there is nothing he can do to bring it about. 'The coming of God's reign is a miraculous event, which will be brought about by God alone without the help of man.'[21]

Since the kingdom of God is God's sovereign act, the church that wishes to see the reign of God spread throughout the world must first of all submit to the reign of God within its own ranks. It must always live and move in complete dependence on God and in faithful obedience to his word. As soon as it tries to extend God's kingdom in a spirit of self-reliance, or by trusting in human wisdom, the battle is lost. And as soon as it tampers with the eternal and God-given message of the gospel of Christ, it has forfeited the Spirit's power, for it is this changeless gospel which is 'the power of God for salvation to every one who has faith'.[22]

In order to proclaim and demonstrate the gospel of the kingdom, Jesus spent much time in prayer. He also taught his disciples that they 'ought always to pray and not lose heart'.[23] In the parable of the unjust judge which follows this statement he concluded, 'And will not God vindicate his elect, who cry to him day and night?... I tell you, he will vindicate them speedily. Nevertheless, when the Son of man comes, will he find faith on earth?' Faith is the one essential that Christ will look for, since God's reign is his sovereign act in the world and therefore we must continually put our trust in him, and in him alone, if his kingdom is to come.

How was the New Testament church able to appeal to the Sovereign Lord for boldness to speak and for power to

---

[16] Luke 14:15-24.
[17] Mark 10:15.
[18] Matthew 6:10.
[19] Matthew 6:33.
[20] Matthew 24:44; 25:1-13; et. al.

[21] R. Bultman, *Theology of the New Testament*, London-New York 1952, I, p. 4.
[22] Romans 1:16.
[23] Luke 18:1-7.

heal so successfully? It was on the grounds that Christ was manifestly the Sovereign Lord in their own lives. As Simon Peter declared to his accusers, 'We must obey God rather than men... And we are witnesses to these things, and so is the Holy Spirit whom God has given to those who obey him.'[24] The early Christians *devoted* themselves 'to the apostles' teaching and fellowship, to the breaking of bread and the prayers.'[25]

How slow the church is to accept the reign of God with consistency! How many meetings of church councils, chapters, synods or fraternals pay anything more than lip-service to the priority of prayer? How many congregations really apply themselves to serious biblical study and persistent prayer? Isaiah, viewing from his prophetic stance the spiritual state of Israel, lamented, 'We have become like those over whom thou hast never ruled, like those who are not called by thy name.' And one of the clearest symptoms of this spiritual decadence was the absence of real prayer: 'There is no one that calls upon thy name, that bestirs himself to take hold of thee.' So the prophet himself cries out to God with the desperate cry of one who knows that unless God works, all is in vain: 'O that thou wouldst rend the heavens and come down, that the mountains might quake at thy presence...[26]

As a matter of great urgency, therefore, absolute priority must be given to earnest, believing prayer (both private and corporate), to serious study of the Scriptures, to the application of the Scriptures to every area of the church's life and the Christian's life, and to constant acceptance of the Lordship of Christ and openness to the power of the Spirit. If God's kingdom is to come in the world, his reign must first come in our lives.

It is good news
The reign of God is primarily for the salvation of sinful men, and therefore is first and foremost good news. It is not, as some of the contemporaries of Jesus, including the Qumran communities, supposed, the release of God's anger and wrath on the impenitent godless. When a Samaritan village would not receive Jesus, and when James and John in their

[24] Acts 5:29, 32.   [26] Isaiah 63:19-64:7.
[25] Acts 2:42.

indignation called out, 'Lord, do you want us to bid fire come down from heaven and consume them?' they were rebuked by Jesus; and some manuscripts add this further reproach, 'You do not know what manner of spirit you are of; for the Son of man came not to destroy men's lives but to save them.'[27] Even if these words are a later gloss, they are certainly consistent with the rest of the Gospel records.

The message of the kingdom is above all *good news* for sinners, an offer of forgiveness, peace and joy. It is symbolised by a wedding feast, by an abundant harvest, by a shelter for the birds of the air, by hidden treasure, or by a pearl of great price.[28] Moreover, it is not a reward for the religious or righteous; it is freely offered to all who 'repent and believe in the gospel'.

For centuries God's people had been waiting for the kingdom of God. They longed fervently for the Messiah to come. 'How beautiful upon the mountains are the feet of him who brings good tidings...who says to Zion, "Your God reigns." Hark, your watchmen lift up their voice, together they sing for joy; for eye to eye they see the return of the Lord to Zion. Break forth together into singing...'[29] 'Arise, shine; for your light has come, and the glory of the Lord has risen upon you...'[30] For centuries the prophecies had poured forth concerning the glorious reign of God, which was certainly coming to his people.

We can understand, therefore, why the people flocked to hear John the Baptist, 'the voice of one crying in the wilderness: Prepare the way of the Lord, make his paths straight... Repent, for the kingdom of heaven is at hand.'[31] We can understand, too, why Jesus told his disciples that it was no time for them to mourn and fast; they should enjoy the festive celebration of a wedding.[32] He assured them that they were blessed by God: 'Blessed are you poor, for yours is the kingdom of God. Blessed are you that hunger now, for you shall be satisfied. Blessed are you that weep now, for you shall laugh...'[33] Satan's downfall had come.[34] God's kingdom was now in their midst.[35]

[27] Luke 9:51-56.
[28] Matthew 13.
[29] Isaiah 52:7-9.
[30] Isaiah 69:1 ff.
[31] Matthew 3:2-3.

[32] Mark 2:18-20.
[33] Luke 6:20f.
[34] Luke 10:18.
[35] Luke 17:20f.

When Jesus brought to people the reign of God, breaking Satan's rule of suffering or sin in their lives, there was immediately an atmosphere of joy, freedom and celebration. The messianic prophecies were being fulfilled: 'Then shall the lame man leap like a hart, and the tongue of the dumb sing for joy.'[36] No wonder they all 'glorified God' when the paralysed man leapt to his feet, picked up his stretcher and walked home.[37] No wonder the seventy returned with joy when they saw the power of the name of Jesus deliver people from demonic bondage.[38] No wonder the cripple at the Beautiful Gate, when healed, entered the temple 'walking and leaping and praising God'.[39] When God's reign comes, it means good news for the poor, release for the captives, recovering of sight for the blind, and liberty for the oppressed.[40] Such is the privilege of belonging to the kingdom of God that a new birth by the Spirit of God is essential. Without this, no one can either see or enter the kingdom.[41] The apostles never forgot this miracle of God's grace: 'He has delivered us from the dominion of darkness and transferred us to the kingdom of his beloved Son, in whom we have redemption, the forgiveness of sins.'[42]

The church's message and image, therefore, must be seen and heard in the first place as joyful good news. It must be positive in its message and ministry to the world. Instead of the gloom and doom all too often associated with it, there needs to be the exuberant and joyful note of celebration. If we communicate to the world in largely negative terms — condemning sin, denouncing society, threatening doom — it will be taken as a declaration of war, not a proclamation of the glorious good news that God reigns and rules and loves, and has come to us in the person of his own Son at infinite cost to bring us abundance of life and fullness of joy. We have 'good news of great joy', and there needs to be some demonstration of the love and joy that we can experience in Christ before the kingdom of God will begin to be attractive to the outsider, prejudiced as he may well be by the depressingly negative and irrelevant image the church has projected for so long.

[36] Isaiah 35:6.
[37] Mark 2:1-12.
[38] Luke 10:17.
[39] Acts 3:1-10.
[40] Luke 4:18.
[41] John 3:3-7.
[42] Colossians 1:13f.

There is indeed the command to repent and to bow to the authority of Christ. Undoubtedly there is also the cry of warning concerning the solemn and righteous judgment of God upon those who will not repent. But even this must be given with the compassionate longing that man's illusion of self-sufficiency must somehow be shattered in order that 'the Lord…may have mercy on him, and…abundantly pardon'.

In his book on the church, Michael Griffiths refers to Allen Ginsberg's poem about a 'love demo' that he wrote in 1966 called 'How to make a March/Spectacle.' Its thesis is that 'demonstrations should lay aside their usually grave and pugnacious quality in favour of festive dancing and a chanting parade, that would pass out balloons and flowers, candy and kisses, bread and wine, to everyone along the line of march — including any cops or Hell's Angels in the vicinity. The atmosphere should be one of gaiety and affection governed by the intention to attract or seduce participation from the usually impassive bystanders — or at least to overcome their worst suspicions and hostilities.'[43] Griffiths went on to comment: 'This is a very attractive illustration of the church as a body of people moving together to a specific goal, as well as increasing their numbers along the route… The institutional church has become so disfigured, and the young generation so disenchanted with it, that we have become unrecognisable.'[44]

The church, of course, should have something far more substantial to offer the world than the 'love demo' advocated by Allen Ginsberg. Instead of ephemeral feelings of good will (the hippie culture failed inevitably because it ignored the truth about man's sinful nature), the church has eternal realities to get excited about. Christians are heirs of God; they have the unsearchable riches of Christ; they should experience the love of God which surpasses knowledge, and the peace of God which passes all understanding. They should rejoice with inexpressible joy in the steadfast love and mercy of God which never end. Rather than offering a poor imitation of the world's transient celebrations, Christians,

[43]Theodore Roszak, *The Making of a Counter Revolution*, Anchor Books 1968, p. 150.

[44]*Cinderella With Amnesia*, I.V.P., 1975, p. 19.

inspired by the creative Spirit of God, should shine with the glory of God and be caught up in worship and praise.

Jesus once lamented the stiff, unbending formality of the religious people of his day: 'They are like children sitting in the market place and calling to one another, "We piped to you, and you did not dance".'[45]

The church that I serve is at the heart of a famous tourist city.[46] It has been our practice for the last few years to express our corporate joy and worship with singing and dancing on the forecourt outside our church.[47] Immediately a crowd gathers, men and women of different nationalities and languages. 'Is it a celebration? Is it a wedding? Is it a festival?' are the questions I am invariably asked by the bystanders. The opportunity is immediately given to explain, in simple terms, that this is what the kingdom of God is essentially like.

The church must above all be loving and unjudging towards a sinful, apathetic and even hostile world. Far from an attitude which criticises and condemns the godless, it must humbly acknowledge that its own moral and spiritual condition is anything but perfect and in constant need of correction and renewal. It must be a church which is always experiencing afresh the joy of God's forgiveness, which never ceases to wonder at the steadfast love and unceasing mercy of the Lord, and which longs to encourage others to 'taste and see that the Lord is gracious'.[48] 'A Church which in these last days does not realise that it is composed of sinful men and exists for sinful men, must grow hardhearted, self-righteous and without compassion, deserving neither the mercy of God nor the confidence of men.'[49] A church which in any measure is submitting to the reign of God in its life must know that, like its own Saviour and Ruler, it is there 'to seek and to save the lost'.

It is the reversal of worldly values
Although the oppressed people of Israel were naturally looking for political liberation from a foreign military power,

[45]Luke 7:32.
[46]St. Michael-le-Belfrey, York.
[47]For a fuller look at these expressions of worship and methods of communication, see pp. 191-197, 222-224, 322-328.
[48]Psalm 34:8.
[49]Hans Küng, *The Church*, Search Press 1971, p. 100.

and some were only too eager to join the spate of violent revolutions that flared up around the time of Jesus, Jesus himself made it clear time and again that his kingdom is not of this world,[50] and that it was not then imminent in its fulfilment.[51] He showed that it had nothing to do with violent action,[52] and that it would be marked by poverty, generosity and suffering[53] rather than concerned with human greatness, power or authority.[54]

Jesus revealed the reign of God as a complete reversal of the aims, ambitions, values and standards of this world. Further, although Jesus was never primarily a social revolutionary, he certainly called for a revolutionary lifestyle which knew no half-measures or compromise in terms of commitment. A man must choose between the reign of God and the reign of the world. If anything mattered to him more than Christ — family, possessions, ambitions, or whatever — he could not be Christ's disciple. It must be a radical discipleship, or nothing at all. For a man to know the privileges of the reign of God in his life, he must put God's kingdom unquestionably and unconditionally first, before money and possessions,[55] before rights and privileges,[56] before family and friends,[57] before personal attitudes and hidden desires.[58] It must be the serious commitment of his whole life, for 'no one who puts his hand to the plough and looks back is fit for the kingdom of God.'[59]

The reign of God includes every part of a man, partly because God is God, and that is his sovereign right (if he is not Lord of all, he is not Lord at all); and partly because God's salvation is for the whole man, wholly separated from sin and selfishness, and wholly able therefore to 'glorify God and to enjoy him for ever'. It is only our inward rebellion and natural self-centredness that spoils our enjoyment of God's love and that prevents us from bringing his love in full measure to a lonely and alienated world.

[50] John 18:36; Luke 23:42;
Acts 1:6.
[51] Luke 19:11.
[52] Matthew 26:52.
[53] Luke 6:20; Matthew 5:40-42.
Luke 12:32f; et. al.
[54] Mark 10:35-45.

[55] Matthew 6:19-34.
[56] Matthew 5:39-41.
Mark 10:42-44.
[57] Luke 14:26f; Matthew 10:34-39.
[58] Matthew 5:21-48.
[59] Luke 9:62.

This is why the conditions of entry into God's kingdom are first *repentance*, a complete about-turn of heart and mind, leading to a radical inward and outward change of direction from sin to God; and secondly *faith* in Jesus Christ, the message of the gospel.[60] This faith is much more than an intellectual assent or an emotional response: it is a surrender of the will and a commitment of the entire person to the saving work and Lordship of Christ.

With this in mind, it is the greatest mistake to water down the cost of Christian discipleship, or to present the church as a club where the degree of commitment depends entirely on personal choice or convenience. The church is not a club; it is the army of Jesus Christ. It is also significant that, throughout the centuries men have responded readily to a strong challenge. Christ frankly told his disciples that he was sending them out as 'lambs in the midst of wolves', that the world would hate them, and persecute them, and those who killed them would think that they were offering God a service.[61] However, they rose to the challenge; and equipped with the power of the Holy Spirit they turned the world of their day upside down and eventually conquered the mighty Roman Empire.

The Church today must constantly examine itself to see how far it has accepted the role of suffering and service that comes with the reign of God. Are its methods and values and ambitions a complete reversal of those of the world? If so, how could it support the use of violence in the fight against political oppression, for example in South Africa? How could it hoard up for itself treasures and wealth above its basic necessities? How could it bestow ecclesiastical honours, position and status, which seem far removed from the character of the Servant? How could the pomp of ecclesiastical titles (the Reverend, the Very Reverend, the Most Reverend, the Lord Bishop, and so forth) possibly contribute towards a caring community or add to the church's relevance in the world? How could many of its members enjoy a considerable degree of personal affluence when the needs of many others in the church are immense, when almost every missionary society is crying out for more money, and when more than thirty

---

[60]Mark 1:15.   [61]Luke 10:3; John 15:18ff; 16:2.

million in the world die each year because they are too hungry to live?

How could the church accept a middle-class mediocrity, tolerated because of its ineffectiveness and worldliness, when the lifestyle and teaching of Jesus was so threatening and disturbing that persecution was inevitable? How could the church become so identified with one political party, or so allied to the status quo, that it ceases to be the prophetic voice that every generation and every culture needs so much? How could the life of the individual Christian, or the relationships between Christians, be so unremarkable as to be indistinguishable from the lives of unbelievers apart from certain credal beliefs?

J.B. Phillips wrote in the Preface to his paraphrase of the Acts of the Apostles: 'Perhaps because of their very simplicity, perhaps because of their readiness to believe, to obey, to give, to suffer, and if need be to die, the Spirit of God found what he must always be seeking — a fellowship of men and women so united in love and faith that he can work in them and through them with the minimum of let or hindrance.' It is the church that is willing to die to worldly standards that will know the power of Christ's resurrection. It may be envied for its depths of loving relationships or for its spontaneous joy; it may be hated and persecuted for its revolutionary lifestyle exposing the hollow values and destructive selfishness of the society it seeks to serve; but it certainly cannot be ignored. When God reigns among his people, they become a city set on a hill and cannot be hid.

It is in the future

The reign of God is eschatological: it is a decisive, future, final event at the end of time.

With the coming of Jesus, 'the Word became flesh and dwelt among us, full of grace and truth,'[62] and Jesus was able to proclaim, 'The time is fulfilled, and the kingdom of God is at hand.'[63] It is both 'now' and 'not yet'. 'The kingdom of God has come upon you,' said Jesus;[64] yet at the Last Supper he told his disciples 'that from now I shall not drink of the fruit

[62] John 1:14. [64] Matthew 12:28; cf. Luke 17:20f.
[63] Mark 1:15.

of the vine until the kingdom of God comes.'[65] It will then 'come with power'.[66]

The church exists in these last days: days which began with the fulfilled reign of God in Christ; days which have continued with manifestations of the reign of God in his church and in his world; and days which will inevitably conclude with the coming reign of God when every rule and every authority and power will be destroyed, and all things will be put under the feet of Christ, including the last enemy of death.[67] Thus the church is, or should be, always on the move. Its structures and institutions are at best only temporary, and must always seek to serve the reign of God as it is demonstrated in power in the world.

A church that forgets this will be unwilling or unable to move. It will cling to its forms of worship and patterns of service, its organisations and traditions, as though these were the ultimate end or aim of the church. Such inflexibility will breed stagnation and sterility. The church that will not listen to the voice of God, or will not respond to the promptings of the Spirit (who is ever the Spirit of movement), will be quite unable to speak with relevance or power to the rapidly changing world in which we live.

'Flexibility, mobility, sensitivity, fluidity — these are some characteristics of an attitude that results in effective action in God's kingdom. Yet they are difficult, and often we would make structures, traditions, or organisation our priority and security. They are valid, but secondary to our availability, our willingness to respond to God according to *his* Spirit, who is often unpredictable and mysterious.'[68] The kingdom of God is always dynamic; it cannot be fossilised even for a moment. It was partly for this reason that Jesus spoke so strongly against the church of his day which had left the commandment of God and held fast the tradition of men,[69] which strained at gnats and swallowed camels, which heaped countless rules and regulations on the breaking backs of the people of God, and whose leaders were greedy for privilege and power within its own moribund ranks of adherents.

[65] Luke 22:18.
[66] Mark 9:1.
[67] 1 Corinthians 15:24-28.

[68] The Editorial from *Towards Renewal*, Issue 6, Spring 1976.
[69] Mark 7:8; cf. vv. 9-13.

In his book *Paths to Power*, A.W. Tozer shrewdly commented that

> the Church began in power, moved in power and moved
> just as long as she had power. When she no longer had
> power she dug in for safety and sought to conserve her
> gains. But her blessings were like the manna: when they
> tried to keep it overnight it bred worms and stank...In
> Church History every return to New Testament power has
> marked a new advance somewhere, a fresh proclamation
> of the gospel, an upsurge of missionary zeal; and every
> diminution of power has seen the rise of some new
> mechanism for conservation and defence.[70]

It is the church which seeks first the kingdom of God that
will experience this constant, fresh effusion of the Spirit's
power. It will also be the church that is free: free to serve God
and the people of God, free to serve the world in terms that
are relevant for each generation, free to move at the leading
of the Spirit, free to explore fresh presentations of the
unchanging message of the gospel, free to overcome the
ravages of sin, suffering and death through the cross and
resurrection of Christ, free to live and to love, knowing that
God's kingdom *will* come and that nothing can stop it.

Such a church can never die. If it is willing to go often
through the painful process of metamorphosis, and to cast off
the chrysalis of the structures and trappings that have ceased
to be relevant, there is every confidence that something new
and beautiful will emerge which will more perfectly and
more suitably express the reign of God for today's world. The
church which so lives and moves in the Spirit will, for all its
many faults and failings, always be to the praise of God's
glory.

[70]Op. cit., Oliphants 1964, p. 10.

CHAPTER FIVE

The Church of God

THE WORD 'CHURCH' popularly embraces a variety of concepts. Probably most people think at once of a building — St. Andrew's Church, St. Mark's Church. In that sense, of course, the New Testament Christians never went to church at all. Apart from the temple and the synagogues, which were used by Christians before the rift came from Judaism, no buildings were set aside solely for the purpose of worship until the fourth century. Today, the proliferation of church buildings in many parts of the world has caused one writer to comment: 'While God waits for his temple to be built of love, men bring stones.'

Another familiar idea of the 'church' is a denomination. People ask, 'Which church do you belong to? Baptist, Anglican, Methodist, Roman Catholic...?' Or we may use the word for the institution; and in that sense the word is not currently a popular one in many circles. 'Jesus Christ was fantastic,' said Mick Jagger of the Rolling Stones, 'but I do not like the church. The church does more harm than good.' A student, when asked 'What do you think of the church?' replied, 'Not much! It doesn't scratch where I itch!'

Others speak of the church as the ordained ministry: 'Peter is studying theology; he is going into the church.' According to this interpretation the church is seen very much like practising law, or teaching: it is the domain of the paid professional. It is the vicar who preaches, visits, counsels, organises and evangelises. He is paid to do it, and trained to do it; and the faithful are expected primarily to occupy the pews. Although they may give a helping hand from time to time, they are not required to do more than that; they are not 'in the church'.

Sometimes the word 'church' is used to refer to a particular service of worship: 'Are you going to church tonight?' This is much nearer one meaning of the word in the Scriptures. Paul wrote to the Corinthians, 'When you assemble as a church, I hear that there are divisions among you...'[1] Here he was thinking specifically of meetings for worship and prayer, the Lord's Supper in particular.

Meaning of the word 'church'
Our English word 'church', like the German *kirche*, Swedish *kyrka*, Slav *cerkov* and Scottish *kirk*, stems from the Byzantine Greek form *kurike*, meaning 'belonging to the Lord'.

On the other hand, several European languages derive their word for 'church' from the Greek *ekklesia*. The French *église*, Spanish *iglesia*, Italian *chiesa*, Latin *ecclesia* and Welsh *eglwys* all come from *ekklesia*. It is this word *ekklesia* that Jesus used when he spoke of the 'church'. We find it in the highly controversial passage in which Jesus said that he would build his church 'on this rock',[2] as well as in a passage about discipline when he said that the sin of an unrepentant brother should be told to the church.[3]

The word *ekklesia* has a Greek background. William Barclay describes its usage in the following way:

In the great classical days in Athens the *ekklesia* was the convened assembly of the people. It consisted of all the citizens of the city who had not lost their civic rights. Apart from the fact that its decisions must conform to the laws of the State, its powers were to all intents and purposes unlimited. It elected and dismissed magistrates and directed the policy of the city. It declared war, made peace, contracted treaties and arranged alliances. It elected generals and other military officers. It assigned troops to different campaigns and dispatched them from the city. It was ultimately responsible for the conduct of all military operations. It raised and allocated funds. Two things are interesting to note. First, all its meetings began with prayer

[1] 1 Corinthians 11:18.   [2] Matthew 16:18.
[3] Matthew 18:17.

and sacrifice. Second, it was a true democracy... It was an assembly where everyone had an equal right and an equal duty to take part.[4]

The word comes three times in Acts 19 referring to a secular assembly which was thrown into confusion over Paul's ministry at Ephesus.[5] For the Greeks the meaning was clear: the citizens were the *ek-klétoi*, those called out and summoned together by a herald. Thus the *ek-klesia* referred to 'those who have been called out', the gathering of 'those who have been summoned together'. Moreover, *ekklesia* referred to each particular gathering; there was no continuing *ekklesia* between sessions.

Turning to the New Testament, *ekklesia* is used in four different ways.

First, it is used of the *universal church*, the entire company of believers, both living and dead. God has made Christ 'the head over all things for the church'; it is 'through the church' that the manifold wisdom of God might now be made known; and God's glory is to be 'in the church'.[6] Second, it is often used of a *particular local church*, such as the church at Cenchreae, Corinth, Thessalonica, or Laodicea.[7] Third, it can mean the *actual assembly* of believers in any place, as they meet together for worship.[8] Fourth, it can apply to a small house church, the regular meeting place for a small group of believers in any one town or city.[9] However, whatever the size, it always speaks of the coming together of God's people in answer to his call, in order to meet with God in the company of each other and to meet each other in the presence of God.

ISRAEL — A SHADOW OF THE CHURCH

Ekklesia has also a Hebrew background. In the Greek Septuagint it translates the Old Testament Hebrew word

[4] *A New Testament Wordbook*, S.C.M. Press 1955, p. 34.
[5] Verses 32, 39, 41.
[6] Ephesians 1:22; 3:10, 21; cf. 1 Corinthians 10:32; 12:28; Philippians 3:6; Colossians 1:58, 24

[7] Romans 16:1; 1 Corinthians 1:2; 1 Thessalonians 1:1; Colossians 4:16.
[8] 1 Corinthians 11:18; 14:19; 23.
[9] Romans 16:5; 1 Corinthians 16:19.

qahal, which again comes from the root meaning 'to summon'. It is frequently used for the 'assembly' or 'congregation' of the people of Israel, the word occurring over seventy times in the Septuagint, and the *ekklesia* and *qahal* word groups in the old and New Testaments coming more than seven hundred times. Michael Griffiths notes four aspects of God's summoning of the congregation of Israel.[10] It may be helpful to expand a little on the distinctions that he makes. In them we shall find four vital aspects of the New Testament church, for Israel's experiences as the congregation of God in the Old Testament were recorded for the church's instruction and warning.[11]

Called out

Israel were God's 'called out' ones. God said of them, 'When Israel was a child, I loved him, and out of Egypt I called my son.'[12] What a marvellous shadow of the New Covenant church! God brought Israel through a process of physical salvation. They were released from physical bondage in Egypt (which represents, in the Bible, the kingdom of this world). They underwent a physical baptism at the Red Sea.[13] Moreover, no sooner were they released from their bondage of Egypt than Pharaoh and all his armies sought to recapture them, even as Satan is quick to try to bring the new Christian back into the bondage of sin. For the next forty years — a number which often denotes trial in the Bible — they journeyed in the wilderness where dangers and deprivation lurked; yet as they looked to God he provided their every need. Finally, they entered their earthly inheritance of the Promised Land. All of this was a physical shadow of the spiritual exodus from sin that the Christian church experiences.

Notice how Israel's salvation was wholly the sovereign act of God. They were utterly unable to free themselves from bondage. It was the miraculous intervention of God that freed them. They could not pass through the Red Sea in order to escape from Pharaoh by their own efforts; it was God who parted the waters and defeated Pharaoh for them. Throughout their journeyings it was God who protected them and

---

[10]Op. cit., p. 15f.
[11]1 Corinthians 10:1-11.

[12]Hosea 11:1f.
[13]1 Corinthians 10:2.

provided for them. Without him they could not have survived the pilgrimage, for he was their very sustenance. And finally it was God who brought them across Jordan and gave them possession of the Promised Land.

The church is the 'called out' people of God. The term 'church of God' is in fact by far the commonest description of the church in the New Testament.[14] The church belongs to God, has come from God, and owes every good gift that it enjoys to God. Without the love of God, the initiative of God, the salvation of God, the revelation of God, and the call of God, there would be no church. When party-spirit crept into the Corinthian church, Paul chided them for their fleshy cult of human personalities and their failure to realise that everything comes from God. 'What then is Apollos? What is Paul? Servants through whom you believed, as the Lord assigned to each. I planted, Apollos watered, but God gave the growth. So neither he who plants nor he who waters is anything, but only God who gives the growth... For we are God's fellow workers; you are God's field, God's building.'[15] And although the church is sometimes called the 'church of Christ,' or the 'body of Christ,' it is the divine origin and life of the church that is being stressed repeatedly.

Hilaire Belloc used to say that, when he considered the manner in which the Roman Church had been conducted, and by whom, he realised that it must have been divinely inspired to have survived at all. No doubt the same could be said of all other denominations. Nevertheless the church, for all its crass follies, crimes and weaknesses (which are only to be expected from what is a fellowship of sinners), has constantly displayed the miracle of divine grace shining through the gloom of human imperfections. This is the ultimate answer to those who enquire pessimistically if the church has any future in tomorrow's world.

Seeing the church as God's church can be a comfort when the going is tough or disappointing. Often, after a hard and barren evangelistic service or mission I have had to remind myself of the sovereignty of God. Although it may be right to ask some searching questions, it is wrong to let our adversary,

[14] 1 Corinthians 1:2;
2 Corinthians 1:1;
(Galatians 1:13;)

1 Thessalonians 2:14; 1 Timothy 3:5, 15.
[15] 1 Corinthians 3:5-9.

'the accuser of our brethren', drive us into depression or despair. The Lord reigns! It is his work, his grace and his power that counts. We can never be more than his servants who seek to obey their Master as they work within his church.

This truth can also be a corrective when the going is good and fruitful. We, in ourselves, are nothing, and can do nothing without him. It is only God who gives the growth. Often, in times of obvious blessing, I have said firmly in prayer: 'Not to us, O Lord, not to us, but to thy name give glory... This is the Lord's doing; it is marvellous in our eyes'.[16]

Knowing that it is always God's church can also prove a challenge to us. How far are we really depending upon him, trusting in him, praying to him for the life and power that we all need? What place has corporate prayer in our fellowship? To what extent do we give ourselves to earnest, believing prayer? Or do we, to be honest, conduct our lives and work as though the situation was largely in our hands?

The description 'church [ekklesia] of God' continually reminds us that it is by the sovereign act of God that we have been called to be a special people for God's own possession. Let us never look to our own size or strength, but simply to his sovereign grace. 'It is because the Lord loves you.'[17]

Called for

God's people were called for a relationship with him. This was the basis of the covenants established with Abraham and Moses. Abraham became the 'friend' of God. Israel entered into covenant relationship with him, whereby he dwelt in their midst. The pillar of cloud and fire represented God's presence among them. When the pillar moved, they moved; when it stood still, they made camp. At Sinai God instructed them to make a tabernacle in which his presence would dwell. Thus wherever Israel went God was with them, and they enjoyed a relationship with him.

Likewise, Christ called his disciples 'my friends'. Christians are 'called [by God] into the fellowship of his Son, Jesus Christ our Lord.'[18] Now that we have been 'born anew', we

[16]Psalm 115:1; 118:23.   [18]1 Corinthians 1:9.
[17]Deuteronomy 7:6-8.

are to 'come to him, to that living stone...; and like living stones be built into a spiritual house...to offer spiritual sacrifices acceptable to God through Jesus Christ.'[19] It is significant that when Jesus called the twelve apostles, he called them to him and appointed them 'to be with him'; and it was only from this primary fellowship with him that they were sent out to preach and heal.[20] The church must never become a religious society for good works; at the heart of it all is this personal and corporate relationship with God.

Called together

Israel's calling was into a new community, and God called them together. They partook of the Passover together. They left Egypt together. They went through the baptism at the Red Sea together. They ate and drank together: 'and all ate the same supernatural food and all drank the same supernatural drink'.[21] They marched together, facing foes and trials together. They experienced God's miraculous power together. And they entered the Promised Land together.

The call of God is not purely a private affair. Abraham's calling entailed the promise of descendants like the sand and stars in number, comprising a great family of children. When we become Christians we also become a part of that Abrahamic family.[22] That we are in one great family is also evident from the fact that God speaks of us all as his sons, and the New Testament continually refers to us as brothers and sisters in Christ. So we find that after the church began 'the Lord added to their number [i.e. to the church] day by day those who were being saved'.[23]

Howard Snyder, in his paper for the Lausanne Congress on World Evangelisation in 1974, wrote: 'The church is the only divinely-appointed means for spreading the gospel...Further, evangelism makes little sense divorced from the fact of the Christian community... The evangelistic call intends to call persons to the body of Christ...Biblical evangelism is church-centred evangelism. Evangelism should spark church growth, and the life and witness of the church should produce evangelism. In this

[19] 1 Peter 1:23; 2:4f.
[20] Mark 3:13-15.

[21] 1 Corinthians 10:4.
[22] Galatians 3:29.
[23] Acts 2:47.

sense the church is both the agent and the goal of evangelism.[24]

Further *ekklesia*, like 'congregation', refers both to *particular gatherings* of God's people and to the *continuing community* of believers in any one area. The *'gatherings'* remind us that the corporate activities of God's people are really important. In no New Testament sense can a person claim to belong to a local church ('St. Luke's is my church') if he seldom or never gathers with the rest of God's people in that place. That is why the writer to the Hebrews exhorted the Christians not to neglect 'to meet together, as is the habit of some,' but to encourage one another by their regular worship and fellowship.[25] Further the *'community'* reminds us that each local church must learn to live as a true community seven days a week, and not just have a nodding acquaintance with one another for an hour or two each Sunday. Relationships must be built up in love, personal needs met by the sharing of gifts, and practical help offered by a caring fellowship giving loving service in the name of Christ.

However, community is not to be confused with activity. Many churches that abound with activities have little or no sense of community. Community depends on relationships. Whatever else we may do, the development of right relationships within a church is of paramount importance. We must learn to love one another and to accept one another just as we are. We need to forgive one another and to ask forgiveness from one another. Our lives must be shared together, with all their faults and failings; otherwise the gospel of a loving and forgiving God will be empty words. The well-known American psychiatrist, Dr. Mowrer, once explained to a group of church leaders why he was an atheist: the church had failed him and many others he knew because it had never learnt the secret of community.

This has been particularly true of Protestant churches. 'Protestantism in general has emphasised the individual over the community. Too often the church has been seen more as a collection of saved souls than as a community of interacting personalities. But the model of Christ with his disciples, the example of the early church, and the explicit teaching of

[24]Op. cit., p. 327.   [25]Hebrews 10:25.

Jesus and Paul should call us back to the importance of community. Fellowship and community life are necessary in order to prepare Christians for witness and service. Every Christian is a witness in the world, but his effectiveness depends largely on his sharing the enabling common life of the church.'[26]

Jeff Schiffmeyer, from the Church of the Holy Redeemer, Houston, Texas, once put it vividly like this: 'The effectiveness of our ministry depends on the fervency of our love for one another.'

Called to

When God called Abraham, it was to a future inheritance. 'By faith Abraham obeyed when he was called to go to a place which he was to receive as an inheritance.'[27] So too Israel was called to journey towards a specific goal, the land of Promise. And it is no different with the church. We have been called out of spiritual Egypt for our journey towards a future inheritance. Thus Paul urged Timothy to 'take hold of the eternal life to which you were called.'[28] We are presently heirs of God and joint-heirs with Christ, and the Holy Spirit is the first instalment of our promised inheritance.

Obedience to this call will never be easy, and suffering has always been a mark of God's people as they journey to the promised land. 'After you have suffered a while, the God of all grace, who has called you to his eternal glory in Christ, will himself restore, establish, and strengthen you.'[29] Unfortunately, the trials that come upon us frequently cause us to become discouraged so that we do not make the progress we should. The setting forth of the great inheritance that awaits the church needs therefore to figure prominently in our teaching and exhortation, as the apostles constantly realised. Indeed it was this clear vision of the future that enabled Jesus himself to endure sufferings. The writer of Hebrews speaks of 'Jesus the pioneer and perfector of our faith, who for the joy that was set before him endured the cross, despising the shame, and is seated at the right hand of the throne of God.'[30]

[26] Howard Snyder, *Let the Earth Hear His Voice*, World Wide Publications, p. 333.
[27] Hebrews 11:8.
[28] 1 Timothy 6:12.
[29] 1 Peter 5:10.
[30] Hebrews 12:2.

When a church has a vivid picture of the goal ahead its members will be able to say with Paul that all the 'sufferings of this present time are not worth comparing with the glory that is to be revealed to us.'[31]

We can never afford to lose sight of the fact that the church has been called to an inheritance, and that we are journeying continually. *Ekklesia*, like the kingdom of God, is something dynamic. The traditional picture of a static church, solid in its establishment, conservative in its attitudes, entrenched in familiar patterns of work and worship, is a gross distortion of the church as it is meant to be and as pictured in the Bible. The Old Testament speaks of the 'church in the wilderness', the New Testament of 'aliens and exiles'[32] — members of the household of God, yes, but travelling through the desert wastes of this world and through the valleys of the shadow of death until the consummation of all things in Christ, when the kingdom of the world becomes the kingdom of our Lord and of his Christ. It is therefore a people on the move, delivered from Egypt, summoned at Sinai to meet with God, and called to go with him to the land of promise. It must never become a people that settles down in the wilderness, but always alive and alert, pressing on 'toward the goal for the prize of the upward call of God in Christ Jesus.'[33]

The temptation, however, is always to look back, and not to move with the cloud and fire of God's presence. Like an immature or insecure adult clinging to the memories of childhood, the church can cling to the past and hold on to forms and structures that were meaningful yesterday. In terms of music, language, dress, style of presentation, methods of teaching, the decoration of church buildings and church halls, the format of church magazines, and the appearance of church bookstalls (if they exist at all) and of church notice-boards — all so often proclaim with one accord that God is the God of yesterday; he is not to be looked for, expected, or to be found today. And that, for the church of the living God, is tragedy.

Often throughout the history of the church the pattern has been the same: God breathes into his church fresh life by the

[31] Romans 8:15-18.
[32] 1 Peter 2:11.
[33] Philippians 3:14.

renewing power of the Holy Spirit: man likes what he sees, organises it, regiments it; and the patterns therefore continue for decades, if not for centuries, after the Spirit has quietly made his departure. God's plan for continuous renewal becomes the Church's Society for Historic Preservation. The aliens and exiles have settled down in the world that is not their home; and, buried beneath an avalanche of synodical reports, liturgical reforms, ecumenical debates and ecclesiastical paraphernalia, they are virtually unable to listen to, or respond to, the gentle but urgent promptings of the Holy Spirit.

However, that is not what it should be. The church must learn to be on the move, always relevant for today's world. If it cannot speak in the language and culture of this present generation, whom it has been called to serve, it is tragically out of touch, not only with the world of today but also with the God of today. Of course God himself never changes. His love and truth endure for ever. Yet our understanding of him, and his communication through us, should be changing all the time.

That is the adventure of faith that the church is called to make. In the words of Leslie Newbigin, 'The church is the pilgrim people of God. It is on the move — hastening to the ends of the earth to beseech all men to be reconciled to God, hastening to the end of time to meet its Lord who will gather all men into one.'[34]

---

[34] *The Household of God*, S.C.M. Press 1953, p. 25.

CHAPTER SIX

The People of God

No DESCRIPTION OF the church so emphasises the dignity, value, and privilege of its members as the phrase 'the people of God'.

The psalmist, gazing up into the night-sky at the tiny pinpricks of light shining down upon him, cried out to God in his majesty, 'When I look at thy heavens, the work of thy fingers, the moon and the stars which thou hast established; what is man that thou dost care for him...?' That the infinite creator God should bother about man at all seemed to him incredible. Yet the good news which Jesus Christ brought to the world reveals something even more astonishing about God's concern for man. Through his grace we can become his very own sons and daughters, so that we can look up into his face and cry 'Abba! Father!' Such is the incredible relationship that God has brought us into as 'his people'.

In today's world, feelings of loneliness and alienation are everywhere to be found, leaving a flood of depression and despair. What is at the root of this tragic state of affairs? A fundamental cause is that there is little or no sense of 'belonging'. The emergence and often breakdown of the isolated, nuclear family has meant that the wider sharing in a community has largely been disbanded.

In contrast, the heart and core of God's message to man through the Scriptures is that he desires a people — a community — to share in his life. Alan Stibbs once wrote, 'God made man for himself. The chief end of God in the creation of man was to have a people of whom he could say: I am theirs and they are mine. I will be their God, and they shall be my people.'[1] He continued: 'It is therefore God's unmistakable purpose to have a people of his own, and by his amazing grace it is the utterly undeserved privilege of all who belong to Christ to belong to this community, the people of God.'[2]

This concept of the church as 'the people of God' — as God's new society, his family, his community — breaks upon many today as the most thrilling 'good news' they could ever hear. And what a transformation it can bring when a person knows that he belongs to God and to his people for ever! In an age of isolation, the joy of really belonging to God and of being a part of his people throughout the world — a belonging which depends not on earning acceptance, but on receiving freely of God's love — is one of the most relevant features of the Christian message of good news. 'See what love the Father has given us, that we should be called children of God: and so we are.'[3]

From beginning to end, the Bible reveals that one of God's greatest desires is that human beings, insignificant as we are, might enter into such a relationship with him that he might call us 'his people'. In one of the earliest chapters of the Bible, in Exodus 6:6f, God declared to a group of men and women: 'I am the Lord, and I will bring you out from under the burdens of the Egyptians, and I will deliver you from their bondage, and I will redeem you with an outstretched arm and with great acts of judgment, and I will take you for my people, and I will be your God.' Then at the very end of the Bible, in Revelation 21:3, we read: 'Behold, the dwelling of God is with men. He will dwell with them, and they shall be his people, and God himself will be with them.' This basic concept runs throughout the Scriptures.

Israel as the people of God
The references to this theme even in the Old Testament are far too numerous to give in any detail. In revealing himself to Israel, God showed that he was their Lord, Creator, Father, Judge, King, Helper, Redeemer, Shield, Defence, Rock and Stronghold. Conversely Israel is seen as the people of God, his

---

[1] Alan Stibbs, *God's Church* I.V.P., p. 7.

[2] *Ibid.*, p. 10.

[3] 1 John 3:1.

possession, his own, his servant, his son, his vine, his vineyard, his flock, and his bride. The Israelites, therefore, as God's servants, sons and daughters, are a chosen people, holy, righteous, just and upright. They have been brought into a convenant relationship with God, and their life is inextricably bound up in his. Throughout the passages which speak of this relationship, two truths stand out.

First, we see clearly the *sovereignty of God*. Of his own free choice and mercy, God delivered his people out of Egypt, established his law and covenant with them at Sinai, led them into Canaan, gave them a kingdom, sent to them his prophets, rescued them from exile, promised them a new and better covenant, and, when the time was fully ripe, sent forth his own Son. Always it was his initiative, his choice, his love and his mercy.

In contrast, the reaction of God's people to his astonishing grace was lamentable: one continuous story of failure, disobedience, rebellion, murmuring, betrayal, backsliding, infidelity, apostasy and sin. Inevitably, they experienced the chastenings of God. Yet shot through the sternest judgments were the promises of mercy and restoration if they would turn back to him. 'My people are bent on turning away from me', he cried, 'so they are appointed to the yoke, and none shall remove it. How can I give you up, O Ephraim!... My heart recoils within me, my compassion grows warm and tender...'[4]

Secondly, therefore, we see the *salvation of God*. 'I will sprinkle clean water upon you, and you shall be clean from all your uncleannesses, and from all your idols I will cleanse you,' he promised. 'A new heart I will give you, and a new spirit I will put within you; and I will take out of your flesh the heart of stone and give you a heart of flesh. And I will put my spirit within you, and cause you to walk in my statutes and be careful to observe my ordinances. You shall dwell in the land which I gave to your fathers; and you shall be my people, and I will be your God.'[5]

This was the message that must have healed the wounded heart of the prophet Hosea. Through the unfaithfulness of his wife he experienced something of the agonising pain that the

[4]Hosea 11:7f.

[5]Ezekiel 26:25-28; cf. 11:19f; 14:11; Jeremiah 7:23; 24:7; 30:22; 32:37-40; et. al.

spiritual adultery of God's people must have meant to God himself. Yet through the prophetic names Hosea was told to give to his children, pointing to their salvation, he learnt that although God's people should be 'Not pitied' and 'Not my people' due to their unfaithfulness, God in his mercy still longed to have pity on them and to call them 'sons of the living God' if they would but return to him.

The church as the people of God

The apostle Peter centuries later referred to the prophetic names of Hosea's children in the context of the gospel of Christ. Quoting from the book of Hosea he wrote, 'Once you were no people but now you are God's people; once you had not received mercy but now you have received mercy.'[6] In the light of this strong theme of the people of God throughout the Old Testament, it is not surprising to find the same concept carried over into the New. The church, by faith in Jesus the Messiah, became the true Israel, the true people of God. The church is seen in unbroken continuity with the old covenant; with the promises, prophecies and sacrifices being supremely fulfilled in Jesus Christ.

What is surprising about the New Testament people of God is that Gentiles are now included. The introduction of the Gentiles into the church came as a bombshell. Immediately after Pentecost there was probably little to distinguish the church from the rest of the Jewish people, apart from the new joy and love that the disciples had experienced so abundantly with the coming of the Holy Spirit. They still met in the temple,[7] and submitted to many of the Jewish customs and regulations. Jesus had declared that he had not come to abolish the law and the prophets,[8] and the first Christian community continued to observe the Jewish practices. The shock to Peter's religio-cultural system when he saw the vision in Acts 10 of the animals in a great sheet is a reminder that even the apostles did not appreciate the full implications of the gospel all at once. Clearly they saw themselves as the new and true Israel; and it was only baptism in the name of Jesus, 'breaking bread' in conscious

[6] 1 Peter 2:10.   [8] Matthew 5:17f.
[7] Acts 2:46.

memory of the Last Supper, and their devotion to the apostles' teaching and fellowship and the prayers, that began to give them a distinctive look from the rest of Israel.

After the Council of Jerusalem, however, the break with the old Israel was now certain. Yet even so, Paul, unexpectedly the apostle to the Gentiles, strongly argued the case that nothing fundamentally new had been done that was not already there in the Old Testament Scriptures. 'It is not as though the word of God had failed,' he pointed out to the church at Rome. 'For not all who are descended from Israel belong to Israel, and not all are children of Abraham because they are his descendants; but "Through Isaac shall your descendants be named." This means that it is not the children of the flesh who are the children of God, but the children of the promise...'[9] And again, writing to the churches in Galatia, 'Thus Abraham "believed God, and it was reckoned to him as righteousness." So you see that it is men of faith who are the sons of Abraham. And the scripture, foreseeing that God would justify the Gentiles by faith, preached the gospel beforehand to Abraham, saying, "In you shall all the nations be blessed." '[10] Paul went on to end his letter by referring to the church metaphorically as the 'Israel of God'.[11]

The rejection of Israel and selection of the church points us once again to the *sovereignty* and *salvation* of God in his dealings with his people. It is God who is seen always to be taking the initiative, whether it be in the calling of the Jews or Gentiles. Zechariah was told concerning the salvation of the Jews that his son John would 'turn many of the sons of Israel to the Lord their God, and he will go before him in the spirit and power of Elijah, to turn the hearts of the fathers to the children, and the disobedient to the wisdom of the just to make ready for the Lord a people prepared.'[12] And when John was born Zechariah himself prophesied, 'Blessed be the Lord God of Israel, for he has visited and redeemed his people... And you, child, will be called the prophet of the Most High; for you will go before the Lord to prepare his ways, to give knowledge of salvation to his people in the forgiveness of their sins.'[13]

[9] Romans 9:6-8.
[10] Galatians 3:6-8.
[11] Galatians 6:16.

[12] Luke 1:16f.
[13] Luke 1:68, 76f.

Then concerning the Gentiles, the angel said to the shepherds, 'I bring you good news of great joy which will come to all the people';[14] and later still Simeon praised God for his salvation 'which thou hast prepared in the presence of all peoples, a light for revelation to the Gentiles, and for glory to thy people Israel.'[15]

Thus in his sovereign grace, God offers salvation to Jew and Gentile alike, so that together in Christ they become 'God's own people'.[16] Several consequences follow on from this.

Consequences of being God's people

When God called Israel to be his Old Testament people, it was not with the intention that they should selfishly bask in his abundant blessings. Certainly we can enjoy God's favour as the people of God, but the scriptural principle is that we are to love our neighbours as ourselves. The calling of God is to share sacrificially his love and gifts with the needy and suffering world around us.

Moses told Israel, 'Behold, I have taught you statutes and ordinances as the Lord my God commanded me, that you should do them in the land which you are entering to take possession of it. Keep them and do them; for that will be your wisdom and your understanding *in the sight of the peoples*, who, when they hear all these statutes, will say, "Surely this great nation is a wise and understanding people".'[17] Through Israel, God himself would be glorified in the eyes of other nations.

What then, is the purpose of *our* calling as God's New Testament people? Like Israel, we are called to be God's new society in the world. 'But you are a chosen race, a royal priesthood, a holy nation, God's own people, that you may *declare* the wonderful deeds of him who called you out of darkness into his marvellous light... Beloved, I beseech you as aliens and exiles to abstain from the passions of the flesh that wage war against your soul. Maintain good conduct among the Gentiles, so that in case they speak against you as wrongdoers, they may see your good deeds and *glorify God* on the day of visitation.[18] It is God's intention that as his people

[14] Luke 2:10.
[15] Luke 2:31f.
[16] 1 Peter 2:9.

[17] Deuteronomy 4:5-6.
[18] 1 Peter 2:9, 11f.

we should glorify him in the world. He has commissioned us to reveal him through our corporate life as his 'own people' to a world that does not know him.

Jesus himself said, 'You are the light of the world. A city set on a hill cannot be hid. Nor do men light a lamp and put it under a bushel, but on a stand, and it gives light to all in the house. Let your light so shine before men, that they may see your good works and give glory to your Father who is in heaven.'[19] It is always true that our lives speak more loudly than our words. By using the illustration of light, Jesus was showing the powerful impact true Christian living can have. Yet tragically we have been more often foghorns than lights. How frequently we hear people say that Christians fail to practise what they preach! Unless we glorify God in our lives, our words will be wasted. 'What the world needs to see,' said Duncan Campbell, 'is the wonder and beauty of God-possessed personalities; men and women with the life of God pulsating within, who practise the presence of God and consequently make it easy for others to believe in God.'[20]

Paul reminded 'all God's beloved in Rome' that they were 'called to be saints'.[21] And a saint, in the New Testament sense, is not someone who is known for his super-piety; he is simply a true Christian who is 'set apart' from sin for God. He has been called out of darkness into God's marvellous light. He has been called into the people of God, and his life must show something of the new family likeness.

Writing to the church at Corinth Paul uses a chain of Old Testament quotations to remind the Christians that they are to be separated from the spiritually and morally pagan society around them in order to be the temple and people of the living God: '"I will be their God, and they shall be *my people*. Therefore come out from them, and be separate from them, says the Lord, and touch nothing unclean; then I will welcome you, and I will be a father to you, and you shall be my sons and daughters, says the Lord Almighty".'[22] Again, writing to Titus, Paul stressed the need to renounce irreligion and worldly passions, and to live sober, upright, and godly

[19] Matthew 5:14-16.
[20] Quoted in his biography
by Andrew Woolsey,
Hodder & Stoughton p. 177.
[21] Romans 1:7.
[22] 2 Corinthians 6:16-18.

lives in this world,' as we wait for the coming of Jesus Christ, 'who gave himself for us to redeem us from all iniquity and to purify for himself *a people of his own* who are zealous for good deeds.'[23] As we live as his people, God will be glorified in the world, and people will want to know about the One who lives through us.

God's call is for a corporate life

Once a congregation grasps that God has called us collectively as his people so that his glory might be seen in us, that congregation may well be transformed. For too long the world has looked upon the church as buildings or as professional clergy. It is time that, as in New Testament days, all Christians are seen as the people of God — God's new society.

This is something not readily understood in educated western culture, where the emphasis is extravagantly on the individual — one of the reasons for the chronic and cosmic loneliness that plagues our society today. The root of all sin could be called independence; and it is for this reason that God calls us not only into a personal relationship with himself, but at the same time into a corporate relationship with the rest of the people of God. We are to be dependent upon him; and, in the right sense, dependent on one another. In the west we tend to confuse the words 'personal' and 'private'. Certainly our faith is to be a personal faith; but it is not to be private. The New Testament knows nothing of solitary religion. The Lord adds to the church those who are being saved; and as Howard Snyder has pointed out, 'There is no salvation outside the Church unless the body of Christ be decapitated, separated from the Head. The Church is the body of Christ; the community of the Holy Spirit; the people of God.'[24]

The church is emphatically *not* an agglomeration of pious individuals who happen to believe the same gospel. Yet all too often Christians talk about '*my* Christian life, *my* faith, *my* salvation, *my* relationship with God.' Passages about the work and gifts of the Holy Spirit, about spiritual warfare, about

[23]Titus 2:11-14.   [24]Spoken at the Lausanne Congress for World Evangelisation, 1974.

guidance or prayer, are often applied in an individualistic way. The letters of Paul and Peter are often expounded as though addressed to individual Christians, whereas the vast majority of them were written to churches. 'How many times does the word "saint" occur in the text of the New Testament?' asks Michael Griffiths. 'Get hold of a concordance and you will discover that the plural form "saints" occurs some sixty-one times. Only once (Phil. 4:21) is the singular used and that is in the phrase, "greet every saint"! The concept of a solitary saint is foreign to the New Testament writers.'[25] We are born again by the Spirit into the family of God; we are called by Christ to belong to the people of God. 'The Church begins, not with a pious individual, but with God. The pious individual cannot by himself achieve the transformation of isolated sinful men into the people of God. How could an atomised crowd of pious individuals be a home for the homeless and isolated men of today?'[26]

The church is also a community of sinners. We are 'called to be saints', but are perhaps increasingly aware that we are a fellowship of sinners. There is the constant need for repentance and renewal, and we stand daily at the need of God's mercy and grace. We can never claim to have 'arrived'; and Paul knew the need to go on pommelling his body and subduing it, 'lest after preaching to others I myself should be disqualified... Therefore let anyone who thinks that he stands take heed lest he fall.'[27]

Richard Wurmbrand once said, 'I'm so glad that the Church is not perfect; for if it were, I could not be a member of it. And I want to be a member of the Church.' It was probably for this reason that Jesus taught so much about the need to forgive, if need be, seventy times seven. There is only one realistic way in which to make progress, and that is to accept and love each other with unjudging friendship, and to exhort one another 'every day'.[28] We all need one another, and together we all need the Lord's grace. And that is what he has promised to the people of God.

---

[25]*Cinderella with Amnesia*, I.V.P., p. 24.
[26]Hans Küng, op. cit., p. 24.

[27]1 Corinthians 9:27; 10:12.
[28]Hebrews 3:12ff.

BUILDING COMMUNITIES

The whole concept of community begins with the nature of God himself. It exists in perfect form within the mystery of the Trinity, and it is this relationship of love that God wants to see entwined in and through his own people. When Jesus prayed that his disciples would all be one he went on to explain what he meant by this (insofar as we are able to comprehend it): 'even as thou, Father, art in me, and I in thee, that they may be in us... That they may be one even as we are one, I in them and thou in me...'[29] That is why the existence of the Christian community of the church in its ideal form is the fullest revelation of God that the world can at present see. His glory is to be seen in the church, shining out into the world.

Not only in biblical days, therefore, but throughout the centuries, for both theological and practical reasons God's people have formed themselves into communities to express their distinct identity as the family of God. Often thrown together by persecution or by the pagan society in which they have lived, Christians have deliberately developed an alternative way of life.

In the earlier centuries one notable example of this was Benedict of Nursia (c.480-c.547), who fled from the degeneracy of Rome, where he was studying, to live a hermit's life in a cave at Subiaco. After a brief experience in a monastery, he set up twelve small monastic communities and later established the monastery of Monte Cassino, where he remained until his death. It was there that he composed his Rule of life, based partly on those of John Cassian and Basil of Caesarea. This Rule became in time the constitution for the Order of Benedictines and has since provided the definitive rule for most western communities and monasteries.

At various points in this chapter we shall look at some of his principles, not least because the desire for community existence has been growing rapidly in recent years, partly owing to the increasing isolation and depressing destruction of meaningful relationships in our present society.

[29] John 17:21f.

The Pressures of today
There are a variety of reasons for the breakdown in today's
relationships: the constant mobility of jobs, the de-
personalisation of human beings in our computerised society,
the sex revolution encouraging extra-marital sexual experiences, the increase of material goods as a substitute to real
communication, and so on. But one of the problems is the
modern attitude to marriage itself. For many it has become a
form of escapism, an answer to the problems for unfulfilled
personalities. Graham Pulkingham rightly has commented:

> For many marriage has become the last desperate hope for
> a dependable relationship. It then becomes a kind of
> hiding place for people and is presented as the ideal love
> relationship. In most cases marriage doesn't measure up to
> these expectations. It becomes a sad knot of periodic
> pleasure which holds things together, a possessive relation-
> ship which produces jealousy, exclusiveness, and hostile
> and destructive tensions...it appears as the only option, the
> last, desperate hope of finding meaningful personal rela-
> tionships in life...[30]

It can be destructive to the forming of genuine Christian
community if marriage is taken as an exclusive relationship.
Apart from any other tension, those who are not married feel
deeply that loving and dependable relationships are denied
them from the start. What we need to see is that this concept
of the small nuclear family – mum, dad and two kids — is
comparatively modern, stemming largely from the days of the
industrial revolution when families were scattered in the
pursuit of jobs. The extended family was the norm in Bible
days (see the references to 'households'); it remained the
norm for many centuries afterwards and still is the case today
in certain parts of the world. It is true that the members of
these households were largely blood-relations but some of the
tensions of the small, modern family were considerably eased.
When battered wives and battered babies are an increasing

[30] *New Covenant* magazine, December 1971, p. 11; quoted by Michael
Harper, *A New Way of Living*, Hodder & Stoughton, p. 150.

tragedy in our present-day society, we cannot claim that all is well. In 1977 England and Wales had a divorce rate of almost one in two — one of the highest in the world.

Those with tensions in their marriage should not take on a community situation in order to solve their problems. This could prove disastrous. It may even be that they need to seek counselling themselves before considering the responsibilities of this lifestyle.

When, however, some (at least) of these small units can be expanded, so that a genuine Christian community of brothers and sisters in Christ can be formed, albeit around a nuclear unit, the possibility of new, deep and caring relationships on a wider basis becomes a vital part of the good news of the gospel.

Apart from community, what real support can be given to the numerous single and divorced members of many churches? What realistic care can be given to the single parent, to the widow or widower? What about those who have suffered from mental illness, those who have been emotionally crippled by deep hurts or starved of love, those who find forming relationships more difficult than most? As good as the welfare system may be in those countries where it exists at all, it is impossible for such a system to escape from the ethos of the 'institution'. If it is God's plan to set the solitary in families, what practical measures can the local church take to see that this actually happens — perhaps starting within its own ranks? And it is by no means only the elderly who are lonely today. Christian ministers and clergy, not to mention their wives, can often suffer acutely in this way.

The call for some sort of community life becomes even more insistent when there is a growing shortage of full-time workers — or money — for the life of the church. When groups of people live together, however, it is possible to set aside both money and manpower for the kingdom of God.

In the house in which I live, it has been our practice for the last five years to have anything up to six or seven living with my wife and two young children, and to share together on the principle of the 'common purse'. At the time of writing we have two salary-earners (a teacher and myself) plus a student with a grant. Together we are able to support the household

of ten, setting aside four or five for full-time Christian work.
We have nothing to boast about. We have made almost every
mistake in the book. The need to forgive and be forgiven is
constantly with us. But we have learnt a great deal about
ourselves, about one another, and about how to live together
as a small community of God's people gathered in this house.
It has not been easy. It is not for everyone. It is not even the
'best' or 'most spiritual' way of doing things! But it is a valid
form of lifestyle in this twentieth century, and fruitful for
those who are called into it.

It is, moreover, one modest way in which we can challenge
the standards of the affluent societies in which we live.
Instead of the constant pressing claims for a 'higher standard
of living' — claims which relate mostly to the acquisition of
more material possessions and have little to do with real life
— the conscious adoption of a different lifestyle can demonstrate the much more important qualities that should become
our priorities in this impersonal and fractured world. This is
an age when we need to live much more simply and to learn
again how to be creative with what we have, instead of
discarding something as soon as it begins to look worn and
torn. If for no other reason, we must live more simply in order
to give much more generously to the millions who scarely live
at all. As an invaluable side-product, the working together on
various tasks, especially if they are for the benefit of others,
can create a new quality of relationships that have often been
lost through the domination of television in the home, with
the consequent impossibility of any real communication.

No form of community living is easy, however! What we
have found interesting is that many of the problems we have
faced — problems which are common to many such groupings and which have sometimes brought them into suspicion
or disrepute — could have been avoided if the remarkably
wise sixth-century Rule of Benedict had been known or
followed more closely.

Leadership
The church is not a democracy, and Benedict saw clearly the
need in each community for a clearly defined and respected
leader who was finally responsible for the decisions and
well-being of its members. His leadership must be expressed

by example as well as words. He should be a man of spiritual maturity with a growing gift of discernment, and not afraid to exercise discipline with both gentleness and firmness. Benedict in fact spoke of the necessity of the 'knife of amputation' or 'the rod' for those who could not be led by other means! Yet to err on the side of mercy was preferable in cases where decisions were difficult.

At various times throughout the centuries to the present day, we have tended to think of communities as somewhat rare groupings of those who have been specially called into this way of life, in contrast to the life of most local churches. More recently, however, several churches have formed small communities — often called 'extended households' — within their own local setting. In our own church in York we now have some six or seven of these, with probably several more coming into being in the near future. In each of these groupings the matter of leadership remains crucial, and in an extended household, where there will usually be several others gathered around a nuclear family unit, it will naturally be the spiritually mature husband and wife who will exercise the joint headship of the family. Good leadership will again be marked by example, gentleness and discipline. If there are several such households in one church, it is good for the leaders to get together at regular intervals to share common problems and to encourage one another in their responsibilities.

Most monastic communities also have the healthy practice of a 'visitor', who may often be the local bishop. Because of the pressures of living closely together there is a real value, both for the leader and for any member of the community, to be able to consult the 'visitor' when certain specific needs arise. Within the extended household the same principle holds good. We have often found it beneficial in our situation to refer to some mature Christian leader outside the house to whom personal problems or household difficulties can be taken. In our case it is another elder in our church. From his objective standpoint various tense situations can more easily be resolved, although it goes without saying that confidences must be very strictly observed.

Community life
Prayer and work have always been the twin marks of

Christian communities. Benedict wrote: 'As the prophet says, "Seven times in the day do I praise thee." We will complete this sacred number seven if, at lauds, at the first, third, sixth, ninth hours, at vesper time and at compline we carry out the duties of our service. Idleness is the enemy of the soul. Therefore at fixed times, the brothers should be busy with manual work; and at other times in holy reading... The brothers shall take turns to wait on each other so that no one is excused from kitchen work, unless prevented by sickness or taken up with some vital business...' Similar patterns of life are familiar with most religious orders.

The details will doubtless be different, but the principles behind this also make much sense in the extended household. Regular prayer needs to be the basis of our common life. 'The family that prays together stays together.' The reason some experiments in modern community living have failed — sometimes disastrously so — is often due to the failure to realise that it is only the life of Christ among us that can keep us together. Just as God's people were often scattered when they disobeyed their Lord in Old Testament times, so households can fall apart unless Christ himself is maintained at the centre of our relationships. A leader of another community once shrewdly asked me, 'Have you come to that point in your relationships when you *have* to depend on the Holy Spirit?'

In practice we find that first thing in the morning (7 a.m.) is the only time when we can regularly be together, and each member of the household is encouraged to share something from the Bible that God has been speaking to them about over the last twenty-four hours. There is no compulsion about this, but it is a way of encouraging one another to maintain our personal relationship with Christ each day. We are not to depend *too* much on the support of our corporate life. Although Bible study groups still have a real place in the life of a church, we have found that this 'sharing' of verses and passages from the Scriptures has considerably helped us to *listen* to what God is saying to us in our personal readings. Then, together, we often gain some insight into what he is saying to us as a community. This Bible sharing is turned into prayer, as we pray for one another, the needs of those in the church, and the wider needs of missionaries and nations, as time allows. The whole practice normally takes about forty minutes, and has become the most important part of our life together in Christ.

Practical work is also vital. Each member of the household has his or her own jobs, and we all take our turns with the various 'chores'. Some careful planning of this is essential to avoid the opting out by some who may feel that they are under more pressure than others (we can all feel that only too often!) resulting in the willing few taking more of the load than they should. Particular personal needs are taken into consideration as they arise.

Defining aims
The ultimate aim of Benedict was that 'God may be glorified in all things'. He saw this not in terms of a narrow piety, but in the redeeming of the whole of life for God so that man might become more fully human. It was through the monasteries based on his Rule that much pagan literature has been preserved for future generations and that agriculture and a host of useful crafts were encouraged. The purpose was to give a meaningful direction to the life of an individual and to make each person more aware of the needs of his neighbour, quite apart from the direct worship and service of God.

Similar aims need to be defined in the communities of today. In our household we have three main priorities, which have often to be checked.

First we come together to support the main ministry that the house represents. With us this ministry is largely directed towards needs of the church and of the mission teams that go out from York to help with the wider mission of the church in other parts of the world. Each household, however, has a slightly different aim. One supports a Christian shop which sells coffee, meals, clothes, books and crafts; it is also a very good meeting place for Christians from various churches and for talking with those who have not yet found Christ. Further, it releases various helpers for the mission teams. Another household aims primarily to support the particular needs of those within the house, although there will necessarily be some healthy outlets outside its own ranks. Another feels a primary call to offer frequent hospitality to many visitors who come here. The important point is to know what the primary aim of the house may be, and to realise that this role may change continuously over the years.

Secondly, we seek to support the needs of the children in the house. Often questions are asked about this, and there is a danger that children of a nuclear family can suffer if adult needs dominate the energies of that household. In practice, it is unwise having disturbed adults living within a community for any length of time if any of the children are under twelve years of age, and households have to be firm in saying 'no' to desperate pleas for help. This may sound hard, but every grouping has limitations which must humbly be accepted. That is why we still very much need one another within the wider church.

Children must never be made to feel second-class citizens to the real work of the house. Each child is a complete although immature person, made in God's own image. One vital role of the household is to serve their younger brothers and sisters in Christ, encouraging them to discover their potential as God has made them, and to see them grow into mature people. As far as the devotional life of the household is concerned, we feel in our situation that forty minutes each day is too long for small children, so my wife and I read and pray more briefly with them before they go off to school.

Thirdly, we aim to support one another within the house. Every person has problems, and it is often in a community situation that some of the deep-seated problems which need to be dealt with emerge in order to be healed. We must learn therefore to accept each person as they are and not as we would like them to be. We must bear with one another in a constant spirit of forgiveness, love and patience, although gently encouraging each individual to face up to his problems, and not to run away from them. What many of us find, when we begin more deliberately to open up our lives to one another, is how intrinsically selfish most of us are! It is comparatively easy to be gracious to one another at church meetings when we see each other for such a short time. But in an extended household, some of our selfishness quickly comes to the light, and many of us have to learn in a much deeper way than ever before how to serve one another with the humility and gentleness of Christ. In many nuclear units the 'no-go' areas are repressed but never resolved.

That is why in community we need so urgently the help of his Spirit to maintain his life among us!

Developing relationships

No relationships can be taken for granted. They must all be worked at with much prayer and patience. Because of the business of most people in a community situation it is the quality of our time together, rather than quantity, that is important. It is all too easy 'switching off' from others or throwing a protective shell around one's inner self. When we are truly open to each other — an essential in good relationships — we make ourselves vulnerable. We shall often be humbled and need to repent. We shall often be hurt. The constant temptation is to erect a polite wall, within which we may still do the tasks that are strictly required of us, but we cease to relate at any depth to those around us. We become instead an atomised group of individuals, which soon destroys the life of the community. It is not that the need for privacy is denied. In fact it is most necessary for individuals to have time to think, read, pray and relax on their own or together in twos or threes. But we are still members of one another, and need to maintain a constant openness to each other if the life of the Spirit has any chance to flow among us, thereby making us into an effective body of Christ.

Benedict knew the absolute need of this. 'Although the principle of leadership was firmly maintained in his Rule, he saw the need of the community to take its full part in making decisions. Not only should 'all be called to council', but 'God often reveals what is better to the younger'. He therefore stressed that the older members should mix freely with the younger to build up the strength of relationships in the community through which the will of God could be discovered and achieved more clearly.

In view of this, each of his communities had to be in part selective. Although a man might be initially invited to join, if after a time it was seen that he could be a disruptive influence, he 'should be told politely to depart'. Later, once a man had become a full member of the community, if he acted in any way which seriously upset the common life or became an attitude of rebellion, he would first be admonished, then given more severe punishment, and then if necessary dismissed. In each community situation there has to be a constant willingness to crucify personal ambitions and individualistic talents for the benefit of the whole, if the risen life of Christ is to appear. A clear mark of maturity is seen in the readiness to recognise one's faults and to be willing to admit them. Further, if we wish others to accept our faults, we in turn must be able to accept theirs.

In households, the same wisdom applies. Very few realise the degree or implications of commitment involved when they first join, and usually members experience three stages. First there is the 'honeymoon' period where the sense of love is overwhelming compared with the loneliness that may previously have been known. After a time this can turn into a 'nightmare' as the irritations, frustrations and loss of independence erupt to the surface. It is sometimes during this period that individuals wish to opt out, and for this reason it is a good practice to invite people originally on a six-month 'trial' (from both points of view) before a more serious commitment into the household is made. Thirdly, these traumas, which can be exceedingly painful at the time, will pass into the period of 'realism' when we consciously accept one another as we are, warts and all, and begin to rely more specifically on the grace of God to hold relationships together.

The wider community of the church

So far we have related the principles of the Benedictine Rule to the slightly wider concept of what could — and I believe should — become a much more common community lifestyle within the ranks of most local churches. I have tried to indicate how this could be a practical way of helping those who are lonely and in need of extra support, and also of releasing many more active workers for the mission of the church, without the crippling financial drain of normal salaries, as low as they are for most ordained ministers.

I have also stressed, however, that this is by no means the only or the best way of doing things. It is 'best' for those who are called into it, but for others the more conventional nuclear family unit will still have a vital part to play in today's society – not least when close family relationships are being broken up increasingly all the time.

Our focus on the extended household has nevertheless

illustrated what the church needs to become in a wider setting. As local churches we need much more consciously to become a warm and accepting community of the people of God, where the outsider feels welcomed, loved and served. The most practical expression of this, for most churches and in the first instance at any rate, may be in the context of home meetings, which we shall look at more fully later in the book. There should also develop a community sense of the people of God in any given locality — village, town, city, district, county or diocese. If any mark is to be made on the political and social scene, corporate action on this scale will almost always be necessary. I have also seen the undoubted value of city missions where numerous churches from all denominations and traditions come together to witness to their corporate faith in the risen Christ, even though those churches may still have serious differences at other levels. The impact of such a united effort can be considerably more than the sum of the individual churches doing their own thing.

In other words, it would be a mistake to limit the concept of 'community' either to the traditional and special monastic orders or to the more recent development of extended households. God calls all his people to become the community of God, even though obviously the levels of commitment within that community will necessarily vary continually. My fingers typing this manuscript are working' very closely together. My toes at this moment are not involved! Yet they are part of the same body, and the whole would be seriously handicapped without some sort of definite commitment and co-operation existing under the leadership of the head.

In all this, especially as our commitment to one another deepens (and in most church circles this is an urgent imperative), it is vital that we all find our security in the love of God as his children. If we are firmly rooted and grounded in his love, any changing of roles will not be a basic threat to our identity. We are first and foremost *his* people and *his* possession, and it is only if we have failed to grasp this or maybe lose sight of this, that we shall be distressed by any uprooting that may take place from one part of God's family to another. As important as our relationships together need to become, they should never be a substitute for our relationship with God himself. When Abraham left his homeland and all that had been his security over generations, he did not know where he was going. But he did know *with whom* he was going, and that was sufficient for him.

Further, the degree of commitment to one another as the people of God may sound very strange bells in the minds of many good churchmen. In the British scene at least, we have kept ourselves to ourselves, even within the church. Our friendships and meaningful relationships still largely depend on questions of culture, education and background, and all this is the very opposite of what we should become in Christ.

When my wife and I moved to York we were lonely to begin with because we found so few to whom we could naturally (i.e. culturally) relate. Some time later the reality of being brothers and sisters in God's family hit us with altogether new force. Here were our real roots — not in the educational and social background to which we originally belonged. Although we have no doubt much still to learn about this, the joy of discovering new depths of relationships within God's family — relationships made possible due to a quality of his love that cannot be found anywhere else in the world — became a most liberating experience for us. When our roots are in the love of God, and when our deepest commitments are both to him and to others within his family, we shall find this both exhilarating and dangerous. But that is how God is able to dwell in the midst of his people.

CHAPTER SEVEN

The Body of Christ

WE TURN TO the most familiar picture of the church in the new Testament: the body of Christ. Although the phrase never once occurs in the Gospels or in Acts, Paul refers to the church in this way in his letters to the Romans, Corinthians, Ephesians and Colossians. For him this metaphor expressed more graphically than anything else the essential unity both between Christ and his Church, and also between the members of his church. In the Greek language the word 'body' was commonly used to describe the unity of anything which consisted of various members (e.g. the State, a melody, a vine), and therefore it was an obvious word to use for those who had become one in Christ.

Moreover, 'the body of Christ' is a particularly apt phrase in the New Testament, as sometimes it refers to the sacrificial death of Christ on the cross ('you have died to the law through the body of Christ');[1] sometimes it describes the fellowship experienced in the Lord's Supper ('the bread which we break, is it not a participation in the body of Christ?');[2] and more often it refers to the body of believers whose unity was made possible through that cross and is beautifully expressed in that fellowship meal.

The meaning of the body of Christ
Paul clearly has in mind something more than the sum of believers in one place. Had this been his intention he would probably have referred to the body of Christians; but in fact

[1] Romans 7:4; cf. Hebrews 10:10. [2] 1 Corinthians 10:16; cf. 11:23-29.

he specifically writes about the body of Christ. It seems clear that he is speaking of an *organic unity*, in which Christians not only belong to Christ and to one another within his body; they also abide in him and find life in him. Without Christ, and for that matter without his body, there is no true salvation. This needs once again to be thoroughly grasped by Christians in an age when many see the church as little more than a club. A 'club', according to my dictionary, is 'an association of persons united by some common interest, meeting periodically for co-operation or conviviality.' But this club-mentality will not do for the church. The church is the body of Christ, and Christians are inescapably and organically members of it.

Some go even further and talk of the body of Christ as Christ's continuing incarnation on earth, or the resurrected form of Christ on earth. Hans Küng even says that 'Christ does not exist without the Church'.[3] Yet quite clearly, as the second Person of the Eternal Godhead, Christ has a distinct existence from the church, even though it is undoubtedly true that 'the Church does not exist without Christ.' The One who could say, 'Before Abraham was, I am', could certainly add 'Before the church was, I am', or 'Apart from the church, I am'. To identify Christ with the church is a dangerous extension of a powerful analogy, and it can lead to much confusion over the question of authority. To those who maintain that what the church says, Christ says, the reply could well be: 'Which church?' or 'What *does* the church say?' Such an identification with Christ and his body also makes it difficult to explain the manifest sins and corruptions of the church. It is still very much a body full of spots and wrinkles.

Paul does however seem to get very near this teaching at times. For example he writes to the Corinthians: 'For just as the body is one and has many members, and all the members of the body, though many, are one body, so it is with Christ.'[4] Notice, he does not say 'so it is with the church.' In fact, the last few words in the Greek are even more striking. They read: 'so also the Christ'. When quite plainly he is talking about the church, why does Paul write 'the Christ'? It is because, as he goes on to explain in that chapter, 'you are the body of Christ and individually members of it.' Although

---

[3] Op. cit., p. 234.   [4] 1 Corinthians 12:12.

Christ is quite distinct from the church, as the body of Christ the church should be a powerful testimony to the reality of the risen Christ today. And that will be true only when individual Christians, or groups of Christians, lose their independence and learn again what it means to belong to one another and to share together their common life in Christ as members of his one body.

Universal or local?

In his letters to the Ephesians and Colossians, Paul uses the expression 'the church, which is his body' primarily in the sense of the universal church. Because of the particular problems facing the Christians at Ephesus and Colossae, he wants to assure them that the whole cosmos is still in the hands of Christ. Christ is 'far above all rule and authority and power and dominion', and God 'has made him the head over all things for the church, which is his body'. Indeed, it is through the church that the manifold wisdom of God might now be made known to the principalities and powers in the heavenly places. Christ 'is before all things, and in him all things hold together. He is the head of the body, the church; he is the beginning, the first-born from the dead, that in everything he might be pre-eminent.' Paul urges the Christians not to be deceived by gnostic heresies, but to hold fast to the Head, 'from whom the whole body...grows with a growth that is from God.' In these letters, it is Christ's headship over the whole church and his authority over all things for the whole church that is the important point. The 'body of Christ' is the universal church.

In the letters to the Romans and Corinthians, however, Paul is much more preoccupied with the harmony and order of the local body of Christians. There had been divisions over the personalities of various leaders, disputes over the gifts and ministries of the Holy Spirit, and confusion and discord at the Lord's Supper. He writes therefore to remind them that they, as a local church, are the body of Christ. The members of the body are different, and must be so, but they all belong to the one body. The hands and feet, eyes and ears all have their essential part to play. Even the weakest members of the body are 'indispensable'. Their relationships must be right with one another, 'for any one who eats and drinks without discerning the body eats and drinks judgment upon himself.'

From this particular analogy Paul emphasises three main truths about the church. First, he outlines the necessary spiritual growth into unity and maturity that the whole body must make together. Second, he describes the variety of gifts that God has given to enable this united body to make its growth. And third, he reminds his readers of the supreme authority of the Head of the body, Jesus Christ. Let us therefore look at each of these in turn.

1. GROWTH INTO UNITY AND MATURITY

In Ephesians 4 Paul presents a marvellous picture of the church, as the body of Christ, growing 'to mature manhood, to the measure of the stature of the fullness of Christ.' For this growth to take place, a number of elements are necessary.

United in love
Unity in a church can never for a moment be taken for granted. The whole history of the people of God, from Genesis to the present day, shows that the devil will do everything he possibly can to divide God's family; this is the surest way of destroying the work of God on earth. Therefore, although unity has been restored and made possible for us through the cross of Jesus Christ, we, on our part, must be 'eager to maintain it'. The leaders of a church should see this as one of their top pastoral priorities.

Whatever our differences, we all need one another and we all belong to one another. 'For just as the body is *one* and has many members, and all the members of the body, though many, are *one* body, so it is with Christ. For by *one* Spirit we were all baptised into *one* body...and all were made to drink of *one* Spirit... As it is, there are many parts, yet *one* body...'[5]

True unity is founded on love. Therefore it is essential that the members of a church develop a strong love for each other. This is the only way in which unity can be maintained. Indeed Paul begs them to forbear one another in love, 'eager to maintain the unity of the Spirit in the bond of peace'. The context of this exhortation is particularly interesting. Paul has

[5] 1 Corinthians 12:12f, 20.

just confidently asserted that God 'by the power at work within us is able to do far more abundantly than all that we ask or think', and so 'to him be *glory in the church* and in Christ Jesus to all generations, for ever and ever'. Notice that God's glory, which means the visible manifestation of his invisible nature, is to be in the church. But that is possible only when the church is strongly united in love. 'Behold, how good and pleasant it is when brothers dwell in unity!... For there the Lord has commanded the blessing...'[6]

True Christian love begins with commitment and issues in practical service. As it is not possible to be equally committed to every Christian, the practicalities of this must first be worked out in local areas or small groups.

In our own church the congregation is divided into 20-25 area groups, and within those groups (not more than 20 in size ideally) we are learning to share our lives together, to borrow cars, tools or household appliances, to be aware of the financial needs of each member of the group and to supply needs as they arise. Our homes are open to one another, and we try to help in the sharing of hospitality, or in caring for one another when anyone falls sick.

Each group is also expected to help in the wider work of the church. Due to the many visitors who come to York we offer buffet lunches each Sunday during the summer months. Members of the fellowship bring picnic lunches to share in common, and the groups take it in turns to organise and serve the food — to give only one small example.

Love also includes constant forgiving. The closer we draw together, the more easily we may hurt one another, and the more often we shall have to forgive and be forgiven. Although this must be encouraged on a continuous basis, we find it helpful every now and then to provide special opportunities for putting right some of the tensions within relationships during the 'Peace' in our services of Holy Communion. Christ has told us to leave our gifts at the altar and first be reconciled to our brother before we do anything else. Right and loving relationships need to be watched and worked at all the time if the bond of peace and true love is to prevail within a church.

[6]Psalm 133.

Love needs expression, too. Dutiful service is not enough in today's cold and impersonal world. Often a touch, an arm around the shoulder, a warm handshake, a gentle embrace or a gracious smile — all these can both express and increase the reality of love within the body of Christ. If it is to be God's love that is flowing, care must be taken to see that these are genuine and in the Spirit. But much of the accusation of the church being 'God's frozen people' is due to the inbuilt reserve that is a cultural characteristic of the British — and some other nations, too!

Equipped for ministry

The whole church should be *equipped* for the work of ministry: 'And his gifts were that some should be apostles, some prophets, some evangelists, some pastors and teachers, to equip the saints for the work of ministry, for building up the body of Christ.' It is a travesty of the true nature of the church to think of the ministry only in terms of the theologically trained leaders. All the saints, or Christians, are to be involved in the work of ministry. All are called to serve within the body of Christ. There are some specialist gifts and ministries, certainly, but these are simply to equip everyone for a definite role and task within the church. No one is to be a passenger. All belong to the crew.

Growth in knowledge

All must *grow in their knowledge* of Christ and of his word: '...until we all attain to the unity of the faith and of the knowledge of the Son of God, to mature manhood, to the measure of the stature of the fulness of Christ; so that we may no longer be children, tossed to and fro and carried about with every wind of doctrine, by the cunning of men, by their craftiness in deceitful wiles.'

Numerous teachings and philosophies abound today. Some are proclaimed within the Christian church, yet are far from God's own revelation in the Scriptures. Others stem from religious sects which proliferate; others are avowedly secular and atheistic.

More than ever, the Christian must know what he believes and why he believes it. There will be no stability or maturity until he is well established in the truth of God's word, and until he has a deep and growing experience of this truth in his own life. That is why Paul commended the Ephesian elders 'to God and to the word of his grace, which is able to build you up and to give you the inheritance among all those who are sanctified.'[7] Regular Bible study, personally and in small groups, constant teaching and training, and the prayerful application of the Bible in our lives and relationships, is vital in any true growth towards Christian maturity. Many churches find some form of 'Bible partnership' schemes, with two Christians (one mature, the other less mature) reading and studying together, particularly fruitful.

Speaking the truth in love
The church must learn to 'speak the truth in love'. There is the need to be open and honest in all our relationships. The East African revival spoke often about 'walking in the light' with one another. Only in this way could real fellowship be maintained, both with God and with his people. Sometimes it is necessary to warn, to rebuke, or to exhort; but always it must be gently and in love: 'Brethren, if a man is overtaken in any trespass, you who are spiritual should restore him in a spirit of gentleness. Look to yourself, lest you too be tempted. Bear one another's burdens, and so fulfil the law of Christ.'[8]

Full commitment
Christians must learn to be *100 per cent committed* both to Christ and to his body: 'We are to grow up in every way into him who is the head, into Christ, from whom the whole body, joined and knit together by every joint with which it is supplied, when each part is working properly, makes bodily growth and upbuilds itself in love.' We need to be as committed to one another as we are to Christ, and so play our full part in the life and work of the church. This will require a constant review of priorities, and a continual willingness to submit fully to Christ, and also to one another out of reverence for Christ. It will not be easy. It will demand all that we have, all that we are. Christ never welcomed or encouraged cheap

[7] Acts 20:32.   [8] Galatians 6:1f.

discipleship. Only in a full-blooded devotion to him and to his body will the living Christ be seen in this world.

The Communist revolution of this century, too, has demanded unhesitating obedience. An American student wrote a letter to his fiancée breaking off his engagement:

> We Communists have a high casualty rate. We are the ones who get shot at, hung, jailed, lynched, tarred and feathered, slandered, ridiculed, and fired from our jobs, and in every other way made as uncomfortable as possible. A certain percentage of us gets killed or imprisoned; we live in virtual poverty. We turn back to the Party every penny we make above what is necessary to keep us alive.
>
> We Communists don't have the time or money for many movies or concerts or T-bone steaks or decent homes or new cars. We've been described as fanatics; we are fanatics. Our lives are dominated by one overshadowing factor: the Struggle for World Communism!
>
> We Communists have a philosophy of life which no amount of money could buy. We have a cause to fight for, a definite purpose in life. We subordinate our petty personal selves into a great movement for humanity. There is one thing about which I am in earnest: the Communist Cause! It is my life, my business, my religion, my hobby, my sweetheart, my wife, my mistress, my bread and my meat! I work at it in the daytime and dream of it at night! Therefore I cannot carry on a friendship, a love affair, or even a conversation, without relating everything to this force which both guides and drives my life... I have already been in jail because of my ideas, and if necessary I am ready to go before a firing squad.

No wonder this revolution has swallowed up more than half the world since its explosion in 1917. The same total commitment is required by the liberation armies and movements that have recently sprung up all over the world. And it is often in the absence of such a challenge by the church that men and women, and especially young people, have turned to the cults and sects and political groups that demand full-blooded discipleship and a totally new way of living.

2. GIFTS OF THE SPIRIT

In order to mature the body, God has given a variety of gifts
to the members. Today, however, there is widespread ignorance of these gifts, and many even discount the validity of
some of the gifts and despise those who use them.

Paul, in 1 Corinthians 12:4ff, stresses that *all* these gifts are
from *God*. They all come through, or according to, or by, the
same Spirit. Indeed he mentions all three persons of the
Trinity in verses 4-6, the earliest trinitarian reference in the
New Testament. Therefore, in the light of God's clear
sovereign action with these gifts, which this passage maintains
so strongly, no one can say quite arbitrarily that certain gifts
such as prophecy or tongues died out with the apostles and
are not for today. Rather, 'all these [gifts] are inspired by one
and the same Spirit, who apportions to each one individually
as he wills'. Thus if all these gifts are from God, all are good,
and none is to be despised, including the gift of tongues. To
despise, or even to disparage, certain gifts is to quench the
Holy Spirit.[9]

Variety of gifts
Some Christians talk of 'the nine gifts', referring to those
mentioned in 1 Corinthians 12:8-10: wisdom, knowledge,
faith, healing, miracles, prophecy, discernment, tongues and
interpretation. But in the New Testament there is no sharp
distinction between 'natural' and 'supernatural' gifts, even if
some (such as those just mentioned) demonstrate a more
unusual manifestation of the Spirit. It is therefore a mistake
to talk of 'the nine gifts'. In verse 28 of that same chapter
there is a mixture of the so-called natural and supernatural
gifts, some of which are mentioned in verses 8-10, and some of
which are not (apostles, teachers, helpers, administrators).
There are also further lists in Romans 12, Ephesians 4 and 1
Peter 4, and there is no suggestion that these lists are
complete. Indeed, Paul talks of the *charisma* (meaning the gift
of God's love) of forgiveness, of eternal life, of leadership, of
marriage, of celibacy, or the *charisma* resulting from Christian
fellowship. The variety is considerable.

[9] See 1 Thessalonians 5:19f.

What, then, makes something a 'gift of the Spirit'? It is not some strange, inexplicable, supernatural quality. Rather, something becomes a gift of the Spirit when it fulfils two functions.

First, it must *glorify Christ*. 'No one can say "Jesus is Lord" except by the Holy Spirit';[10] and in one way or another the Spirit will always seek to glorify Jesus, for that is his supreme work.

Second, it must *edify the body of Christ*. 'To each is given the manifestation of the Spirit for the common good.'[11] Paul later stresses the absolute importance of this no less than seven times in 1 Corinthians 14. Arnold Bittlinger wrote: 'Gifts are functions of the body of Christ. They are his eyes, hands and feet, with which he acts and moves on earth. When gifts are no longer an expression of Christ's actions, then they are not only useless but harmful in their effect. They are counterfeits which offer my neighbour nothing, but positively deceive him.'[12]

If any gift or ability, therefore, is used to glorify Christ and to edify his body, it becomes a gift of the Holy Spirit. Of course there must be some conscious dependence on God, together with the inspiration of the Holy Spirit, before a natural ability becomes a true spiritual gift. Without this, the gift can all too easily become an occasion for self-display. Our attitudes to these natural talents are important. Do I see my talent as '*my* gift', so that I am looking for personal fulfilment for *my* gift? Or do I see it as entirely a gift from God, which he could remove at any moment, and must consequently be used humbly and prayerfully to his glory and for the benefit of his people? Only then can it become a genuine spiritual gift. Arnold Bittlinger has described such a gift as 'a gratuitous manifestation of the Holy Spirit, working in and through, but going beyond, the believer's natural ability for the common good of the people of God.'[13] If these gifts are thus for the benefit of the church, it is important to understand them, to have a right attitude towards them, and to make full use of them.

[10] 1 Corinthians 12:3.
[11] 1 Corinthians 12:7.
[12] *Gifts and Graces*,
Hodder & Stoughton p. 81.
[13] *Gifts and Ministries*,
Hodder & Stoughton, p. 20.

Every gift important

Human nature is naturally inclined towards feelings of inferiority and superiority. When one person has a particular gift which another does not possess, it is easy to forget that every gift comes only by the grace and sovereignty of God. It was because the Corinthians lost sight of this that Paul had to deal with feelings of inferiority and superiority among them.

Paul addresses himself first to those who suffer from an *inferiority complex*. 'If the foot should say, "Because I am not a hand, I do not belong to the body," that would not make it any less a part of the body. And if the ear should say, "Because I am not an eye, I do not belong to the body," that would not make it any less a part of the body... If all were a single organ, where would the body be? As it is there are many parts, yet one body.'

In many churches there are Christians who feel on the fringe because of this sense of inferiority. Because they do not possess much knowledge about their faith, and do not have the obviously needed gifts such as preaching or playing the organ, they feel inferior. However, imagine if you can a congregation that consisted entirely of preachers or organists! Some theological colleges might approximate to this, but how inadequate this would be as the body of Christ! Each local church needs the widest range of gifts imaginable — some more obviously 'spiritual' and some more obviously 'practical', although it is impossible to make such a distinction. Every person and every gift is vital. After all, 'God has arranged the organs in the body, each one of them, as he chose.'

Paul next speaks to those who suffer from a *superiority complex*. 'The eye cannot say to the hand, "I have no need of you," nor again the head to the feet, "I have no need of you." On the contrary, the parts of the body which seem to be weaker are indispensable... [Indeed] God has so composed the body, giving the greater honour to the inferior part, that there may be no discord in the body, but that the members may have the same care for one another.' In other words, the members of a local church *ought* to be 'one body', regardless of their different gifts, because they already *are* 'one body' in Christ. To be a Christian is to be 'in Christ'; and to be 'in

Christ' also means to be in 'one body in Christ', as Paul expresses it in Romans 12:5.

Use of gifts

Once the importance of all of the gifts is recognised, three consequences follow:

(i) *We should appreciate them.* Inferiority and superiority complexes would never arise if we all appreciated one another's gifts and saw each gift as a cause for rejoicing and thanksgiving, not as a reason for jealousy or pride. 'If one member is honoured, all rejoice together,' because all gifts become 'our' gifts, since we all belong to one body. If one member, for example, begins to show evangelistic or prophetic gifts, all should rejoice since the whole fellowship will be enriched and strengthened by these gifts. Through whom the gifts are given is not the important point; the essential truth is that all gifts are 'for the common good', to edify the body of Christ.

Paul rapped the foolish Corinthian Christians over the knuckles for their rivalry and party-spirit. They were boasting of the different personalities and gifts of their leaders. What a silly and unspiritual thing to do, he wrote. 'Let no one boast of men. For all things are yours, whether Paul or Apollos or Cephas... all are yours; and you are Christ's; and Christ is God's.'[14] The very differences between Paul, Apollos and Cephas meant an enriching variety for the whole church. When seen in this way, all three leaders were God's gift for the benefit of the whole church, and therefore of every member of that church. If the Corinthians failed to see this, they had not begun to see what it meant to belong to the body of Christ or to the temple of the Holy Spirit.

Today, the cult of personality is rife, especially within certain sections of the church. Such immature rivalry is a mark of the lack of real spirituality within the church. If we are guilty of this, we are 'behaving like ordinary men'. The same is true of tensions between churches in the same town or city, or between clergy and ministers. Once we have in any way grasped what it means to belong to the body of Christ, we ought to thank God for one another, and for the great

[14] 1 Corinthians 3:21-23.

variety of gifts and ministries that God gives within his church.

(ii) *We should earnestly desire them*, especially the gift of prophecy and any others which excel in building up the church. Paul is quite insistent that Christians should not sit back and 'let God give them a gift if he wants to'. Not at all! 'Earnestly desire the higher gifts... Earnestly desire the spiritual gifts, especially that you may prophesy... Earnestly desire to prophesy...'[15] In practice, the congregation needs to pray specifically for all the gifts of the Spirit to be given in order to build up the body of Christ, and each Christian needs to discover and then use his God-given gift. That gift will need to be recognised and tested by others within the congregation, especially by the leaders, but encouragement should be given constantly. It should also be part of the leader's responsibility to spot the gifts that God may well be giving to different members of Christ's body, even before those members are aware of those gifts themselves.

In order to encourage gifts to grow and develop within a church, the following guidelines may be of some help. First of all, clear, biblical teaching on this subject is essential. This whole area can easily lead to deception and counterfeits, abuses and tragedies, which is the reason why some Christian leaders prefer to keep clear of this subject altogether. There may also be misunderstandings and fears, usually due to ignorance, and positive and sensitive teaching will help to build a good foundation for any further developments. Secondly, work hard to create a true body of Christ, where the atmosphere is one of love and acceptance, so that, if and when there are some manifestations of the Spirit, people are not frightened of making mistakes, nor of being corrected. We are simply a family learning to talk with, and listen to, our heavenly Father, and then to share together what he is saying to us. Of course mistakes will be made; but the alternative is not to start at all, and that is a mistake! Thirdly, help people to see that the gifts are all expressions of the compassion of Christ, and in no sense a display of superior spirituality. Therefore, as certain needs arise, such as when praying for a special task or for a person who is sick, it is the most natural

[15] 1 Corinthians 14:1.

time to ask God to speak to us and to move amongst us in a clear, sovereign way. Fourthly, encourage worship and praise in times of prayer. Consciously focus on the Lord, so that we are able to receive whatever he wants to give or say to us. Fifthly, encourage Christians to share what they have: 'When you come together, each one has a hymn, a lesson, a revelation, a tongue, or an interpretation. Let all things be done for edification.'[16] The first attempts to prophesy, for example, may not be immensely profound; but equally the same could be said of the first talks and sermons of someone who might later become a great preacher. Even the powerful prophets of the Old Testament sometimes brought a very simple message: 'Then Haggai, the messenger of the Lord, spoke to the people with the Lord's message, "I am with you, says the Lord."'[17] That was all! Therefore don't dismiss some simple prophetic word on the grounds of being 'trite', as I have so often heard from various Christian leaders who are sure they know best! Lastly, encourage everyone to pray much for the gifts which will most of all strengthen the body of Christ.

(iii) *We must use these gifts*: 'Having gifts that differ according to the grace given to us, let us use them.'[18] In the parable of the talents the message is clear: if God has given us anything at all, it must be made to work. We are all stewards of God's gifts, and these gifts are all expressions of his love, as he reaches out in and through the body of Christ for the benefit of others. Further, when God is clearly active within his body, and when that activity reveals his love, the impact on the surrounding community will be considerable. There is nothing like the obvious, loving activity of God for drawing people to Christ. As Juan Carlos Ortiz has commented, 'God has revealed to us a new dimension of the Kingdom. We love people. We want to bring them into a group where their needs will be met. They come to the group not because we call them ("Don't forget to come. Please come, promise me that you will come."). No, they come because they cannot help coming, because here they find a new kind of love. They become part of a caring family moving in the Holy Spirit.

[16] 1 Corinthians 14:26.   [18] Romans 12:6.
[17] Haggai 1:13.

This family is sensitive to and can help supply their social, material and spiritual needs. They become brothers and sisters in a family of love.'[19]

It follows that each member should offer what gifts he has for the benefit of the whole body. It does not matter how 'spectacular' or 'unspectacular' the gift may be. Every part is vital for the body to work properly.

Further, Paul said that 'if one member suffers, all suffer together.' This is often taken to mean that if, for example, one member is sick, all should feel sympathy. No doubt that is true, but it is not the main purpose of Paul's remark. My hand suffers when it is not working as it should — perhaps it is paralysed. In that case, if my hand suffers, my whole body suffers because it loses the service of the hand. Similarly if one member of the body of Christ is not playing his full part in the life of that body, the whole body will suffer. We must all be fully involved within the body of Christ, because we *are* fully involved, whether we like it, or realise it, or not. No one can opt out without the whole body suffering as a result.

Complete in Christ

Each individual *ekklesia* (local church, groups of churches, or denomination) is not *the* church, but *fully represents it*. For example, each local church is not just a section of the whole church, and the whole church is not just the sum of all the local churches. Instead, the *whole* gospel, the *fullness* of God, the *finished* work of Christ together with the 'immeasurable greatness' of his resurrection power, the *complete* gift of the Holy Spirit together with the full range of his gifts and ministries, and the 'very great promises' of God offering *full* salvation — all these are available in every place, wherever the church, great or small, is to be found. 'Where two or three are gathered in my name, there am I in the midst of them,' said Jesus;[20] and he is the undivided Christ. All power has been given to him.

Thus the local church does not merely *belong* to the universal church as some junior, smaller and greatly inferior part of the whole; the local church *is* the church and is

---

[19]*A Call to Discipleship*,   [20]Matthew 18:20.
Logos 1975, p. 106.

therefore *complete* in Christ: 'In him the whole fullness of
deity dwells bodily, and you have come to fullness of life in
him,'[21] wrote Paul to the Christians at Colossae who were
being deceived into believing that there was something more
to be had apart from Christ. Not so! God has blessed
us in Christ with *every* spiritual blessing;[22] there is nothing to discover for our spiritual well-being that is outside
him.

This is not to encourage a spirit of independence or
anarchy on the part of the local church towards the wider
church (deanery, district, diocese, denomination, or the
universal church). Respecting and obeying the God-given
leaders in the church is very much to be found in New
Testament teaching. But it is to encourage the members of
each local church to realise and enjoy the full inheritance
that is already theirs in Christ, to grow up into full maturity,
and to play their full part in the mission of the church to the
world.

This is a truth which needs to be clearly grasped by smaller
and perhaps struggling congregations. The temptation will
always be to look enviously, and maybe despairingly, at
larger and seemingly thriving churches in the area. Why
don't they send some of their many gifted workers to help
these smaller churches? Sometimes, perhaps, that is right and
necessary; but *each* local church needs to realise the immense
potential that exists within the body of Christ in that place. If
those Christians can be genuinely open to God, deeply
committed to Christ, and filled with his Spirit, all that is
necessary for building up that body into spiritual maturity is
there already. Certainly help from other Christians or
churches can be stimulating and valuable. But it is a mistake
to feel inferior and inadequate, looking too quickly to help
from outside, when God has already promised us all the
spiritual resources that we need in Christ. Probably very
few churches have begun to realise the potential for spiritual
gifts and ministries that already exist within the congregation. Given the right incentive and encouragement,
many a minister might discover a whole range of gifts,
at least in embryo, which would considerably enrich

[21] Colossians 2:9f.   [22] Ephesians 1:3.

the worship and ministry of that church. Of course such a discovery might threaten his own 'indispensable' role in every part of the church's work! But that is a risk that needs to be taken for the health of that body of Christ.

Testing gifts

In the New Testament there are numerous warnings about false prophets and teachers — warnings that are still highly relevant for today. Part of the confusion over the 'charismatic renewal' has been due to some spurious manifestations of so-called spiritual gifts. When one man told me that he had 'been in Pentecost for the last twenty years', during which time he had 'specialised in exorcisms', I found all the red lights flashing in my mind! The sad story of the Montanists in the second century shows the need for wise discernment and firm leadership in this whole area. At the same time, part of the tragedy with the Montanist movement was the over-reaction by the rest of the church, resulting in the quenching of the prophetic spirit for centuries. As Michael Green rightly comments: 'How much better it would have been for the church at large if the Montanists had determined to submit to the authority of Scripture, and to resist the temptation to be exclusive and write off other Christians. How much better if the Catholics had stressed tests for the genuineness of prophecy rather than writing off the whole movement, good and bad together.'[23]

What are these tests that we can apply to a person, or to a movement, when the claim is to be under the inspiration of the Holy Spirit? There are at least seven guidelines that can sharpen our discernment.

1. *Is Jesus Lord of that person's life?* No one can say that Jesus is Lord except by the Holy Spirit. Paul was no doubt referring not just to the credal statement that 'Jesus is Lord', which anyone can *say*, but to the reality of that lordship in that person's life.

2. *Is Jesus acknowledged as perfect Man and perfect God?* 'By this you know the Spirit of God; every spirit which confesses that

[23]*I Believe in the Holy Spirit*, Hodder & Stoughton, p. 173.

Jesus Christ has come in the flesh is of God.'[24] Down the pages of church history, there have always been some who have questioned or denied either the humanity or the divinity of Jesus. Scripture makes it clear that both together are true; and since the whole Christian faith rests solidly on the person of Jesus Christ, a right belief about his human-divine nature is crucial.

3. *Is the manifestation of the gift in accordance with the Scriptures?* When Samuel said to Saul, 'You have rejected the word of the Lord', the next thing we read is that 'the Spirit of the Lord departed from Saul'.[25] The Scriptures are the final court of appeal for the truth or falsehood for what may be claimed as a word or revelation from the Lord.

4. *Is there true holiness and godliness about that person?* No one will be perfect, and it is a well-known saying that great men have great faults because of the great powers latent within them. Nevertheless, in his warning about false prophets Jesus said, 'You will know them by their fruits.'[26] The New Testament especially mentions self-centredness, covetousness and immorality as common marks of the false prophet.

5. *Is there submission to church leaders?* One of the marks of being filled with the Spirit is to be 'subject to one another out of reverence to Christ';[27] and this would apply in particular to submission to leaders. The spirit of independence (often the same as rebellion) is certainly not the mark of someone who is truly under the control of the Holy Spirit.

6. *Is the church edified through this gift?* As we have seen, this is Paul's repeated emphasis in 1 Corinthians 12 and 14. Spiritual gifts are never for personal display or for sensational titillation. Unless they help the church and its members to grow up into Christ they are useless and deceptive. Paul warned Timothy about those who came with endless speculation, which only led to vain disputes about words, and in no way helped towards true godliness.

7. *Is love the controlling factor?* This is always the supreme mark of the Spirit of God, and without it we are nothing, and have nothing, of any value in the sight of God.

[24] 1 John 4:2.
[25] 1 Samuel 15:26; 16:14; cf. 1 Corinthians 14:36-40.
[26] Matthew 7:15-20.
[27] Ephesians 5:21.

When any church opens itself more fully to the wide range of spiritual gifts — and rightly so — the leaders need to covet the ability to distinguish between the spirits. If these tests are applied prayerfully and sensitively, and if correction, teaching and encouragement are given in love, there is every possibility that the shared ministry of that church will be immeasurably enriched. 'Make love your aim, and earnestly desire the spiritual gifts.'

3. AUTHORITY OF THE HEAD

We have already seen that we are 'to grow up in every way into him who is the head, into Christ.' Writing to the Colossians, who were in danger of slipping away from the centrality of Christ into gnosticism, Paul again stresses the same point: 'He is before all things, and in him all things hold together. He is the head of the body, the church; he is the beginning, the first-born from the dead, that in everything he might be pre-eminent... Let no one disqualify you, insisting on self-abasement and worship of angels, taking his stand on visions, puffed up without reason by his sensuous mind, and not holding fast to the Head, from whom the whole body nourished and knit together through its joints and ligaments, grows with a growth which is from God.'[28] All too quickly we give the glory, which belongs to Christ alone, to images, buildings, religious works of art, musical excellence, or to man who is at best a poor and unprofitable servant of Christ. Although God's people are clearly to respect and obey those who are over them in the Lord, Christ is still the Head of the body and the Lord of the church. Any attitude or tendency which takes the pre-eminence away from Christ and places it elsewhere is to write the obituary ICHABOD over that church: 'the glory of the Lord has departed'. As God blesses and prospers a work, this will be one of its greatest dangers. Wise are the leaders and members of the body of Christ who are determined, at whatever cost, to give the glory to Christ and to none other.

[28]Colossians 1:17f; 2:18f.

CHAPTER EIGHT

The Building of God

CLOSELY ALLIED TO the body metaphor, the church is also the building of God. 'We are... God's building... You are God's temple.'[1] The roots of this analogy are obviously in the tabernacle and temple of the old covenant, together with the Mosaic patterns of sacrifice and priesthood.

However, with the coming of Christ and the birth of the church these institutions of the old covenant disappeared, a theological fact which was sealed historically by the destruction of Jerusalem in AD 70. Christ is our great high priest, and there is now neither need nor room for any other priest. He has also once for all become our perfect sacrifice for sin, so that no further sacrifice for sin is required or permissible — although God's people in thanksgiving for all that Christ has already done should offer him the sacrifice of their bodies[2] and the sacrifice of their praise.[3] It can also be said that Christ is the fulfilment of the tabernacle and temple.

Speaking of Jesus, the writer of Hebrews stated: 'Through the greater and more perfect tent (not made with hands, that is, not of this creation) he entered once for all into the Holy Place... For Christ has entered, not into a sanctuary made with hands, a copy of the true one, but into heaven itself, now to appear in the presence of God on our behalf.'[4] Further, during his own ministry Jesus said, 'Destroy this temple, and in three days I will raise it up.' The Jews could not understand what he was talking about since it had taken

[1] 1 Corinthians 3:9, 16.
[2] Romans 12:1.
[3] Hebrews 13:15.
[4] Hebrews 9:11f, 24.

forty-six years to build Herod's temple, but, explained John, 'he spoke of the temple of his body'. [5]

Not only is Christ now the great high priest, the finished sacrifice, and the true tabernacle and temple of God, the church is 'God's house', [6] a 'holy temple', [7] and a 'dwelling place of God in the Spirit.' [8]

Not a material building
The tabernacle, and later the temple, were central to Israel's worship. Even Jesus when on earth upheld the temple as the Father's house. Israel's worship was however principally of a physical nature, centred on the offering of physical sacrifices, the strict observance of days, and various teachings about 'touch not, taste not, handle not'. The Old Covenant enabled them to enjoy an arm's-length relationship with God, which was designed especially for a nation in which the Holy Spirit did not yet abide.

Although right up until the time of his death Jesus taught men to honour the temple, he did begin to speak of a far superior kind of worship to come with the inauguration of the New Covenant. This would no longer be centred on the physical. The woman of Samaria, perceiving Jesus to be a prophet, raised the age-old question of the correct location for worship. Jesus primarily answered by saying that the time was coming — and it did come on the day of Pentecost, after he ascended to heaven — when even the temple would have no real relevance in worship. Instead, the true worshippers would worship in spirit and truth.

This new kind of worship, experienced by only a few in the Old Testament, would mean that men would no longer need holy buildings in order to worship the holy God. Instead they themselves would be made holy by the indwelling presence of the Holy Spirit. Sacrifices, too, would no longer be impersonal, since Christians were to be themselves living sacrifices. Neither would there be a need for Israel's holy days to sanctify God's people, because the blood of Christ and the Holy Spirit would sanctify them.

[5] John 2:19-22.
[6] Hebrews 3:6;
1 Timothy 3:15.

[7] Ephesians 2:21;
2 Corinthians 6:16.
[8] Ephesians 2:22.

Could it be that many in our congregations today overlook this simple but profound teaching of Jesus in John 4, still tending to think of a church building as a kind of temple? Is it misunderstanding on this point that causes many to be reluctant to allow a more modern use of buildings?

Ever since the Old Testament symbols were fulfilled in Christ and in his church, the church has faced constant temptations to bring back the institutions that Christ has fulfilled and removed; and she has, to a large extent, fallen to these temptations.

We see today, for example, a professional priesthood as a class distinct from the rest of the people of God. Indeed in many sections of the church there is explicit teaching of the sacrifice of the mass or eucharist. Of course, hundreds of thousands of church buildings have also mushroomed all over the world.

The tragedy is that the return to the institution has always resulted in a diminishing of spiritual life and power. A missionary travelling in India wrote down his impressions a few years ago: 'Vying for a place on the skyline with the minarets of Hindu temples and Muslim shrines, were the galaxy of Church steeples, many of which were quite new or just being built. In most of these places the new church was by far the most outstanding and most pretentious of all the buildings in the area. Obviously built with the maximum of foreign funds and the minimum of local help, these monuments stood out as bastions of a watered-down faith in a last-ditch stand to defend denominationalism and missionaryism.'

Material church buildings can often be no more than monuments of religion. They can often fail to speak of the reality of the living God. And this is not surprising, since that is the privilege and responsibility of God's people when they truly become the temple of the Holy Spirit. God dwells now with his people as they come together as a believing community. The Holy Spirit 'dwells with you, and will be in you,' promised Jesus.[9] Further, 'if a man loves me, he will keep my word, and my Father will love him, and we will come to him and make our home with him.'[10] 'Do you not

[9] John 14:17.   [10] John 14:23.

know that you are God's temple and that God's Spirit dwells in you?'[11] Church buildings, then, are in no way essential to the nature of the true church.

A *building* is no longer the temple or house of God: it is God's *people* who are now so called. A *building* is not to be a 'holy place'; rather God's *people* are called to be a holy people. Certainly, from a purely practical point of view, buildings may be necessary for a meeting-place of God's people; but all too easily they can become the first step towards the static institutionalism that Christ came to abolish.

When we look at the Old Testament, it seems that God deliberately chose a *tabernacle* as the symbol for his presence among his people because of its mobility. For forty years God's people moved when God moved, and the tabernacle was carried easily with them. From the very start, God intended that his dwelling should be in the midst of his people;[12] but because of the sin and rebellion in their hearts, his habitation had to be symbolically expressed in the tabernacle. Therefore the design of the tabernacle was given in great detail by God to Moses. Even the ark of the covenant, the special symbol for God himself, was essentially mobile: 'You shall put the poles into the rings on the sides of the ark, to carry the ark by them.'[13]

The solid and permanent structure of the *temple*, on the other hand, was not primarily God's plan, but David's. Indeed, God 'protested' to David: 'Would you build me a house to dwell in? I have not dwelt in a house since the day I brought up the people of Israel from Egypt to this day, but I have been moving about in a tent for my dwelling...'[14] God allowed a temple to be built, through David's son, just as he allowed his people to make for themselves a king. However, both these were his permissive will, and not his original intention. In fact Stephen, at the climax of his charge, saw the building of the temple as the high point of Jewish intransigence — a remark which understandably infuriated his accusers.[15]

---

[11] 1 Corinthians 3:16.
[12] Exodus 25:8.
[13] Exodus 25:14.
[14] 2 Samuel 7:5f.
[15] Acts 7:46ff.

In his book *People-Centred Evangelism*, John Havlik summed it up like this: 'The church is never a place, but always a people; never a fold but always a flock; never a sacred building but always a believing assembly. The church is you who pray, not where you pray. A structure of brick or marble can no more be a church than your clothes of serge or satin can be you. There is in this world nothing sacred but man, no sanctuary of man but the soul.'[16]

A new look at church buildings

In a powerful critique of present-day church buildings, Howard Snyder raises the following points:

First, church buildings are *a witness to our immobility*... Christians are to be a mobile people... The gospel says, 'Go,' but our church buildings say, 'Stay'. The gospel says, 'Seek the lost,' but our churches say, 'Let the lost seek the church'.

Second, church buildings are *a witness to our inflexibility*... The Sunday morning service allows the direct participation of only a few — dictated by the sanctuary layout... Communication will be one-way — dictated by architecture and the PA system...

Thirdly, church buildings are *a witness to our lack of fellowship*. Church buildings may be worshipful places, but usually they are not friendly places. They are uncomfortable and impersonal. Church buildings are not made for fellowship... Homes are. And it was in homes that early Christians met to worship (Acts 2:42; 5:42)... A stranger may attend a Christian church for weeks and never encounter the winsome, warm, loving fellowship that draws a person to Christ. Such a situation would simply have been impossible in AD 100.

Fourth, church buildings are *a witness to our pride*. We insist that our church structures must be beautiful and well-appointed — which usually means expensive — and justify this on the grounds that God deserves the best. But such thinking may be little more than the rationalising of

[16]Nashville: Broadman press, p. 47.

carnal pride... A gospel with the New Testament dynamic does not need to make a good impression on the world through the appeal of an attractive building. That is rather like wrapping a diamond in tin foil to help it sell. In fact, a fine church building may simply attract the Pharisees and repel the poor... If buildings are to be built, let them speak of God, not of middle-class bourgeois values.

Finally, church buildings are *a witness to our class divisions*. The early church was composed of rich and poor, Jew and Greek, black and white, ignorant and educated. But our modern church buildings advertise to the world that this is not true today. A sociologist can take a casual look at ten church buildings and their denominational brand names and then predict with high accuracy the education, income, occupations and social position of the majority of their respective members. In the light of the New Testament, this ought not to be. [17]

Howard Snyder is of course particularly emphasising one side of the coin, since it is also true, in the words of Marshall McLuhan, that 'the medium is the message'. The presentation and context of the message is of considerable importance for today's world. A dirty and unkempt church building is no witness to our majestic creator God. A cold and dingy church is no welcome to an outsider. Nevertheless, a grossly inordinate amount of time and money is spent on building new churches, or repairing old ones — time and money which could be much more profitably spent on releasing and training men and women for ministry within God's church and on building up the people of God into a true living temple, the dwelling place of God in the Spirit.

Howard Snyder concludes his challenge in this way: 'It seems to me that any church which

> spends more on buildings than on outreach
> holds all its gatherings only in "the church"
> puts construction before missions and evangelism
> refuses to use its building for anything other than "sacred" functions

[17]*New Wineskins*, Marshall, Morgan & Scott, pp. 61-65.

measures spirituality by the number of human bodies
present within the four walls

has an edifice complex and is almost totally ignorant of what
the Bible means by *the church*.'[18]

For the first two centuries, the church met in small groups
in the homes of its members, apart from special gatherings in
public lecture halls or market places, where people could
come together in much larger numbers. Significantly these
two centuries mark the most powerful and vigorous advance
of the church, which perhaps has never since been equalled.
The lack of church buildings was no hindrance to the rapid
expansion of the church; instead, in comparison to the
situation after AD 200, it seemed a positive help.

The colourful Argentinian pastor, Juan Carlos Ortiz,
closed his church building for a month to see if the church
could survive under times of persecution. It continued to
flourish in the numerous small cell groups within the
congregation, and 'more money came in during that month
than ever before!'

It is hardly realistic to suggest that we should at once sell
all our buildings and land — although something similar to
this was one of the reasons for the 'great power' and 'great
grace' experienced by the early church![19] However, a careful
reassessment of our building programmes and of our use of
existing structures might well be vital for the health and
progress of God's work. What, then, does it mean for God's
people to become God's building?

Centred on Christ
Christ is both the *architect* and *builder* of his church. 'I will
build my church, and the powers of death shall not prevail
against it.'[20]

Each local church, therefore, needs to come humbly to
Christ to ask for his guidance and direction, and not just to
copy the developments of another place. Although the basic
principles should be the same, the detailed outworking of
those principles will naturally vary. In particular, Christ's

[18]Op. cit., pp. 69f.   [20]Matthew 16:18.
[19]Acts 4:32ff.

timing is all-important. We may be excited by a church that has steadily been built up over the years into an impressive structure, alive with the Spirit of God; but if we try to construct with haste a similar spiritual building in our own area, a sudden collapse of the whole building is not unlikely.

The Scriptures use several metaphors to show how Christ is involved in every part of the building.

First, he is seen as the *foundation* of the building. Paul saw himself, according to the grace of God given to him, as a skilled master builder laying a strong foundation for other people: 'For no other foundation can anyone lay than that which is laid, which is Jesus Christ.'[21] Sadly, it is possible to build a sizable superstructure without checking first the foundations. There are many within the church who are not at all sure about their personal relationship with Jesus Christ. Even if they believe in him and do not doubt the basic truths concerning him, they are not at all sure about his personal reality in their own lives, and they have little experience of the life and power of the Holy Spirit.

A Swiss pastor with a noted counselling ministry amongst Christians once made this comment: 'It is remarkable to note the ignorance of most believers concerning the forgiveness of their sins... When one speaks of an actual personal certainty, and when one asks the direct question, 'Do you know, now, if your sins are forgiven?" nine times out of ten their reply is evasive... Can one be surprised then that the faith of our church members is so dull?'

An Anglican Vicar came to see me about local church renewal. We talked at some length, and finally prayed together. Later he wrote to me, and in his letter he said this: 'Jesus Christ is a reality for me in a new way... Now, for the first time in my life I know him as a person and a friend. For the first time, I think, I can preach him as one with whom we can have a personal relationship, rather than just one who *shows* us a loving Father and the way we must live.' For the first time in his life and ministry, the foundations were secure.

Second, Christ is described as the *cornerstone*, on which the whole building depends. 'Come to him, to that living stone, rejected by men but in God's sight chosen and precious; and

[21] 1 Corinthians 3:11.

like living stones be yourselves built into a spiritual house...
For it stands in scripture: "Behold, I am laying in Zion a
stone, a cornerstone chosen and precious, and he who believes
in him will not be put to shame..."' [22] Peter goes on to say that
those who disobey the word will find Christ a stumbling-
stone, 'a rock that will make them fall'; but for those who
believe, he has 'become the head of the corner'.

Exegetes differ as to the place of the cornerstone in a
building, but it is probably a stone set in the foundations at
the corner which holds everything together and which gives
the walls their line. All other stones are therefore fitted into
this cornerstone, just as all true Christians find their right
place and usefulness in God's building only in relation to
Christ. Paul writes to the Colossians: 'As therefore you
received Christ Jesus the Lord, so live in him, rooted and
built up in him, established in the faith.' [23]

Paul also writes about God's people being 'built upon the
foundation of the apostles and prophets, Christ Jesus himself
being the cornerstone, in whom the whole structure is joined
together and grows into a holy temple in the Lord; in whom
you also are built into it for a dwelling place of God in the
Spirit.' [24] At first sight this passage seems to contradict Paul's
clear statement in 1 Corinthians 3 that there is only one
foundation, namely Jesus Christ. The difficulty arises,
however, because the same building analogy is being used in
two different ways. In the Corinthian passage, Paul and
others were the builders working on the rock-like foundation
of Jesus Christ. In Ephesians 2 Paul saw himself and others as
stones in the building.

J. A. Allen, in his commentary on Ephesians, has put it like
this: 'The Church rests on the total unique Event of which
Christ is the centre, but in which the apostles and prophets,
filled and guided by the Spirit and doing their work in
unique closeness to Christ, had an indispensable and untrans-
missible part.' They, supremely and uniquely have given us
the written word of God, the foundational gift for the church.
It was to them that the mystery of Christ was revealed by the
Spirit; [25] and therefore they, together with the all-important

---

[22] 1 Peter 2:4f.
[23] Colossians 2:6f.
[24] Ephesians 2:20-22.
[25] Ephesians 3:5.

cornerstone, are the beginning of the building on which others were built.

Some commentators have preferred '*keystone*' to cornerstone. The keystone is at the top of an arch and holds the whole arch together. Take the keystone away from its vital position, and the whole arch becomes a rubble of stones. Whether or not this is the correct exegesis, the truth is a profound one: as soon as any church moves away from the centrality of Christ, it at once ceases to be God's dwelling place; spiritual demolition has taken place.

Created by the Spirit

All true believers are being built into a holy temple, said Paul, 'for a dwelling place of God in [or through, or by] the Spirit.' The presence and activity of the Spirit is indispensable before the church can ever be a place where God himself dwells. This is one of the greatest needs in the church today. 'The world is perishing for lack of the knowledge of God, and the church is famishing for want of his presence.'[26]

Zechariah once prophesied about a time of spiritual restoration in Jerusalem: 'In those days ten men from the nations of every tongue shall take hold of the robe of a Jew, saying, "Let us go with you, for we have heard that God is with you."'[27] This will always be the most attractive and persuasive argument for the reality and relevance of God: a sense of his presence in the midst of his people. Indeed, when a local church begins to learn how to live and move in the Spirit, using spiritual gifts to build up the temple of God, an unbeliever or outsider may enter and 'falling on his face, he will worship God and declare that God is really among you'.[28] Everything depends on the presence and power of the Spirit to make the church alive. Our own lives must be filled with the Spirit; our relationships united by the Spirit; our worship infused by the Spirit; our preaching empowered by the Spirit; our understanding illuminated by the Spirit; our activities led by the Spirit. 'You are God's temple and God's Spirit dwells in you.'

A failure to see this truth will lead to constant frustration.

[26] A. W. Tozer.   [28] 1 Corinthians 14:24f.
[27] Zechariah 8:23.

We may adopt new structures, introduce new services, work hard on new plans and construct new buildings; but unless we are constantly experiencing the new wine of the Spirit, all will be in vain.

Today there is no shortage of new ideas, and some of them are necessary if the church is ever to communicate to today's world. However, God has made man with a basic spiritual hunger which cannot be satisfied with anything less than himself. The reports, conferences, commissions and synods of the church can never be a substitute for the living God. Unless we place spiritual renewal within the church as our first and foremost priority, we shall not begin to meet the spiritual hunger that undoubtedly does exist, and we shall wonder why all our efforts and energies seem remarkably unfruitful.

Writing about the generous giving and sharing of the early church, James K. Baxter comments: 'The first Christians did not start to share their goods in a free and full manner till after the bomb of the Spirit exploded in their souls at Pentecost. Before then, they would be morally incapable of this free and joyful sharing. The acquisitive habit is one of the deepest rooted habits of the human race. To say, "This is ours, not mine," and to carry the words into effect is as much a miracle of God as the raising of the dead.'[29]

Consists of living stones

'Come to him, to that living stone, rejected by men but in God's sight chosen and precious,' wrote Peter; 'and like living stones be yourselves built into a spiritual house.'

Evangelism on its own is not enough. It is insufficient calling men and women to come to Jesus. By itself, this is like making a pile of bricks, and we go on adding to that pile as God blesses our evangelistic work. However, we are to build a spiritual house in which we can offer spiritual sacrifices that are acceptable to God, and we can never do that by making a pile of bricks. All living stones, therefore need to be built together and cemented by love and trust. Each stone must find its right place within the building, and each stone is vitally important. If several stones are out of the building, lying on their own, not only are they in the wrong place, and

[29]*Thoughts about the Holy Spirit*, Fortuna Press, New Zealand, p. 11.

useless where they are, but the rest of the building is weakened by their absence.

We must also take care *how* we build on the foundation of Jesus Christ. 'Some will use gold or silver or precious stones in building on the foundation; others will use wood or grass or straw. And the quality of each person's work will be seen when the Day of Christ exposes it. For on that Day fire will reveal everyone's work; the fire will test it and show its real quality. If what was built on the foundation survives the fire, the builder will receive a reward. But if anyone's work is burnt up, then he will lose it; but he himself will be saved, as if he had escaped through the fire.'[30] In other words, the building must be worthy of the foundation. Further, the context shows that Paul has in mind more than just the quality of our own personal life. It is important that we use every gift that God chooses to give us to build up the church in a way that is worthy of Jesus Christ. The work of God must not be superficial, shoddy or cheap. Statistics of conversions may be impressive; but what will count in the long run is how far those converts have been built into the church of God.

I happen to live in York, and it would be something approaching a national disaster if any madman attempted to destroy York Minster. Yet how much more serious it must be to 'destroy God's temple'. If anyone did such a thing, wrote Paul, 'God will destroy him. For God's temple is holy, and that temple you are.'[31] How would it be possible to demolish God's temple?

From the context, it could be through *disunity*. The Corinthian church was split into different factions, each group vying for its own leader. This was not only a fleshly and foolish thing to do — it was possible in this way to destroy 'God's temple' at Corinth.

It could also be through *sin*. In his second letter to the same church, Paul urges them not to be 'mismated with unbelievers'. The purity of their fellowship was of great importance, for 'what agreement has the temple of God with idols? For we are the temple of the living God... Therefore come out from them, and be separate from them, says the Lord.'[32]

[30] 1 Corinthians 3:12-15 (T.E.V.).   [32] 2 Corinthians 6:14-18.
[31] 1 Corinthians 3:17.

Deep, intimate and permanent relationships between Christian and heathen, for example in marriage, could not be permitted.

This is not simply a personal matter, for each Christian is inescapably a part of God's holy temple. Even though the gates of hell cannot prevail against God's church, it is possible to destroy it from within. Gossip, criticism, slander, jealousy, back-biting, bitterness, immorality — these are some of the ways in which we can effectively do the devil's work for him. It was for such sins as these that Christ warned five of the seven churches in Revelation 2 and 3. Although the warning in most cases led to a temporary repentance and revival, the sins of the flesh re-appeared, and the church in that place was in this way destroyed. It is sobering to realise that all seven churches were situated in what is now the western part of Turkey. Today, throughout the whole of Turkey there are only about a hundred Christians in all.

Still under construction

It may often be helpful to remember that most buildings under construction look a terrible mess, at least to the untrained eye, until the last stage is reached. When our kitchen was recently being extended it seemed almost impossible that we would be eating and cooking there within a few days!

The same is true with the church. The dust and dirt, chaos and confusion, may make it hard to believe that this could really be the temple of God. Yet, if we have faith and patience, the architect and builder is hard at work, and knows very well what he is doing. On this earth we can never claim to have 'arrived'. The apostle Paul was well aware of this in his own personal life: 'Not that I am already perfect...; but one thing I do..., I press on toward the goal for the prize of the upward call of God in Christ Jesus.'[33]

As a church, we can never afford to stand still. We can never be complacent. Nor should we ever lose heart. Always our vision should be on the promise of our future inheritance, when we shall 'have a building from God, a house not made with hands, eternal in the heavens'. Until that time, God has

[33] Philippians 1:12-14.

given us his Spirit as a guarantee of the place he has prepared for us.[34]

Abraham, too, once 'looked forward to the city which has foundations, whose builder and maker is God'. He and others 'all died in faith, not having received what was promised, but having seen it and greeted it from afar... Therefore God is not ashamed to be called their God, for he has prepared for them a city.'[35]

The vision of this heavenly city was described by the apostle John: 'And I saw the holy city, new Jerusalem, coming down out of heaven from God prepared as a bride adorned for her husband; and I heard a loud voice from the throne saying, "Behold the dwelling of God is with men..." And I saw no temple in the city, for its temple is the Lord God the Almighty and the Lamb.' On that day our union with God and with one another will be complete: 'He will wipe away every tear from their eyes, and death shall be no more, neither shall there be mourning nor crying nor pain any more, for the former things have passed away.'[36]

If this is our vision and hope, we shall not be discouraged. Rather, we shall seek to pray and work together with God to become that spiritual house that is filled with his praise. That is the privilege of those who have been called to him, in order to be 'joined together into a holy temple in the Lord..., a dwelling place of God in the Spirit'.

---

[34] 2 Corinthians 5:1-5.
[35] Hebrews 11:10, 13, 16.
[36] Revelation 21:2-4, 22.

CHAPTER NINE

The Bride of Christ

HERE IS ONE of the most beautiful analogies for the church, recurring frequently throughout the Scriptures. It speaks of the intimate union between God and his people, enjoyed both personally and corporately now, and one day to be consummated in heaven. 'For your Maker is your husband, the Lord of hosts is his name... For the Lord has called you, like a wife forsaken and grieved in spirit, like a wife of youth when she is cast off, says your God...'[1] 'You shall no more be termed Forsaken, and your land shall no more be termed Desolate; but you shall be called My delight is in her, and your land Married; for the Lord delights in you, and your land shall be married. For as a young man marries a virgin, so shall your sons marry you, and as the bridegroom rejoices over the bride, so shall your God rejoice over you.'[2]

As the bride of God Israel was called into a spiritual relationship marked by absolute fidelity and devotion. She pledged herself unconditionally to him, and waited for his coming with confident and expectant hope. Any disobedience to his word, or any different allegiance or devotion, was therefore to be seen as spiritual adultery — perhaps the most serious of all sins, involving the gravest of consequences. 'Have you seen what she did, that faithless one, Israel, how she went up on every high hill and under every green tree, and there played the harlot?... Because harlotry was so light to her, she polluted the land, committing adultery with stone and tree... Surely, as a faithless wife leaves her husband, so

[1] Isaiah 54:1-8.   [2] Isaiah 62:4f.

have you been faithless to me, O house of Israel, says the Lord.'³

Often the prophets spoke to God's people in this vein, reminding them of the solemn covenant of love which they had broken. God had called them to himself, blessed them with his gifts, enriched them with his glory, and yet they had forsaken him and gone after other lovers who would offer them nothing of real and lasting value. 'Your renown went forth among the nations because of your beauty, for it was perfect through the splendour which I had bestowed upon you, says the Lord God. But you trusted in your beauty, and played the harlot because of your renown, and lavished your harlotries on any passer-by... Adulterous wife, who receives strangers instead of her husband!... Wherefore, O harlot, hear the word of the Lord:... I will give you into the hand of your lovers, and they shall throw down your vaulted chamber and break down your lofty places; they shall strip you of your clothes and take your fair jewels, and leave you naked and bare. They shall bring up a host against you and they shall stone you and cut you to pieces with their swords.'⁴

Most poignant of all is the prophet Hosea who, for the sake of the prophetic message he had come to bring, was called by God into marriage with a harlot who would continue to remain a harlot and become unfaithful to her husband. Here, from the depths of personal and domestic pain, God's word came with great power and feeling, and yet with astonishing tenderness — as from a husband still deeply in love with his unfaithful wife: 'Therefore, behold, I will allure her, and bring her into the wilderness, and speak tenderly to her. And there I will give her her vineyards, and make the Valley of Achor a door of hope. And there she shall answer as in the days of her youth... And in that day, says the Lord, you will call me, "My husband," and no longer will you call me, "My Baal."... And I will betroth you to me for ever; I will betroth you to me in righteousness and in justice, in steadfast love, and in mercy. I will betroth you to me in faithfulness; and you shall know the Lord.'⁵

Nowhere is the warmth, passion and tenderness of this

³ Jeremiah 3.   ⁵ Hosea 2:14-20.
⁴ Ezekiel 16.

relationship between God and his people more clearly seen than in two Old Testament passages, originally conceived as secular poems about human love. These are Psalm 45 and the Song of Solomon. The church that has become cold, hard, efficient (perhaps!), and moralistic, could do no better than to spend time meditating on these poems. What an astonishing thing for the heavenly Bridegroom to say to us, his earthly and faithless bride: 'You have ravished my heart, my sister, my bride, you have ravished my heart with a glance of your eyes, with one jewel of your necklace. How sweet is your love, my sister, my bride!'[6]

The marriage analogy used so frequently for Israel is an important theme for the nature of the church. When Jesus was asked by John's disciples about fasting, he replied, 'Can the wedding guests fast while the bridegroom is with them?'[7] Later, speaking of the wise and foolish virgins waiting for the coming of the bridegroom, he described the kingdom of heaven as a marriage banquet for the King's Son. Paul likewise thought of the church as the bride of Christ on a number of occasions. And in the Revelation of John, the summit of praise in heaven is when 'the marriage of the Lamb has come.'

From this thoroughly biblical picture of the church, three main features stand out.

Moral purity
In Paul's great passage on Christian marriage,[8] it is sometimes difficult to discern whether he is thinking primarily of husband and wife or of Christ and his church. 'For the husband is the head of the wife as Christ is the head of the church, his body, and is himself its Saviour. As the church is subject to Christ, so let wives also be subject in everything to their husbands. Husbands, love your wives, as Christ loved the church and gave himself up for her, that he might sanctify her, having cleansed her by the washing of water with the word, that he might present the church to himself in splendour, without spot or wrinkle or any such thing, that she might be holy and without blemish... "For this reason a man

[6] Song of Solomon 4:9f.   [8] Ephesians 5:22-33.
[7] Mark 2:18-20.

shall leave his father and mother and be joined to his wife, and the two shall become one flesh." This mystery is a profound one, and I am saying that it refers to Christ and the church.'

From these words, and from the context of this passage, it is clear that Paul is concerned with the moral purity of the church. He is telling the Ephesians not to take part in the 'unfruitful works of darkness, but instead expose them'; not to be foolish, but to understand what the will of the Lord is; not to get drunk with wine, but to be filled with the Spirit.

However, there should be nothing cold or hard about moral purity within the church. That was the error of the Pharisees. They were quick to judge and slow to forgive, thereby showing themselves far removed from their Lord, whom they professed to worship with such diligent devotion. In contrast, Christ himself was totally without sin yet immensely attractive to sinners. As a light attracts moths on a warm summer evening, so Christ drew to himself such a mixed and notorious circle of friends that he was called by respectable people (and they meant it as a term of derision) 'the friend of sinners'. Dostoevsky once said about Jesus: 'I believe there is no one lovelier, deeper, more sympathetic, and more perfect than Jesus. I say to myself, with jealous love, that not only is there no one else like him, but there could never be any one like him.'

In the same way, the moral purity of the church must never become critical and censorious, upholding the *status quo* of bourgeois morality, condemning every departure from established conventions. There is nothing lovely and sympathetic about that. Instead, it should be unashamedly a fellowship of sinners who have learnt, or at least are learning, to forgive and to be forgiven. It is true that the grace of God should be seen by the steady transformation of sinful lives into the image of Christ. But this process will never be complete this side of heaven; and the bride, much loved by the Bridegroom, must not despise members of her own body.

The present Bishop of Woolwich, Michael Marshall, wrote in *Southwark News:*

The measure of the church should be that it brings

together a bunch of people that no other club or society could ever attract into one fellowship. Of course this will include men and women, conspicuous for their good works and their sanctity. But it will also include the struggling and the wayward, the fallen and the weak: this is the stuff of the catholic religion... The main thrust given to the church by our Lord was the good news of forgiveness and healing, and it is very important indeed to return to that with a new scriptural authority and pastoral zeal at a time when love is growing cold and moralism abounding. The lovely thing about being a Christian is that you don't have to be right: you have to be forgiven.

Paul expressly wrote to the Christians at Rome that no longer were they in bondage to the law, for they had 'died' in Christ and the law was binding on a person only during his life. 'Thus a married woman is bound by law to her husband as long as he lives; but if her husband dies she is discharged from the law concerning her husband... Likewise, my brethren, you have died to the law through the body of Christ, so that you may belong to another, to him who has been raised from the dead in order that we may bear fruit for God.'[9]

Here is an astonishing concept, used with great daring by the apostle. Just as the Holy Spirit worked within the body of Mary in order that she might 'bear fruit for God', giving birth to Jesus, so the Spirit works within our hearts when we belong to Christ and are embraced in the arms of his love in order that we too might 'bear fruit for God', producing a life that is increasingly like Christ. Such a life, seen in the individual Christian and in the church, will be both morally pure and, at the same time, winsome, compassionate, forgiving and attractive.

Doctrinal purity

'I feel a divine jealousy for you,' wrote Paul to the Corinthians, 'for I betrothed you to Christ to present you as a pure bride to her one husband. But I am afraid that as the serpent deceived Eve by his cunning, your thoughts will be led astray from a sincere and pure devotion to Christ. For if someone

[9] Romans 7:1-4.

comes and preaches another Jesus than the one we preached,
or if you receive a different spirit from the one you received,
or if you accept a different gospel from the one you accepted,
you submit to it readily enough.'[10] And to the Galatians Paul
declared that 'if any one is preaching to you a gospel contrary
to that which you received, let him be accursed.'[11] Moreover,
Jesus implied that spiritual adultery is even worse, far worse,
than physical adultery. He told the religious leaders of that
day, who were guilty of spiritual adultery, that harlots would
enter into the kingdom of heaven before them.[12]

Who are the spiritual adulterers within the church? From
the Corinthian passage, it is those who are doctrinally
corrupt. Jesus was full of both grace and truth, and the same
must also increasingly be true of the church. Moral purity is
therefore not enough. If the church is to be the faithful bride
of Christ, its doctrinal purity is also extremely important. The
New Testament, however, is quite clear about the need to be
faithful to apostolic teaching. This needs to be stressed in a
day when there has been such a sharp reaction to cold,
doctrinaire orthodoxy that almost anything goes. An article
in *The Times*[13] on the Church of England's Doctrine Commission Report made this comment: 'What the eighteen theologians hold in common is a belief in the likelihood of God, and
reverence for Jesus. They disagree about almost everything
else. An ordinary man in the pew picking up the volume to
discover the bedrock beliefs of his church would find that the
available options are so wide anything goes... The impression
given... is that Anglicanism is a religion without doctrine.'

The same can be said of most other denominations. In 1961
one of the top pollsters in the United States made a survey of
Protestant seminaries. Of ministers in training, 56 percent
rejected the virgin birth of Christ, 71 per cent rejected life
after death, 54 per cent rejected the bodily resurrection of
Christ, 98 per cent rejected a personal return of Christ to this
earth. Although there has more recently been a healthy
return to biblical studies and to a renewed acceptance of the
authority of the Scriptures as the written word of God, there
are still many within the church who question, and some-

[10] 2 Corinthians 11:2-4.   [12] Matthew 21:31f.
[11] Galatians 1:8f.   [13] 16 February 1976.

times categorically deny, the most basic truths of the Christian faith. When 'the serpent deceived Eve by his cunning', he questioned God's word: 'Did God say...?'

Significantly, the first recorded temptation in the New Testament is along precisely the same lines. Twice Satan raised a doubt in the mind of Jesus: '*If* you are the Son of God... *If* you are the Son of God...'[14] His tactics seldom change; and Paul was afraid lest the Corinthian church should be led astray from a sincere and pure devotion to Christ, seen especially in the doctrinal content of the gospel received and preached. Peter also saw that those who twisted the teaching given in Paul's letters did so 'to their own destruction, as they do to the other scriptures.'[15] God looks for both moral and doctrinal purity within his church. We need to be full both of grace and truth, if we are to be the bride who is ready for her Bridegroom.

Having said that, no Christian, and no church or group within the church, can claim absolute purity in either realm. If we say we have no sin, we deceive ourselves; and concerning our understanding of the truth, at best we see 'in a mirror dimly'. We know and understand only in part. In no way can we say that we have arrived or are already perfect. Those who are zealous for holiness or for truth need to temper their zeal with humility. We all have much to learn; we all have many faults; we all can learn from one another. No man, no group, has a monopoly of God's truth or of God's Spirit. Spiritual arrogance is the mark of the Pharisee. It is sterile and offensive, both to God and man. The bride is not yet ready for her wedding day.

Love
This, surely, is what a bridegroom looks for most of all in his bride. Beauty and faithfulness are important, yes; but above all he looks for love.

The marriage relationship essentially is one of love. This love has as its basis a wholehearted and lifelong commitment. It does not depend on feelings. But something would be sadly amiss if the feelings were never there. There must be a warm and deep devotion in the relationship, which is something

[14]Genesis 3:1; Matthew 4:3, 6.   [15]2 Peter 3:16.

different from the fulfilment of respective roles. Paul, in his classic passage,[16] made it clear that spiritual gifts, understanding, knowledge, faith, generosity, sacrifice, are nothing by themselves without love.

In the message to the church at Ephesus, the risen Christ commended them for their hard work, their patient endurance, their doctrinal purity. 'But,' he went on to say, 'I have this against you, that you have abandoned the love you had at first.' The church at Ephesus had for years been one of the showpieces of the Christian faith. Their activities and maturity had proved an inspiration for many. Yet in spite of all this, they were nothing without love. They were commanded by Christ to repent. 'If not, I will come to you and remove your lampstand from its place.'[17] Can the marriage ever take place if the bride has lost her love for the bridegroom?

The Bible daringly indicates that our love for the Lord should be one of great intimacy. The essence of the life that God has planned for us is that we should *know* God and his Son Jesus Christ, and the word that John uses[18] is the word (although common enough) that is often used for a man knowing his wife in the most intimate sexual relationship within marriage. We are called to delight ourselves in the Lord; and 'as the bridegroom rejoices over the bride, so shall your God rejoice over you.'[19]

Fervent love, proved by unswerving faithfulness, should be the attitude of the church towards her heavenly bridegroom; and, in return, the promise is that God will continuously pour his love into our hearts by the Holy Spirit. Have we learned to love Christ so deeply that he can expect our faithfulness, no matter what the personal cost may be?

Accounts of outstanding faithfulness abound in many parts of the world where following Christ means a willingness to be faithful unto death. It has been estimated that there have been more Christian martyrdoms during this twentieth century than during the entire history of the Christian church put together. The following example is typical of the total

[16] 1 Corinthians 13.   [18] John 17:3.
[17] Revelation 2:1-7.   [19] Isaiah 62:5.

sacrifice that many are being called to make for the sake of the Master who laid down his life for us all:

I write of pure love in Red China. A pastor and two Christian girls were sentenced to death. As on many other occasions in Church history, the persecutors mocked them. They promised to release the pastor if he would shoot the girls. He accepted.

The girls waited in the prison yard for the announced execution. A fellow-prisoner who watched the scene from his prison cell described their faces as pale but beautiful beyond belief; infinitely sad but sweet. Humanly speaking, they were fearful, but they decided to submit to death without renouncing their faith. Then, flanked by guards, the executioner came with a revolver in his hand: it was their own pastor.

The girls whispered to each other, then bowed respectfully before the pastor. One of them said:

'Before being shot by you, we wish to thank you heartily for what you have meant to us. You baptised us, you taught us the way of eternal life, you gave us Holy Communion with the same hand in which you now have the gun. May God reward you for all the good you have done us. You also taught us that Christians are sometimes weak and commit terrible sins, but they can be forgiven again. When you regret what you are about to do to us, do not despair like Judas, but repent like Peter. God bless you, and remember that our last thought was not one of indignation against your failure. Everyone passes through hours of darkness. We die with gratitude.'

They bowed again. They knew it was the Lord who had provided that suffering should come when they would feel it most: in the betrayal of their pastor.

The pastor's heart was hardened. He shot the girls. Afterwards he himself was shot by the Communists. This happened in Kiangsi.[20]

I wonder how many of us have thought of faithfulness to Christ in such terms. We may think of faithfulness to

[20] From *Voice of the Martyrs*, No. 2, 1977.

scriptural truth, faithfulness in attending services, faithfulness towards our own tradition, but how far have we seriously considered faithfulness to the point of intense suffering, maybe even death?

Such a supreme sacrifice may not be required of many of us. But it will be possible only if we have learnt to obey Christ daily and to love him most of all in our lives. He asks, in response to his total, sacrificial and steadfast love towards us, nothing less than the willing and joyful response of our whole heart — for we are to be his bride!

In his book *The Church before the Watching World*, Francis Schaeffer puts this in a telling and forceful way:

We must ask, 'Do I fight merely for doctrinal faithfulness?' This is like the wife who never sleeps with anybody else, but never shows love to her husband. Is that a sufficient relationship in marriage? No, ten thousand times no. Yet if I am a Christian who speaks and acts for doctrinal faithfulness but do not show love to my divine bridegroom, I am in the same place as such a wife. What God wants from us is not only doctrinal faithfulness, but our love day by day. Not in theory, mind you, but in practice. Those of us who are children of God must realise the seriousness of modern apostasy; we must urge each other not to have any part in it. But at the same time we must be the loving, true bride of the divine bridegroom in reality and in practice, day by day, in the midst of the spiritual adultery of our day. Our call is first to be the bride faithful, but that is not the total call. The call is not only to be the bride faithful, but also the bride in love.[21]

Any bride preparing for her wedding day has to see to many demanding details. Yet they should not be a burden to her, but rather expressions of her love for the bridegroom. As Christians, we have a glorious wedding day to look forward to. It is literally out of this world. 'Then I heard what seemed to be the voice of a great multitude, like the sound of many waters and like the sound of mighty thunderpeals, crying, "Hallelujah! For the Lord our God the Almighty reigns. Let

[21]Op. cit., Inter-Varsity Press, 1972, p. 51.

us rejoice and exult and give him the glory, for the marriage of the Lamb has come, and his Bride has made herself ready; it was granted her to be clothed with fine linen, bright and pure" — for the fine linen is the righteous deeds of the saints. And the angel said to me, "Write this: Blessed are those who are invited to the marriage supper of the Lamb." '[22]

Such a hope as this should be a constant encouragement for us to prepare ourselves for that glorious day, and especially to deepen our love for him who first loved us.

[22] Revelation 19:6-9.

CHAPTER TEN

The Army of God

AT A MAJOR charismatic conference in Rome in 1975, with 10,000 present, a number of prophecies were given, including this one: 'Because I love you, I want to show you what I am doing in the world today. I want to prepare you for what is to come. Days of darkness are coming on the world, days of tribulation — buildings that are now standing will not be standing; supports that are there for my people now will not be there. I want you to be prepared, my people, to know me, to cleave to me, and to have me in a way deeper than ever before. I will lead you into the desert — I will strip you of everything that you are depending upon now, until you depend just on me. A time of darkness is coming on the world, but a time of glory is coming for my Church. I will pour out on you all the gifts of my Spirit. I will prepare you for a spiritual combat. I will prepare you for a time of evangelism that the world has never seen. I speak to you now on the dawn of a new age for my Church. Prepare yourselves for the action that I begin. Things that you see around you will change. The combat that you must enter now is different, and you need wisdom from God that you do not yet have. Open your hearts to prepare yourselves for me, and for the days I have now begun. My Church will be different, my people will be different. Difficulties and trials will come upon you. They will send for you to take your life, but I will support you. Come to me now. Band yourselves together now around me. I am calling you to receive my power. I am forming a mighty army. I am renewing my people — I will free the world.'

The church of the New Testament must never forget its role as the army of God. Paul urged Timothy to 'share in suffering as a good soldier of Christ Jesus. No soldier on service gets entangled in civilian pursuits, since his aim is to satisfy the one who enlisted him.'[1] In every age we are to 'fight the good fight of the faith'; and perhaps more than ever that is true of this age. In this century there have been more martyrs for Christ than in the entire history of the Christian church put together. Tens of thousands have been imprisoned for their faith. Numerous churches have closed, or are threatened with closure at this moment. And even in more 'peaceful' situations, millions of Christians are battling against apathy, depression, pessimism, apostasy, doubt, confusion — not to mention the rapid growth of some of the cults and sects, the fresh interest in occultism and witchcraft, the domination of society by the media, and the disarray within the theological ranks of the church.

In a radio broadcast about Christian dissidents in the Soviet Union on June 9th 1977, an Orthodox priest said this: 'We are at the front. In the front line. And this front line is all around us because the enemy has surrounded us on all sides. We are surrounded by the godless. There is not a single place which is free from attack — the press, art, the theatre, schools, official institutions, everything is occupied by the godless. The laws are designed to suffocate religion. We've been at the front for a long time, many of us have been taken prisoner. One might almost say that the whole front has been captured. Anyone who can hear us, respond. Do not believe those who try to dismiss the danger. The aim of the enemy is to destroy us. He has no other aims. But having destroyed us; he will destroy you as well. Listen, listen all those who can hear, we are alive, after all the terrible attacks, after all the awful bombardments, we are *still* alive. But we need help. Help us in every way you can.'

Francis Schaeffer has rightly said, 'This is not an age to be a soft Christian.'

In every battle there are a number of basic principles which are vital to observe if there is to be any possibility of victory.

[1] 2 Timothy 2:3f.

1. KNOW YOUR ENEMY

In the African campaign of the last world war, Field-Marshal Montgomery had a vast photograph of his enemy, General Rommel, pinned up in his caravan. He wanted to be constantly reminded of the enemy he had set out to beat. In the same way, we are not to be ignorant of Satan or his devices.

Many within the church today hold that belief in a personal devil is a hangover from medieval superstition, and is a serious hindrance to the growing up of our faith. However, this is not the first generation to have voiced this opinion. From the days of the early church onwards there have been two equally dangerous errors that Christians have tended to make. The first is to deny the very existence of Satan, and this means to lose the battle before it has even begun. The second is to have an unhealthy interest in Satan, and to see devils and evil spirits behind almost every problem that comes our way. Both errors can lead to disastrous consequences in the spiritual battle in which we are certainly engaged, whether we recognise it or not.

Paul, who after all was a first-rate intellectual of his day, was under no illusion about the reality of his enemy: 'For we are not contending against flesh and blood, but against the principalities and powers, against the world rulers of this present darkness, against the spiritual hosts of wickedness in the heavenly places... Although we live in the world we are not carrying on a worldly war...'[2]

Further, the Scriptures indicate that this spiritual battle, which is always with us, will be considerably intensified in the last of the last days. 'And the great dragon was thrown down, that ancient serpent, who is called the Devil and Satan, the deceiver of the whole world — he was thrown down to the earth, and his angels were thrown down with him... Woe to you, O earth and sea, for the devil has come down to you in great wrath, because he knows that his time is short! And when the dragon saw that he had been thrown down to the earth, he pursued the woman [i.e. the church] who had borne the male child... The dragon was angry with

[2]Ephesians 6:12. 2 Corinthians 10:3.

the woman, and went off to make war on the rest of her offspring, on those who keep the commandments of God and bear testimony to Jesus.'[3]

Biblically and traditionally, the Christian faces a threefold enemy: the world, the flesh and the devil. We shall look at these briefly in turn.[4]

The world

This refers to everything in life which does not come directly under the lordship of Christ. At the beginning of creation, everything that God had made was 'very good'. Any form of dualism, therefore, which sets matter and spirit as opposed to one another, is a false doctrine. Paul called such ascetic or gnostic teaching, which despised marriage and certain foods 'which God created to be received with thanksgiving', nothing less than 'doctrines of demons'.[5] He went on to say that 'everything created by God is good, and nothing is to be rejected if it is received with thanksgiving'. God's creation of the world was planned for his special creation, made in his own image — man. It was all originally made for man's benefit and enjoyment. Because of this, man is to live in complete dependence upon his Creator, and this is an essential factor in man's enjoyment of God's creation.

When man rebelled and disobeyed God, there were two tragic consequences. In the first place, *man's sin brought a barrier between himself and God.* 'Therefore the Lord God sent him forth from the garden of Eden, to till the ground from which he was taken. He drove out the man; and at the east of the garden of Eden he placed the cherubim, and a flaming sword which turned every way, to guard the way to the tree of life.'[6] Since that day, man naturally has no knowledge of God, and no personal experience of the reality of God, until he finds God through Jesus Christ.

The second consequence of the fall is that *man's world was brought under the control of Satan,* and God's kingdom of light became Satan's kingdom of darkness. Genesis 4 becomes a

---

[3] Revelation 12:9, 12-13, 17.
[4] I have written more fully on these in *God's Freedom Fighters*, Movement Books,

10 Cuthert Road, Croydon, CR9 3RB, England.
[5] 1 Timothy 4:1-5.
[6] Genesis 3:23f.

vivid picture of the world, with its negative influence away from God. It is summed up in verse 16: 'Then Cain went away from the presence of the Lord.' Interestingly, the whole chapter speaks about various areas of life no longer under the authority of God, and therefore brought under the control of Satan. It is important to remember that, since the fall of man, 'the whole world is in the power of the evil one'.[7] We need to understand this clearly. It is all too easy to think that on the one hand we have the 'church' with all its blessings; on the other hand, far away, we have the 'world' with its drugs, violence, gambling and sex; and in between there is the perfectly harmless 'no-man's-land' with its working, eating, sleeping, loving and entertaining. In fact that is a false picture, for 'the *whole world* is in the power of the evil one', until it is redeemed by Christ and placed under his control.

In the opening verses of Genesis 4 we see that this applies to *religion and worship*. Cain had his own ideas as to what would be an acceptable offering for God, but it was rejected. It was not that his offering was bad or blasphemous; far from it. But it was still not acceptable in the eyes of God, seemingly because of the arrogance and self-righteousness in Cain's heart.[8]

Unless our activities and worship are centred on Christ, in accordance with God's word, and inspired by the Holy Spirit, they will be of the world and not of God. Religion is all too often a worldly counterfeit of the real thing. Paul wrote to the Colossians, who were in danger of shifting away from a Christ-centred faith: 'If with Christ you died to the elemental spirits of the universe, why do you live as if you still belonged to the world? Why do you submit to regulations, "Do not handle, Do not taste, Do not touch" (referring to things which all perish as they are used), according to human precepts and doctrines? These have indeed an appearance of wisdom in promoting rigour of devotion and self-abasement and severity to the body, but they are of no value in checking the indulgence of the flesh.'[9]

In other words, the world says something like this, 'If you want religion, you can have religion.' So the world offers us

---

[7] 1 John 5:19.   [9] Colossians 2:20-23.
[8] Genesis 4:56; cf. 1 John 3:12.

legalism or asceticism or ritualism or institutionalism — anything which may have the appearance of spiritual wisdom, but which in fact is counterfeit.

All too often the organisations and structures of the church exist for their own sake and have lost their vital spiritual life and power. In that case, they belong to the world. 'The church depends for its very existence upon a ceaseless impartation of fresh life from God, and cannot survive one day without it.'[10] It may still 'hold the form of religion', but it will be the religion of the world and not of God.

Further on in Genesis 4 we see that the 'world' also includes *city-life*. Immediately after Cain went away from the presence of the Lord, he built a city. The cities of today are marked by loneliness, insignificance, apathy, violence, hatred, suspicion, selfishness and despair — the very opposite of the community life planned for us by God, a life marked by love and service.

The 'world' also embraces *agriculture and ecology*. In verse 20 we read that Jabal was 'the father of those who dwell in tents and have cattle'. In recent years in particular, the land has been prostituted and polluted to an appalling degree. To give one tiny illustration: An average issue of the Sunday *New York Times* (92 pages), with its book supplement and magazine, requires 100 acres of forest for its production. Today, not more than one tenth of American forests remain, and the annual loss exceeds the annual growth by over 50 per cent. At least one-half of the fertility of that continent's soil has been dissipated. This is the attitude of the world: using God's gifts without reference to the Giver.

The 'world' also includes *music and culture*. In verse 21 we have Jubal, 'the father of all those who play the lyre and pipe.' Many of the divisions that separate Christians today have little or nothing to do with biblical truth. Often it is the cultural background, musical style, or social class that are far more divisive and damaging. This again is the influence of the world on the life of the church. All too often the missionary work of the church has been seriously hindered by the imposition of a foreign culture which has nothing to do with the basic tenets of the Christian faith. Professor Mbiti, speaking at the Pan-African Christian Leadership Assembly

[10] Watchman Nee, *Love Not the World*, Victory Press, p. 25.

in Nairobi in December 1976, reminded the assembly that conversion took place within a cultural framework, and that each society had to redeem the culture of *that* society for God: 'The gospel has been, and should continue to be, proclaimed within the melodies of our African culture... The gospel does not throw out culture. On the contrary, it comes into our culture, it settles there, it brings its impact on our total life within that culture. God does not want us to be aliens to our culture but only aliens to sin.' There is an urgent need for Christians to get involved in the culture of each society and each generation. Only in this way shall we be able to speak to today's world in terms that can be understood, and so win today's world for Christ.

Genesis 4 also includes a reference to *industry*. In verse 22 we read of Tubal-cain, 'the forger of all instruments of bronze and iron'. This, too, is another major area of life which is very much of the world, and needs to be brought under the control of God. Christians today cannot afford to opt out of Trade Unions in favour of attending the prayer meeting of the local church. It is because of the church's common neglect in these areas that many of the decisions affecting the life of industry and of the nation have been made by atheistic minority groups concerned with the destruction of existing social order. Our guilty silence has meant that the world system is developing with ever-increasing power without God. Even by Genesis 6 the corruption of the world was so great that God had to bring his judgment upon men: 'The Lord saw that the wickedness of man was great in the earth, and that every imagination of the thoughts of his heart was only evil continually. And the Lord was sorry that he had made man on the earth, and it grieved him to his heart. So the Lord said, "I will blot out man..."'

The church, therefore, needs to be fully involved in the world, even though it is not to be *of* the world. As good soldiers of Jesus Christ, we are not to be entangled in civilian pursuits; and we are not to let the world around us squeeze us into its own mould. Instead we are to bring the authority and power of Christ to bear on a world that is his by right.

The flesh
This refers to our natural life, our self-life. It is that part of us

that is naturally self-centred and therefore hostile to God. 'When you follow your own wrong inclinations your lives will produce these evil results: impure thoughts, eagerness for lustful pleasure, idolatry, spiritism (that is, encouraging the activity of demons), hatred and fighting, jealousy and anger, constant effort to get the best for yourself, complaints and criticisms, the feeling that everyone else is wrong except those in your own little group — and there will be wrong doctrine, envy, murder, drunkenness, wild parties, and all that sort of thing.'[11] The truth is that 'the desires of the flesh are against the Spirit'; and therefore to 'set the mind on the flesh is death' since this is hostile to God. 'Those who are in the flesh cannot please God.'[12]

Unless we consciously 'set our mind on the Spirit', seeking daily to 'live by the Spirit' and to 'walk by the Spirit', we shall inevitably slip back into the flesh. There is a constant tug-o'-war beteen the flesh and the Spirit; and unless our will is consciously pulling on the side of the Spirit, it may well be pulling on the side of the flesh.

An understanding of this spiritual battle is crucial in the life of any church. It is possible to be fully and actively involved in good works and religious services, yet to do these things 'in the flesh' and not 'in the Spirit'. If they are done 'in the flesh' there will be, underlying the activities and often unrecognised, a basic self-centredness with its consequent hostility towards God and towards genuine spirituality. This explains why many 'religious' and 'good' people are surprisingly resistant and opposed to the true work of the gospel.

It also serves as a reminder that new schemes, new services, new organisations, are never by themselves the means for spiritual renewal. What is most of all important is that we should learn how to crucify the flesh and to walk in the Spirit.

At the Pan-African Christian Leadership Assembly in Nairobi, the Archbishop of Capetown, Dr. Bill Burnett, surprised the delegates by giving a clear and very personal testimony of his own spiritual renewal, when he was consciously filled with the Holy Spirit whilst praying in his chapel one day. He then went on to say this about the crisis in South Africa: 'Our crises are not basically of tribalism or racism or economics,

[11] Galatians 5:19-21, Living Bible. [12] Romans 8:3-8.

but of faith. Do Christians really trust God? God can deliver people who are locked in unforgiveness.' But he will do so only in the power of the Spirit, not in the energy of the flesh. All other attempts to sort out the tensions, conflicts and hatreds between people inevitably fall short at some point or other because they leave individuals basically self-centred instead of God-centred. It is only the fruit of the Spirit that is 'love, joy, peace, patience, kindness, goodness, faithfulness, gentleness, self-control.'

Until there is a genuine spiritual renewal within people and within communities, nothing will be fundamentally changed. This has been the sad and repetitive story of the bitter and violent revolutions that have so dominated this century. An old saying makes this wise comment: 'The man who sets out to change society is an optimist; but the man who sets out to change society without changing the individual is a lunatic.' And the individual can be changed only when he comes to the cross of Christ to receive forgiveness for his sins and to be crucified with Christ. It is only by dying to self that we are able to live in the Spirit.

The devil
He is the mastermind behind all the evil in the world. In the Scriptures, he is called the *ruler of the world*, who seeks to influence and control governments, world powers, and those in authority at all levels in society. That is why the church is to pray regularly for rulers and 'for all who are in high positions'.

He is the *prince of the power of the air*, who seeks to manipulate the philosophy, the thought-forms, the moral standards of our life, often through the influence of the media. In an almost unthinking and subliminal way, the impact of television (especially), radio, press, theatre and cinema can change radically the beliefs and values of a society within a remarkably short period of time.

He is the *god of this world*, who can blind the minds of unbelievers, often by the paralysis of apathy, and who can change the patterns and structures of society so fast that many are left bewildered and depressed. Alvin Toffler writes of those who 'cannot cope rationally with change', so that they fall into 'drug-induced lassitude, video-induced stupor, alcoholic haze — when the old vegetate and die in loneliness'. [13]

He is the *angel of light,* who works through false teachers and false prophets, often infiltrating into the heart of the church, twisting and distorting the gospel of Christ.

He is the *father of lies,* who will cause you, if he can, to doubt God's word, to question God's love, to deny God's control, to disbelieve God's faithfulness.

He is a *murderer from the beginning,* who is always out to destroy God's work and God's church.

He is the *slanderer and accuser,* who will make Christian to mistrust Christian, suspecting the worst instead of believing the best, and who will impose an intolerable sense of guilt and condemnation when God has forgiven and forgotten.

He is the *serpent,* trained in subtlety and disguise, so that some of our most powerful temptations come from the least expected sources.

He is the *roaring lion,* who can spring sudden and fierce attacks, so that we are startled by overwhelming depression that pins us down, or by overpowering feelings of lust, greed, anger, jealousy, ambition, resentment, that leave us wounded and helpless. Always he is prowling around. When Satan presented himself before the Lord, in the introduction to the book of Job, 'the Lord said to Satan, "Whence have you come?" Satan answered the Lord, "From going to and fro on the earth, and from walking up and down on it." ' [14]

A Scotland Yard Inspector was once asked if he believed in the devil. He replied like this: 'Yes, I do, although I have never seen him. Sometimes in London there is an outreach of petty crime, and the quality of the criminals caught show that they are not intelligent enough to have planned the crime. So we know that there is a new leader, and we open a new file, "Mr. X". We then build up a picture of what he is, and from that we seek to find him. In the same way, as I cross-examine people on how they got into the mess they are in, I find there is a "Mr. X" who is twisting our lives. That "Mr. X" is the Devil.'

It is vital that we should know our enemy. We must not be ignorant of Satan or of his devices.

[13]*Future Shock*, Bodley Head, p., 325.   [14]Job 2:2.

2. FOLLOW YOUR LEADER

Christ is called the 'Captain of our salvation'. [15] He is the one who has enlisted us. Therefore our primary aim should be to please him and to follow him.

In any army, submission and obedience to those in authority are crucial to the efficiency and fighting power of that army. It is significant that the regiments with the finest battle honours are also the regiments with the strictest discipline. The ability to obey an order without questioning or challenging it (let alone ignoring or disobeying it) is an essential mark of the good soldier.

The same is true in the spiritual realm. A Roman centurion once sent a message to Jesus to ask if he would heal his servant who was dying. Jesus went towards the centurion's house. He was intercepted by a message from the centurion, who begged Jesus not to trouble himself in coming to the house. 'But say the word, and let my servant be healed. For I am a man set under authority, with soldiers under me: and I say to one, "Go," and he goes; and to another, "Come," and he comes; and to my slave, "Do this," and he does it.' We are told that Jesus then marvelled at the centurion. 'I tell you, not even in Israel have I found such faith.' And the servant was healed instantly. [16] Such discipline and obedience is excellent soil in which a strong and healthy faith can grow; and, as John tells us, 'this is the victory that overcomes the world, our faith.' [17]

In the army of God, then, we must learn — painfully perhaps — this vital principle of *submission*.

Naturally we are *to submit to Christ* in everything. We are to 'take every thought captive to obey Christ.' [18] If we are consciously disobeying him in any area of our life, we cannot hope to fight successfully in our spiritual battles.

That was the lesson that God's people had to learn over and over again in the Old Testament. Sometimes they went confidently into battle against their enemies, only to suffer humiliating defeat. So they asked God for the reason for this. Normally it was because of some sin or disobedience within

[15] Hebrews 2:10, A.V.   [17] 1 John 5:4.
[16] Luke 7:1-10.   [18] 2 Corinthians 10:5.

their ranks, and until that matter was put right God's victory would not be with them. 'Submit yourselves therefore to God. Resist the devil and he will flee from you,' writes James. [19] But it must be that way round. Unless we learn to submit to God of our own free will, God may have to knock us into submission. He loves us too much not to chasten us when we are being foolish. 'He disciplines us for our good, that we may share his holiness. For the moment all discipline seems painful rather than pleasant; later it yields the peaceful fruit of righteousness to those who have been trained by it.' [20]

We are also *to submit to those over us in the Lord*. 'Obey your leaders and submit to them; for they are keeping watch over your souls.'[21] Paul also urged the young church at Thessalonica, where clearly there was some tension between the leadership and the rest of the church (faults were on both sides, it seems, and this is nearly always the case): 'We beseech you, brethren, to respect those who labour amongst you and are over you in the Lord and admonish you, and to esteem them very highly in love because of their work.' [22]

Neither of these exhortations say anything about 'providing you agree with their decisions'. That is not the point at issue. The leaders of a church will not always be right. There may often be a need to talk and pray things through, until the will of the Lord is more clearly seen for that church. But that is no excuse for rebellion, inward or outward, silent or vocal.

Until we learn to submit to those who are over us, the Lord cannot and will not bless our work and worship. Although the time came for Jesus, as Son of God, Prophet, Priest and King, to make some stinging remarks to the Jewish leaders concerning their hypocrisy and unbelief, for many years he humbly submitted himself to the worship and leadership of his day. It was his regular custom to go to the synagogue at Nazareth on the Sabbath Day, and to travel to the Temple at Jerusalem for the great festivals. This is a point worth remembering when we become impatient with the church where we worship, or with the leadership of that church.

The leaders, in turn, are expressly commanded not to be 'domineering' over those in their charge, but to be examples

---

[19] James 4:7.
[20] Hebrews 12:10f.

[21] Hebrews 13:17.
[22] 1 Thessalonians 5:12f.

to the flock. They must learn that ministry means service. They are to care for their flock, to feed them, guide them, teach them, shepherd them, be very gentle with them, and to be patient with all. [23]

We must also learn *to submit to one another*, out of reverence for Christ. Significantly, this command comes immediately after the exhortation to go on being filled with the Spirit. [24] One healthy sign of a truly Spirit-filled church is this atmosphere of loving submission to one another, in an attitude of thanksgiving and praise, all out of reverence for Christ. It is the very opposite of what sometimes happens after claims of spiritual blessing: the unhealthy individualism, when each person does his own thing, or each group does its own thing, 'because the Spirit said so'.

In a thoroughly practical manner, Paul applies this principle of mutual submission to all areas of life. Wives are to be 'subject to your husbands, as to the Lord'; children are to 'obey your parents in the Lord'; slaves are to be 'obedient to those who are your earthly masters...as to Christ.' Peter adds, 'you that are younger be subject to the elders'; and Paul reminds Christians living in Rome, the seat of pagan rulers, 'let every person be subject to the governing authorities.' [25]

When relationships are right, 'submission' in the Christian army does not mean becoming a doormat so that others can wipe their feet on you. Of course, if the leadership is not spiritual it could become something like this, and Jesus himself had to learn to be reviled without reviling back. When he suffered at the hands of the authorities over him, he did not threaten, but trusted himself to 'him who judges justly'. [26] Christians may at times be called to suffer for Christ in similar ways, even within the church. However, when relationships are basically right, albeit imperfect, submission becomes a place of protection and safety. This can be clearly seen in Paul's teaching about husbands and wives.

Not to submit means an unecessary exposure in battle. If we have wilfully and disobediently removed ourselves from the shelter that God has given us, we are on our own and

[23] See 1 Peter 5:2f; Acts 20:28ff; 1 Thessalonians 5:14ff; et.al.
[24] Ephesians 5:18-21.
[25] Ephesians 5:22-6:9; 1 Peter 5:5; Romans 13:1ff.
[26] 1 Peter 2:22.

should not be surprised if we encounter spiritual attacks which overwhelm us. It is no doubt for this reason that Paul gives his fullest and clearest instruction about spiritual warfare following his detailed teaching about relationships and submission at home and at work. We are simply asking for trouble, in our personal lives and in our church, if our relationships are not right, and if we are not submitting to one another out of reverence for Christ.

Because Simon Peter would not listen to the warnings of Jesus, he denied his Master three times. Because the Christians at Corinth would not accept the apostolic authority of Paul, many of them were severely chastened. Because some of them ignored the authority of their leaders, and did their own thing, even at the Lord's supper, they became 'weak and ill, and some have died.'[27]

It is impossible to over-estimate the importance of right relationships, particularly in this matter of loving and willing submission to one another. Unless the members of a body work in harmony together, submitting to the head and to each other, the result is ugly and grotesque. It certainly will not reveal to the world the beauty and glory of Christ.

3. PUT ON YOUR ARMOUR

The classic passage for this is Paul's teaching to the church at Ephesus.[28] It is worth stressing that he was writing to a church, and not just to an individual, as frequently this passage is expounded in a very personal way. It is together that we must stand against the wiles of the devil. It is together that we must be strong in the Lord. It is together that we must put on the whole armour. That is why our relationships together need to be guarded so closely. A break in the ranks weakens the whole defence.

Further, all the armour is needed, as is indicated by the single Greek word *panoplia*. One part protects the heart, but not the head; another the head, but not the heart. We need every single piece. Notice, too, that it all comes from God. He wants to bring us to the point where we are consciously depending on him for all our needs. We are not playing

[27] 1 Corinthians 11:30.   [28] Ephesians 6:10-20.

religious games; we are not even fighting against flesh and blood. We are contending against an immensely powerful spiritual army, and we need to realise our total weakness without God. Almost every part of the armour mentioned by Paul is to be found in the Old Testament as the armour of the Messiah. [29] Christ has already proved himself victorious in the fight, and we are to use the well-tried armour and weapons that are his. Let us consider the armour briefly. From the different phrases that Paul uses in 1 Thessalonians 5:8 we cannot be dogmatic over any exegesis, but the following suggestions may be helpful.

The girdle of truth

In Isaiah 11:5 the word 'faithfulness' is used, not 'truth'. Paul is probably thinking here not about doctrinal truth, but about integrity and sincerity. There should be a 'ring of truth' about our relationships within the body of Christ. We need to be open and honest with one another, walking in the light as God is in the light. Only in this way can we have fellowship with him and with one another, and such fellowship, marked by mutual love and trust, is essential if we are to win any battle. The belt for the soldier held everything else together. In spite of our many faults and failings, we must have a basic integrity towards God, and trust one another's integrity. It is only with a pure heart, a good conscience and a sincere faith that we can wage a good warfare. Although we shall often have to forgive one another, a confident and mutual trust in each other's sincerity before God is vital. Everything else will depend on this.

The breastplate of righteousness

This speaks of lives that are right with God and with man. Paul once said, 'I always take pains to have a clear conscience toward God and toward men.' [30] If anyone's life is not right with God and men, there will be a crack in the breastplate, a chink in the armour, and therefore an obvious target for the enemy. Personal sin is not a private matter. It is the church that must put on the breastplate of righteousness; and this means that my sin can make the whole church vulnerable to

[29] Isaiah 11:5; 52:7; 59:17.   [30] Acts 24:16.

the devil's attacks. Others are always saddened and weakened by our sins, especially when they become an open offence to the congregation. The whole of Israel suffered through the sin of Achan. The entire life of a local church can likewise suffer from unconfessed sin which is festering somewhere within the congregation. If one part of my body is sick, my whole body suffers. Our corporate righteousness is a crucial factor in the spiritual battle, and a healthy church will always be a disciplined church.

The shoes of peace

Paul writes: '...having shod your feet with the equipment of the gospel of peace.' The Roman soldier wore heavy sandals, equivalent to the army boots of today. Isaiah spoke of the beauty upon the mountains of those 'who bring good tidings, who publish peace... [and] salvation.'[31] Many liberation armies of today offer a peace which is little more than mockery and dictatorship. But Christ truly came to bring peace, and we need to be equipped and ready to take this good news wherever God sends us.

The heavy Roman sandal meant mobility for the soldier. It enabled him to move quickly and easily over rough, unfamiliar ground. As soldiers of Jesus Christ, we need to move quickly to bring God's peace to a rapidly changing situation. It is not that the gospel should change, but our presentation and approach must change if we are to speak to today's world. The battle is raging today, and God's peace is for today. God forbid that we should spend our time trying to fight today's battles with yesterday's tactics. That is the way to defeat, not victory.

The shield of faith

The Roman shield was large and oblong, offering the soldier complete protection, especially if he crouched down a little. When all the soldiers were standing side by side, the shields formed a solid wall which effectively stopped all the arrows fired by the enemy. An individual on his own was still extremely vulnerable to any flanking attacks, but a company of soldiers standing close together could offer one another

[31] Isaiah 52:7.

excellent defence. So it is with the church. We are not meant
to stand on our own. We must stand together, fight together,
and protect one another with the shield of faith. Faith is
happily infectious. We can encourage one another to trust in
the Lord. As we care for one another, pray for one another,
and share God's word with one another, so we are lifting up
that shield which can quench all the flaming darts of the evil
one. As we share and bear one another's burdens, we can
stand together fully protected against every fiery attack. No
weapon that is formed against us shall be able to prosper.

The helmet of salvation

This is to protect the mind and our whole attitude towards
the Christian faith. If Satan cannot succeed in other ways, he
will try to make us tired, weary, discouraged and disillusioned. Often the psalmist asked questions like this, 'Why do
the wicked prosper and the righteous suffer?' The answer to
that is to take up the helmet of salvation. Paul declared, 'I
consider that the sufferings of this present time are not worth
comparing with the glory that is to be revealed to us.'[32] He
looked ahead to the glorious future when at last we shall see
Jesus face to face, when all the sufferings of the present world
will be lost in that first moment's welcome in heaven.

Paul knew what it was to be beaten and buffeted more
than most. His testimony in 2 Corinthians 11 gives us an
indication of the astonishing suffering he endured for the sake
of the gospel of Christ. However, defeat never entered his
head. He was protected by the helmet of salvation: 'This
slight momentary affliction [!] is preparing for us an eternal
weight of glory beyond all comparison... Who shall separate
us from the love of Christ?... In all these things we are more
than conquerors through him who loved us.'[33]

There is a tendency in some sections of the church to be
vocal about failure and defeat. We tell one another how we
have failed to do this and that, and it no doubt is supposed to
be a mark of humility and penitence. Perhaps it is a reaction
against the triumphalism which can be very superficial.
However the apostles, although personally very honest about

[32] Romans 8:18.

[33] 2 Corinthians 4:17;
Romans 8:35, 37.

their own sinfulness, spoke with unshaken confidence in the victory of Jesus Christ. They knew that Satan was defeated and that God was on the throne. In literally everything he would work for good with those who loved him.

The sword of the Spirit

The classic example of this is when Christ overcame his adversary in the wilderness temptations by thrusting him away with the sword of the Spirit, which is the word of God. He countered all three temptations by saying 'It is written... It is written... It is written...', quoting from Deuteronomy 6 and 9, which had no doubt recently been on his mind. A good working knowledge of the Scriptures will frequently be invaluable in spiritual warfare.[34] Our thoughts are not God's thoughts, and our ways are not God's ways. Often the devil will want us to think and act according to our own wisdom and strength, but this will nearly always be fatal. We must learn to think biblically, and to let the word of Christ dwell in us richly, in all God's wisdom. In so doing, we shall become much more skilled in using the sword of the Spirit, and therefore less easily tricked by the wiles of the devil.

The same sword is also to be used, of course, to set others free from spiritual snares and bondage. It is the way God can cut through the blindness, the excuses, the arguments of men and women, until their lives are 'open and laid bare' before God; only when this happens can he heal and cover us with his righteousness.

At the same time the combination between the sword and Spirit is all-important. It is often said, 'All word and no Spirit, we dry up; all Spirit and no word, we blow up; both word and Spirit, we grow up.' There is much truth in this catchy saying. It is only as we allow the Spirit within us to use the sword that the word of God becomes 'living and active, sharper than any two-edged sword, piercing to the division of soul and spirit, of joints and marrow, and discerning the thoughts and intentions of the heart.'[35]

Further, even with this piece of the armour of God, there is still a corporate application. It is when we have the high praises of God in our throats that we have two-edged swords

[34] See also I Peter 3:15.   [35] Hebrews 4:12.

in our hands;[36] and such praises, based on the promises of God's word, are much more effective when sung together. It was when the singers began to sing and give praise together, saying 'Give thanks to the Lord, for his steadfast love endures for ever,' that God gave his victory to Jehoshaphat and the army of Israel.[37]

The church that builds its life on the teaching of the Scriptures is always likely to be a strong and stable church when it comes to spiritual battles. 'For whatever was written in former days was written for our instruction, that by steadfastness and by the encouragement of the Scriptures we might have hope.'[38]

4. USE YOUR WEAPONS

With the exception of the sword of the Spirit, all the pieces of armour are naturally defensive. However, God also supplies us with offensive weapons which 'have divine power to destroy strongholds.'[39] Particularly are these valuable in clearing the pathway through to the knowledge of God: 'we destroy arguments and every proud obstacle to the knowledge of God, and take every thought captive to obey Christ.' Again, it is worth looking at these weapons briefly.

Prayer and praise
Immediately after Paul's detailed description of the armour, he says this: 'Pray at all times in the Spirit, with all prayer and supplication. To that end, keep alert with all perseverance, making supplication for all the saints.'[40] Jesus also told his disciples to 'watch and pray' when he knew they were about to be severely tested. It was because they failed to pray that they failed the test. The armour and the weapons by themselves are not magical. Can they by themselves fight a battle? Of course not! They need to be controlled by a living and powerful person before they can be of any use at all, in spite of their potential.

In the same way, even with all God's armour in place and

36 Psalm 149:6.
37 2 Chronicles 20.
38 Romans 15:4.
39 2 Corinthians 10:3-5.
40 Ephesians 6:18.

his sword in our hands, we still need to be spiritually alive and alert in the battle. We still need the power of the Holy Spirit. We are to be strong *in the Lord.*

Richard Wurmbrand once described how he learnt this truth amidst fourteen years of torture within communist prisons:

> In prison we unlearnt Theology, and we learnt Theos, the One about whom Theology speaks... Christians sought comfort in a Bible verse. We knew verses like, 'My grace is sufficient for thee' and 'The Lord is my Shepherd'. But Christians found no comfort in Bible verses. It is not written anywhere in the Bible that the verse will be sufficient for you. It is only God's grace that is sufficient. It is nowhere written in the Bible that the twenty-third psalm will lead you into green pastures. It is only the Lord who will lead you into green pastures.

It is only by prayer that spiritual realities become alive within us, and that we become alert to the spiritual battle.

Praise, too, is of special importance. When Paul and Silas were smarting under the lash, their feet fastened to the stocks, their bodies locked away in prison, and the future as black as the night, they began to sing praises to God. Not only were they inwardly delivered from fears and depressions, God wonderfully released them and converted the jailer and his household as a bonus! I doubt if either Paul or Silas on their own would have had the courage to sing praises at midnight in a situation like that. But corporately, this weapon of praise was marvellously used.

The cross of Christ

The cross has often been a banner for the Christian solider, but the significance of this emblem has not always been clear. To quote a parody of a well-known hymn:

> Onward Christian soldiers,
>   Each to war resigned,
>   With the cross of Jesus
>   Vaguely kept in mind.

Many travesties of the real Christian battle have taken place throughout church history, with the cross seen as a rallying-point, the Christian's national flag. Appalling crimes and acts of violence have subsequently been committed in the name of Christ.

In all these sad events, men and women have lost sight of our true conflict, which is not against flesh and blood but 'against the principalities, against the powers, against the world rulers of this present darkness, against the spiritual hosts of wickedness in the heavenly places.'

In talking about Christ's death on the cross, Paul said this to the Colossians: 'He disarmed the principalities and powers and made a public example of them, triumphing over them in him.'[41] It is in knowing that Satan has already been defeated on the cross, and that he has no power or authority over us if we are trusting in Christ and in his victory on the cross, that we can go with absolute confidence into the thick of the battle. On numerous occasions when I have felt desperate and utterly weak in some situation, I have found God's peace and victory at the cross of Christ. Even in the fiercest conflicts, such as an exorcism of someone who has been completely under Satan's control, the power of the cross is quite astonishing. Making the sign of the cross, reading verses about the cross, claiming prayerfully the victory of the cross — all these can have a quite devastating effect in controlling the most bizarre manifestations of the evil one.

The gifts of the Spirit

Paul once urged Timothy to wage a good warfare 'in accordance with the prophetic utterances' and 'inspired by them'.[42] When Timothy was set apart for the leadership of the church at Ephesus, the council of elders laid hands upon him,[43] and words of prophecy were uttered. Because these came as God's special word to Timothy for the special task confronting him, he was to remember those words and let them inspire him, especially in the midst of spiritual battles.

Before I have gone out from my church to lead various missions, the elders have frequently gathered round me, laid

[41]Colossians 3:15.   [43]1 Timothy 4:14.
[42]1 Timothy 1:18.

their hands on me, and quite often a word of prophecy has been given. Since this word has been of particular relevance for that particular task, I have taken care to remember what was said and to pray over it many times on that mission. It has always proved a means of special encouragement and strength.

It is not only prophecy that is valuable in the battle. It may be words of knowledge or wisdom, giving us insight into a situation beyond our normal understanding. It may be healing — three or four times I have been instantly healed from flu or some other affliction in order to be fit for a mission. The liberating gift of tongues, too, can refresh and edify us in the battle. Many Christians who have experienced exceptional times of testing have said that they doubt if they could have survived apart from this gift of tongues.

Think, too, how many Christians have been encouraged in the fight by loving and generous hospitality, by the ministry of intercession, by wise counsel, by sacrificial service — the 'foot-washing' ministries which can be such a blessing within the body of Christ. It is not just the more spectacular gifts that are valuable in this context, but every gift that is edifying for the church. They are all specifically given to strengthen the church in the battle.

The fellowship of Christ

Throughout this chapter we have repeatedly noticed the vital role of our fellowship in Christ to withstand the assaults of the enemy. 'Two are better than one... For if they fall, one will lift up his fellow; but woe to him who is alone when he falls and has not another to lift him up... And though a man might prevail against one who is alone, two will withstand him. A threefold cord is not quickly broken.'[44] It was doubtless for this reason that Jesus sent out his disciples two by two,[45] and we see the same pattern continuing, whenever possible, in the Acts of the Apostles. We are not meant to battle on our own. If there is no alternative, God's grace will certainly be sufficient for us; but there is a special sense of Christ's presence promised when two or three are gathered in his name.

[44]Ecclesiastes 4:9-12.   [45]Luke 10:1.

The Christian who neglects or avoids real fellowship with other Christians has only himself to blame if he finds the battle excessively tough. In the New Testament church, the severest form of discipline was to exclude someone from the fellowship of believers. This was tantamount to handing him over to Satan, since the offender would no longer be protected by the body of Christ from Satanic attacks. Yet sometimes this was necessary 'for the destruction of the flesh', and in order that the offender might 'learn not to blaspheme'.[46]

That is why we need to be open and honest with one another. We must share, with at least one other Christian, the particular areas of temptation and trial that we find the hardest. We need to pray specifically for one another, and 'exhort one another every day..., that none of you may be hardened by the deceitfulness of sin.'[47]

A disciplined life

Although the battle is the Lord's and the victory is the Lord's, we still need to be thoroughly trained and disciplined as soldiers in the army of Christ. Thinking of the famous Isthmian Games (second only to the Olympic Games) that were held every three years at Corinth, Paul wrote to the church in that city about the spiritual contest in which they were all engaged. 'Every athlete exercises self-control in all things. They do it to receive a perishable wreath, but we an imperishable. Well, I do not run aimlessly, I do not box as one beating the air; but I pommel my body and subdue it, lest after preaching to others I myself should be disqualified.'[48]

The astonishingly rigorous and disciplined training schedule for an athlete who is out to win should be a constant challenge and rebuke to the flabbiness and laziness of many Christians. Everything, even a good and harmless pursuit, is put to one side if it might in any way hinder the training. The Christian likewise is to lay aside not only every sin, but also every weight which might hold him back as he seeks to run the race, looking to Jesus.

This truth is a healthy corrective to the emphasis so often

---

[46] 1 Corinthians 5:5;
1 Timothy 1:20.

[47] Hebrews 3:13.
[48] 1 Corinthians 9:25-27.

heard about coming to Jesus who will meet your every need. That is admittedly one side of the coin; but 'in the Bible,' said Dr. Martyn Lloyd-Jones in one of his sermons, 'I find a barracks, not a hospital. It is not a doctor you need, but a Sergeant Major. Here we are on the parade ground slouching about. A doctor is no good; it is discipline we need. We need to listen to the Sergeant Major: "Yield not to temptation, but yield to God." That is the trouble with the church today; there is too much of the hospital element; we have lost sight of the great battle.'

We must also learn, however, to be encouraged, and to encourage one another, in the Lord. We may have many knocks and many defeats; but these are only to make us rely not on ourselves but on God.[49] We need to meditate on passages such as Romans 8. 'If God is for us, who is against us? He who did not spare his own Son but gave him up for us all, will he not also give us all things with him?'

The last decade or so has witnessed many encouraging signs of spiritual renewal. Thousands of Christians from all traditions are discovering again what it is to worship God with unrestrained joy, praising him in music, song and dance; they have experienced afresh the love of God, spilling over into the community and drawing Christians together in a new joyful unity in Christ; the Scriptures have become alive; witness has become the spontaneous overflow of spiritual life; prayer has become a delight; service towards others has sprung from a new devotion to Christ.

Yet, at the same time, the spiritual warfare has been growing in intensity. Many Christian leaders involved in this renewal have experienced personal battles of a degree not known before, often in the area of their own home. Others have learnt that the way of Christ did not end at Jordan when the Spirit descended upon him in that breathtaking moment. Jordan led immediately to a prolonged period of great testing in the wilderness; and thereafter to a time of suffering, pain, loneliness, rejection, exhaustion, until the crisis of Calvary. All this was necessary before there could be any resurrection or any outpouring of the Spirit. The Christian who really wants to follow Jesus must be ready for a similar pattern.

[49] 2 Corinthians 1:9.

God is preparing an army to fight against the powers of darkness that rage in the world. Translated into the area of spiritual conflict, the words of Winston Churchill, in a famous speech in the House of Commons on the 13th May 1940, at the start of the Battle of Britain, could hardly be bettered: 'I have nothing to offer but blood, toil, tears, and sweat. We have before us an ordeal of the most grievous kind. We have before us many, many long months of struggle and suffering. You ask what is our policy; I will say: "It is to wage war, by sea, land and air, with all our might and with all the strength that God can give us, and to wage war against a monstrous tyranny, never surpassed in the dark, lamentable catalogue of human crime." '

CHAPTER ELEVEN

The Spirit in the Church

THE GRAND THING the church wants in this time is God's Holy Spirit. You all get up plans and say, 'Now if the church were altered a little bit, it would go on better.' You think that if there were different ministers, or different church order, or something different, then all would be well. No, dear friends, it is not there that the mistake lies; it is that we want more of the Spirit... That is the church's great want, and until that want be supplied, we may reform, and reform, and still be just the same. All we want is the Spirit of God.

That could well be a tract for our times. In fact it was written by Charles Spurgeon on 31st August 1857. In every age the Holy Spirit is indispensable to the life and health of the church.

The church was born of the Spirit on the day of Pentecost, as described in Acts 2. Before that date the disciples had certainly known spiritual fellowship with Christ and with one another; they had experienced the illumination and power of the Spirit on a variety of occasions; they had been specifically taught about the Spirit, and had been promised God's gracious gift of the Spirit for themselves. Yet, although the Spirit had clearly been *with* them before Pentecost, he was not abiding *in* them. His action had been as in Old Testament days: coming upon certain people at certain times for certain occasions.

It was only at Pentecost that the prophecy of Joel was

fulfilled, when God poured out his spirit 'upon all flesh', sons and daughters, young men and old men, menservants and maidservants. 'For the promise is to you and to your children and to all that are afar off, every one whom the Lord our God calls to him.' From that moment on, the church learnt to live and move and pray in the Spirit. It realised (as did the prophets of the Old Testament) that it could grieve or quench the Spirit. One way or another, it became impossible to think of the church without the Spirit. Take him away, and you have no church: an institution, an organisation, a building, a structure, perhaps; but no church of the living God. Yet Dr. Carl Bates once commented, 'If God were to take the Holy Spirit out of our midst today, about 95 per cent of what we are doing in our churches would go on, and we would not know the difference.' Several clergy have told me that, in their opinion, that remark is absolutely true. At the same time it is important not to identify the church with the Spirit, nor subordinate the Spirit to the church.

Distinct from the church

The Spirit is the third Person of the Godhead; and thus has an independent and eternal existence apart from the church. Nowhere in the New Testament do we find any reference to the 'Spirit of the church'. He is always the Holy Spirit, or the Spirit of God, or the Spirit of Christ. He never becomes the property or possession of the church, let alone one particular group within the church. Although we are commanded to be filled by him, we no more 'possess' him than we possess the air when our lungs are filled with air. Rather, he wants to possess us, in order to teach us, guide us, empower us, equip us and use us as he wills. One reason for the church's confusion about the Spirit may be that he is often thought and spoken of as an impersonal 'it' — a divine influence, a spiritual power. In this way we can easily think of possessing *it*, or of wanting more of *it*; instead of desiring that *he* should have more of us.

There are two areas in particular where we need to remember the sovereignty of the Spirit as the third Person of the Trinity. First, the church neither controls nor confines the Spirit. There is no guaranteed bestowal of the Spirit at baptism, confirmation or ordination. There is no assured

presence of the Spirit for the preacher or pastor, priest or
bishop purely on the grounds of the office he holds in the
church. When Simon the sorcerer wanted for himself the
power to bestow the Spirit on anyone he wished, he was told
forthrightly to repent. The Spirit will not be tied to the
church, nor to any ecclesiastical office within the church.
Certainly the Spirit is not arbitrary or capricious in his
actions; he has given us in the Scriptures clear conditions on
which he has promised to work. At the same time, 'the Lord is
the Spirit, and where the Spirit of the Lord is, there is
freedom.'[1] The church which tries to tie the Spirit to its
institutionalised forms, to its traditional patterns, or to its
doctrinal statements, will quickly find itself moribund and
powerless. True spiritual life and freedom will come only
insofar as the church submits to the Spirit, listens to the Spirit
and obeys the Spirit. At every stage we must learn to hear
what the Spirit is saying to the churches, even if that word is
sometimes a word of rebuke, or a warning of judgment. God
gives the Spirit to those who obey him.

Second, no group within the church can claim a special
monopoly of the Spirit. All true Christians have the Spirit
within them: 'Anyone who does not have the Spirit of Christ
does not belong to him.'[2] Certainly some Christians may
obviously be filled with the Spirit: the church at Jerusalem
was asked to 'pick out from among you seven men of good
repute, full of the Spirit...'[3] That these men were Spirit-filled
must, in some way, have been obvious for others to see. At the
same time, it is dangerous when some Christians claim a
special possession of the Spirit in a way that is not available
for the ordinary Christian. It was such a proud boast that led
to *gnosticism*, which assumed superior enlightenment for the
initiated; and later to *Montanism*, and to the long succession of
cults and sects, all of which claim divine authority for freshly
revealed teachings that are beyond, and often contradictory
to, God's self-revelation in the Scriptures. Equally dangerous
are those theologians who sit loose to biblical authority, who
treat the Scriptures as of largely historical interest condi-
tioned by the cultural context of the time, and who talk and

[1] 2 Corinthians 3:17.   [3] Acts 6:3.
[2] Romans 8:9.

write as though they possess a revelation beyond the teaching of Christ and the apostles.

The author and giver of life

The Spirit is not an optional extra for the church, as though the church could jog along fairly happily on its own. The truth is that the church is totally dependent on the Spirit for the whole of its life. It is created by the Spirit, and it must be continuously sustained and renewed by the Spirit. 'The church depends for its very existence upon a ceaseless impartation of fresh life from God, and cannot survive one day without it.'[4] As a living body dies the moment its breath has gone, so the church becomes a dead institution the moment the Spirit makes his departure. As there is no entrance into the kingdom of God 'unless one is born of water and the Spirit',[5] so there is no life within the kingdom unless the Spirit is continuously maintaining that life.

It is therefore of paramount importance that every church should not only understand the person and work of the Spirit, but be open wide to his invigorating power. All our activities in the church become empty and meaningless without the Spirit. 'The written code kills,' wrote Paul, 'but the Spirit gives life.'[6]

The foremost task of the church is to *worship God*. But real worship is never easy; in fact it is impossible without the Holy Spirit: 'God is spirit,' said Jesus, 'and those who worship him must worship in Spirit and truth.'[7] It is only the Spirit within us that can genuinely cry out 'Abba! Father!'

The next most important task of the church is to *witness to Jesus Christ*. Again, no one finds this easy; and therefore Jesus promised his disciples the power of the Spirit in order to be his witnesses. Indeed, they were to stay put until they had been 'clothed with power from on high.'[8]

Preaching, too, urgently needs a 'demonstration of the Spirit and of power' if the faith of those who respond is to rest in the power of God and not in the wisdom of man.[9] Our understanding of God's word and ways also needs the

[4] Watchman Nee.
[5] John 3:5.
[6] 2 Corinthians 3:6.

[7] John 4:24.
[8] Acts 1:8; Luke 24:49.
[9] 1 Corinthians 2:4f.

illumination of the Holy Spirit, since 'no one comprehends the thoughts of God except the Spirit of God.'

Any effective *ministry* that is able to build up the body of Christ is also entirely dependent on the Holy Spirit. It is the 'manifestation of the Spirit' that is for the common good and the various gifts of the Spirit are inspired by the Spirit in order to build up the church.[10]

True *prayer*, also, needs the direct assistance of the Holy Spirit. We are to 'pray at all times in the Spirit'; and if we are conscious of our weakness in the realm of prayer, 'the Spirit helps us in our weakness; for we do not know how to pray as we ought, but the Spirit himself intercedes for us with sighs too deep for words.'[11]

Guidance, too, is the work of the Spirit of God, 'for all who are led by the Spirit of God are sons of God.'[12] Throughout every part of our personal and corporate life, we need to learn to 'walk by the Spirit', be 'led by the Spirit', and 'live by the Spirit', so that the 'fruit of the Spirit' may be increasingly seen in our lives.[13] He alone is the author and giver of life.

Dr. Stuart Blanch, in one of his monthly newsletters to the York Diocese, once remarked, 'There is a sense in which we are back to the apostolic age when apostles could not look for privilege, could not demand a hearing, and stood before an indifferent or hostile community solely in the power of the Spirit given to them.' I know of several other church leaders who have said that unless there is shortly a renewal by the Spirit in the churches under their care, those churches will soon be digging their own spiritual graves. At a recent clergy conference, a depressing number of junior clergy were seriously worried by their fears of future redundancy.

However, the church that re-discovers the life of the Spirit is far from lost. In his fascinating book *A New Pentecost?*, Cardinal Suenens wrote,

The Church has never known a more critical moment in her history. From a human point of view, there is no help on the horizon. We do not see from where salvation can come, unless from HIM; there is no salvation, except in his

[10] 1 Corinthians 12:4-11.   [12] Romans 8:14.
[11] Ephesians 6:18; Romans 8:26.   [13] Galatians 5:16-25.

name. [Yet] at this moment, we see in the sky of the Church
the manifestations of the Holy Spirit's action which seem
to be like those known to the early Church. It is as though
the Acts of the Apostles and the letters of St. Paul were
coming to life again, as if God were once more breaking
into our history.'[14]

Not all Christians see today's situation as clearly as this.
How many Christians are deeply concerned about the
desperate state of any church which has its doors and
windows closed to the fresh wind of the Spirit? How many
even know when the doors and windows *are* closed? How
many realise what 'manifestations of the Holy Spirit's action'
are taking place today in different parts of the world?
How many seriously long for and pray for a powerful
spiritual renewal or revival? How many understand that
only this will save the church from death and the world from
disaster?

A BBC interviewer, who would I think call himself an
agnostic, told me recently that he was appalled by the trivial
irrelevance of the Church of England's General Synod's
debates that he had to cover once for Radio 4. A headmaster
of a famous public school said that he longed for a clear
prophetic voice to be heard again in the church: for someone
with the spiritual strength and stature of Jeremiah or Amos
or John the Baptist, who can cut through the polite niceties of
respectable church affairs, and who can call the church to
repentance and to a pining after the Spirit's life. A vicar of a
country parish, detecting considerable spiritual hunger in the
area (a fact I witnessed for myself during a visit), lamented
that, while the laity were longing to move forward, the local
clergy in that area were dragging their feet. They seemed
either unaware of the critical times confronting the church, or
unwilling to receive the 'kiss of life' that the Spirit alone
could give.

The Spirit of truth
Jesus promised his disciples that 'when the Spirit of truth
comes, he will guide you into all the truth; for he will not

[14]Op. cit., Darton, Longman & Todd, p. 90.

speak on his own authority, but whatever he hears he will speak, and he will declare to you the things that are to come.'[15] Both this statement and the daring comment in 1 John 2:27 that 'you have no need that anyone should teach you; as his anointing teaches you about everything' have, not surprisingly, been the favourite texts of those who have claimed new and intriguing revelations, ignoring the teachers given to the church by God. However, Jesus went on to say about the Spirit that 'he will glorify me, for he will take what is mine and declare it to you.' Hans Küng comments helpfully on this point:

> What the free Spirit of God has to reveal to the Church is therefore not *new* revelations, *new* doctrines, *new* promises, which go beyond things that Jesus himself said or even complement and add to them. It is not said of the Spirit that he will lead the Church into *new* truth, but into *all* truth... Jesus is followed by no new revealer: in him, once for all, the revelation of God is given to the world. This revelation is of course inexhaustible. But the new insights bestowed on the Church by the Spirit do not add to or surpass what Christ himself revealed. They can only be a recollection of what Jesus said: the Spirit will 'bring to remembrance' what Jesus said (14:26); he will not speak 'on his own authority', but only say what he has 'heard'... The Spirit cannot say *more* than Jesus; for in his leave-taking Jesus says: 'all that I have heard from my father I have made known to you' (15:15). The Spirit cannot give a *new revelation*, but through the preaching of his witnesses he will cause everything that Jesus said and did to be revealed *in a new light*.[16]

The Spirit of God is therefore bound to the word of God, as the word is inspired by the Spirit, and God is not a God of confusion. 'All scripture is inspired by God [*theopneustos* — God-breathed].'[17] The Spirit is not confined to the word; he speaks to us in a great variety of ways apart from the Scriptures; but these will not be at variance with the

---

[15] John 16:13; cf. 14:17; 15:26; 1 John 4:6.

[16] Op. cit., p. 201f.

[17] 2 Timothy 3:16.

Scriptures, which are for us the supreme objective authority of God's self-revelation.

From this, at least two important points follow. First, with the close link (but not identification) between the Spirit and the word, the illumination of the Spirit is absolutely necessary before the word can rightly be understood. Spiritual truths must be spiritually discerned.[18] Secondly, since 'the whole counsel of God' is immeasurably rich, it is impossible to hold every truth in perfect balance all the time. The Spirit will therefore be constantly giving fresh insights into certain aspects of God's truth which have been forgotten or neglected, and which are of particular relevance for *today's* situation. It is a great mistake to fight yesterday's battles; rather we need to discern what special emphasis the Spirit is drawing to our attention for today.

It is also a mistake, of course, to take some fresh insight given by the Spirit, and then concentrate on this to the virtual exclusion of everything else. For example, if the Spirit brings back to the church certain gifts which have been largely dormant, such as prophecy, healing and speaking in tongues, it is only playing into the devil's hands to exalt these gifts (or maybe the nine listed in 1 Corinthians 12:8-10) as though they were the only gifts worth bothering about, thereby ignoring gifts of teaching, evangelism, helping or administration. Nevertheless, within the whole range of God's truth, we need to discern which are the particular areas we need to concentrate on at any one time in order 'to grow up in every way...into Christ.'[19]

The Spirit of mission
This was the primary purpose of the gift of the Spirit upon the disciples at Pentecost. He came to equip them for mission. Certainly he gave them fresh life and led them into all the truth, he filled them with joy and praise, and created them into a loving, caring fellowship; but first and foremost he made them into missionaries. Any claimed experience of the Spirit which does not enrich the missionary and evangelistic work of the church is suspect. He comes in power that we

[18] 1 Corinthians 2:7-14;   [19] Ephesians 4:15.
Ephesians 1:16ff.

may powerfully witness to Christ. He dispels our fears that we may boldly proclaim Christ. When Peter stated that God gives the Spirit to those who obey him, the context makes it clear that he was talking about obeying God in the task of preaching Christ.[20] In the New Testament, Matthew and Mark, John and Paul, and Luke in particular, stress the immediate and direct link between the Spirit and mission.[21] Thus the church that is spiritually alive must be profoundly concerned with the work of communicating Christ; it cannot do otherwise when the Spirit is present in power.

One important consequence of all this is that it is the Spirit who rightly initiates evangelism. In the upper room, it was not that Peter and the apostles held a committee meeting and decided that they ought to hold a mission in Jerusalem. They were simply obeying Christ's command to stay in the city until they had been 'clothed with power from on high'.[22] Then, when the promised power of the Spirit came upon them, they were so controlled by the love of Christ that nothing could stop them.

All too often in today's church missions are man-initiated, man-organised, and man-centred. Indeed, when a church writes to an evangelist, asking him to lead an evangelistic mission, it may well be that the first absolute essential is for spiritual renewal to occur within that church. Unless the Spirit is already at work within the congregation, equipping them with the power that is necessary for mission, all evangelistic efforts, however well planned and executed, will be largely in vain.

Moreover, the initiative of the sovereign Spirit may well upset ecclesiastical tidiness, cut across traditional patterns, and perhaps become a threat to some of the leaders of the church. It was not easy for the twelve to accept the Spirit-inspired missionary work of Saul of Tarsus, one-time persecutor of the church. It could have been humbling for the Jerusalem leaders to hear of the Spirit leading Philip to the Ethiopian eunuch, or empowering him for that astonishing mission in Samaria. It was perhaps a sobering fact that the

[20] Acts 5:32.
[21] For fuller treatment, see
I Believe in the Holy Spirit,
by Michael Green,
Chapter 5, Hodder & Stoughton.
[22] Luke 24:49.

apostles were kept in Jerusalem following the martyrdom of Stephen while the Spirit scattered the ordinary believers and enabled them to preach the good news of Christ all the way to Antioch. None of these exciting and fruitful initiatives had been planned from the top. They were all examples of the wind of the Spirit, who blows where he wills.

The Holy Spirit will never be bound or boxed into the tidy categories of our small minds. He is the Spirit of the eternal God, whose primary concern is that God's people should get on with the task of mission; and sadly that concern or that initiative will not always be found amongst the leadership of the church. Instead there can be disapproval, or even opposition, to the missionary zeal of the Spirit. No doubt some of the motives and methods of today's evengelism leave much to be desired; but we need again the outlook of the early church, who were so fired with the Spirit of mission that they could only rejoice whenever Christ was proclaimed.[23]

The Spirit of love

We shall return to this again in the last chapter of this book, but love undoubtedly is the hallmark of the Spirit's presence within any church. Other groups may display great missionary enthusiasm and a ringing conviction about their own doctrinal position; but only the Spirit of the living God will consistently witness to Jesus Christ and pour out upon his disciples, insofar as they are willing to receive this, an ever-fresh effusion of God's love.

It is, in the first instance, a love for God the Father and for God the Son. But if this love for Christ is to mean anything at all, it must spill over into love for other people, especially for our brethren in Christ. Bitterness, anger, slander and gossip all grieve the Holy Spirit.[24] Jealousy, suspicion and a negative attitude towards other Christians all quench the Holy Spirit.[25] It makes no sense to say that we love Christ if we do not love the members of his body. Or, as the apostle John expressed it in his usual striking way, 'If any one says, "I love God," and hates his brother, he is a liar; for he who does

[23]Philippians 1:18.   [25]1 Thessalonians 5:19-22.
[24]Ephesians 4:25-32.

not love his brother whom he has seen, cannot love God whom he has not seen.'[26]

Today there is a widespread spiritual hunger. Disenchanted by the poverty-stricken philosophies of materialism or nihilism, many are seeking for personal significance, for spiritual values, for some kind of spiritual reality that is greater than themselves. Basically, whether this is consciously realised or not, people are hungry for God. However where can they find him or see him? Again the apostle John brings us back to the heart of the matter: 'No one has ever seen God; if we love one another, God abides in us...'[27]

It is this love, when seen in Christian relationships and in a local church, which is the surest sign of the reality and presence of God. It makes for instant communication, regardless of any cultural or radical differences which might exist. An outsider, coming into a service of worship, may not begin to understand the hymns, the prayers, or the sermon. But if the love of God is clearly manifested in that church, its impact will be immediate. The world today is suffocated with words, but starved of love. A truly loving fellowship will therefore act like a magnet. Nothing can be a substitute for love; it is the greatest thing in the world, and it is the foremost concern of the Holy Spirit to pour God's love into the hearts of his people. Without that love we are nothing, and have nothing to offer to a hungry world.

[26] 1 John 4:20. [27] 1 John 4:12.

PART III

THE LIFE OF THE CHURCH

CHAPTER TWELVE

Worship

THE PRIMARY TASK of the church is to worship God. Even before the obvious evangelistic and missionary work, God's people are called to be a worshipping community. Having come to Jesus, that 'living stone', Christians are to be 'like living stones built into a spiritual house.' For what purpose? 'To be a holy priesthood, to offer spiritual sacrifices acceptable to God through Jesus Christ.'[1]

Throughout the New Testament the emphasis is the same. 'We who first hoped in Christ have been destined and appointed to live for the praise of his glory.'[2] 'Do you not know,' asked Paul to the church at Corinth, 'that your body is a temple of the Holy Spirit...?' This temple, as all other temples, is primarily set aside for the worship of God. This is the chief end of man: 'to glorify God and to enjoy him for ever.'

Evangelistic or social activities can never be a substitute for this. If we neglect our foremost calling, we become spiritually arid in ourselves, we have nothing of lasting value to offer the world, and we dishonour God.

What is worship?
Our present-day English word comes from the Anglo-Saxon *weorthscipe*, which means 'to attribute worth to something'. Worship means worth-ship, to give someone the honour or worth that is due to his name.

We find this thought constantly reflected in the psalms. 'For

---

[1] 1 Peter 2:9f.   [2] Ephesians 1:12.

great is the Lord, and greatly to be praised; he is to be feared above all gods... Ascribe to the Lord the glory due to his name...'[3] 'Extol the Lord our God, and worship at his holy mountain; for the Lord our God is holy!'[4] 'Let them praise the name of the Lord, for his name alone is exalted; his glory is above earth and heaven.'[5]

The roots of Christian worship are to be found in the Old Testament. Even after Pentecost, the disciples of Christ followed the pattern and attitude of their Master, in that they worshipped God in the temple and synagogues, as well as in their own homes. For them, there was no sudden break from the style of worship that had been familiar to them for centuries. Gradually they came to see the implications of Christ's coming to fulfil the Old Testament sacrifices, but many basic principles of worship applied to the old and new covenants alike.

There are two main Hebrew words for worship. The first is *hishahawáh*, which literally means 'a bowing down', a prostration before God, as a sign of profound respect and humility. This aimed to lead people to an immediate and deep awareness of the holiness of God and the sinfulness of man. 'O come, let us worship and bow down, let us kneel before the Lord, our Maker! For he is our God, and we are the people of his pasture, and the sheep of his hand.'[6] In 2 Kings 17:36 God made a covenant with his people, saying to them: 'You shall fear the Lord, who brought you out of the land of Egypt with great power and with an outstretched arm; you shall bow yourselves to him, and to him you shall sacrifice.' And when Jehoshaphat was encouraged by the prophetic word concerning the Lord's victory in the forthcoming battle, 'Jehoshaphat bowed his head with his face to the ground, and all Judah and the inhabitants of Jerusalem fell down before the Lord, worshipping the Lord.'[7]

In the New Testament, too, there is a frequent link between 'bowing down' or 'falling down' and 'worshipping the Lord'.[8] Always we need to spend time humbly realising

[3] Psalm 96:4, 8.
[4] Psalm 99:9.
[5] Psalm 148:13.
[6] Psalm 95:6f.
[7] 2 Chronicles 20:18.

[8] For example, Matthew 2:11; 4:9; Acts 10:25; I Corinthians 14:24f; Revelation 4:10; 5:14; 7:11f; 11:16; 19:5, 10; 22:8.

the greatness and holiness of our God before we can begin to
offer him our praise and thanksgiving. We must first be still,
in silent adoration, and know that he is God.

The second Hebrew word for worship is *abodáh*, meaning
'service'. Thus true worship involves not only praising God
with our lips, but also serving him with our lives. The
combination is perfectly expressed in Psalm 116:16f: 'O Lord,
I am thy servant; I am thy servant, the son of thy handmaid.
Thou hast loosed my bonds. I will offer to thee the sacrifice of
thanksgiving and call on the name of the Lord.' Such service
is willingly and gladly offered because of the glorious nature
of our God, and because of the gracious gifts that he bestows
so freely upon his children.

It is therefore God himself who initiates worship. It is
simply our response to all that God has shown us of himself
and done for us in our lives. Indeed, until the Spirit of truth
reveals to us the nature and activity of God, we cannot truly
worship him at all. 'God is Spirit, and those who worship him
must worship in Spirit and truth,' said Jesus.[9]

It was God who inspired Israel to worship, and who gave
them precise instructions concerning the way in which to
worship. He prescribed to them the pattern of sacrifices that
were acceptable to him. Later Christ had to rebuke the
Pharisees on the grounds that much of their worship was
based on the precepts and traditions of men, and not on the
word of God.

True worship, then, must be firmly based on the nature
and revelation of God and on his creative and redemptive
acts. William Temple once wrote this:

> Worship is the submission of all our nature to God. It is the
> quickening of conscience by his holiness; the nourishment
> of mind with his truth; the purifying of imagination by his
> beauty; the opening of the heart to his love; the surrender
> of will to his purpose — and all this gathered up in
> adoration, the most selfless emotion of which our nature is
> capable and therefore the chief remedy for that self-
> centredness which is our original sin and the source of all
> actual sin.[10]

[9] John 4:24.   [10] *Readings in St. John's Gospel*,
                                        Macmillan 1939, p. 68.

Both the 'bowing down' and the 'serving' are essential and complementary aspects of worship. We need to come together with the rest of God's people, both to offer him praise and to build one another up in love. Colin Buchanan once said that worship means 'relating to each other in the presence of God, and relating to God in the company of each other.' From this we see that the matter does not begin and end with what we do in a church building for an hour or two a week. The church is a community, and we worship God by our service within the community seven days a week. The whole of our work, and every aspect of our lifestyle, can and should express our worship of God. It is our total response to the total giving of God in his love to us.

Describing the daily work and music workshops of the Christian community at Post Green, Dorset, a writer commented: 'Worship is the symbolic expression of the community's life. As such, it is necessary for all to work out their grumbles and grievances so that when we come together in worship we come in unity and love. The attitude in which we come, how we use the time and the priority each person gives to it, is of prime importance. It takes fully committed and given individuals knit together to become a worshipping corporate body.'[11]

Why worship?
I have often been asked by young people about this. If God wants us to praise him all the time, is he not proud and self-centred? After all, if we as humans have any streak of humility about us, we do not want to be praised and thanked all the day long.

Whenever we make God in our own image ('*my* idea of God is…') there will be problems. God alone is worthy of all praise and honour; he knows that to worship him in the Spirit is the greatest experience that man can know on earth. It is the very essence of heaven. It is only when we learn to glorify him that we can begin to enjoy him for ever. There is no relationship so intensely satisfying and enriching as our personal and corporate relationship with God; and it is only when we open

[11] *Towards Renewal*, Issue 7, Summer 1976.

our hearts to him in loving adoration that God, in turn, pours
his love into our hearts by the Holy Spirit.

C.S. Lewis once expressed his own doubts concerning the
reasons for God wanting us to worship him. He felt it was as if
God were saying, 'What I most want is to be told that I am
good and great.'

> I had never noticed that all enjoyment spontaneously
> overflows into praise unless (sometimes even if) shyness or
> the fear of boring others is deliberately brought in to check
> it. The world rings with praise — lovers praising their
> mistresses, readers their favourite poet, walkers praising the
> countryside, players praising their favourite game — praise
> of weather, wines, dishes, actors, motors, horses, colleges,
> countries, historical personages, children, flowers, moun-
> tains, rare stamps, rare beetles, even sometimes politicians
> or scholars. I had not noticed how the humblest, and at the
> same time most balanced and capacious, minds, praised
> most... I had not noticed either that just as men spontan-
> eously praise whatever they value, so they spontaneously
> urge us to join them in praising it: 'Isn't she lovely? Wasn't
> it glorious? Don't you think that magnificent?' The
> psalmists in telling everyone to praise God are doing
> what all men do when they speak of what they care
> about.[12]

The psalmist cannot stop extolling God: 'O give thanks to
the Lord, for he is good, for his steadfast love endures for ever'
— a refrain he repeats no less than twenty-six times in that
one psalm alone![13] He wants us not only to understand the
goodness and steadfast love of the Lord, but to appreciate and
experience this for ourselves. Again C.S. Lewis helpfully
comments, 'Therefore praise not merely expresses, but com-
pletes the enjoyment... In commanding us to glorify him,
God is inviting us to enjoy him.'[14]

When the Spirit was poured out on the disciples on the day
of Pentecost, they were so overwhelmed with the love of God
that spontaneously they worshipped him in languages given
to them by the Spirit. They could not but praise him for his

[12] *Reflections on the Psalms*,   [13] Psalm 136.
Fontana 1961, p. 80.   [14] Op. cit., p. 95.

mighty works. When the Spirit enters the heart of an individual, the 'witness' of that is that he cries out with joy 'Abba! Father!'[15] When the Spirit fills the fellowship of a local church, the natural expression of this is in 'psalms and hymns and spiritual songs, singing and making melody to the Lord with all your heart, always and for everything giving thanks in the name of our Lord Jesus Christ to God the Father.'[16] Here, in each case, the worship and enjoyment of God are inextricably mixed.

However, the fact is that we may not always feel like this, and if worship were confined to spontaneous expressions of joy it might be very limited indeed. There is another side of the coin to be considered.

Worship involves sacrifice

Even when worship is a natural overflow of our love for God, it will, and should, cost us something. David once said, 'I will not offer to the Lord that which costs me nothing'.[17] Worship that costs us nothing is worth precisely what it costs! In the New Testament, there are three main sacrifices that should be part of our worship of God.

1. *The sacrifice of our bodies.* After Paul's magnificent exposition of the gospel in the first eleven chapters of his letter to the Romans, during which he spelt out the universal fact of sin, the atoning sacrifice of Christ's death, the sufficiency of faith for salvation, the glorious liberty of the children of God, and the astonishing wisdom of God in his dealings with men, he went on to make this appeal from his heart: 'I appeal to you therefore, brethren, by the mercies of God, to present your bodies as a living sacrifice, holy and acceptable to God, which is your spiritual worship.'[18]

The idea of a living sacrifice would have been especially striking to any Jew, who was familiar with dead sacrifices being offered up to God. It meant the total and unreserved surrender of a life to God. In Paul's mind there was nothing vague about this. It involved being constantly transformed into the likeness of Christ, and totally committed to the body of Christ, offering every God-given spiritual gift for the

15 Romans 8:15f.   17 2 Samuel 24:24.
16 Ephesians 5:18-20.   18 Romans 12:1.

benefit of the whole. It involved love and service, prayer and patience, joy and hospitality, forgiveness and peaceful relationships. No, it would not be easy; but set alongside the amazing mercy of God through the sacrifice of his own Son, no response on our part could be too great.

'True worship is at cost. This is something that still needs to be learned on a day when men take churchgoing lightly, when they will go to church only if it is easy, if the church is near, if the choir is good, if the preacher is approved, if the congregation is socially acceptable, if the weather isn't bad, if friends haven't dropped in for a visit, and if any of a 101 other things haven't stopped them. If worship means a real effort, then men today are often most disinclined to make it.'[19]

We need urgently in the church today men and women of the calibre of C.T. Studd who once said, 'If Jesus Christ be God and died for me, then no sacrifice can be too great for me to make for him.' It is in this vein that Paul indicated that he worshipped God through his 'priestly service of the gospel of God,'[20] and through his being 'poured as a libation upon the sacrificial offering of your faith.'[21] Because he was determined to be faithful unto death, he saw this, too, as the 'point of being sacrificed.'[22] In both life and death he was courageously concerned that Christ should be honoured in his body, no matter what the personal cost might be to himself.[23] All this is included in the worship of God by the sacrifice of our bodies.

2. *The sacrifice of our possessions.* 'Do not neglect to do good and to share what you have,' urged the writer to the Hebrews, 'for such sacrifices are pleasing to God.'[24] Christ and his apostles always took the question of money and possessions seriously, 'for where your treasure is, there will your heart be also.'[25]

William Temple once called Christianity the most materialistic of all religions, since the practical outworking of it touches every area of our daily life. Christians are not to form themselves into a holy ghetto, safe from the strains and stresses of the world. The majority are to work out their high

[19] Leon Morris, *Christian Worship*, Falcon, p. 12f.
[20] Romans 15:16.
[21] Philippians 2:17.
[22] 2 Timothy 4:6.
[23] Philippians 1:20.
[24] Hebrews 13:16.
[25] Matthew 6:21.

calling in Christ in the midst of a busy, competitive and unjust society, applying the principles of love and generosity even when it comes to 'filthy lucre' (as the Authorised Version scornfully translates money on five occasions). However, there is nothing unspiritual about the right handling of money. Jesus spoke more often about this subject than he did about heaven or most other 'spiritual' subjects, because he knew that money is one of the commonest rivals to God. He personalised it, using an Aramaic word for wealth, 'mammon', because it so often becomes a god, an object for worship. 'No one can serve two masters,' he warned; 'for either he will hate the one and love the other, or he will be devoted to the one and despise the other. You cannot serve God and mammon.'[26] Although money itself is neutral, 'the love of money is a root of all evil;' and by craving for it, some have wandered from the faith and pierced their hearts with many sorrows.[27]

When the possession of money is seen as an opportunity for generous giving, it becomes a source of great blessing. 'Give, and it will be given to you; good measure, pressed down, shaken together, running over, will be put into your lap. For the measure you give will be the measure you get back.'[28] Further, in the two main passages on this theme, 2 Corinthians 8 and 9, Paul referred to the wonderful giving of the Macedonian church as 'the grace of God' or 'this gracious work'. He urged the Corinthians to follow the example of the Macedonians, for 'you will be enriched in every way for great generosity, which through us will produce thanksgiving to God; for the rendering of this service [leitourgia, the word from which liturgy is derived, indicating that giving can be a part of our worship] not only supplies the wants of the saints but also overflows in many thanksgivings to God. Under the test of this service, you will glorify God...'[29]

Many churches today are facing a financial crisis, in common with the rest of the world. However, the real question is not how to raise money. It is how to release the money that is already there in the pockets, property and possessions of the members and institutions of the church.

[26] Matthew 6:24.
[27] 1 Timothy 6:10.
[28] Luke 6:38.
[29] 2 Corinthians 9:11-13.

There would be little or no problems if we learnt again to worship God by the sacrifice of our possessions.

It is alleged that the Pope was once showing Thomas Aquinas the fabulous treasures of the Vatican. 'The Church can no longer say "Silver and gold have I none,"' said the Pope. Aquinas, quick on the mark with that partial quote from Acts 3, replied, 'Neither can it say, "In the name of Jesus of Nazareth rise up and walk!"'

How the church can justify the hording of silver and gold when confronted daily with the needs of the Third World, let alone the constant cutting back of missionary societies through lack of funds, is impossible to answer. Critics are right in pointing the finger. There is little doubt what the prophets of the Old Testament would have made of this.

It is equally hard to justify the constant buying of new cars, fitted carpets, colour television sets, new furniture, or luxury foods in order to keep up with the affluence of the west, when knowingly millions of our brethren in Christ have barely enough to eat.[30] God's question through Haggai still has great relevance: 'Is it time for you to dwell in your panelled houses, while this house [the house of God, which today is the church] lies in ruins?... You have looked for much, and, lo, it came to little; and when you brought it home, I blew it away. Why? says the Lord of hosts. Because of my house that lies in ruins, while you busy yourself each with his own house.'

Let us then look at Paul's two great chapters on giving, as he draws lessons from the Macedonian church.

First, it was *in response to God's love*. Paul never specifically refers to the word 'money' or any of its equivalents. He writes: 'we want you to know, brethren, about the grace of God which has been shown in the churches of Macedonia.' The Christians there had so responded to the grace or love of God in their hearts that they 'overflowed in a wealth of liberality'. Great generosity of this kind is one of the surest signs of the grace of God in the hearts of his people.

A diocesan bishop once told me about two churches in his diocese that had experienced spiritual renewal recently. One of the most convincing evidences of this renewal, he said, was

[30] For a searching biblical study on this theme see *Rich Christians in an Age of Hunger* by Ronald J. Sider, Hodder & Stoughton, 1978.

their astonishing giving: it was far beyond all the other churches in his diocese. One church, rooted in an ordinary housing estate, had increased its giving from £3,000 to £30,000 within three or four years.

The measure of God's love is that he gave his only Son, and the proof of the love of God in our hearts today will always be seen in terms of giving. Therefore if the church is looking for more money, it must first give attention to a much greater need — spiritual renewal. It is when Christians and churches experience afresh the love of God, and begin to worship him with their whole being, that anything can happen, not least in the context of money.

Around Christmas, one student gave me a huge sum of money (for her at any rate) for the work of the church. She enclosed this note: 'I'm afraid I can't give him gold, frankincense, myrrh, or even a lamb, as an expression of my worship this Christmas, but please accept the enclosed as an expression of my truly thankful heart.' There, in her cheque, was abundant evidence of the grace of God in her heart. Indeed, if our giving is not marked by great generosity, we might well question how much of the love of God we really know in our hearts, if any at all. Lack of Christian giving is one of the first signs of spiritual decay in a person's life.

Secondly, the giving of the Macedonians was *in spite of hard times*. 'For in a severe test of affliction, their abundance of joy and their extreme poverty have overflowed in a wealth of liberality on their part.' When faced with economic crises and spiralling inflation, the obvious temptation is to cut back on our giving. But the opposite should be true. We should cut back on our spending and increase our giving to cover the obviously greater financial needs of the church throughout the world.

The trouble is that we are so swayed by worldly standards. Social and cultural values very largely determine the extent of our spending, and therefore of our giving. The standard of living of the New Testament is clear: it is *enough*. 'God is able to provide you with every blessing in abundance, so that you may always have *enough* of everything and may provide in abundance for every good work.'[31] If, by any chance, there is an abundance one year, it should make little or no difference to

---

[31] 2 Corinthians 9:8

our living standards. But it should make a considerable difference to our giving. 'As a matter of equality your abundance at the present time should supply their want, so that their abundance may supply your want, that there may be equality.' In this way there will develop a mutual interdependence within the church, which will help to unite us in love. Therefore we need to learn to be content with enough — Paul calls that 'food and clothing' — and everything over 'enough' is to give away. Each person must determine humbly before God what 'enough' means in his situation; but there is no doubt that most Christians, in the west at any rate, have far more than enough and give far less than they could.

When John Wesley was at Oxford, he had an income of £30 a year. He lived on £28, and gave £2 away, which was 15 per cent. Some years later his income had increased four times to £120 per annum. He still lived on £28, and gave £92 away, which was almost 77 per cent. Tragically today there are not many Christians who tithe, giving even 10 per cent of their income, let alone 15 per cent, not to mention 77 per cent! We have forgotten the New Testament standard of *enough*. We have neglected to *worship* God sacrificially by our money and possessions.

Thirdly, the Macedonians gave *in proportion to their means*. 'For they gave according to their means, as I can testify, and beyond their means, of their own free will.' Again, each Christian must decide how much should be set aside for God's work. A woman once asked her husband, 'Can you give me a little money?' He replied, 'Yes, how little?' That is so often the attitude of church members today. 'How little can I give with a clear conscience?'

The Jews gave by law one tenth, which was their tithe. They considered that they only started to give to God when they gave more than a tenth. If that was their response 'under law', and God now gives us freedom 'under grace', it should certainly be a freedom marked by generosity! Think of it like this: if our wages or salary were ten times the amount we give to God each week, would we be well off? Good stewardship means thinking through these facts and figures very carefully, and then going 'beyond our means', gladly and cheerfully, on top of any painless figure that we have worked out. In many churches there is also great value in covenanting, although Christians are sometimes nervous of this, perhaps through ignorance or misunderstanding. Simple teaching on this whole matter will prove helpful.

Fourthly, the Macedonians gave *in sympathy with obvious need.* They begged earnestly 'for the favour of taking part in the relief of the saints'. Although they themselves were afflicted and poverty-stricken, they pleaded for the privilege of sharing what little they had with their Christian brethren in Jerusalem who were suffering on account of the famine there.

The annual report of the World Bank stated in 1976 that approximately 650 million people have incomes of under £24 a year. The developed countries offer 0.33 per cent of their gross national product to help the poor, and this percentage is likely to decrease. Today the needs of the Third World are known by all. We easily forget, sometimes conveniently so; but if we are spiritually alive, we must care about those in need. 'If any one has the world's goods and sees his brother in need, yet closes his heart against him, how does God's love abide in him?'[32]

Fifthly, their giving was *an evidence of their commitment.* 'First they gave themselves to the Lord and to us by the will of God.' No matter how much we worship God by our giving, it will always be an inadequate response to his infinite love towards us. 'For you know the grace of our Lord Jesus Christ, that though he was rich, yet for your sake he became poor, so that by his poverty you might become rich.' Our giving to God must always be seen in the light of the incarnation and humiliation of Jesus Christ, as he gave himself willingly for our sake, even to the extent of the bitter pain and shame of the cross.

God looks, therefore, not first and foremost for our money, but for the worship of our hearts and lives, the reality of which will partially be expressed by the generosity of our giving. Gifts of money without this commitment to Christ and to the body of Christ will always be an unacceptable substitute. The Pharisee gave 'tithes of all that he possessed'; yet it was the sinful tax-collector who was justified because he threw himself on the mercy of God. Once again, it is not our activity nor our giving that God looks for in the first instance. It is the worship of the whole of our being.

[32] 1 John 3:17.

This worship is expressed not only in the sacrifice of our bodies and our possessions. It is also seen in —

3. *The sacrifice of our praise.* 'Through him [Jesus] let us continually offer up a sacrifice of praise to God, that is, the fruit of lips that acknowledge his name.'[33] Again we need to look at this carefully, as the music and singing in our churches are not always expressive of true worship. The Jews had three main words for praise: *hálal*, which is to do with 'making a noise'; *zámar*, which describes the singing or playing of music; and *yàdâ*, which refers to bodily actions and gestures which often accompany praise. Let us look at these in turn.

First, we have '*making a noise*'. 'Make a joyful noise to God, all the earth; sing the glory of his name; give to him glorious praise!'[34] Singing has always been a basic ingredient of praise. Jesus sang a hymn with his disciples at the Last Supper.[35] Paul and Silas sang hymns at midnight in the jail at Philippi.[36] Paul often wrote about the importance of singing within the fellowship of a church. 'When you come together, each one has a hymn, a lesson…'[37] He told the Ephesian Christians to go on being filled with the Spirit, 'addressing one another in psalms and hymns and spiritual songs, singing and making melody to the Lord with all your heart.'[38] In similar vein, he urged the Colossians to 'sing psalms and hymns and spiritual songs with thankfulness in your hearts to God.'[39] This would help them considerably in maintaining their unity and love in Christ. James, too, encouraged those who were cheerful to 'sing praise'.[40] Individual or corporate singing can strengthen faith. By lifting our voices we can lift our hearts to God.

Usually there should be good theological content in our songs of praise, so that it is more than a mere sound to stimulate our emotions. The hymns written at the time of the Reformation, or during the revival through Wesley and Whitefield, became a major factor in the work of the Spirit in both personal and national life. Most scholars accept that several passages in the New Testament are examples of early Christian hymnology. To give a few examples, translated in forms which illustrate the point:

[33] Hebrews 13:16.
[34] Psalm 66:1f.
[35] Matthew 26:30.
[36] Acts 16:25.
[37] I Corinthians 14:26.
[38] Ephesians 5:19.
[39] Colossians 3:16.
[40] James 5:13.

Ephesians 5:14

> Awake, O sleeper,
> From thy grave arise.
> The Light of Christ upon thee shines.

I Timothy 3:16

> He was manifested in the flesh,
> Vindicated in the Spirit
> Seen by angels,
> Preached among the nations,
> Believed on in the world,
> Taken up in glory.

Philippians 2:6-11

> He, although he was in the divine form,
> Did not think equality with God a thing to be grasped;
> But surrendered his rank
> And took the role of a servant;
> Becoming like the rest of mankind,
> And appearing in a human role;
> He humbled himself,
> In an obedience that went so far as to die.
> For this God raised him to the highest honour,
> And conferred upon him the highest rank of all,
> That, at Jesus' name every knee should bow,
> And every tongue should own that 'Jesus Christ is Lord.'

Other passages have also been suggested as possible examples of early hymns.[41]

One Christian leader said recently: 'I don't mind who writes the theological books, so long as I can write the hymns.' Significantly, the present renewal of the Spirit is marked by a fresh upsurge of hymns and spiritual songs. Some of these songs may be in the form of simple and repetitive worship choruses whose theological content is dwarfed by the great hymns of Luther or Wesley. Yet in a day when the speed of life is increasing all the time, there is something to be said

---

[41] Colossians 1:15-20; Hebrews 1:3; John 1:1-14; 1 Peter 1:18-21; 2:21-25; 3:18-22; Revelation 5:9f, 12; 12:10-12; 19:1ff. See *Worship in the Early Church* by Ralph Martin, Marshall Morgan & Scott, pp. 39-52.

for what amounts to a sung meditation, for example repeating slowly and thoughtfully a simple but profound statement that 'Jesus is Lord'. The psalmist knew the value of this; and some of the greatest works of praise, such as in Handel's *Messiah*, repeat the same few words and phrases time and time again. It is not always necessary to write a solid 'body of divinity' into every spiritual song.

It may be here that we need to learn from the culture of other Christians. An English observer of a revival meeting in East Africa commented: 'Their joy was so obviously spontaneous and unaffected, and, although I sometimes felt myself irritated by their constant repetitions of a single chorus or verse of a hymn, I could not honestly doubt their reality and earnestness, or the depth of their experience of Jesus Christ.' In most traditional western churches, you will not be irritated by constant repetitions; but sadly you may not find this infectious joy or depth of spiritual experience. Also, when the theological understanding of most congregations is frighteningly small, I wonder what helpful thoughts pass through the minds of most people when they sing

> Consubstantial, co-eternal,
> While unending ages run?

And is it true that the love of sinners 'can ne'er forget the wormwood and the gall'? Examples like this abound in most hymn books; and although many good and meaningful hymns do exist, it would be wrong to despise the simpler expressions of worship.

Secondly, praise may include '*playing an instrument*'. Psalm 150 alone speaks of trumpet, lute, harp, timbrel, strings and pipe, and loud clashing cymbals. Elsewhere we read of the psaltery, sackbut, dulcimer, flute, organ, horn, cornet, bells and tabret. In other words, virtually any instrument can be used in the praise of God.

Although most churches leave it to one man and one instrument, the organist on his organ; there are probably people sitting in almost every congregation that could play some instrument or other, and the creation of a small orchestra might considerably enrich the worship of that church. In our church in York we have a Family Service orchestra each Sunday morning, consisting mostly of children, and sometimes an adult orchestra in the evening. We also have a musical and singing group that leads some of the current songs of renewal that are better accompanied by guitar than by organ. Also, for many hymns and songs there is no reason why the organ, orchestra and singing group should not play together, as often in our services they do. In this way more people are drawn into an active part in the service and are given an opportunity for worshipping God with the particular gifts that he has given them. Some of the instruments that are currently being used in our church include: organ, piano, violin, viola, double bass, flute, oboe, clarinet, trumpet, trombone, euphonium, recorder, guitar, tambourine, maracas, coconut shells, bells, claves, bongos, and glokenspiel!

Thirdly, praise may well be expressed in *moving the body*. The value of dance and movement is being re-discovered by many churches today, after a nervous start some years ago. Father Lucien Deiss of Cincinnati, Ohio, wrote a book called *Dancing for God*, which the World Council of Churches described as a 'do-it-yourself manual of liturgical dances'. The report from the W.C.C. went on to say, 'The manual provides the necessary rudiments to master such choreographic movements as the "clergy stomp", the "step curtsey", the "paddle turn", and the "kneel and incense step".' The reporter seemed a little sceptical of the value of dance!

Dance, nevertheless, was a natural expression of worship for God's people for centuries in the days of the Old Testament. Miriam led the women in praising God with timbrel and dance after the triumphant crossing of the Red Sea;[42] David 'danced before the Lord with all his might' as the ark of God was brought into Jerusalem, even though his wife despised him for doing so.[43] The psalmist exhorted God's people to 'praise his name with dancing'[44] and to 'praise him with timbrel and dance'.[45] Jeremiah described the restoration of Jerusalem as a time of joyful praise: 'Then shall the maidens

[42]Exodus 15:20f.　　　　[44]Psalm 149:3.
[43]2 Samuel 6:14-23.　　　[45]Psalm 150:3.

rejoice in the dance, and the young men and the old shall be merry.'[46] These and other references indicate that there was nothing special or unusual about dance as a form of praise. It was the natural language of the body as every part of man's being was brought into the worship of his Creator and Redeemer. After all, spiritual worship includes using our bodies to the glory of God.

Some have argued that in the New Testament there is no specific reference to dance. However, there was dancing as part of the celebration when the prodigal son came home,[47] and it seemed such a common part of life that it entered into children's games.[48] It would be strange if this perfectly natural and wholesome expression of joy and praise should cease when Jesus came to bring his people fullness of joy. Added to that, the New Testament describes a pioneer missionary situation, with the church meeting primarily in the homes of believers. Perhaps there were other priorities to concentrate on to begin with; perhaps the homes were too small for this form of worship; perhaps dance or movement happened spontaneously, but it was never written about as it was never a problem in the early church. Most of the specific instructions of Paul were written to correct abuses that had developed. Indeed, some commentators suggest that when Paul spoke about singing psalms,[49] he included the manner and style in which the psalms were sung, namely accompanied by musical instruments and, often, dance.

Be that as it may, there is little doubt that dance today is a perfectly valid form of praise and worship, especially in a generation that is increasingly word-resistant and that responds quickly to the language of movement. The Spirit of God is a Spirit of movement, and the formal and static nature of much of the worship of the church today does not help to communicate the reality of the living God and the vitality of those who have come alive in him.

Having experienced the place of dance within regular Christian worship for several years now, I am personally

---

[46] Jeremiah 31:13.
[47] Luke 15:25.

[48] Matthew 11:17; Luke 7:32.
[49] Ephesians 5:19; Colossians 3:16.

convinced that this biblical expression of praise is both meaningful and important for our present generation.[50] Not every Christian will find it easy to adjust to the idea of movement in a church service. Some have been profoundly embarrassed by the 'Peace' in an Anglican communion service when they have been asked to shake hands with the person standing next to them. Anne Long writes: 'There are those who are very scared of anything moving in a service — either emotionally (such as the sermon), or physically (such as the kiss of peace or a dance). Some want a service that is safe and completely predictable where they can keep their liturgical masks in position and not relate to others. Certainly meeting each other in the presence of God can be very embarrassing if people are unsure about either God or each other.'

What is clear from the Scriptures is that worship should be a delight, not a duty. The great Jewish feasts were times of exuberant joy and heartfelt celebration. Some of them contained an element of sorrow and repentance for sin; but this led to the joy of knowing God's forgiveness and mercy. They were always intended to be great and glorious festivals.

It is true that the prophets sometimes spoke disparagingly of religious feasts, but that was only when they had lost their spiritual content and had degenerated into an empty and worldly ritual. For the man whose heart was set on God, there was no greater joy than coming to worship him, especially in the presence of his people, as the psalmist made so clear: 'I was glad when they said to me, "Let us go to the house of the Lord!"'[52] 'How lovely is thy dwelling place, O Lord of hosts! My soul longs, yea, faints for the courts of the Lord; my heart and flesh sing for joy to the living God.'[53] Further, when he was depressed, the psalmist remembered with longing how he once 'led them in procession to the house of God, with glad shouts and songs of thanksgiving, a multitude keeping

[50]I have written more fully about dance in *I Believe in Evangelism*, Hodder & Stoughton, pp. 160-162. See also *Praise Him in the Dance*, by Anne Long, Hodder & Stoughton, 1976.
[51]Op. cit., p. 25.
[52]Psalm 122:1.
[53]Psalm 84:1.

festival.'[54] How many of us have experienced 'glad shouts of thanksgiving' in our worship today?

The early church, too, was well-known for its love feasts, *agapai*, which were essentially times of unaffected joy in fellowship with God and with one another. Of all the accusations against Christians, one of the most tragic came from Nietzsche when he said that Christians had no joy. Infectious joyful delight in God's presence needs urgently to be recaptured by the church of today. If emerging from our inhibitions and stiff formality is not easy for some of us, we need to remember that true worship demands sacrifice.

Conclusion

The church is essentially a worshipping community of those who believe in Jesus Christ. They are called together for this purpose, and to neglect this primary task is to dishonour God and maybe to forfeit his grace and power in all the work that is done in his name. It is as we honour him that he will honour us. Three features need to be remembered.

First, true worship must always be *directed towards the living God*. It is not a performance in order to display the talents of priests, preachers, musicians, singers, dancers, or anyone else. Unlike any other religion in the world, the Christian church from its birth at Pentecost was marked by the presence of its living Lord, and everything that is worthy of the name of worship must be directed wholly towards him. The aim of worship is to glorify God, and him alone, and to lead worshippers to an increased awareness of his presence with his people. The hymns, prayers, preaching and sacraments should all combine to magnify the Lord. 'O magnify the Lord with me, and let us exalt his name together.'[55] That is worship.

Second, true worship should always *edify the body of Christ*. It is never meant to be dominated by one specialist who is doing all the work on behalf of everyone else. Worship should be the corporate expression of the praise of God's people. It should be a people's service.

In almost the only verse giving instructions to Christians about what they are to do when they come together, Paul makes this point clear: 'When you come together, each one

[54] Psalm 42:4.   [55] Psalm 34:3.

has a hymn, a lesson, a revelation, a tongue, or an interpretation' — in other words, everyone, as far as possible, taking an active part. Then Paul goes on to stress this: 'Let all things be done for edification.'[56] In that one chapter he explicitly emphasises that point about edifying the body of Christ no less than seven times, and implicitly talks about it throughout the whole passage. Here is the test for the content of any act of worship.

Ralph Martin notes three main components: *charismatic*, involving 'enthusiastic praise and prayer under the direct afflatus of the Spirit', together with other spiritual gifts; *didactic*, covering 'all ministry in intelligible speech which aims at clarifying the will of God'; and *eucharistic*, which includes thanksgiving, praise and prayer, sometimes in the distinctive setting of the Lord's Supper. Whatever details may be included, the unity of all believers present, and the upbuilding of the whole church, is of considerable importance, 'that together you may with one voice glorify the God and Father of our Lord Jesus Christ.'[57]

Third, true worship always *depends on the presence of the Holy Spirit*. We must 'worship by the Spirit of God', as Paul wrote to the Philippians.[58] Without his active presence we cannot communicate with God at all, or offer anything that is worthy of his name. It is through the Spirit that we have access to the Father. He is the one who inspires our prayer and praise, who opens our minds and hearts and voices, who helps us to understand the word of God, who convicts of sin, and who bestows gifts for the common good. He is the very breath and life of any true worshipping community.

The church that is seeking for renewal in its worship must first seek for renewal in its experience of the Holy Spirit. Liturgical revision may be a helpful aid to worship, but it can never be a substitute for a fresh effusion of the Spirit's power.

[56] 1 Corinthians 14:26.　　　[58] 3:3 (margin).
[57] Romans 15:6.

CHAPTER THIRTEEN

Preaching

'BEWARE OF ANY course on *How to Preach: By One who Knows.*
The creature is an impostor! No man knows how to preach.
You will have to reckon with this significant, disconcerting
fact, that the greatest preachers who have ever lived have
confessed themselves poor bunglers to the end, groping after
an ideal which has eluded them for ever... It is one thing to
learn the technique and mechanics of preaching: it is quite
another to preach a sermon which will draw back the veil and
make the barriers fall that hide the face of God.'[1]

A preaching church

The church of the New Testament was unquestionably a
preaching church. Although the birth of the church in Acts 2
began with praise, it continued with preaching. It was not
sufficient for the Holy Spirit to fall on the disciples, prompting
them to worship God in languages given by the Spirit; Peter
stood up to preach. And it was only when the crowd heard the
proclamation of Jesus Christ crucified and risen that they were
'cut to the heart' and cried out 'What shall we do?' It was not
enough for the cripple to be healed miraculously at the Gate
Beautiful, causing him to go into the temple 'walking and
leaping and praising God'; Peter again stood up and preached.
The response, following the preaching of Christ in the context
of the Spirit's power, was something like 5,000 converted.

Wherever the apostles found an opportunity to preach the

[1] James S. Stewart, *Preaching*, The Teach Yourself Series, Hodder &
Stoughton Ltd, London, 1955, pp. 89, 91.

gospel, they were not slow in taking it. When faced with the leaders who were responsible for the crucifixion of Jesus, Peter, filled with the Holy Spirit, proclaimed fearlessly the uniqueness and authority of Christ, 'for there is no other name under heaven given among men by which we must be saved.'[2] Nothing could stop them. Even when they were all scattered through persecution, 'those who were scattered went about preaching the word.'[3]

Luke, in fact, lays such stress on the preaching ministry of the New Testament Church that he uses no less than thirteen different Greek words to describe the variety and richness of their verbal proclamation: they preached, heralded, testified, proclaimed, taught, exhorted, argued, disputed, confounded, proved, reasoned, persuaded and pleaded. Elsewhere in the New Testament the apostles announced, explained, confessed, charged, admonished, rebuked — about thirty different terms are used in all.

Luke also emphasises the thoroughness with which they taught the word of God. At Corinth, Paul stayed for eighteen months for this one supreme purpose. At Ephesus, he argued in the hall of Tyrannus every day for two years; and some manuscripts add that it was from the fifth to the tenth hour, which amounts to some 25,000 hours of gospel peaching! This meant that Paul hired this public lecture-room from 11 a.m. to 4 p.m., which was probably the only period he was able to book it, since it coincided with siesta time at Ephesus — the worst possible time for taking part in a five-hour seminar. While the rest of the Ephesians slept, he continued this tremendously demanding ministry because he knew the power of God's word to bring people to a vital experience of Christ and to change their lives. Luke tells us the result of those two years: 'All the residents of Asia [Minor] heard the word of the Lord... [so that] the word of the Lord grew and prevailed mightily.'[4]

Significantly the churches that are growing today are, in the vast majority of cases, the churches where preaching and teaching are taken seriously. Thomas Goodwin used to say: 'God had only one Son, and he made him a preacher.'

The church of today needs largely to recover its confidence

[2] Acts 4:8-12.   [4] Acts 19:8-20.
[3] Acts 8:4.

in the proclaimed word of God. The gospel is still 'the power of God for salvation.'[5] Christ is still 'the power of God and the wisdom of God'; and the preaching of Christ and him crucified is still the way in which there can be a 'demonstration of the Spirit and of power.'[6]

Yet recently many have lost confidence or interest in the regular preaching ministry of the church. In a vivid passage, James Stewart paints the 'disillusioned preacher':

> No longer does the zeal of God's house devour him. No longer does he mount the pulpit steps in thrilled expectancy that Jesus Christ will come amongst his folk that day, travelling in the greatness of his strength, mighty to save. Dully and drearily he speaks now about what once seemed to him the most dramatic tidings in the world. The edge and verve and passion of the message of divine forgiveness, the exultant, lyrical assurance of the presence of the risen Lord, the amazement of supernatural grace, the urge to cry 'Woe is me if I preach not the Gospel!' — all have gone. The man has lost heart. He is disillusioned. And that, for an ambassador of Christ, is tragedy.[7]

What is preaching? Bernard Manning once defined it as 'a manifestation of the incarnate Word, from the written word, by the spoken word'. It is God communicating himself to man through human agencies in the power of his Spirit. It may be helpful examining some of the words used in the New Testament for the task of the preacher.[8]

1. HERALD

A divine message
It has been common to draw a distinction between preaching and teaching — between *kerygma* (public proclamation) and *didache* (ethical instruction). C.H. Dodd, who has most

---

[5] Romans 1:16.
[6] 1 Corinthians 1:22-2:5.
[7] Op. cit., p. 19.

[8] I am indebted to the study by John R.W. Stott in *The Preacher's Portrait*, Tyndale Press 1961, for some of the ideas in this section.

thoroughly developed this distinction,[9] has defined the *kerygma* as 'the public proclamation of Christianity to the non-Christian world'; and Alan Richardson described it as 'the telling of news to people who had not heard it before.' The differentiation between these two words has almost certainly been over-pressed, however, as both in the Gospels and in Acts the words are sometimes used interchangeably.

Nevertheless, the verb *kerysso*, meaning 'to proclaim as a herald', comes more than sixty times in the New Testament, and gives us a vital insight into the character of preaching which needs to be recovered by the church today. This form of preaching is not a detached and theoretical discourse, addressed dispassionately to a closed group of convinced believers, as is so often the image of preaching. Instead, it is 'a proclamation made by a herald, by the town crier, in the full light of day, to the sound of a trumpet, up-to-the-minute, addressed to everyone, because it comes from the King himself.'[10] The herald, therefore, carries with him the authority of the King in his message. He is not proclaiming his own ideas or opinions, but the mighty acts of God. He has God's word laid upon him, and is called to be absolutely faithful to the message that is not his, but God's. He is consequently expecting some response. He is summoning men to repent, or beseeching them to be reconciled to God. In this way, God is making his own appeal through the preacher: 'So we are ambassadors for Christ, God making his appeal through us. We beseech you on behalf of Christ, be reconciled to God.'[11]

J. I. Packer has described the authority of the herald in this way: 'Paul, in his own estimation, was not a philosopher, not a moralist, not one of the world's wise men, but simply Christ's herald. His royal Master had given him a message to proclaim; his whole business, therefore, was to deliver that message with exact and studious faithfulness, adding nothing, altering nothing, omitting nothing.'[12] Whether people want to hear the message, or enjoy listening to it, is not the point. It is a message from the King.

There have been several attempts to summarise the *kerygma*

[9] See *The Apostolic Preaching and its Developments*
[10] C. Senft, article 'Preaching' in *Vocabulary of the Bible*, edited by

J.-J von Allmen, Lutterworth 1958.
[11] 2 Corinthians 5:20.
[12] *Evangelism and the Sovereignty of God*, I.V.P., p. 43.

of the early church, and C.H. Dodd has suggested these themes as the most common in apostolic preaching:

(i)   The age of fulfilment has dawned: the Old Testament prophecies have been realised; the hope of Israel is now a present fact.

(ii)   This fulfilment is shown by the life, death and resurrection of Jesus the Messiah.

(iii)   In virtue of his resurrection he is exalted as Lord.

(iv)   The Holy Spirit's presence in the church is a token of God's favour towards his people.

(v)   Christ will come again as Judge and Saviour.

(vi)   There is an appeal for repentance, an offer of forgiveness and the gift of the Holy Spirit, and an assurance of salvation.

Dr. R.H. Mounce has criticised this summary by saying that the apostolic *kerygma* was not 'a sort of stereotyped six-headed sermon', but 'a proclamation of the death, resurrection and exaltation of Jesus, that led to an evaluation of his person as both Lord and Christ, confronted men with the necessity of repentance, and promised the forgiveness of sins.'[13] No summary can serve as more than a rough guide, and clearly there was a warmth and passion and spontaneity in the preaching in Acts which cannot be strait-jacketed in a neat formula.

Paul indicates that the essential elements of his message were the death and resurrection of Jesus Christ. 'For I delivered to you as of first importance what I also received, that Christ died for our sins in accordance with the scriptures, that he was buried, that he was raised on the third day in accordance with the scriptures.'[14] This was the heart of the gospel 'by which you are saved.' Elsewhere he wrote, 'we preach Christ crucified... We preach Jesus Christ as Lord.'[15]

What is clear is that all true apostolic preaching contained the essential *kerygma*, the proclamation of Jesus, crucified and risen, as Saviour and Lord, followed by an appeal to respond to Christ in repentance and faith. 'It is preaching for a

[13] *The Essential Nature of New Testament Preaching*, p. 84.
[14] 1 Corinthians 15:3-5.

[15] 1 Corinthians 1:23;
2 Corinthians 4:5.

verdict. Heralding is not the same as lecturing. A lecture is dispassionate, objective, academic. It is addressed to the mind. It seeks no result but to impart certain information and, perhaps, to provoke the student to further enquiry. But the herald of God comes with an urgent proclamation of peace through the blood of the cross, and with a summons to men to repent, to lay down their arms and humbly to accept the offered pardon.'[16]

It is quite wrong to make an appeal without declaring first some content of the gospel. There must be a basic integrity about the preacher as he tries to inform the mind before moving the will. His first responsibility is to declare what God has done in Christ; only then can the invitation be fairly made.

At the same time, it is equally wrong to proclaim the gospel without issuing some appropriate appeal. God's truth is to be obeyed. If we are hearers of the word, and not doers, we are only deceiving ourselves. The herald should therefore expect something to happen as a result of his preaching. He should not be afraid of emotion, since often the heart must be stirred before the will can be moved. He must eschew all forms of emotional-*ism*; but if he has clearly proclaimed the truths of God's grace in Jesus Christ, it is hard to see how emotion can fail to be present if any of the hearers show signs of spiritual life.

We see this appeal to practical action, based on God's saving acts in Christ, in most of the epistles in the New Testament. 'With eyes wide open to the mercies of God, I beg you, my brothers, as an act of intelligent worship, to give him your bodies...'[17] Paul had just been outlining in considerable detail, covering eleven chapters, the astonishing mercy of God to those who are guilty before him and who deserve only his judgment; and it is only with their eyes wide open to this that the Christians at Rome are exhorted to present their bodies to God. In the remaining part of this letter, Paul explains what this means in thoroughly practical terms.

A.W. Tozer once voiced the feelings of many Christians who have sat through appeals for money, evangelism, service or prayer, without being given any adequate motivation: 'I am tired of being whipped into line, of being urged to work

[16] John R.W. Stott, ibid., p. 37.   [17] Romans 12:1, J.B. Phillips.

harder, to pray more, to give more generously, when the speaker does not show me Christ.'

The preacher's primary task must be to exalt Christ, to give a fresh vision of Christ, for it is only the love of Christ that will effectively motivate God's people into an ever-increasing, sacrificial service for the Master. A young man felt strongly that God was calling him into the ordained ministry of the Church of England. He said that the call came during a sermon he had heard. He was asked the name of the preacher. 'I don't remember,' he replied. 'All I know is that the preacher showed me Jesus.'

A divine compulsion

The herald should also have a sense of divine compulsion with regard to his preaching. The disciples once pursued Jesus and told him, 'Every one is searching for you.' But Jesus had no intention of changing his plans because of this. He replied, 'Let us go on to the next towns, that I may preach there also.'[18] When Peter and John were charged not to speak or teach at all in the name of Jesus, they boldly replied, 'We cannot but speak of what we have seen and heard.'[19] Paul, too, knew that the love of Christ left him no choice: 'For necessity is laid upon me. Woe to me if I do not preach the gospel!'[20] And he reminded the Corinthian church how he had come into their city 'in much fear and trembling'.

William Barclay has commented on this phrase:

It was what has been called 'the trembling anxiety to perform a duty.'... The preacher who is really effective is the preacher whose heart beats faster while he waits to speak. The man who has no fear, no hesitancy, no nervousness, no tension, in any task, may give an efficient and competent performance; but it is the man who has this trembling anxiety...who can produce an effect which artistry alone can never achieve.[21]

Campbell Morgan said that he frequently felt like a man being led to the slaughter when he went into the pulpit to preach.

[18] Mark 1:37f.
[19] Acts 4:18-20.
[20] 1 Corinthians 9:16.
[21] *The Letters to the Corinthians,* St. Andrew Press, p. 27.

Yet the herald accepts the strain of this because of his royal commission. He must pray over his message until it becomes a 'fire in his bones', a passionate conviction within him that what he is declaring is not only the truth, but the truth given to him by God to deliver on that particular occasion to that particular group of people. There must be an urgency about the message, and a ringing persuasiveness which can come only from one who knows that he has a message from God. He is to speak in the presence of God and in the name of Christ. He is to be the mouthpiece of God. 'I charge you in the presence of God and of Christ Jesus who is to judge the living and the dead, and by his appearing and his kingdom: preach the word, be urgent in season and out of season, convince, rebuke, and exhort, be unfailing in patience and in teaching.'[22] Nothing could be more compelling than that.

2. STEWARD

'As each has received a gift,' wrote Peter, 'employ it for one another, as good stewards of God's varied grace: whoever speaks, as one who utters oracles of God.'[23] 'This is how one should regard us,' wrote Paul, 'as servants of Christ and stewards of the mysteries of God. Moreover, it is required of stewards that they be found trustworthy.'[24] A steward is a trustee and dispenser of someone else's goods.

Trustee
The preacher, therefore, has been entrusted with the sacred deposit of God's truth, as revealed in the scriptures; and, as Paul counselled young Timothy, he must 'follow the pattern of the sound words... [and] guard the truth that has been entrusted to you by the Holy Spirit who dwells within us.'[25] He is a *trustee* of God's mysteries; and *mysterion* in the New Testament is not some strange and inexplicable phenomenon, but a truth that has been unveiled and made known. The 'mysteries of God' are therefore his open secrets, his self-revelation recorded for us, by the inspiration of the Spirit, in

[22] 2 Timothy 4:1f.   [24] 1 Corinthians 4:1f.
[23] 1 Peter 4:10f.   [25] 1 Timothy 1:13f.

the Scriptures. As Jesus once said to his disciples, 'To you it has been given to know the secrets of the kingdom of heaven.'[26]

Consequently, the preacher must take care not to distort God's word by his own opinions, or by the traditional views of others. It is possible to 'make void the word of God' by holding to the tradition of men.[27] It is possible to be ensnared by 'philosophy and empty deceit', and those who twist the Scriptures do so to their own destruction.'[28] It is a solemn thing to be entrusted with God's message, which, by its very power, can bring both life and death, salvation and judgment, to those who hear. Paul was acutely aware of this awe-inspiring responsibility for the preacher: 'Who is sufficient for these things? For we are not, like so many, peddlers of God's word; but as men of sincerity, as commissioned by God, in the sight of God we speak in Christ.'[29]

Dispenser

The steward is also a *dispenser*, who must know how to handle and dispense his Master's goods in the best and most helpful way. He must listen carefully to his Master's instructions, and try to discern the particular and immediate needs of the household. At all costs he must refuse to 'practise cunning or to tamper with God's word;'[30] instead there must be 'the open statement (*phanerosis* = manifestation) of the truth.' The preacher's task, as steward, is therefore to unfold the Scriptures, so that the truth becomes manifest or plain. Every sermon should, to some extent at least, be expository. Contemporary illustrations can serve to show the relevance of the word of God; but the preacher is never there to give his own thoughts on the political or social issues of the day. He is a dispenser of the word of God. He must not shrink from declaring anything that is profitable for the family of God, and eventually aim to declare the whole counsel of God, since it is the word of his grace that is able to build up the household in spiritual strength and health.[31]

The preacher must therefore work hard to provide thoroughly digestible food, attractively presented. He must

[26] Matthew 13:1.
[27] Mark 7:8-13.
[28] Colossians 2:8; 2 Peter 3:16.
[29] 1 Corinthians 2:16f.
[30] 2 Corinthians 4:2.
[31] See Acts 20:20-32.

gauge the spiritual appetite of his hearers, and speak in such a way that all are able to receive it. Charles Spurgeon used to say to his students: 'If a learned brother fires over the heads of his congregation with a grand oration, he may trace his elocution, if he likes, to Cicero and Demosthenes, but do not let him ascribe it to the Holy Spirit.' Martin Luther likewise insisted on a basic simplicity: 'A preacher should have the skill to teach the unlearned simply, roundly and plainly; for teaching is of more importance than exhorting. When I preach, I regard neither doctors nor magistrates, of whom I have above forty in the congregation. I have all my eyes on the servant maids and the children. If the learned men are not well pleased with what they hear, well, the door is open.' John Wesley wrote in his preface to a volume of sermons, 'I design plain truth for plain people... I labour to avoid all words which are not easy to be understood.'

Such simplicity is not easily attained. Anyone can be complicated, anyone can be trite. But to preach profound truths in a way that all can understand requires considerable study. The preacher must know, as far as is possible, the personal and corporate needs of his congregation. It is not just the truth of the message that is important, but its particular relevance. He must also know how to handle the word of God in such a way that he will not deface the truth, but still be able to make it fit into the needs of his hearers.

Paul urged Timothy to be 'a workman who has no need to be ashamed, rightly handling the word of truth.'[32] John Stott helpfully comments on this verse:

'The verb, *orthotomounta*, [rightly handling] means literally, 'cutting straight'. It was employed of road-making and is, for instance, used in the LXX of Proverbs 3:6: 'He will make straight (AV, direct) your paths.' Our exposition of the Scripture is to be so simple and direct, so easily intelligible, that it resembles a straight road. It is easy to follow it. It is like Isaiah's highway of the redeemed: even 'fools shall not err therein'. Such straight cutting of the Word of God is not easy. It requires much study,...not only of God's Word but of man's nature and of the world in

[32] 2 Timothy 2:15.

which he lives. The expository preacher is a bridge builder,
seeking to span the gulf between the Word of God and the
mind of man. He must do his utmost to interpret the
Scripture so accurately and plainly, and to apply it so
forcefully, that the truth crosses the bridge.[33]

Student

The poverty of preaching in much of today's church is
probably due to the poverty of Bible study. If the preacher is
to dispense God's word effectively week after week, year after
year, and still remain fresh and relevant, there will be no
substitute for the dogged discipline of daily study. He must
learn to grasp the broad sweep of scriptural truth as well as
examining carefully the detailed text. He must ask himself:
'What is the meaning of this word or phrase? What is its
relevance and application to my life, and to the needs of this
particular part of the body of Christ? How can it be
explained and illustrated?'

We need to be soaked in the Scriptures. We must 'let the
word of Christ dwell in us richly in all wisdom'.[34] We shall
need modern translations and commentaries, the original text
(if we understand it!), a lexicon, a concordance and a Bible
dictionary. Most of all we need the illumination of the Holy
Spirit. Our aim is not to produce a commentary on the
passage in question, but to discover and deliver God's
message for the occasion. With some confidence we should be
able to stand up and say, as it were, 'Thus says the Lord'.

We need increasingly today a prophetic note in our
preaching. Orthodoxy by itself can be dry and barren. We
need instead, in the context of biblical truth, to discern what
the Lord is saying to this particular group at this particular
moment in time. It is impossible to give equal balance to the
whole counsel of God at the same time. Different aspects of
God's truth need to be stressed on different occasions. What is
the Spirit saying today to the churches? What emphases
should we concentrate on? What is the word of the Lord for
now? There should be an arresting (and no doubt often a
disturbing) relevance about the preached word of God.

[33] Ibid., p. 24f.   [34] Colossians 3:16.

For this to be true, praying over the Bible and listening to the Spirit of God as he speaks to our minds through the written word will prove essential if we are to dispense anything of value when we preach. George Whitefield once described his own way of studying the Bible: 'I began to read the Holy Scripture upon my knees, laying aside all other books, and praying over, if possible, every line and word. This proved meat indeed and drink indeed to my soul. I daily received fresh life, light and power from above. I got more true knowledge from reading the book of God in one month than I could ever have acquired from all the writings of men.' Perhaps for this reason it is small wonder that Whitefield became the prince of preachers in his day.

A good steward will so discipline himself in his study of the Bible, and in his reading of other books, newspapers and magazines, filing potential material carefully, that he will never go to his cupboard and find it bare. The larder will always be well stocked. His difficulty will not be in finding something to preach, but in choosing from the wealth of material that already exists. Jesus once said that 'every scribe who has been trained for the kingdom of heaven is like a householder who brings out of his treasure what is new and what is old'.[35] A wise steward will do exactly the same with the treasures of God's word.

He will need to discern how much can be swallowed and digested at any one time. The danger in many biblically-based churches is that of developing a congregation of sermon-tasters. People listen to a stirring message on prayer on Sunday morning; they are challenged by a call to repentance on Sunday evening; they study the complexities of personal witness in a discipleship group on Tuesday; they are stimulated by an exposition from Isaiah on Thursday; and they are enthused by a spiritual renewal rally on Saturday. And all this is on top of their own personal study of the Scriptures, which happens to be in Leviticus that week!

At the end of all that, how much of God's word has effectively taken root in their hearts? When most of that Bible teaching will be 'one-way' (preacher to a passive congregation), how much has really been assimilated? Is there really

[35]Matthew 13:52.

any chance for it to be lived out in the lives of God's people? The steward of God's word will need to think carefully about the diet and menu if he is to serve the household of God.

In a radical re-appraisal of the preaching ministry in a local church, Juan Carlos Ortiz has suggested that there should be only about six different sermons a year, giving time for the truth to be thoroughly digested and applied before going on to something new.

3. WITNESS

Some years ago, at the New Delhi Assembly of the World Council of Churches, D.T. Niles said this: 'Like Peter, we are all in the courtyard of the judgment hall where Jesus is on trial.' That is a truth that we often forget. Jesus is still on trial in the court of world opinion. He is the one who is being accused in the world today. He, of his own choice, is delivered up into the hands of a secular, godless and often hostile society. He is being judged by the world, and a verdict is being passed against him. That is why we must speak out clearly and boldly, or else share in Peter's denial.

The work of the Spirit
What we need to see clearly, as it is not always obvious on the surface, is that the world (meaning everything in society that does not come directly under the Lordship of Christ) is always hostile to Christ. 'The whole world is in the power of the evil one,' said the apostle John.[36] Jesus constantly warned his disciples about this: 'If the world hates you, know that it has hated me before it hated you... Because you are not of the world,... the world hates you... If they persecute me, they will persecute you...'[37] And it is in this context of the world's enmity towards God the Father and God the Son that Jesus declares that the counsel of defence in this trial is the Holy Spirit. He is the *Parakletos*, the Advocate; and he is the Advocate, in the first instance, not of the Christian but of Christ: 'He will bear witness to me,' said Jesus. Insofar as we grasp this point, and allow the Spirit to work in our own lives, then we too can share in this task: 'You also are witnesses.'

[36] 1 John 5:19.   [37] John 15:18ff.

We see this strikingly illustrated on the day of Pentecost when the Spirit was first poured out on the disciples. Although Peter briefly explained that this was the fulfilment of the prophecy of Joel, he went on, in the power of the Spirit, to bear witness to Jesus. He preached about the uniqueness of Jesus, the ministry of Jesus, the crucifixion of Jesus, the resurrection of Jesus and the exaltation of Jesus. His whole message could be summed up in his closing sentence, 'Let all the house of Israel therefore know assuredly that God has made him both Lord and Christ, this Jesus whom you crucified.' Although the dramatic experience of that day was undoubtedly the gift of the Holy Spirit, it is equally clear that the Holy Spirit came in power, as Jesus had promised, to enable them to be witnesses to Jesus. Certainly Luke emphasises the place and activity of the Holy Spirit throughout the life and growth of the early church; but this was to enable the church to preach Christ. When they were filled with the Holy Spirit in Acts 4, 'with great power the apostles gave their testimony to the resurrection of the Lord Jesus.'

From these basic truths about the witness of the Spirit and the witness of the disciples, two consequences follow.

In the first place, there must be an *empowering work of the Spirit within the preacher*. A witness is called to give first-hand evidence of what he has personally seen and heard. Second-hand evidence is not acceptable. His witness is valid only if he has a personal experience of the object of his witness; and as Christians we are called by God to witness to his Son in the power of his Spirit.

John the Baptist once declared, 'I saw the Spirit descend as a dove from heaven, and it remained on him... I have seen and have borne witness that this is the Son of God.'[38] Jesus told Nicodemus, 'We speak of what we know, and bear witness of what we have seen.'[39] The apostles were equally emphatic: 'We were eye-witnesses of his majesty,' said Peter.[40] 'The life was made manifest, and we saw it, and testify to it,' wrote John.[41]

The preacher's authority will depend not only on the authority of the message that has been entrusted to him; it

[38] John 1:32-34.
[39] John 3:11.
[40] 2 Peter 1:16.
[41] 1 John 1:2.

will also lie in his personal experience of that message. A man cannot preach Christ unless he knows Christ; he cannot witness to the power of the Holy Spirit, unless he knows that power in his own heart; he cannot talk about prayer, unless he knows the reality of personal communion with God. Spiritual truths must become a part of a man before they can be effectively preached by that man. He must speak of what he knows, or it would be better for him not to speak. As Ignatius of Antioch once expressed it: 'It is better to keep silence and to be, than to talk and not to be.'

Moreover, if a man is to preach about following Christ, and about being crucified with Christ there will necessarily be, in one way or another, some sufferings in his own life. Witness, in the New Testament, was closely linked with suffering, as the Greek word for a witness, *martus*, clearly indicates. The witnessing church was the suffering church, and sometimes the ultimate sacrifice was paid by those who were 'faithful unto death'. If the truths of God's word are to become flesh and blood, some pain is unavoidable. 'The man, the whole man, lies behind the sermon. Preaching is not the performance of an hour. It is the outflow of a life. It takes twenty years to make a sermon, because it takes twenty years to make a life.' Perhaps this is something of an overstatement, since Peter did not require twenty years before preaching at Pentecost! But he did have a very real experience of what he was testifying to through the equipment of the Spirit's power. Without this, his words would have been totally lacking in conviction. Most people instinctively recognise the man who really knows what he is talking about, since he is speaking from an obvious personal knowledge of the subject in question.

At the same time, *the Spirit must also be at work within the congregation* if the preaching is to be really effective. Preaching is a corporate activity. As Dr. Coggan has put it: 'Any preacher of experience will bear witness to this fact that in Church A one Sunday, having prepared himself and his sermon with care and prayer, he finds that his words rebound like a fives ball from the wall of the court. In Church B the following Sunday, the preparation of himself and of his sermon having been the same as during the previous week, he finds a receptivity to the Word of God and a response to it so manifest and real as to be almost tangible. What is the reason for this? No doubt many facts are involved. I suspect, however, that one of the most important is this — the members of the congregation A have never grasped the fact that preaching is a function, a corporate activity of the Church... But at Church B the members of the congregation know that prayerful dedication on the part of the preacher is not enough — something is demanded of them. Preaching is a corporate activity.'[42]

Certainly it was the corporate witness of the early church that helped the apostles to preach so effectively. In the passage quoted above from Acts 4, for example, it was because the whole church 'lifted their voices *together* to God' in prayer, because 'they were *all* filled with the Holy Spirit', and because 'those who believed were of *one* heart and soul, and...they had everything in *common*,' that the apostles were able 'with great power' to give their testimony to the resurrection of the Lord Jesus — and Luke adds, 'great grace was upon them *all*.'

Within our congregation at York, I have often experienced the vast difference in the preaching ministry between the times when we have been spiritually alive and the times when we have been spiritually sleepy or dead. The renewal of preaching must be linked with renewal of the church; and, if the Spirit is active, the one will help towards the other.

The exaltation of Christ

In the second place, *a true witness must at all costs seek to exalt Christ in his preaching.* The pulpit is a perilous place for those who are ambitous for themselves and for power over people. Popular preachers are all too often idolised by their followers and exalted to a pre-eminence that belongs to Christ alone. Some of the great conventions and conferences of the church display a degree of speaker-worship that must surely be offensive to God and grieving to the Holy Spirit.

We need to hear again the Father testifying to Jesus: 'This is my Son,...; listen to *him!*' And we need to remember that the work of the Spirit is likewise to glorify him. John the Baptist understood this, and resolutely refused to accept any glory that belonged to Christ alone. He knew that he had

[42] *Stewards of Grace*, pp. 87f.

come to bear witness to the light. 'He was not the light, but came to bear witness to the light.' He was content to be 'a voice crying in the wilderness.' He constantly pointed to the one, 'the thong of whose sandal I am not worthy to untie.' When John's disciples complained that many were leaving him to follow Jesus, John accepted this as a necessary part of his role as a witness: 'You yourselves bear me witness, that I said, I am not the Christ, but I have been sent before him. He who has the bride is the bridegroom; the friend of the bridegroom, who stands and hears him, rejoices greatly at the bridegroom's voice; therefore this joy of mine is now full. He must increase, but I must decrease.'[43] This perfectly expresses the task of a witness. His whole ambition is to testify to Christ, to draw people to Christ, to encourage people to follow Christ, to help them to love Christ and to worship Christ. It used to be said of Samuel Rutherford that he showed his hearers the loveliness of Christ.

A witness, therefore, must learn first to be a worshipper himself. He must so love Christ that his greatest joy is found when others come to love Christ too. King David once wrote in the psalms, 'Look to him, and be radiant.'[44] A true witness will be so focussed upon Christ that there will be a radiance in his life as well as in his preaching; and it is this radiance that will be more convincing than the greatest eloquence or preaching techniques.

Dr. W.T. Stace, Professor of Philosophy at Princetown University, for a long time was an agnostic. To him, religion was no more than myth and make-believe. Mystical experiences were simply subjective illustrations. He wrote and argued like this for many years. Then he began an intensive study of the lives of the true saints of God. Out of his painstaking research came the revolutionary truth that impressed him above all else. It was the radiance of Spirit-filled Christians. Many of them suffered more than most human beings, and sometimes died agonising deaths. Yet through their most appalling ordeals their spirits shone through with a glorious lustre that defied extinction. Professor Stace was convinced that such radiant sufferers drew on supernatural and inexhaustible resources. This brought him to Christ.

[43] John 1:27; 3:28-30.   [44] Psalm 34:5.

The preacher, as a witness, must pray for the same radiance to shine from his whole being. A noted intellectual at Cambridge University, Dr. Charles Raven, once described a preacher he heard: 'The sermon was as an argument puerile, but the man was aflame, radiating a power of loving that filled his simple words with meaning and with an atmosphere of worship. Here was a man not only passionately convinced of the gospel, but, for whatever the words mean, God-possessed... Here was the real Christianity that had changed the course of human history: if this man were deluded, I should almost be content to share this delusion. The scoffer stayed to pray.'[45] That preacher, whose name significantly is not recorded, illustrates what it means to be a witness to Christ.

4. SERVANT

In similar vein to the concept of a witness, a servant is someone of no importance in himself. In humble obedience he is simply required to speak and act in his master's name. In this way his master speaks and acts *through* him. That is why Paul could describe Apollos and himself as 'servants through whom you believed.' A servant is nothing, and has nothing of himself. Everything he is and has comes from his master. If the preacher, then, is to know the power of God working through him, creating faith and strengthening faith in his hearers, he must rely wholly on those factors that are linked with the power of God. Today there is a power crisis in the church. In how many meetings and services can the outsider know that 'God is in this place'? How often do men and women find Christ through our preaching — not only through special evangelistic efforts? To what degree are the lives of our congregations being transformed into the likeness of Christ through the regular teaching of his word? We live in a spiritually hungry society in which many, especially young people, are looking for spiritual reality. In how many churches can they find unmistakable evidence of that reality and power? Is it obvious that God is with us? Jesus told his disciples to stay put until they were 'clothed with power from

[45] *A Wanderer's Way.*

on high;'[46] otherwise it would be useless trying to preach the gospel to all nations.

At best the task of communicating Christ to the world is a most exacting and demanding one. Paul well knew the dangers of spiritual depression, when he was tempted to lose heart.[47] There were two main reasons for such a temptation.

In the first place, the preacher has to contend with spiritual blindness on the part of the unbelievers. 'The god of this world has blinded the minds...to keep them from seeing the light of the gospel of the glory of Christ.' However, as Paul had received his ministry by the mercy of God, he was determined not to lose heart.

In the second place, the preacher may often be physically, mentally and spiritually exhausted. I am more prone to depression after preaching than at almost any other time, simply because it is utterly exhausting work. Nevertheless, wrote Paul, 'we do not lose heart. Though our outer nature is wasting away, our inner nature is being renewed every day.'

Since, then, this work of preaching is so demanding, how can we make sure that our labour is not in vain? No one wants to become an ecclesiastical barrel-organ, rustily churning out the same religious platitudes Sunday after Sunday to an elderly and rapidly diminishing congregation. How can we know something of the power of God in our preaching, so that we can truly be 'servants through whom you believed'? There are three sources of power available to the preacher, and they need to go together.

The power of the gospel

'I am not ashamed of the gospel' wrote Paul to the Romans. '*It* is the power of God for salvation to every one who has faith.'[48] God's word is always powerful, and Paul often witnessed its revolutionary work in the lives of those who heard and received it. 'Our gospel came to you not only in word, but also in power and in the Holy Spirit and with full conviction... When you received the word of God..., you accepted it not as the word of men but as what it really is, the word of God, which is at work in you believers.'[49]

[46] Luke 24:49.
[47] 2 Corinthians 4.

[48] Romans 1:16.
[49] 1 Thessalonians 1:5; 2:13.

When God speaks, anything can happen! The whole world was created by the word of God. In the first chapter in the Bible we find this repeated refrain: 'God said... And it was so.' God's word is like the snow and the rain that come down from heaven, said Isaiah. It causes the ground to 'bring forth and sprout'. It never returns empty; it always accomplishes what God purposes, and prospers wherever he sends it.[50] By the same word Jesus healed the sick, made the lame to run, the deaf to speak, and the dead to rise.

The servant of God who sets his mind to preach the word of God will almost invariably see God at work before long within his congregation. That word is 'like fire,...like a hammer which breaks the rock in pieces.'[51] It is 'living and active, sharper than any two-edged sword, piercing to the division of soul and spirit, of joints and marrow, and discerning the thoughts and intentions of the heart.'[52] It can cut through the apathy, blindness and hardness of any person's life. If we depart from the authority of God's word, as given in the Scriptures, we abandon a vital source of power that God has provided for his church.

The power of the cross

When Paul came to the notoriously evil city of Corinth, he knew he faced an exceptionally difficult task. The Greeks invented a new word, 'to Corinthianise', which meant 'to go to the devil', as the city was so full of evil of every description. How could Paul possibly see the power of God at work in that situation? He tells us clearly in the first two chapters of his first letter. He was determined to eschew the showy eloquence of the 'debater of this age' for one overwhelming reason: 'lest the cross of Christ be emptied of its power. For the word of the cross is folly to those who are perishing, but to us who are being saved it is the power of God.' And although the Jews kept on demanding signs before they were prepared to believe, and the Greek sophists were interested only in 'wisdom', Paul concentrated on the message of 'Christ crucified, a stumbling block to Jews and folly to Gentiles, but to those who are called, both Jews and Greeks, Christ the power of God and the wisdom of God.'

[50]Isaiah 55:10f.   [52]Hebrews 4:12.
[51]Jeremiah 23:29.

The preaching of the cross humbles the sinner, cuts the ground of pride from under his feet, shows him the foolishness of trusting in his own good works for salvation, and reveals the only path by which a sinner may come to God. In some magnificent words of Emil Brunner:

In the cross of Christ, God says to man, that is where you ought to be. Jesus, my Son, hangs there in your stead. His tragedy is the tragedy of your life. You are the rebel who should be hanged on the gallows. But lo, I suffer instead of you and because of you, because I love you in spite of what you are. My love for you is so great that I meet you there, there on the cross. I cannot meet you anywhere else. You must meet me there by identifying yourself with the one on the cross. It is by this identification that I, God, can meet you in him, saying to you as I say to him: my beloved son.'

The preaching of such a message, which is at the heart of the gospel, will always see the power of God.

The power of the Spirit

Again, Paul at Corinth knew that it was no good relying on 'lofty words of wisdom'. 'My speech and my message [Jesus Christ and him crucified] were not in plausible words of wisdom, but in demonstration of the Spirit and power, that your faith might not rest in the wisdom of men but in the power of God.'

It was clearly the power of the Spirit that made the first disciples so fruitful in the proclaiming of Christ. It was this power that made them bold in the presence of their accusers, and in the face of great opposition and persecution. It was this power that brought conviction of sin, of righteousness and of judgment, as Jesus had promised. If we lack this power of the Spirit, our preaching and our labours will all be in vain. He alone can make the written word the living word. Only the Spirit can quicken the conscience, illuminate the mind, reveal Christ, create the new birth, bring assurance of salvation, and instruct the believer. The preacher must seek for continuous renewal of the Holy Spirit in his own life before he can bring God's life to anyone else. He is only a servant, and God alone gives life and growth. 'I planted,

Apollos watered, but God gave the growth. So neither he who plants nor he who waters is anything, but only God who gives the growth.'[53]

However, the servant of God's word must not fulfil his task with unthinking obedience. Obviously it would be useless delivering God's message in English when addressing those who understood only Chinese; and it is almost as meaningless quoting texts, especially from the Authorised Version, to those who are totally ignorant of the Scriptures, even when the language is technically the same. What matters is the degree of communication that takes place. The message must always be God's message, but the way it is presented must vary in virtually every situation.

Elsewhere[54] I have tried to widen our whole concept of 'the word of God', so that the communication of this word to man must not be thought of solely by the image of the preacher in the pulpit. I have tried to show that the word of God spread rapidly in the first century by preaching and teaching (often in thoroughly secular situations, not just in religious buildings), by a loving and united church, by signs and wonders, by prayer and praise, by prayerful re-organisation, by social action and service, by suffering, and, above all, by the power of the Holy Spirit. Given the divine message, which must not be tampered with, the vital question is, how can this message be most clearly understood by this particular group of hearers?

5. COMMUNICATOR

In an age when people are numbed by the bombardment of technical jargon and empty promises, other forms of communication may be necessary to illustrate or support the verbal presentation of the message. With the immeasurable influence of radio and television, plays, films and documentaries have become a normal part of our everyday life. It has been calculated that, on average, the vast majority of the population in the developed countries watch three hours of drama each night, seven days a week, and almost 365 days a

[53] 1 Corinthians 3:6f.

[54] *I Believe in Evangelism*, Hodder & Stoughton, pp. 45-62.

year. A child growing up in today's world may well spend ten years of his life in front of the box.

One obvious result of this is that, in spite of the enormous sums of money spent on general education, with the resulting decline in illiteracy, we have still produced a generation that is increasingly *non*-literate. The spoken or written word by itself makes less and less impact on our modern society. All the communicators of today have to be influenced by the essential nature of television, or else they fail entirely to communicate with any but a tiny section of society.

This is a vital fact that the church has been tragically slow to realise, or at least to accept. Most churches rely heavily on the spoken or written word for communication, and then wonder why so few people find the Christian faith to be relevant. The truth is that we live in a world that is almost dominated by drama, and it is only when the church comes to terms with this in any serious and realistic way that it will be able to speak in the 'language' of today. If it fails to do this, any effective heralding of God's word will be severely handicapped. The church, in the eyes of the world, will be limping slowly along, supported on the crutches of past methods, and quite unable to keep up with the rapidly increasing speed of change within our culture.

This basic truth applies to Christian education at all levels, not least as far as children are concerned. The old-style Sunday School class, with a strong emphasis on Bible-words and often very little activity, becomes largely meaningless and irrelevant. Children up to the age of eleven have a natural flair for drama and movement. In churches where these natural gifts are encouraged, instead of suppressed, children may gain a much quicker grasp of the teaching of the Bible, with its absolute relevance to the world in which they live; and, what is just as important, they are much more likely to develop a positive and healthy attitude towards the church, seeing God's family as a place where the best of life can be experienced and enjoyed to the full.

In our church at York we have a Children's Workshop each week. The basis for each evening will almost certainly be some biblical passage or Christian truth. However, children are taught how to relate to one another, how to pray aloud

together, how to express their worship in dance and movement, as well as in song. Then there will be different groups,
with some acting out the Bible story, others making banners
or visual aids — sometimes baking bread for a coming Family
Communion Service, with an explanation, while they are
doing it, of the meaning of this sacrament. The variety is
endless, and many churches are finding this a much more
fruitful method of instruction for the children and young
people of today.

Such visual and dramatic forms of communication are, of
course, by no means new. In biblical days it was not unusual
for the prophets to dramatise their message, sometimes in
extremely vivid and colourful ways; and Jesus, in his superb
teaching ministry, was constantly making use of various forms
of visual aid. Many of his parables were probably told in this
way.

Eugene Nida, in his book *Message and Mission*, describes an
anthem in a Baptist Church in the Belgian Congo some years
ago:

Just before the choir arose to sing, a man came forward
and placed a large basin of kerosene on the pulpit and set a
match to it. As the flames leapt up the choir began to sing
an anthem, written by the African director—

> The city that forgot God
> Gomorrah, Gomorrah,
> The city that forgot God...

Over and over and louder and louder they rang out until
suddenly the choir stopped singing, and in the distance
some choir members who had slipped out of the choir
began to wail, scream and cry somewhere in the background. Then as the lamentation in the distance died away
the choir took up the theme again —

> The city that forgot God
> Gomorrah, Gomorrah,...

More and more quietly they sang, until at last we could
not quite tell when the music ceased. It was an unforgettable communication.

I am not suggesting that this particular anthem might be suitable for Matins in an English country church, although I was at one Anglican family service where two constructed houses were set on fire, and the flames, illustrating the testing of our works by fire, leapt alarmingly high, with ashes floating gently onto the heads of those present! I will not forget that in a hurry! But the congregation, on the whole, was not amused!

I wonder, however, how often the congregation leaves a service with the feeling that it has just experienced 'unforgettable communication'? Having witnessed something of the potential of mime and drama, not to mention music and dance, when it comes to effective communication both within and without a church building, I am convinced of the need to explore prayerfully and sensitively other forms of presentation in addition to the conventional sermon from the pulpit. Nothing can or should replace the straight proclamation of God's word, but there is much that can illustrate it most effectively. Mistakes will no doubt be made, but the alternative is to cling fiercely to traditional forms for fear of making a mistake — and that is a mistake in itself! Given the necessary context of much prayer and love, the determination to be true to the Scriptures, the desire to glorify Christ, and the willingness to give and receive correction when necessary, there is much that can be done to make the church's communication of the gospel far more powerful than it is at present. As with other issues, the children of this world are so often wiser than the children of light.

Much of the biblical record is highly dramatic in character, and trying to present it purely in sermon form is like trying to present a beautiful country scene on a black-and-white photograph. However artistic, the smells and colours and distances will all be lost. The use of drama, therefore, can bring to life Jonah's predicament as a reluctant missionary, Ezekiel's vision of dry bones, Job's anguish in the midst of suffering, Zacchaeus' astonishment in the sycamore tree, the servant's unforgiveness, the rich farmer's folly, the bearing of our sin by Jesus on the cross, or the mixture of wonder and excitement surrounding the resurrection. All these can be made to live, not least for today's generation, by the sensitive use of drama. Potential gifts, in terms of writing, acting, making costumes and simple scenery, can be developed, and will consequently enrich the corporate preaching of that local church. Moreover, such drama is highly suitable for the streets and in secular situations where the traditional style of preaching is largely irrelevant.

Dance, too, can speak powerfully of the life and joy that God calls us to experience in Christ. Movement, for many people, can have a silent eloquence that on occasions is even more expressive than words. We recognise this in everyday life with a gesture, a handshake, a kiss. Too often the church is pictured by stiff and motionless bodies which, by their unbending formality, do not speak of the God of action and the Spirit of movement. We need to understand the culture of today. What speaks to today's world? What is meaningful for today? God forbid that the church should hide the living word of God in the coffin of yesterday's cultural patterns. Whether we like it or not, for most people outside convention-al church-ianity the medium *is* the message, and therefore the church, if it is to be faithful to its preaching commission, must give urgent attention to its methods of communication.

The ministry of preaching, then, is one of the most demanding of all ministries within the church, and one that today needs to be re-discovered, in all its variety, relevance and power. P.T. Forsyth used to say, 'With preaching Christianity stands or falls, because it is the declaration of a gospel. Without the faithful proclaiming of Christ in the power of the Spirit, the church could never have survived.'

Certainly 'every one who calls upon the name of the Lord will be saved.' But, as Paul rightly asked the Christians at Rome, 'How are men to call upon him in whom they have not believed? And how are they to believe in him of whom they have never heard? And how are they to hear without a preacher? And how can men preach unless they are sent? As it is written, "How beautiful are the feet of those who preach good news!"… So faith comes from what is heard, and what is heard comes by the preaching of Christ.'[55]

[55] Romans 10:13-17.

CHAPTER FOURTEEN

Sacraments

AUGUSTINE, THE FIFTH-CENTURY bishop of Hippo in North Africa once stated: 'Our Lord Jesus Christ hath knit together a company of new people by sacraments, most few in number, most easy to be kept, most excellent in signification.'

The sacraments in Protestant churches are the 'effectual signs of grace' that were instituted by Christ, namely baptism and the Lord's Supper. They are the outward and visible signs of the blessings of the gospel that are given by God's grace and received by faith. Thus both sacraments are primarily sacraments of God's grace, not of human activities. Even in the realm of faith, they are not signs of our personal belief, but of God's good will towards us. That is an important point that we shall return to later.

It is, then, unfortunate that the sacraments in Western Christendom have frequently been the source of bitter controversy. Often 'the word' has been set in opposition to the sacraments, so that some have stressed the one, and some the other.

It seems that part of the trouble is that we have regarded the sacraments as institutions *of* the church and *within* the church; and it may well be that some of this tension would be resolved if, with the Eastern Orthodox Church, we saw the church in itself as the sacrament of Christ's presence and action in the world. As Alexander Schmemann writes: 'Orthodoxy is presented usually as specialising in "mysticism" and "spirituality" as the potential home of all those who thirst and hunger for the "spiritual banquet". The Orthodox Church has been assigned the place and the function of the "liturgical" and "sacramental" Church, *therefore* more or less indifferent to mission. But all this is wrong...'[1]

In spite of the secularism and hedonism of this present age, the spiritual hunger of people — including those right outside the ranks of the church — is increasing noticeably. However, with the secular theologians emptying the gospel of the divinity of Christ and authentic spiritual experiences in an attempt, albeit sincere, to make the Christian message more acceptable and rational to twentieth-century man, the religious search has turned sharply from the ordinary, secularised church to the mysticism of the east — transcendental meditation, occultism, and the like. A renewal of the true sacramental life of the church, as opposed to sheer superstition and idolatry (which so revolted the Reformers), would enhance, not detract from, the mission of the church in our spiritually starved society.

Let us look, however, at the two sacraments instituted by Christ, both of which have been so hotly debated over the centuries.

1. BAPTISM

The verb *baptizo* was used in pre-Christian Greek to mean 'plunge, sink, drown, drench, overwhelm'. A person could be overwhelmed (lit. baptised) by debts, sorrow, calamity; or overcome (lit. baptised) by wine or sleep. Euripedes in the Orestes uses *bapto* when water is splashing into a ship, but *baptizo* when the ship is waterlogged or sinking.

The verb is also used in pre-Christian Judaism, and once again means 'overwhelm, immerse'. 'Lawlessness overwhelms [lit. baptises] me, says Isaiah in 21:4. In 2 Kings 5:14 Naaman 'dipped' [lit. baptised] himself seven times in the Jordan — clearly for him an immersion! Proselytes, too, were baptised. The males were first circumcised before entering the fold of Judaism; but all, whether male or female, adults or children, were then baptised in the presence of witnesses before presenting the sacrificial offering. The Rabbis used to say, 'When he has been baptised, he is regarded in all respects as an Israelite.' As his Gentile impurities were washed away, he was considered as 'a newborn child'. Paul also described the

---

[1]*For the Life of the World*, S.V.S. Press 1963, p. 21.

Israelites as 'baptised into Moses in the cloud and in the sea.'[2]
This is an interesting use of the word signifying personal
involvement in someone who was effectively their saviour —
a theme which Paul develops much more fully when he talks
about being baptised into Christ. It is worth noting that their
outward baptism into Moses (through the crossing of the Red
Sea) did not guarantee their final salvation, for 'with most of
them God was not pleased; for they were overthrown in the
wilderness.' The whole passage is cited as a warning to those
who were trusting for salvation in their participation in the
sacraments of baptism and the eucharist.

The distinctive Christian use of baptism, however, is seen in
two main ways. In the first place, no man baptised himself. It
was always something that was done by another, since baptism
is essentially a sign of what God has done for us in Jesus Christ.
This is in striking contrast to the baptism of a proselyte to
Judaism, who always washed himself. In the second place, the
noun *baptisma* is specifically Christian. It is not to be found
anywhere before its occurrence in the New Testament.

The first reference in the New Testament is to the baptism of
John, which was known as a 'baptism of repentance',[3] preparing
people for God's kingly rule and the coming of the King. It was
a baptism 'for [*eis* — with a view to] the forgiveness of sins'. It
did not automatically convey that forgiveness, but helped those
who were so baptised to acknowledge their need of forgiveness
and to turn away from their sins.

It therefore took John by surprise when Jesus himself
submitted to this baptism;[4] but Jesus did so in order to
identify himself with the sinners he had come to save. He had
to be 'numbered with the transgressors'.[5] As the heavens
opened and the Spirit came down upon him, a voice from
heaven assured him of his role as both the Son of Psalm 2:7
and the Servant of Isaiah 42:1: 'Thou art my beloved Son;
with thee I am well pleased.'[6] Jesus later identified himself
with sinners in the fullest and most profound sense possible
when on the cross he 'became sin' for us; and it is worth
noticing that on two occasions Jesus spoke about his coming
death in terms of baptism: 'I have a baptism to be baptised

[2] 1 Corinthians 10:2.
[3] Luke 3:3; Acts 13:4.
[4] Matthew 3:13ff.
[5] Isaiah 53:12.
[6] Mark 1:10f.

with.'[7] It was through his baptism of suffering on the cross, when he took upon himself the full consequences of our sin, that forgiveness was made possible. Moreover, that forgiveness, symbolised by water baptism, could be received only through repentance and faith.

From the record in John's Gospel, it is not clear whether Jesus baptised his own disciples.[8] There are too many linguistic, textual and historical difficulties for any definite conclusions. It seems more certain that Jesus commanded his followers to go 'and make disciples of all nations, baptising them in the name of the Father and of the Son and of the Holy Spirit.'[9] Yet this passage, too, has been questioned for numerous reasons — textual, literary, historical and theological. However it fits in well with all that has gone before in the Gospels, and with apostolic practice and teaching in the rest of the New Testament. Further, if it is true, as some maintain, that these words come from the evangelist and not from Jesus, and that this trinitarian baptismal formula was not used by the church until the second century, we are faced with other problems. The words are found in all the manuscripts; and it is hard to see why Matthew inserted them if, at the time, they formed no part of the church's liturgy. Admittedly the baptisms recorded in Acts were 'in the name of the Lord [Jesus]' and not in the name of the Trinity; but these were baptisms for those who already possessed a basic belief in the one true God before they heard the good news of his Son Jesus Christ. Thus baptism in his name was the all-important issue; and it is quite possible that both Luke and Paul meant, by baptism in the name of the Lord Jesus, Christian baptism as opposed to any other, and were not primarily concerned about the precise formula used at the time of that Christian baptism. Further *Didache* 7:1, a first century text, records baptism in the three-fold name. This may not settle all the difficulties surrounding this matter in the New Testament, but there is no convincing argument against accepting those words in Matthew as the authoritative words of Jesus himself.[10]

[7]Luke 12:50; cf. Mark 10:38.
[8]John 3:22-26; 4:2.
[9]Matthew 28:19.

[10]For a fuller treatment of this issue see *Baptism in the New Testament*, by G.R. Beasley-Murray, London 1962, pp. 77-92.

When we turn to the significance of baptism, we see that in the first place it speaks of, and seals, *union with Christ*. This is such an important part of the meaning of baptism that we repeatedly find the expression 'baptism into [*eis*] Christ'. By the means of God's grace, through repentance and faith, outwardly symbolised by baptism, a man is brought *into* Christ, so that Paul's most frequent description of a Christian is 'a man in Christ'.

This sacrament is therefore the sacrament of justification, since justification describes the right standing of a sinner before God once he has been incorporated into Christ. He is accepted 'in the Beloved'. Moreover, union with Christ automatically includes membership in the body of Christ. It is impossible to be 'in Christ' without being a member of his body. Paul therefore writes to the Corinthian Christians, who were prone to setting up divisions within their fellowship: 'For by one Spirit we were all baptised into one body — Jew or Greeks, slaves or free — and all were made to drink of one Spirit.'[11] And to the Galatians he wrote: 'For as many of you as were baptised into Christ have put on Christ. There is neither Jew nor Greek, there is neither slave nor free; for you are all one in Christ Jesus.'[12]

In the second place, baptism signifies the *forgiveness of sins*. Peter urged the crowd on the day of Pentecost to 'repent, and be baptised...in the name of Jesus Christ for [*eis*] the forgiveness of your sins.'[13] Later, Paul recounted how Ananias had come and told him, 'Rise and be baptised, and wash away your sins, calling on his name.'[14] Paul wrote to Titus about the 'washing of regeneration';[15] and the writer to the Hebrews spoke of 'our hearts sprinkled clean from an evil conscience and our bodies washed with pure water.'[16] The allusion to baptism is clear, and the symbolism obviously expressive of the complete cleansing of sin that God offers all who come to Christ, on the basis of the death of his Son.

In the third place, baptism speaks of the *gift of the Holy Spirit*. At the start of Christ's ministry, John was requested to baptise Jesus, and he witnessed 'the Spirit descend as a dove from heaven'. John went on to explain: 'He who sent me to

---

[11] 1 Corinthians 12:13.
[12] Galatians 3:27f.
[13] Acts 2:38.

[14] Acts 22:16.
[15] Titus 3:5.
[16] Hebrews 10:22.

baptise with water said to me, "He on whom you see the
Spirit descend and remain, this is he who baptises with the
Holy Spirit." [17] Jesus himself told his disciples, shortly before
his departure from them: 'John baptised with water, but
before many days you shall be baptised with the Holy
Spirit.' [18] The fulfilment of this for the disciples was clearly at
Pentecost; and when Peter exhorted the crowd to repent and
be baptised for the forgiveness of their sins, he added, 'and
you shall receive the gift of the Holy Spirit'.

Baptism with the Holy Spirit
Recently there has been much debate about the phrase 'the
baptism of the Holy Spirit', and this is not the place to enter
into a detailed argument as to its meaning. [19] However, let me
repeat one or two pointers in the discussion that I made in my
book *One in the Spirit*. [20]

First, the term 'baptism' is unquestionably linked with
initiation; and therefore in one sense, at least, every Christian
is baptised in the Spirit. Union with Christ, the forgiveness of
sins and the gift of the Spirit are all symbolised by baptism,
and baptism is for all who are in Christ Jesus. We have every
spiritual blessing in Christ. Every true Christian is indwelt by
the Holy Spirit.

Second, we have already seen that the verb 'to baptise'
conveys the thought of 'to overwhelm, immerse, drench'; and
it is equally clear that the promised baptism of the Spirit at
Pentecost resulted in an overwhelming of the Spirit, an
overwhelming of the love and power of God which transformed the lives and witness of those disciples. They had a
vital experience of the Spirit, something far more than an
intellectual grasp of their theological status in the sight of
God. It is no doubt dangerous trying to describe the precise
nature of their experience — so much depends on purely
human factors. Nevertheless, if you take the experience of the
Spirit out of the pages of the New Testament, you are left
with virtually nothing. These pages are shot through with
superlatives: the peace which passes understanding, the love

[17] John 1:33.
[18] Acts 1:5.
[19] See *I Believe in the Holy Spirit* by Michael Green, Hodder & Stoughton, chapter 8.
[20] Hodder & Stoughton, pp. 65-70.

which surpasses knowledge, unutterable and exalted joy. Lesslie Newbigin has rightly commented: 'Theologians today are frightened of the word "experience". I do not think it is possible to survey the New Testament evidence...without recognising that the New Testament writers are free from this fear. They regard the gift of the Holy Spirit as an event which can be unmistakably recognised.'[21]

From this we see that the word 'baptised' speaks both of 'initiated into' and of 'overwhelmed by' — the one a status, the other an experience. Confusion arises when either is stressed at the expense of the other. For example, it is possible to think of the overwhelming of the Spirit as something entirely separate from, and subsequent to, Christian initiation; whereas the two, ideally and potentially, though not necessarily experientially, are one. On the other hand, it is possible so to stress that the Christian has 'got it all' by being baptised into Christ, that the overwhelming of the Spirit is never experienced.

The difficulty lies in the fact that Christian initiation, symbolised and sealed by water-baptism, is a united cluster of distinct concepts, including forgiveness, justification, regeneration, death, burial and resurrection with Christ, adoption, the gift and baptism of the Spirit. These concepts are not identical, either in meaning or experience. Although they all form one united cluster which belongs to all those in Christ, they can be examined separately, and they may be experienced separately. Depending on a person's initial understanding, repentance and faith, and depending too on the spiritual health of the fellowship into which that new believer comes, it may be quite possible for him to experience initially the regenerating work of the Spirit; then later to experience great assurance as the Spirit enables him to grasp the significance of justification; and later still to be overwhelmed by the love of God, poured in by the Holy Spirit, issuing in new joy and freedom and praise. These are all part of the single cluster of concepts which rightly belong to initiation, but may not be all experienced at the time of initiation.

It is not helpful, therefore, either to deny the significant experience which some, for the reasons given above, may call

[21]Quoted by Michael Harper, *Walk in the Spirit*, Hodder & Stoughton, p. 9.

'the baptism of the Spirit', nor to teach dogmatically the need for a two-stage or even three-stage experience for every Christian. God works in different individuals in different ways and at different times; and the New Testament's usage of these terms relating to the Spirit's work is not always so cut-and-dried as some would make out.

Certainly there is no room for complacency, regardless of past experiences. No Christian has yet 'arrived'. We all need to strain forward to what lies ahead, and to press on towards that goal.[22] For the sake of harmony within certain sections of the church, it may be preferable to avoid the phrase 'the baptism of the Spirit', if it is being used to describe an experience of the Spirit subsequent to conversion. It is interesting that neither John Stott, the leader of conservative evangelicals within the Anglican Church, nor Cardinal Suenens, a prominent figure of the charismatic renewal within the Roman Catholic Church, like the term 'the baptism of the Spirit' used for this purpose; and anyway, when the promise of Jesus in Acts 1:5 was fulfilled at Pentecost, Luke records that they were all *filled* with the Spirit. Elsewhere he writes about receiving the Spirit, or the Spirit falling upon them. Although it is important to understand and use the terms rightly, it would seem unwise to take issue over the phrase 'the baptism of the Spirit', from whatever standpoint, when much greater harmony can be achieved and maintained by referring to the need of being 'filled with the Spirit'. This clearly is a constant need for every Christian and for every church.[23]

Water Baptism
Returning briefly to water-baptism, it is worth considering the effect of the sacrament. What is the relation between the sign and the thing signified? Three main views have been expressed within the church.

First, there is the view that the sign always conveys the gift — *ex opere operato*. However, the objection to this idea of 'baptismal regeneration' is that a great many people who have been baptised are clearly not regenerate if the 'tests of life' given in the New Testament are anything to go by. Jesus

[22]Philippians 3:8-16.   [23]Ephesians 5:18.

warned us about the danger of doing all the right things 'in
his name' without coming to know him personally.[24] Paul,
too, stated that the external and physical sign of the old
covenant, namely circumcision, meant little in itself. 'He is a
Jew who is one inwardly, and real circumcision is a matter of
the heart, spiritual and not literal.'[25] Moreover, justification is
always by grace through faith, and never through baptism.
This is so consistently taught throughout the New Testament
that when Peter uses the story of the ark and the flood as a
picture of Christian baptism, and when he adds 'Baptism,
which corresponds to this, now saves you', he sees the need to
clear himself of any misunderstanding that he is teaching
'baptismal regeneration' by continuing: 'not as a removal of
dirt from the body but as an appeal to God for a clear conscience, through the resurrection of Jesus Christ...'[26] What
matters in salvation is the clear conscience, made possible
through the death and resurrection of Jesus Christ, and
appropriated by repentance and faith. Baptism then acts as an
'appeal' or 'pledge' or 'seal' of this, but, in itself, it does not
effect salvation. This was the truth that Simon the sorcerer had
to learn after being baptised in the name of Jesus Christ.[27]

Second, there is the opposite view, that the sign effects
nothing at all; it is simply a bare token and no more.
However, it is hard to justify this view from the New
Testament where water-baptism is linked very closely with
the blessings of the gospel. We have already seen how Peter
said to the crowd, 'Repent, and be baptised...for [eis — with
a view to] the forgiveness of your sins.' It is pre-empting the
value of a sacrament to say that it is a bare sign, and no more.
In daily life, a handshake is not only a sign of friendship, it
may enhance the friendship; a kiss is not only a sign of love, it
will very likely increase that love. Sacramental actions of all
kinds frequently increase or strengthen the reality that they
signify. That surely is true of the two sacraments instituted by
Christ. The eucharist, for example, is one place where we can
feed upon Christ in our hearts by faith; it is not simply a bare
remembrance of his death. Both sacraments are outward signs
through which God acts.

[24] Matthew 7:21-23.   [26] 1 Peter 3:20f.
[25] Romans 2:29.   [27] Acts 8:13, 21.

Thirdly, there is the view already expressed in this chapter, that the sign signifies the gift, and seals or pledges it. Baptism thus becomes the sacrament, or solemn pledge, of the new covenant. It is like a title deed to some property. Conditions must still be fulfilled, and the new owner must still 'experience' or possess the property for himself. It is not enough to possess the title deed. Yet that deed is a most important document, and will be the necessary 'appeal' or 'pledge' should the ownership of the property be questioned.

Much of the confusion surrounding water-baptism arises from a lack of understanding of this 'covenant theology'. For example, it is commonly believed by many that the Church of England has always taught 'baptismal regeneration'; and certainly the 1662 Prayer Book gives that impression when, immediately after a child has been baptised, the priest shall say, 'Seeing now...that this child is regenerate...' However, the original drafter of this service was a man called Martin Bucer (1491-1551), who was one of the leading Reformers and at one time Regius Professor of Divinity at Cambridge. It was there that he influenced the 1549 Book of Common Prayer, including this particular statement in the baptism service. Now Bucer was a 'Calvinist' in his theology, and in fact Calvin sat at his feet when he was teaching in Strasbourg from 1538-41; and it is virtually certain that Bucer did *not* believe in baptismal regeneration. Further, the bishops at that time who accepted this service of baptism were, for the most part, Calvinist in their theology, and they too did not believe in baptismal regeneration.

So what did Bucer mean by this statement, which has unfortunately caused such confusion for many years? He was simply better versed in 'covenant theology' than most of us today. The nature of faith in the Bible is that we take a promise of God, claim it for ourselves, and then dare to believe the truth of it even before (perhaps long before) the fulfilment of the promise is worked out in our experience. For example, Mary, in the *Magnificat*, praised God that he *had* done great things for her, when, at the time, she had only the promise of the angel to show for it. Now since baptism is the sign or pledge of the covenant promises of God, as soon as that person (or child) has been baptised we can look forward in daring faith to the fulfilment of those promises in

experience. It may be some time before that fulfilment is
worked out. If the conditions are not fulfilled, the promises
will not be fulfilled. But in daring faith, based on the
covenant promises of God and sealed with the sign of the
covenant, we say 'seeing now...that this child is regenerate...'
Within the context of covenant theology, that makes a lot of
sense; but divorced from that context, it can be thoroughly
misleading and has, sadly, confused many about the significance of this sacrament.

Concerning the mode of baptism, whether immersion or
sprinkling, the Scriptures are not emphatic. There is little
doubt that immersion was the norm for most people. Not
only does the word 'baptise' mean 'immerse', or at least
'intensively dip', but death to the old life and rising to the
new is most clearly symbolised by going right under the water
and coming up again as a 'new creation in Christ'. It could be
assumed that Jesus himself was baptised by immersion,
though, interestingly enough, one of the oldest pictures of his
baptism shows Jesus standing rather less than knee-deep in
the river Jordan, with John pouring water over his head![28]
Certainly baptism, as recorded in the New Testament, does
not demand immersion, and it could be argued that it was
unlikely that the Philippian jailer and all his household were
immersed when baptised in the middle of the night. In fact
the earliest reference to the mode of baptism that we have in
the Christian church comes in the *Didache* (c. AD 85): 'Baptise
in this way... Baptise in the name of the Father and of the
Son and of the Holy Spirit, in running water. But if you have
not running water, baptise in other water; and, if thou canst
not in cold, in warm. If you have neither, pour water thrice
on the head in the name of the Father and Son and Holy
Ghost.' As the vicar of two Anglican churches, I am content
to pour water in this way over the heads of those being
baptised; but I should also very much like to have a
baptismal tank for use where it seemed appropriate! A few
churches are being built with both a font and a tank, and it is
a pity that this is not more frequently the policy.

Furthermore, baptism, whatever the mode, can be received
only once. The New Testament expects all believers to be

[28] In the Catacomb of St. Callixtus, Rome.

baptised, but it knows nothing of Christians who are rebaptised. There are always three elements which go together to make a man a Christian. On man's side, there is repentance and faith; on God's side, there is union with Christ, membership of the body of Christ, forgiveness of sins and the gift of the Holy Spirit; on the church's side, there is baptism as the pledge of God's grace. Baptism may precede regeneration, or follow it, or even never lead to it (for lack of repentance and faith on man's side). However, even when baptism precedes regeneration, there is no case for what amounts to rebaptism. As Michael Green has put it: 'Baptism, like justification, is *once for all*. It is unrepeatable. You can no more be rejustified than you can be rebaptised. Both ideas make nonsense.'[29] Baptism can be neither revoked nor removed. A man can only acknowledge his baptism or deny it.

2. THE LORD'S SUPPER

Here is *the* fellowship meal and the central act of worship of the church. Michael Griffiths puts it in this way:

> An individual body is a body all the time, not just at mealtimes. But meals are essential if that body is to continue in health, to grow and to develop to maturity. A family is a family all the time, not just when it meets together for meals. It is when the family is doing things together that its ties as a family are strengthened. You look at the faces of your parents and your children with fresh love and joy, and a fresh understanding of what it means to belong to each other. A congregation is a congregation all the time, even when it is scattered among secular society, but it is when it assembles together as the Lord's people on the Lord's day that it is able to realise and appreciate its unique community — and most significantly when it meets to eat together symbolically in the Lord's supper.

This meal is based, of course, on the last meal that Jesus shared with his disciples;[31] and it immediately became the

[29]Op. Cit., p. 13.
[30]*Cinderella with Amnesia, I.V.P.,*
1975, p. 122f.
[31]Mark 14:17-26; Luke 22:14ff.

focal point of fellowship and worship in the early church. Luke records how the first disciples 'devoted themselves to the apostles' teaching and fellowship, to the breaking of bread and the prayers... And day by day, attending the temple together and breaking bread in their homes, they partook of food with glad and generous hearts (or with unaffected joy, N.E.B.), praising God...'[32] Some have drawn conclusions about 'communion in one kind only' from the fact that the cup is not mentioned in such passages;[33] but probably there is no significance to be drawn from this. The term 'breaking of bread' was a common expression for the whole fellowship meal, and Luke in Acts never mentioned the cup at all. What is more important is the joy and praise that accompanied such meals, as they experienced the presence of the risen Christ amongst them, and the fellowship of the Holy Spirit. Certainly, a few years later, when Paul wrote to the church at Corinth (probably around AD 55), the Lord's Supper was very much part of the life of a local church, although at Corinth there were various abuses that needed correction.

The Last Supper that Jesus had with his disciples was a festive farewell meal which was clearly linked with the thoughts of the Passover. Professor Jeremias has drawn up eleven parallels between the setting of the Last Supper and the setting of the Passover, and undoubtedly the links are strong. It is also clear that paschal ideas were in the thoughts and words of Jesus as he sat with the Twelve; and Paul later described Jesus as 'our paschal lamb' who had been sacrificed for us. 'Let us, therefore, celebrate the festival, not with the old leaven, the leaven of malice and evil, but with the unleavened bread of sincerity and truth.'[34]

Since Jesus told his disciples at the table, 'I have earnestly desired to eat this Passover with you before I suffer,' it is important to understand something of the Passover Feast if we are to grasp the significance of the Lord's Supper. The Jewish festival called the worshipper to look in four main directions.

It called him to *look back* by remembering God's mercy when he delivered his people from the land of bondage. A vital part of the ritual was the telling of the story of the

[32] Acts 2:42, 46.
[33] See H. Lietzmann, *Expository*
Times, LXV, pp. 333ff.
[34] 1 Corinthians 5:7.

This was never omitted on the assumption that everyone
present knew the story well enough. The youngest child present
would be instructed that, at a particular point, he was to ask
certain questions. The reply to these, given by the celebrant,
told the story of God's wonderful salvation from Egypt.

However, it was not just a remembrance; in a sense God's
people were called to relive their deliverance. The bitter
herbs forcefully reminded them of the bitterness of the
bondage that their fathers suffered in Egypt; and the cups
spoke of their coming salvation. The Rabbis instructed the
Jews in a rubric: 'In every generation a man must so regard
himself as if he came forth out of Egypt;' and every member
of the household had to eat the Passover as if he were taking
part in, or reliving, his own deliverance from bondage. The very
word *Haggadah* is taken from the Hebrew of Exodus 13:8: 'And
you *shall tell* your son on that day, "It is because of what the
Lord did for me when I came out of Egypt".' The words 'me'
and 'I' indicate the strong personal involvement that the Jews
were expected to feel with God's salvation for his people.
Moreover, the head of the household held a loaf in his hand,
and said, 'This is the bread of affliction which our fathers ate
when they came out of Egypt.' Literally, of course, it was not
the bread eaten by their fathers, but it symbolised and
represented that bread, and thus it helped the Jew to share
vividly with the experience of his fathers. This point is
important when we come to understand the meaning of the
words of Jesus at the Last Supper: 'This is my body... This is
my blood...'

The Passover also called the Jew to *look in*, by purifying
himself and his household from anything that was evil. Before
the Feast could take place there was a day of purification
(following a time of thorough spring-cleaning) when the head
of the house would perform a little ritual. He would take a
light in one hand and a pair of tongs in the other, and
systematically search through the house, looking for any scrap
of leaven. He probably never found any, since the house had
been thoroughly cleaned already; but the symbolism is clear.
Leaven was a sign of corruption or evil; and before the
Passover Feast could be held in that house, every trace of
corruption had to be removed.

Thirdly, the Jew was called to *look around*. In no sense was this Feast a private affair. It involved the whole household, children and all; and it was the custom to invite any stranger, who might be away from his family at that time, to join in with the family celebration and rejoicing.

Fourthly, the Jew was called to *look forward*, by waiting for the messianic age, when God's purposes for Israel would be fulfilled. An extra place would therefore be laid, with an empty chair opposite it, as they waited for the coming of Elijah, the forerunner of the Messiah. As expressed in the *Haggadah*: 'This year we are here: next year in the land of Israel! This year we are slaves: next year free men!' They were looking forward to future salvation.

Turning to the Lord's Supper, the parallels become clear. The Christian is called first to *look back*, and to remember with thanksgiving God's mercy to his people when he delivered them from the bondage of sin through the once-for-all death of his own Son. It is truly a *eucharist*, a thanksgiving: 'Do this in remembrance of me.'[35]

In the Anglican/Roman Catholic *Agreed Statement on the Eucharist* it is remarkable and encouraging to read these forceful words: 'Christ's redeeming death and resurrection took place once and for all in history. Christ's death on the cross, the culmination of his whole life of obedience, was the one, perfect and sufficient sacrifice for the sins of the world. There can be no repetition of or addition to what was then accomplished once for all by Christ.' This *agreed* Statement may come as a shock to some Protestants who have their own very different ideas about the most recent theological thinking in the Catholic Church concerning the finished work of Christ on the cross.

However, the tokens of bread and wine at the Lord's Supper, as with the sacrament of baptism, are not 'bare signs'. They are a solemn pledge of God's mercy and forgiveness offered to the sinner on the grounds of Christ's death. The believer is encouraged to 'relive' the personal application of the cross: Christ has died for *him*, and has suffered for *his* sins, that *he* might live. The personal receiving of the bread and wine emphasises this truth.

[35] See 1 Corinthians 11:20-34.

Secondly, the call is to *look in*, by allowing a time for self-examination before taking the tokens of Christ's death and of God's forgiveness. The necessity of this is stressed by Paul in forceful terms: 'Whoever, therefore, eats the bread or drinks the cup of the Lord in an unworthy manner will be guilty of profaning the body and blood of the Lord. Let a man examine himself, and so eat of the bread and drink of the cup. For any one who eats and drinks without discerning the body eats and drinks judgment upon himself. That is why many of you are weak and ill, and some have died.' Paul was referring to specific abuses of drunkenness and greed which were corrupting the Lord's Supper into an immoral orgy. As with the symbolic day of purification, we must have a time of 'spring-cleaning' in our own hearts, allowing the light of the Spirit of Christ to search for any trace of remaining sin, before we take part in the Lord's Supper. We cannot of course make ourselves clean; but we can confess and bring out into the open anything that we know is wrong, in order that God might forgive and cleanse. That is the significance of those words of Paul already quoted: 'Cleanse out the old leaven …as you really are unleavened. For Christ, our paschal lamb, has been sacrificed. Let us, therefore, celebrate the festival, not with the old leaven, the leaven of malice and evil, but with the unleavened bread of sincerity and truth.'

Thirdly, the call is to *look around*, by enjoying the fellowship of God's family assembled together for the meal. Our unity is expressed by taking part in the same meal, eating the same bread and drinking from the same cup: 'The cup of blessing which we bless, is it not a participation in the blood of Christ? The bread which we break, is it not a participation in the body of Christ? Because there is one bread, we who are many are one body, for we all partake of the one bread.'[36] Our fellowship, therefore, is first and foremost with the living Christ himself, who is present at that meal, but it is also with one another. It should be a love-feast, when we experience the love of God binding us together in Christ. It is very much a family meal.

Fourthly, the call is to *look forward*: 'For as often as you eat this bread and drink the cup, you proclaim the Lord's death

[36] 1 Corinthians 10:16f.

until he comes.' Jesus had said to his disciples: 'Truly, I say to you, I shall not drink again of the fruit of the vine until that day when I drink it new in the kingdom of God.'[37] With the assurance of Christ's living presence with his disciples now, the Christian community can rejoice that the reign of Christ has already begun. It can therefore look forward, full of confidence and hope, to the marriage feast of the Lamb. Once again, the links with the Passover Feast are instructive. We believe that the Messiah has come; but at the Lord's Supper we should still have this sense of anticipation, and be ready for his return in glory. The old Aramaic cry 'Marana-tha', meaning 'Our Lord, come',[38] is especially appropriate for this Christian celebration.

Over the years there have sadly been persistent and heated controversies over the words 'This is my body, this is my blood.' What is the significance of the copula 'is'? The fact is, Jesus almost certainly never used this word since it would be omitted in Aramaic, and Jesus spoke Aramaic. It would be more accurate to translate the words: 'This bread — my body; this cup — my blood.'

The Council of Trent (1545-63) declared that Christ is 'truly, really and substantially contained in the sacrament under the appearance of sensible things... By the consecration of the bread and wine a change is brought about of the whole substance of the bread into the body of Christ our Lord and of the whole substance of the wine into the body of his blood. This change...is called transubstantiation.' The metaphysical philosophy underlying this view was called 'realism', which distinguished the outward form of an object from its inward substance. For example, a table could be accurately described as a piece of wood supported by four legs, and the exact measurements, colour, and weight could be given. However, according to this philosophy, there was also a 'tableness' about it; and it was this inward and real substance that could change while the outward form remained the same. In this way the bread could become the body of Christ, and the wine become the blood of Christ.

However, the philosophy of 'nominalism' developed, which challenged this distinction between a substance and its

[37] Mark 14:25.   [38] 1 Corinthians 16:22.

'accidents' (outward form). William of Ockham (c. 1280-c. 1349) maintained the basic principle that 'what can be done with fewer assumptions is done in vain with more' (called 'Ockham's Razor', since it cut away the non-essentials in philosophy and metaphysics). From this, there was no justifiable reason for talking about the 'breadiness' of the bread together with its external form. By 1500 this view was widely accepted, and it paved the way for Luther and others to repudiate the doctrine of transubstantiation, and to look afresh at the true interpretation of the words 'This is my body, this is my blood.'

The key most probably lies in the use of the food and drink in the Passover ritual. As the 'bread of affliction' clearly *represented* the bread eaten at the time of the exodus and redemption of God's people from Egypt, so the bread taken by Jesus *represented* his body which was about to be broken for the redemption of God's people from sin. It is interesting that Luke refers to his impending death as his *exodus* 'which he was to accomplish at Jerusalem'.[39] In the same way, the wine, or cup, *represented* his blood which was about to be poured out in death, fulfilling the sacrifices for sin under the old covenant. Since Jesus was standing there in flesh and blood when he uttered those words, their interpretation would have been no more confusing to the disciples than my showing you a photograph and saying 'This is my wife'. It is unfortunate that the church has so often forgotten the original setting of the Lord's Supper, with Christ fulfilling the role of the paschal Lamb, and injected complex metaphysical concepts which there is no reason to suppose Christ ever intended.

In most recent Roman Catholic thinking there are significant changes in the interpretation of Christ's presence in the eucharist, although further clarification would be much desired. *The Agreed Statement on Eucharist* states that 'communion with Christ in the eucharist presupposes his true presence, effectually signified by the bread and wine which, in this mystery, become his body and blood.' It is these last five words which cause difficulty for some. There is a footnote here to stress that these words 'affirm the *fact* of Christ's presence and of the mysterious and radical change which

[39] Luke 9:31.

takes place. In contemporary Roman Catholic theology it is not understood as explaining *how* the change takes place.' The Statement further emphasises that 'Christ is present and active, in various ways, in the entire eucharistic celebration. It is the same Lord who through the proclaimed word invites his people to his table, who through his minister presides at that table, and who gives himself sacramentally in the body and blood of his paschal sacrifice.' Some of these phrases need to be examined carefully, but contemporary Roman Catholic theology has moved a long way from the rigid doctrine of transubstantiation of 1500. And at the same time evangelical and reformed theologians have perhaps a much richer and fuller grasp of sacramental theology than has been understood over the centuries. If there is not yet unanimity, the areas of agreement are considerably greater than could have been imagined possible only a few years ago.

The nature of Christ's presence in the sacrament has been a matter for fierce and often bitter theological debate from the time of the Reformation onwards. Without going into the complexities of this, and without naïvely presuming to solve the debate in a couple of sentences, the Passover may still yield some light on the subject. For although the meal was instituted as a memorial of the great Exodus, it was not a *bare* memorial. Those taking part in the feast not only looked back to the past, remembering what had happened; in some sense, as we have already seen, they relived the past and were caught up into God's redeeming action. Likewise, the Lord's Supper is more than the bare memorial that Zwingli taught. The believer not only remembers the once-for-all sacrifice of Jesus Christ for the sins of the world, represented by the bread and wine; in one sense he relives the events of the Upper Room and Calvary, and shares both in the redeeming work that was then accomplished and in the Redeemer himself, since he is clearly present at that fellowship meal. We really can 'feed on him in our hearts by faith with thanksgiving'.

Hans Küng summarises the central importance of this meal for the Christian church in this way:

So much is clear: the Lord's Supper is the centre of the Church and of its various acts of worship. Here the Church is truly itself, because it is wholly with its

Lord; here the Church of Christ is gathered for its most intimate fellowship, as sharers in a meal. In this fellowship they draw strength for their service in the world. Because this meal is a meal of recollection and thanksgiving, the Church is essentially a community which remembers and thanks. And because this meal is a meal of covenant and fellowship, the Church is essentially a community, which loves without ceasing. And because finally this meal is an anticipation of the eschatological meal, the Church is essentially a community which looks to the future with confidence. Essentially, therefore, the Church must be a meal-fellowship, a *koinonia* or *communio*; it must be a fellowship with Christ and with Christians, or it is not the Church of Christ. In the Lord's Supper it is stated with incomparable clarity that the Church is the ecclesia, the congregation, the community of God.'[40]

Further, it is when we really come together as the body of Christ, in love and fellowship with our Lord and with one another, that we can expect Christ to move with power among us. If we are truly committed to one another and are willing to lay down our lives for one another however painful this may be, the life of the risen Christ will be manifested among us.

It is quite often at this service that I have seen unbelievers brought to faith in Christ; others are convicted of sin and drawn back to the Saviour; others are healed. It is especially appropriate, in the context of this service, when God's people are gathered together around his table, to pray for the sick; and it is the normal practice in our own church to lay hands on those in any form of special need when they come to the communion rails to receive the bread and the wine. Always, I believe, God blesses them when they come to him in faith, and sometimes quite specific answers to prayer are given.

On the grounds of Christ's finished work on the cross, together with his resurrection, ascension and the gift of his Spirit, it is at this fellowship meal that he stretches out his hands to us, and says in his love: 'Come; for all is now ready.'

[40]Op. cit., p. 233.

CHAPTER FIFTEEN

Ministry and Leadership I

IT IS PROBABLY here, more than in any other area of the Church's life, that we need to look with fresh understanding and re-examine, critically and biblically, the traditional patterns that have been passed down to us over the centuries.

Fundamental questions are being asked today. What is ordination? Should women be ordained? Should the permanent diaconate be restored? What is the place of bishops? Are there any apostles, prophets or healers today? What about auxiliary ministry? Should there be a professional ministry at all? If so, how does this combine with the 'every-member ministry' of the early church?

No one can claim that the familiar picture of the parish priest, working faithfully but single-handed in, say, a parish of 20,000, comes anywhere near the rich concept of Christian ministry put forward in the New Testament. If some within the church are slow to see this, those outside the church are quick to expose the anachronism of much of the existing structure.

One writer put it like this: 'The Anglican priests of England, a motley band of underpaid and generally frustrated men, provide some of the most poignant casualties of the 20th century... They are like armless lifeguards trying to save the drowning. They become priests because they believe they can help people through God — and they find themselves trapped in an archaic structure. There is nothing wrong with their message, and very little wrong with them. Their methods of communication, though, are appalling.'[1] The

[1] *The Weekend Telegraph.*

reason this writer describes the ordained priesthood as 'armless lifeguards' is that in all too few churches is there any real idea of a shared ministry and a shared leadership.

Changing the analogy, the vicar or minister is usually the bottleneck, if not the cork, of his church: nothing can go in or out except through him. No meetings can take place unless he is the leader or chairman. No decisions can be made without his counsel and approval. I know of some parishes where the laity cannot meet even for Bible study or prayer unless the vicar is present.

We could illustrate many a local church like this:

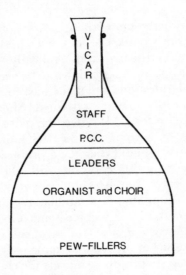

This bottle concept of the church makes growth and maturity virtually impossible. Members are unable to develop into the God-given ministry they could well experience because, in structure and in practice, there is room for only one minister. It is no doubt because of this that the fire of the Spirit has resulted in the bottle exploding into numerous house fellowships or house churches where there is room for growth and for the sharing of ministry. Unless there are new wine-skins for the new wine of the Spirit, some bursting out is almost inevitable.

At a time when there is a considerable shortage of clergy
and an even greater shortage of money with which to pay
them, there is an urgent need to look again at the principles
of the New Testament. Not that we shall find here a fixed
pattern for the church's ministry: we shall not. And of course
the numerous denominations today all turn to the New
Testament to support their particular emphases — not least
in the realm of ministry. However, a fresh and prayerful look
at the scriptural principles may help us to see the adjustments
that we must surely make at this present time.[2]

1. MINISTRY

Two basic principles stand out from the New Testament

A) *Ministry involves the whole body of Christ*

Speaking of the grace given to every Christian according to
the measure of Christ's gift, Paul wrote: 'And his gifts were
that some should be apostles, some prophets, some evangelists, some pastors and teachers, to equip the saints for the
work of ministry, for building up the body of Christ...'[3] It is
worth stressing that these gifts and ministries are *functions*, not
offices, within the church. They are spheres of ministry, not
status or rank. We shall return to this as it is one of the
commonest misconceptions about Christian ministry today.
Further when Paul says that the various gifts of Christ are 'to
equip the saints' for the work of ministry, the word 'equip'
means literally 'setting bones back into their proper place'
or 'putting something back into its correct position'. It
is also used of fishermen 'mending' their nets. In other
words, the body of Christ can work properly, or 'fish' successfully, only when all the saints are actively involved
in the work of ministry, and not just one or two paid professionals.

Part of the barrier that has no doubt obscured this need for
total involvement has arisen from the common use of words
like 'priest' and 'clergy'. It is worth looking at the meaning
and use of these two terms a little more closely.

[2]For an excellent and fuller study, see *Let My People Grow!* by
Michael Harper, Hodder & Stoughton, 1977.
[3]Ephesians 4:11f.

Definition of terms

The word *priest* today has a different connotation from its original meaning. The word itself comes from the Latin *presbyter* and from the Greek *presbuteros*, simply meaning 'elder' — although later it was used to describe the leader of a community. However, in its modern usage the term 'priest' seems to be derived more from the actual Greek word for priest, *hiereus*, with all its Old Testament connotations. Yet turning to the New Testament, *hiereus* is never used for someone who holds a distinct office in the church. Not once does it describe a class or caste of people separate from the laity of God. Instead, all God's people are 'a chosen race, a royal priesthood.'[4]

The writer to the Hebrews made it obviously clear that Christ, by fulfilling the priesthood of the Old Testament, also finished with it. 'He has no need, like those high priests, to offer sacrifices daily, first for his own sins and then for those of the people; he did this once for all when he offered up himself.'[5] He is now the eternal high priest in the heavens. All earthly and human priesthood has now once for all been fulfilled and finished by that unique, final and unrepeatable sacrifice of our great high priest who is 'a priest for ever... The former priests were many in number, because they were prevented by death from continuing in office; but he holds his priesthood permanently, because he continues for ever. Consequently he is able for all time to save those who draw near to God through him, since he always lives to make intercession for them.'[6]

The finished sacrifice of Christ means that no further sacrifice for sin is required or permitted today; the perfect priesthood of Christ means that there is therefore no need, and no room, for any priestly office within the church. There is now only one mediator between God and man.

The word *clergy* comes from the Latin *clerus* and from the Greek *kleros*, meaning 'lot' or 'inheritance'. Its link with the concept of ministry comes from Acts 1:17 and 26, when the

[4] 1 Peter 2:9.   [6] Hebrews 7:21-25.
[5] 7:27; cf. 9:24-28; 10:19.

apostles had to find a successor to Judas, 'for he was numbered among us, and was allotted his share (*ton kleron*) in this ministry... And they cast lots (*klerous*) for them, and the lot fell on Matthias.' In the time of Origen, in the third century, *kleros* had become an established term for those who held office in the church, as opposed to the rest of God's people. By the fourth century, the unbiblical and tragic distinction between priest and people was widely accepted.

Interestingly, the term 'layman' (*laikos*), which the Greeks used to refer to the uneducated masses, is not to be found anywhere in the New Testament. It does however occur in I Clement, at the end of the first century, where it applies to the 'simple faithful' in contrast to the educated priesthood of the Jews; and in the third century the term was commonly used in the context of the church.

Inevitably there developed a split between the 'clergy' (the educated religious leaders, such as monks) and the 'laity'. The 'clergy' soon became a distinguished class, marked by certain privileges, immunities, dress, titles, culture and liturgy (in Latin). They were the educated section of the church, who could read and write Latin. On the other side were the 'laity', both ignorant and uneducated (*idiotes*), who could not be expected to understand the finer points of the faith, and who must therefore be guided and directed by the 'clergy'. It is interesting to note that Boniface VIII, in a constitution of 31 July 1297, made this comment: 'The fact that the laity is hostile to the clergy is something which antiquity has handed on to us clearly enough.'

When rightly understood, *kleros* refers to the share in the inheritance of God which belongs to *all* those in Christ, and this is its essential New Testament meaning. Paul urges the Colossians to give 'thanks to the Father, who has qualified us to share (*tou klerou*) in the inheritance of the saints in light.'[7] Peter strongly rebuked Simon the sorcerer by telling him that he had 'neither part nor lot (*kleros*) in this matter.'[8] In other words, Simon had no share in God's gifts in Christ, since his heart was not right with God. Paul recounted that God had sent him to the Gentiles 'to open their eyes, that they may turn from darkness to light and from the power of Satan to

[7]Colossians 1:12.   [8]Acts 8:21.

God, that they may receive forgiveness of sins and a place
(*kleron*) among those who are sanctified by faith in me.'[9]
Kleros, then, does not refer to a special office in the church.

In the biblical sense, all Christians are priests and clergy,
and this is a crucial starting-point if we are to re-discover the
true concept of ministry and leadership within the church.
Through the gifts of God's Spirit, various ministries will
develop within a local church[10] which are in no way confined
to a paid, professional, theologically-trained and episcopally-
ordained ministry. The two-class system of priest and people,
clergy and laity, professional and amateur, has been disastrous in stifling the growth of the church and in quenching
the life of the Spirit. It is partly for this reason that the great
variety of spiritual gifts has been so little understood and
experienced by the body of Christ as a whole.

God's call is to all people alike

All priests are the people (*laos*) of God, and all the people are
priests of God, so that collectively we are 'a royal priesthood'.[11] A special class or caste is 'out'. Not only has the
middle wall of partition been broken down; *all* distinctions
have gone: 'there is neither Jew nor Greek, there is neither
slave nor free, there is neither male nor female; for you are all
one in Christ Jesus.' The church has been crippled by
clericalism for far too long, resulting in a largely passive and
theologically uneducated laity who leave it to the paid
professional to get on with his job. The New Testament
church would not have understood this attitude at all. All
together were the *laos* of God, 'a chosen race, a royal
priesthood, a holy nation, God's own people.' The work of the
church should be the work of the whole people of God.
Certainly there are different gifts, functions, and ministries
distributed by the Holy Spirit; but the glory of the church lies
partly in its unity in diversity. The different gifts, when
rightly used in love to build up the body of Christ, are
complementary and valuable; but they are God's gifts to his
people, without any hint of priestly distinction.

When we consider the special functions normally reserved

[9] Acts 26:18.

[10] Ephesians 4:11; 1 Corinthians
12:8-10, 28; Romans 12:6-8.

[11] 1 Peter 2:9.

for the ordained ministry, it is impossible to find any biblical authority for this. Is it only the priest who can *absolve sins?* James tells us to confess our sins to one another, and to pray for one another, that we may be healed. It is the prayer of a righteous man (regardless of ordination) that has great power in its effects.[12]

Is it only the priest who can *baptise?* In the New Testament it seems that almost any believer could baptise. Certainly it was not the prerogative of the apostles. Paul could not remember too clearly whom he had baptised, but it was only a few at Corinth: 'For Christ did not send me to baptise but to preach the gospel.'[13] In Acts 8, it was Philip who baptised believers in Samaria, even though this was the country which the Jews had viewed with such suspicion and hostility for centuries. In Acts 9, it was Ananias, that comparatively unknown disciple living at Damascus, who baptised the future leader of the Christian Church, Saul of Tarsus. In Acts 10, Peter commanded the first Gentile converts to be baptised; but Luke does not make it at all clear that Peter himself baptised them. Presumably who carried out the baptism was not the important matter (providing it was by someone acting in solidarity with the Christian community); the significant factor was that these Gentiles had been baptised in the name of Jesus Christ.

Again, is it only the priest who can *celebrate Holy Communion?* If, as most commentators think, 'breaking bread in their homes'[14] refers to a simple communion service, then undoubtedly this was something done by young converts. It was very much a 'lay celebration'. In these days when one ordained clergyman is in charge of several churches, do the faithful really have to wait for two or three weeks before they can remember Christ's death through the sacrament, and feed on him in their hearts by faith? Providing the necessity for church discipline is still remembered, what is the theological objection to any mature Christian, ordained or not, leading such a service? The work of the church is the work of the whole people of God.

It is interesting that in the Anglican/Roman Catholic

[12] James 5:16.   [14] Acts 2:46.
[13] 1 Corinthians 1:14-17.

Agreed Statement on Ministry the point is made that 'he who has oversight in the church...should preside at the celebration of the eucharist'; but the Statement says nothing of the necessity for an ordained priest to have this responsibility. Ignatius is quoted as saying that the man exercising this oversight in the church should preside and that no other could do so without his consent. But even this leaves open the possibility of a lay celebration if the need is there.

Today, when there is a known shortage of men and money for the 'ministry', it is vital to rediscover the biblical picture of the church that *all* the people of God are to be actively and purposefully involved in the work of ministry. Paul stressed that the special gifts that God has given to the church were 'to equip the saints for the work of ministry.'[15] When this is rightly understood and acted upon in local churches, there should be no shortage of money or manpower at all. Paul envisages the whole church working to build up the body of Christ, and pressing on to 'mature manhood, to the measure of the stature of the fullness of Christ.'[16]

This is particularly urgent in today's world, when enormous changes are taking place in terms of culture, technology, and communication, and these changes are accelerating all the time. Alvin Toffler commented that 'the acceleration of change has reached so rapid a pace that even bureaucracy can no longer keep up.' Therefore for the church to cling to outworn structures and patterns of ministry is to court disaster. 'Biblically it is clear that the Church *should* be structured charismatically, and any Church so structured is already largely prepared to withstand future shock. But churches which are encased in rigid, bureaucratic, institutional structures may soon find themselves trapped in culturally bound organisational forms which are fast becoming obsolete.'[17]

Reshaping structures

Although the Reformation was a time when the heart of the gospel was re-discovered and the glory of God's grace offered

---

[15] Ephesians 4:11f.
[16] Ephesians 4:12f.

[17] Howard A. Snyder, *New Wineskins,* Marshall, Morgan & Scott, p. 176.

freely to us in Christ shone with liberating beauty in the spiritual darkness of the medieval church, there was sadly a failure to come to grips with the doctrine of the church itself. It is true that the Reformers discussed at length what it was that constituted any true church of Jesus Christ; but their primary concern was that of personal salvation. How could a sinner be justified in the sight of a holy God? That was the great question. Practical considerations concerning the structure of the church did not seem to be relevant. As a result, most Protestant denominations have been just as 'priest-ridden' as the Roman Catholics! It is the vicar, the minister or the pastor who has usually dominated the whole proceedings. In other words, the clergy-laity divisions have continued in much the same way as in pre-Reformation times, and the doctrines of spiritual gifts and body-ministry have been largely ignored. Hendrick Hart writes: 'Even though the leaders of the Protestant Reformation sincerely intended to break with the traditional Roman Catholic conception of the church, nevertheless the tradition arising from the Reformation did not succeed in making that break.'[18]

One of the sociological tragedies resulting from this inability to grapple with the nature of the church is that the Reformed churches have largely been middle-class, constantly drawing from the educated section of society that has been content to listen passively to the preacher as he has expounded, often at considerable length and with no small degree of intellectual skill, the intricacies of Christian doctrine as drawn from the Scriptures. Niebuhr has commented: 'The failure of the Reformation to meet the religious needs of peasants and other disfranchised groups is a chapter writ large in history. With all its native religious fervour it remained the religion of the middle class and the nobility.'[19]

It is true that certain groups, such as the Anabaptists, tried to be more consistent in returning to the New Testament

---

[18]*Will All the King's Men...*, Toronto: Wedge Publishing Foundation, 1972, p. 30.

[19]*The Social Sources of Denominationalism*, p. 34.

picture of the church; but, for their challenge, they were persecuted almost to extinction, often at the hands of other Reformers. The Mennonites and Hutterites suffered in a similar way. The Wesleyan revival successfully reached the poorer section of society, and through the 'class-system' the whole concept of shared ministry and leadership came into focus. But this too was rejected by the established church. The Pentecostal revival, which has been the most remarkable Christian movement this century, has also flourished amongst the poor and uneducated, partly because every Christian is seen as a minister of Christ. There is maximum involvement for every member of the body of Christ. Yet, once again, this movement has been severely persecuted, especially in the early days, by the traditional churches.

Ministry means service
Status-seekers keep out! The primary word that the New Testament uses to describe ministry is *diakonia*, meaning 'service'. It is the word that is used for the ministry of Jesus, the Holy Spirit, Paul, Timothy and Epaphras. The other key word that is frequently used is *doulos*, meaning 'slave'. Michael Harper distinguishes the two like this:

> The word *diakonos* is a functional word, meaning a person who renders acts of service to other people, particularly waiting at table. When Jesus said 'I am among you as one who serves' (Luke 22:27), he is using this word. But the word *doulos* is a 'relationship' word. It means literally a 'slave', one who is owned by another person, with no rights or independent status whatsoever. Thus Paul could speak of himself and Timothy as the slaves of Christ (Phil. 1:1)...[20]

One of the greatest objections to the proliferation of ecclesiastical titles within the church is that they all express position, prestige and power — the concept of a ruling class. This is in striking contrast to the concept of ministry given by Jesus. It seems that Jesus and the writers of the New

[20]Op. cit., p. 75.

Testament deliberately avoided the existing variety of religious terms (such as priest, ruler, rabbi, master), which might denote a special and privileged class within the church marked by domination over others, and chose instead *diakonos* and *doulos*, thoroughly secular words for the menial tasks of a slave: washing the feet of the guests, waiting at table, serving food and pouring wine. The masters and guests would lie at the table in the long, expensive and colourful robes, whilst the servants, in simple clothes girded at the waist, had to wait upon them. How very different from the attitudes and dress of many clergy and priests of today! And how very different too from the attitude of Jesus who washed the feet of his own disciples — the most telling illustration of all as to the nature of Christian ministry.

The apostles learnt that great lesson of the Last Supper. At Corinth Paul puts the personalities of the various leaders very firmly in their rightful place: 'What then is Apollos? What is Paul? *Servants!*'[21] Here he uses the word *diakonos*; but in his second letter to the same church he uses *doulos*: 'What we preach is not ourselves, but Jesus Christ as Lord, with ourselves as your *servants* for Jesus' sake.'[22] When writing to the Philippians, he urges them to 'do nothing from selfishness or conceit, but in humility count others better than yourselves... Have this mind among yourselves which is yours in Christ Jesus, who...emptied himself, taking the form of a servant (*doulos*)''[23]

Michael Green has expressed it forcefully like this:

> If the Church as a whole has failed, the ministry has failed even more signally, to exhibit the character of the Servant... Does the vicar give the impression of being the servant of his people? Does he not rather behave, as too often the missionary has behaved, like a little tin god, loving to be recognised and looked up to, anxious that nothing shall go on in his parish without his personal supervision? Is it not an astonishing reversal of the pattern left by Jesus when a bishop, a chief pastor of the flock, is

[21] 1 Corinthians 3:5.
[22] 2 Corinthians 4:5.
[23] Philippians 2:3-5.

glad to be called 'My Lord'? One cannot but help feeling
that the whole gamut of ecclesiastical courtesy titles, 'the
Venerable', 'the Very Reverend', 'the Most Reverend' and
so on, are a hindrance rather than a help in the work of the
ministry. They tend to build an invisible wall between
their bearer and the world at large; much more important,
they tend to make him just a little proud, just a little
pleased with himself, just a little further removed than he
was before from the role of the Servant.'[24]

2. GIFTS

Dr. Coggan once asked, 'Why is it that the Pentecostal
Churches are growing at such a phenomenal rate? Is it
possible that they have the gifts of the Spirit which we have
not?'

Certainly some of them are expanding in a most amazing
way. One church in Korea started from nothing in 1961. By
1969 it had grown to 16,000, and by 1976 to 40,000. They
currently expect 10,000 converts each year. On the principle
of shared leadership and gifts, they have 80 full-time workers,
2,300 deacons, and about 1,500 small groups for study,
fellowship, training and prayer. These groups are growing
and dividing all the time. The main pastor is usually away for
six months in the year on preaching engagements, but the
church continues to flourish. There are no doubt a number of
local factors which help to explain this amazing growth —
but 'is it possible that they have the gifts of the Spirit which
we have not?'

We have already looked at the gifts of the Spirit in Chapter
7. What, then, is the relationship between gifts and ministries?

God in his sovereignty may bestow a gift to the body of
Christ through any member of that body. For example, any
Christian might be used by God to bring a gift of prophecy or
a gift of healing or a word of wisdom. However, when one
Christian is being often used by God to bring one particular
gift, say prophecy, he or she could rightly be said to have

[24]*Called to Serve*, Hodder & Stoughton, p 16.

(or to be developing) a prophetic ministry. As this matures
still further, the church will no doubt recognise this person as
a prophet within that fellowship.

The same could be said with evangelism, teaching, and
pastoral counselling. Paul, in fact, lists five spheres of
ministry, or five callings, which are Christ's gifts (*dorea*, not
charismata) to the church of God: apostles, prophets, evangelists, pastors and teachers. It seems clear from the New
Testament that these were never considered to be *offices* in the
church, but *functions* that enabled the whole body of Christ to
be equipped for the work of the ministry. Indeed, with the
sharing of ministry and leadership in a church we should
expect these different functions to develop as part of the
team-work in that church. In this way, leadership becomes
creative and complementary, not competitive.

In the Anglican/Roman Catholic *Agreed Statement on Ministry*, therefore, questions could well be raised about the
comment that 'The New Testament shows that ministerial
office [italics mine] played an essential part in the life of the
Church in the first century.' Is that really the case? When the
Statement goes on to say that the ministry of the ordained
priesthood 'is not an extension of the common Christian
priesthood but *belongs to another realm of the gifts of the Spirit*'
[italics mine], biblical issues certainly need to be pressed.

Paul writing to the Ephesians, nevertheless, does acknowledge Christ's gifts of the special spheres of ministry to equip
the whole body of Christ. It is worth looking briefly at these
five spheres of ministry in turn:[25]

Apostles. It is important to stress the uniqueness of
the first apostles. In a way that can never be repeated, they
were personally chosen by Christ and were eye-witnesses
of his resurrection. Apostolic teaching had the stamp of
the Spirit's authority in a way that was unique. There
are no successors to the apostles in that sense. There can
be no addition to the doctrinal teaching of the New Testament.

However, apostolic function, as a gift to the church, is

[25] For a fuller study of the five-fold ministry, see *Let My People Grow!*
by Michael Harper, Hodder & Stoughton, Chapter 3.

something different. The word *apostolos* simply means 'messenger' or 'emissary'. Therefore the apostles of today are those who travel as representatives or ambassadors of Christ for the purpose of establishing churches or encouraging Christians in their faith. Undoubtedly the church of today is enriched by those who travel widely, bringing new vision and fresh spiritual life, just as in the first century.

(b) *Prophets.* Once again, there is a foundational gift of prophecy which cannot be repeated or enlarged. The church is 'built upon the foundation of the apostles and prophets, Christ Jesus himself being the cornerstone'. Since the closing of the New Testament canon the church has always suffered when 'prophetic utterances' have been accepted with the same (if not greater) authority as Scripture itself, if contradicting Scripture. Most of the cults and sects have stemmed from the claims of false prophets who have added to or changed the given revelation of God through the Scriptures. This must be totally rejected.

    Nevertheless, the church still has a prophetic role, and there is a secondary sense in which prophecy can be very much part of God's gift in edifying the body of Christ. One of the most urgent needs of the church is to know what the Spirit of God is saying to his people *today*. There is therefore a 'particularity' about prophecy. It is a particular word inspired by God, given to a particular person or group of persons, at a particular moment, for a particular purpose. It is not the same as preaching or teaching, although there may often be some overlap; and effective preaching may at times be prophetic, at least in part. 'Prophecy is distinguished from teaching by its character of a direct message in relation to the situation...and by its reference to a particular divine revelation.'[26]

    A prophet must above all learn to listen to God, discern the voice of God, and then to pass on that word from God to his people. 'A prophet is not a scripture exegete. He knows the scriptures, but he does not teach from his knowledge of the Bible, which is the role of the teacher; he hears that which is particularly appropriate for the hour, and he faithfully passes

[26] *Vocabulary of the Bible*, ed. by J.-J. von Allmen, Lutterworth, p. 348.

on the message to the appropriate quarter, wherever and whoever that may be.'[27]

(c) *Evangelists.* Interestingly, the New Testament refers only to Philip as an evangelist,[28] although Paul also exhorts Timothy to 'do the work of an evangelist'.[29] The scarcity of references to the specialist calling of 'an evangelist' suggests that the whole church was deeply committed to the task of evangelism, with some members no doubt more gifted by God in this respect.

The modern pattern of full-time evangelists should perhaps be seen as a necessary second-best due to the failure of the church concerning its continuous and spontaneous evangelistic work. Moreover, this pattern has at least two unfortunate side-effects: many evangelists are not rooted in a local church situation, and therefore tend to lack the discipline, care and pastoral oversight that they themselves need; further, there can develop amongst many churches a wrong dependence on the specialist evangelist and on the highly concentrated evangelistic mission which can (if not handled carefully) militate against the continuous witness of that church to the surrounding community. Interestingly, as an evangelist, I see my task in missions to be partly, at least, aiming towards the renewal of the church.

We cannot escape the great commission of Christ. Next to worship, evangelism is the primary task of *every* Christian. We can no more 'leave it to the evangelist' than the laity can 'leave it to the clergy'. However, some members of local churches may have an unusual gift of evangelism, and therefore should make themselves available in some measure for the benefit of the wider church.

(d) *Pastors.* Paul urged the Ephesian elders to 'take heed...to all the flock...[and] to care for the church of God.'[30] As with every other gift or ministry, the model is Christ himself, the good shepherd who laid down his life for the sheep. As Jesus taught his disciples in John 10, the caring shepherd 'calls his own sheep by name and leads them out... He goes before

[27] Michael Harper, op. cit., p. 52.   [29] 2 Timothy 4:5.
[28] Acts 21:8.   [30] Acts 20:28.

them, and the sheep follow him, for they know his voice.'

More than ever, the church of today needs to become a caring community where much detailed attention must be given to the pastoral oversight of all within the fold of God's church. We shall look at this more carefully in the next chapter when considering the leadership in a church. But all too often the rebuke from God through the prophet Ezekiel is true: 'You do not feed the sheep. The weak you have not strengthened, the sick you have not healed, the crippled you have not bound up, the strayed you have not brought back, the lost you have not sought, and with force and harshness you have ruled them. So they were scattered, because there was no shepherd.'[31]

We can see from this what a demanding and all-embracing task true pastoral work involves: nurturing, training, encouraging, healing, strengthening, watching, praying, evangelising, leading. With such a stretching ministry it is almost impossible to be a true pastor for more than about a dozen families, perhaps twenty at the most. Therefore if the church is to grow, the number of pastors must increase. Was not this the lesson Moses had to learn when he set leaders over groupings of ten?[32] The apostles too found this essential with the rapid expansion of the church in Jerusalem. They found that the practical needs of some of the widows were being neglected. Since this pastoral care could not go by default, and since the apostles could not give up their primary task of prayer and preaching, they called in others to help with the shepherding. This is the pattern which must develop if the church is to grow.

(e)   *Teachers.* In Chapter eleven we have already stressed the crucial role that preaching and teaching have in the life of any church. It is through the proclaimed word of God that men and women are brought to Christ, faith is strengthened, and Christians are nourished and led into maturity. Group Bible study is also vital, and members of the body of Christ are called to 'teach and admonish one another'.

In addition, the special gift of 'teachers' for the church is of immense importance for the health of that body, as the Pastoral Epistles bear out. For example, 'let the elders who

[31] Ezekiel 34:3-5.   [32] Deuteronomy 1:15.

rule well be considered worthy of double honour, especially those who labour in preaching and teaching.'[33] Timothy, too, is given the most solemn charge 'in the presence of God and of Christ Jesus... [to] preach the word, be urgent in season and out of season, convince, rebuke, and exhort, be unfailing in patience and in teaching...'[34] The high priest complained angrily that the apostles had 'filled Jerusalem' with their teaching; and yet, in spite of beatings and further threats, 'they did not cease teaching and preaching Jesus as the Christ'.[35]

In general terms, the churches today that take this ministry seriously are the churches that are seeing both spiritual maturity and numerical growth. Other factors may be involved as well, but relevant and applied biblical teaching is an indispensable ingredient.

3. AUTHORITY

In almost every area of life the traditional concepts of authority are being challenged, and the church is no exception. Even the powerful authority of the Pope has been questioned since Vatican II, and there has been a 'struggle to re-distribute authority' amongst the Pope, bishops, theologians, priests and laity.

Some of the challenge to the church's authority is well justified. 'There has been a tendency in every age to assimilate the lifestyle of top people in the Church to that of top people in secular society. Senatorial, baronial, aristocratic and managerial patterns have all made their mark upon the office of a bishop.'[36] We need therefore to look at this whole question of authority from the Scriptures.

To begin with, a distinction between two kinds of authority needs to be made. The first is the authority of *official status*, which draws its strength from the institution or structure concerned. The second is the authority of *spiritual reality*, which should be self-evident and a prerequisite of the first.

[33] 1 Timothy 5:17.
[34] 2 Timothy 4:1f.
[35] Acts 5:42.

[36] *The Theology of Ordination*, a report from the General Synod of the Church of England, 1976, p. 13.

In today's climate, when there is an increasing disenchantment with established institutions and a growing hunger for
genuine reality, the second form of authority has considerable
appeal. Ideally there should be no clash between the two. The
church should give official recognition to those in whom the
Spirit of God is manifestly at work, while on the other hand
such people should be willing to submit into the existing
structures, partly as a corrective to the excessive individualism that has weakened so much of the church. It is not
enough to claim divine guidance for one's actions; submitting
to those who are over us in the Lord is a part of God's method
of guidance, as indicated in the Scriptures. Nor is it sufficient
to stand on one's dignity as bishop, priest, deacon or anyone
else; we shall only be 'lording it over' those in our charge
unless the wisdom and power of the Spirit is clearly with us.
In an unhealthy situation, legal authority may frustrate
spiritual authority, and so quench the Holy Spirit; or
spiritual authority may reject legal authority, and this, unless
manifestly right, will grieve the Holy Spirit.

In his commentary on the Anglican/Roman Catholic
Agreed Statement on Authority, Julian Charley makes this helpful
point:

> The authority of Jesus during his public ministry was not
> an assumed role. It stemmed from the reality of who he
> was. When he spoke, it was recognised to have the ring of
> truth and the authority of God. When he healed or
> performed miracles, it was recognised that this was the
> finger of God. When he prayed, it was clear that here was a
> uniquely intimate relationship with God... Yet his min-
> istry all along had been one of sacrificial service and
> humility. Now this should be the pattern of authority in
> the Church, but the underlying principle has far too often
> been forgotten.'[37]

Those, then, who are called to lead in God's church must
do so with a clearly recognised *spiritual* authority, and not
with one that derives purely from the *office* that they bear.
The coming of the Spirit enabled the apostles to preach with

[37]*Agreement on Authority*, Grove Booklet No. 48, 1977, p. 17.

great power. That authority was further manifested in the local churches that sprang up. The congregations were called to obey their leaders, and to be subject to one another out of reverence for Christ. They were to curb their impulsive instincts and learn to be members one of another, since God is not a God of confusion but of peace. Christ is Lord of the church, and it is his authority that has to be accepted and worked out within the congregation.

The apostles clearly were vested with a unique authority in the early church, and their ruling on faith and order was forthright. However, towards the close of the apostolic age, we see Paul urging Timothy and Titus also to take on the full responsiblities of spiritual leadership, and the elders who ruled well were to be considered worthy of double honour. As the church of the second and third centuries decreased in spiritual power, so did its spiritual authority. And in its place institutional and legal authority grew in strength. Since then every fresh surge of spiritual life has however challenged the institutional structures and brought the church back to the power of the gospel. Like our Master, we are to speak what we know, and bear witness to what we have seen.

The emergence and acceptance of spiritual leadership within the New Testament followed a clear and logical sequence. Paul insisted that a man should not be set aside for leadership if he was a recent convert or if his qualifications (moral and spiritual, primarily) were inadequate. The man must first prove himself in the congregation where he is known.

Today there may be practical difficulties in the case of a student who is living and working mostly away from his home situation, but the principle of the local church recognising the gifts and ministries that God is giving to someone is a very important one. The danger has always been that the office and institution of the church stifle the freedom and inspiration of the Spirit. No man has a true spiritual ministry by virtue of his office in the church. He is entirely dependent on the *charisma* of the Spirit.

Michael Harper rightly observes:

The Church can only authorise those whom God has authorised, and can only recognise those whom God has gifted and empowered. No amount of theological training or human pressure can bestow *charisma* on a person. It is the sole gift of God, who gives it sovereignly to whom he wills, and when he wills... The Church is utterly dependent on the Holy Spirit, and without *charisma*, however learned ministers may be, however dedicated and however many of the right hands have been laid on them, their work will be a failure. Much of the Church has yet to learn what this means, and its failure to honour the Holy Spirit is one of the main reasons why it has ceased to grow. The charismatic dimension is a crucial factor in the renewal of the ministry of the Church today.[1]

One of the great advantages of recognising and encouraging the gifts given by God is that a shared ministry will inevitably emerge. It is ludicrous to expect one clergyman or ordained minister to keep four or five country churches spiritually alive, or to make any real impact on a parish of 20,000. Theologically, what is there to prevent a competent layman from conducting baptisms or from presiding at the eucharist? If many are given authority to preach (a much more demanding task) why not conduct a liturgical service in the prescribed manner? Might not many laymen and laywomen be far better at certain kinds of pastoral visiting than the ordained professional? Is it necessary to look for all the gifts in one man? Does this not stifle the immense potential that surely exists within the whole people of God? Further, is the only practical solution to the shortage of clergy and funds the setting up of team ministries or auxiliary ministries? Does this not still perpetuate the unbiblical division between clergy and laity?

Today, the challenge to the church to develop along biblical lines, especially in the pattern of ministry, is of the utmost importance.

4. TRAINING

One humbling truth that we must accept is that the Spirit of God has always used those who are open to him, regardless of certain qualifications.

[38]Op. cit., p. 100.

The missionaries of the Sudan Interior Mission had to leave Ethiopia during the Second World War, and 'only a handful of converts' remained in that country. When the missionaries returned, they found 25,000 new Christians.

The church in Madagascar has a similar story a century before. After the founding of the first churches, the missionaries were expelled in 1845 for twenty-five years. On their return they found that the church had grown tenfold. They set about erecting hundreds of schools, churches, and a theological college. But the expansion of the church has never equalled the time when the missionaries were not there!

The church in China today, by all accounts, is growing spiritually and numerically, in spite of the absence of the professional and trained missionary. For instance, there is a city in South China, with a population of 400,000, where (from carefully checked reports) there are now some 50,000 believers. How many cities in Western Europe can boast of one in every eight being committed to Christ? Admittedly the China Inland Mission had a strong work in that particular city in South China, but that was twenty-five years ago; and during this period, of course, no missionaries have been able to go there. It seems that through radio broadcasts believers have been writing down the Scriptures at dictation speed, and then making copies for others to read. It takes twenty-eight broadcasts for the whole of Matthew's Gospel to be dictated!

In Cambodia, too, we hear of similar encouragements. In 1970, after a time of severe oppression and persecution, there were reported to have been only 700 professing Christians in that country. In 1975, however, it appears that there were some 5,000 to 6,000 who were following Christ.

Such reports have a distinct New Testament flavour, with the church rapidly expanding without any academically trained leadership. In the light of these facts, is the church of today, in nearly all denominations, laying too much emphasis on certain intellectual qualifications when the apostles were much more concerned to find men full of faith and of the Holy Spirit? Most of Jesus' own disciples would have failed dismally according to required standards of today.

Certainly the best available theological education and a clear grasp of the intellectual questions which hinder faith in Christ are necessary to reach a small, sophisticated minority in our present society. But what about the vast majority of ordinary people who are untouched or unimpressed by the church? For them, the vital and convincing factors are spiritual reality, a ringing note of conviction, meaningful and relevant communication, and a visible expression of the gospel in the church. These convey the truth about Christ far more than any closely-reasoned apologetics of the Christian faith.

Moreover, it is tragic to see how uncertain many men are, at the time of their ordination, concerning their personal relationship with Christ and the truth of the gospel. In some circles it is considered a virtue and a mark of humility not to be too sure about anything. The New Testament, in contrast, throbs with the note of assurance. Here were men and women modest about themselves, but in no sense modest about the facts of the gospel. We find great stress on holding fast apostolic teaching, on preaching the word with authority, on convincing those who doubt.

Indeed, the only 'technical' qualification for Christian leadership in the Pastoral Epistles, apart from moral integrity, is 'apt to teach'. In many theological colleges this is largely ignored, and hardly any training in this direction is offered to readers and local preachers. A man may be hopeless as a preacher; he may be useless in personal counselling; he may have little idea about evangelism, and be quite out of touch with unbelievers; he may be opposed to lay training, and even discourage the development of gifts and ministries within his own congregation; but he can still be ordained. So often his theological courses seem to be preoccupied with biblical criticism and liturgical instruction, but how many parishioners have the slightest interest in the literary composition of the Penteteuch?

Academic theology certainly has a vital role to play. I am only too thankful for those who have been theologically equipped to look again at the relations between the Anglican, Roman and Eastern Orthodox Churches. It is their clear and objective grasp of complex theological issues that has led to a new, sympathetic and constructive understanding between these churches in recent years. Others with more limited knowledge might well have clung fiercely to prejudiced positions, instead of realising that *some* of our differences are simply a question of semantics — a misunderstanding of the doctrinal content in the words and phrases that we traditionally use.

Further, a careful study of the original texts, a good knowledge of the cultural and religious background of many words and phrases, and some understanding (at least) of biblical history and the history of the church throughout the centuries will all help towards a more accurate interpretation and application of the word of God.

Most of us naturally cling to what we know, and are nervous of exploring, with an open mind, areas that are much less familiar. Therefore a theological course which makes us read and study outside our present field of knowledge can be extremely enriching. The caricature of the church is all too often that of clergymen pontificating on matters of which they are largely ignorant, and an uneducated and ill-informed leadership does no credit to the church in the eyes of the world. Even in the first-century church, the apostle Paul became such a powerful leader partly because he really knew what he was talking about. His academic training was surely of considerable value both to him and to the rest of the church ever since, and it was no doubt as a result of his training that he was able to apply himself so thoroughly to a fresh study of the Scriptures. Together with the specific revelation given to him by God, he was able to testify, from the Scriptures, to the truths about the kingdom of God and the facts about Jesus. We should in no way despise nor belittle the value of careful and painstaking theological study.

But such an academic approach is by no means necessary in every case for a powerful and effective ministry. Over the years I have met hundreds of men and women who have had no formal theological training at all, but who, through the prayerful study of the Scriptures have a profound grasp of many spiritual issues. They have learnt to apply these truths to their lives and relationships, and they have been given by God an increasingly fruitful ministry. I am certain that some of these Christian workers might well have become *less* effective had they undertaken an academic course of study.

Is there any good reason for removing all who might be used by God in ministry for three years from their local church setting, filling their minds with theology (much of which they may never need to use in daily work), and then sending them to serve their apprenticeship in an area they probably know nothing about? In the early church the leaders were nearly always appointed from the area in which they served. They had the advantage of knowing the local scene intimately, and were therefore naturally placed for fulfilling an effective pastoral and preaching ministry according to the gifts given to them by God. When the professional ordained minister moves around as frequently as he does in most churches, it is hardly surprising that it is extremely difficult to build up the strong and mature relationships that are necessary for the body of Christ to function properly.

Whether or not there has been any formal theological education, the value of 'in-service' training cannot be over-emphasised. With the growing wealth of books, study schemes and training courses available, this should not be too difficult in many countries, although further help could well be given by those with a recognised teaching gift in each area. There are plenty of tape and cassette libraries available, too; and many Christian workers in different and often lonely parts of the world have benefited enormously in this way from more experienced teachers whose ministry has been proved by a wider cross-section of the church.

If the God-given gifts and ministries are to develop for the benefit of the whole church, the fresh stimulation from continuous study, coupled with an ever-ready willingness to learn, is vital. We are all disciples, or learners, to the end of our days. Even the apostle Paul, towards the close of his astonishing ministry, knew that he had not arrived, and was far from perfect. Not only morally and spiritually was he still pressing on to know Christ more and more, his agile mind could by no means fully plumb 'the depth of the riches of the wisdom and knowledge of God!' To dig ever deeper into the unsearchable riches of Christ should be one of the constant joys of the Christian faith.

CHAPTER SIXTEEN

Ministry and Leadership II

ALTHOUGH THE NEW Testament is recording a pioneer missionary situation, so that the patterns of leadership were still emerging, the principles are significantly the ones which make most sense in the church of today.

The stages of development in the early church were fairly obvious. Firstly, *disciples* were made, often resulting from some apostolic ministry. The church at Antioch, for example, started when 'a great number that believed turned to the Lord', and for a whole year Barnabas and Saul 'met with the church, and taught a large company of people; and in Antioch the disciples were for the first time called Christians' (Acts 11:19-26). As these disciples went on with Christ, *gifts and ministries* developed through the Holy Spirit, and Acts 13 opens with a comment about the prophets and teachers in the church at Antioch.

Then, in Acts 14, when Paul and Barnabas returned to Antioch, they 'appointed *elders* for them in every church, with prayer and fasting, [and] committed them to the Lord in whom they believed.' Here we see the necessity for shared leadership even for the youngest and smallest of churches. The church is not a democracy with equal votes for every member on all decisions. The clear principle of headship is true both for the human family and for the family of God, the church. And if the picture of the New Testament church is that of a charismatic community, we must remember that one of God's gifts to the church is the *charisma* of leadership.

It is important to distinguish between the principles that

hold good for the church's leadership in every generation and the details that happened to exist in a certain local church in the first generation. What patterns of leadership are *exemplary* and what are *mandatory?*

For instance, the New Testament terms for elder (*presbuteros*), bishop (*episkopos*) and shepherd (*poimen*) appear to be synonymous,[1] with the result that some would want to see in this fact a rigid blueprint for the church in all ages and thus reject any form of episcopacy as we know it today. The precise nature and function of modern-day episcopacy might need some fresh examination, but clearly the need for trans-church leadership became urgent for the unity of the universal church in the post-apostolic period. Therefore the cry to 'get back to the New Testament church' could lead to the rigid imposition of certain structures which related to the history and culture of the day, but which could be irrelevant for an entirely different setting in the latter part of the twentieth century, not to mention the wide variety of cultures that exist today in different parts of the world.

Andrew Kirk has helpfully suggested six principles of Christian ministry that would appear to be mandatory.[2]

1.   No distinction either in form, language or theory between clergy and laity was ever accepted by the New Testament Church.

2.   The ministry is co-extensive with the entire church (1 Cor. 12:7).

3.   The local church in the apostolic age always functioned under a plurality of leadership.

4.   There are no uniform models for ministry in the New Testament; the patterns are flexible and versatile.

5.   In the New Testament church can be found both leadership and authority, but no kind of hierarchical structure.

6.   There is one, and only one, valid distinction which the New Testament appears to recognise within the ministry, apart from the different functions to which we have been alluding: the distinction between *local* and *itinerant* ministries.

It may be helpful to look at some of the terms used for leadership in the first century church.

[1] See Acts 20:28; 1 Peter 5:1f; Titus 1:5, 7.

[2] Quoted in *Let My People Grow!*, p. 164.

1. ELDERS

Elders are almost always mentioned in the plural in each local church. The only exceptions are the two references to the functions and qualifications of a bishop (= elder),[3] but neither of these imply the existence of a singular leader in a church. John also twice describes himself as 'the elder',[4] but this probably refers to his age and position in the New Testament church towards the end of the first century. Paul does the same, probably for similar reasons, in his letter to Philemon (verse 9). Otherwise we always find that elders, in the plural, were appointed in every church.

Although there might well have been a presiding elder, there is never the slightest hint of a solitary leader (such as *the* vicar, *the* minister, *the* pastor), even in the smallest and youngest churches.[5] Always it was a shared responsibility, thereby giving much mutual encouragement, protection and support. 'If the pastors are not submissive to one another how can they have people submissive under them? The pastor might rebuke his disciples when they are wrong, but who rebukes him when he is wrong?'[6] In practice, it is much better sharing the pastoral load, which can bear very heavily on one man; it is much healthier learning to submit to one another out of reverence for Christ; it is much safer seeking together to know the mind of Christ. It was while the prophets and teachers at Antioch were together worshipping the Lord and fasting that the Lord gave them instructions about the next forward move of the church. 'Where two or three are gathered in my name, there I am in the midst of them,' said Jesus; and the context of that statement concerns the discipline of the church. Nowhere is there any suggestion of a one-man ministry or leadership, except perhaps in the sad and telling comment about Diotrephes, 'who likes to put himself first.'[7] The first hint of monarchical episcopacy was not a happy one!

Turning to the early church fathers, we see that the same

---

[3] 1 Timothy 3:2; Titus 1:7.
[4] 2 John 1; 3 John 1.
[5] See Acts 14:23; Philippians 1:1; 1 Thessalonians 5:12; Hebrews 13:7, 17,24; James 5:14; 1 Peter 5:1.
[6] See Ortiz, *Call to Discipleship*, Word, p. 100.
[7] 3 John 9.

pattern continued, at least until the unfortunate distinction between priest and people developed. The *Didache* (written probably at the end of the first century) exhorts each Christian community to have a proper ministry: 'Appoint for yourselves therefore bishops and deacons worthy of the Lord, men who are meek and not lovers of money, and true and approved; for unto you they also perform the service of the prophets and teachers. Therefore despise them not; for they are your honourable men along with the prophets and teachers.'

The principle of shared leadership is axiomatic.

This is not to say that the creative contribution of a gifted leader will not be of a key importance to the growth of a church; nor that a theologically equipped leader and teacher will not play a big part in the maturing of a church; nor that in our society a church may not function much more efficiently if it has a full-time stipendiary executive officer; nor even (for the sake of argument) that the presidency at the eucharist may not be located at least normally in one particular person. It is rather to say that we should not look for all those functions to be fulfilled by the same person, but rather that there should be a genuinely corporate leadership of the local church exercised by its elders. There is no place for the traditional concept of the clergyman. There is no theology of ordination. The emperor has no clothes![8]

If some find this de-bunking of traditional ordination too extreme, the sharing of leadership and ministry should still be a matter of foremost concern in the biblical re-structuring of today's church.

The role of an elder is a demanding and challenging one: he is to lead, to teach, to work hard, to set an example, to tend the flock of God, to encourage, to pray for the sick, to have authority over others and to exercise discipline, to evangelise and to be well thought of by outsiders.[9]

[8] John Goldingay, *Authority and Ministry*, Grove Booklet, p. 24.
[9] Acts 20:18ff; 1 Thessalonians 5:12-14; 1 Timothy 3:1-7; 5:17; Titus 1:9-11; Hebrews 13:7; James 5:14-16; 1 Peter 5:1-3.

This, of course, is the picture of the complete elder, and not every elder would be expected equally to fulfil all these functions, although a group of elders together would approximate more to this ideal. Nevertheless the personal standard required by an elder is a very high one in the pastoral epistles: personal holiness, generous hospitality, aptitude for teaching, discipline at home, spiritual maturity, gentleness, and a good reputation in the community.

It is a sad departure from the New Testament picture that the unique functions of the ordained ministry in today's church, at least in Roman Catholic and Anglican circles, are conducting services and presiding at Holy Communion, pronouncing absolution, and baptising infants and adults. In the meetings for worship in the early church everyone had (or certainly could have) a contribution.[10] The Lord's Supper seemed normally a 'lay celebration'.[11] When Paul had to correct disorders in the Corinthian church he wrote to the whole congregation, not specifically to the leaders. Even in that confused situation he did not suggest that the leadership should take over the conduct of the services.

With regards to confession and absolution, James instructs the Christians to confess their faults to one another, and to pray for one another.[12] There is never a hint of any 'priestly' function for this, since all Christians are priests in the New Testament era. Baptism, too, as we have seen in an earlier chapter, seems not to have been the prerogative of the leaders of the church, although clearly church discipline in all these matters was and is important.

There is one further consequence of a shared leadership: why should the presiding elder (vicar or minister) of a local church be expected to move every 3, 5 or even 10 years to another (better?) living? Together with the other leaders in that church, he is called to be a spiritual father to the family of God in that place. What human family benefits if the father moves on to another family when he feels it is time for a change? In an age when the rapid mobility of families is one of the major factors in the breakdown of community life, it is perhaps even more important that the leadership of local

[10] 1 Corinthians 14:26.   [12] James 5:16.
[11] Acts 2:46.

churches should be willing to stay for at least some considerable time. Some stability is urgently needed if the church is
ever to become, in any real sense, the community of God that
is so desperately needed in today's unstable world.

2. DEACONS

These were regarded as a supportive ministry to the eldership
of a church. Some have traced their origin to Acts 6 when,
with the rapid growth of the church in Jerusalem, the twelve
apostles found that they could not preach the word of God
and 'serve tables' at the same time. Both were valid and
important aspects of service; but since the apostles knew that
their foremost priority must be prayer and 'the ministry of
the word', it was vital that others should take on the more
practical ministry that was necessary for the widows. The
qualifications of the seven appointed were spiritually of a
high level: they had to be 'men of good repute, full of the
Spirit and of wisdom.' Further, they were not restricted to the
purely practical jobs in the church. Stephen, 'full of grace
and power, did great wonders and signs among the people',
and Philip became well-known for his evangelistic gifts.

Whether or not the deacons stem from the Acts 6 situation,
it seems that they were largely responsible for the administrative, financial and business side of the church. Their qualifications, from the Pastoral Epistles, were mainly personal
holiness and family discipline.[13] Women, too, could almost
certainly fulfil this role,[14] whereas it seems that the elders
were all men. We shall look at this more carefully later in this
chapter.

3. BISHOPS

During the period AD 70-150 it is noticeable that the terms
'bishop' and 'elder' ceased to be interchangeable. Instead,
there was only one bishop for each Christian community, and
the beginnings of a professional ministry became apparent.
Ignatius of Antioch (writing between AD 98 and 117) in
particular made a clear distinction between the bishop and

[13] 1 Timothy 3:8-13.   [14] 1 Timothy 3:11; Romans
16:1-2.

presbyters (or elders), with only one bishop to each church. He further separated the ministers and laity in a way that is not to be found in the New Testament, apart from the recognition of leaders within each church. He referred to '*one* eucharist, *one* body of the Lord, *one* cup, *one* altar, and therefore *one* bishop together with the presbyterium and the deacons, my fellow servants' (*Philad.* 4:1). Here is the earliest reference to a three-tiered hierarchy within the church. The split between clergy and laity had begun.

Certainly in New Testament days there were some, namely apostles, prophets, evangelists and teachers, who travelled widely, setting up churches, encouraging Christians, teaching the faith, correcting abuses; and it was through their work that the unity and catholicity of the early church was maintained, in spite of considerable diversity of emphasis. This was also clearly one of the functions of the emerging bishops, who were called to shepherd a number of churches in a given area.

The value of present-day episcopacy along such lines cannot be denied; and it is interesting to note that virtually every other denomination, including the present-day house-church movement, has discovered the necessity of developing some structure that is remarkably similar to the basic concept of episcopacy.

What is important is that bishops should be spared the enormous administrative and committee work that so often enslaves them, in order to concentrate on the leadership and pastoral work that should be their prime function. The role of *pastor pastorum* is of the utmost importance within the church.

This is what the Anglican/Roman Catholic *Agreed Statement on Ministry* so interestingly stresses: 'An essential element in the ordained ministry is its responsibility for "oversight" (*episcope*).' However, the Statement does not say the same about bishops (*episcopoi*). Whereas the *function* seems once again a vital ingredient of a healthy and united church, the *office* — particularly an office stemming from a direct pipe-line transmission of ministerial authority from the apostles through a line of bishops (a theory which cannot be substantiated) — is not cited as being essential to the church. This is a healthy trend, apparently leaving the door open for the recognition of other ministries which have not come through these ecclesiastical channels but which seem clearly to have been called by God.

In practical terms for any bishop to fulfil his much-needed pastoral oversight in any satisfactory way, areas of responsibility would need to be much smaller in most cases, and careful thought should be given to the sustaining and developing of the bishop's own spiritual life. There is a real danger that the bishop of today could be a figurehead of the 'establishment', whose task seems to be to uphold the *status quo*. He is isolated from any local body of Christ and is therefore deprived of the continuous worship and ministry of such a body. He is expected to be 'all things to all men' to such an extent that it is difficult for him to take a clear lead with some of the spiritual issues of the day. The pressure is on him to 'sit on the fence' in a cautious and guarded manner. His commission to 'hold up the weak, heal the sick, bind up the broken, bring again the outcasts, seek the lost' can all too easily be buried underneath a welter of ecclesiastical machinery. Of course, there are some outstanding exceptions to this, but the immense demands made of bishops today make it almost impossible for them to fulfil the vital role that they still have within the church without an intolerable strain on their physical health or spiritual vitality.

4. THE MINISTRY OF WOMEN[15]

It would be honest and important to say from the start of this section that, even during the writing of this book, I have been re-thinking my whole position towards the ministry of women. I can only write what at this stage I personally believe to be true, although (as on other issues) I trust I am open to correction and to fresh illumination by the Spirit of truth.

It is partly because of the present 'revolution' in my own thinking that, again at the time of writing, the church I serve in York does not yet reflect some of the ideas I suggest; and it is also fair to say that another reason for this is that our

[15]For the best and most balanced view on this subject that I have read, see Michael Harper, *Let My People Grow!*, Hodder & Stoughton, Chapter 8.

present eldership is still looking carefully into this whole question.

I have always held, as a basic principle in the development of our church, that we should be 'eager to maintain the unity of the Spirit in the bond of peace'; and to force my own position on to the congregation when the leaders are not yet agreed would be disastrous. 'The Lord reigns'; and his sovereign timing in all such matters is an extremely important factor in the growth or renewal of any church.

Though the institutional church has not always followed suit, the attitude and teaching of Jesus, together with the practice of the early church, brought immense liberation to women. No other major religion in the world gives such dignity to women as the Christian faith.

When we look at the New Testament, in spite of the oft-quoted Pauline strictures about the role of women, written as a corrective to certain abuses (it is always a mistake to take a corrective and use it as a normative), there is no question about the vital place that many women occupied in terms of Christian ministry. There were not a few women who ministered to the needs of Jesus himself, especially Mary and Martha, and also Mary Magdalene. We later find women working alongside men as fellow-labourers in the gospel. Women, as well as men, could pray and prophesy in a church assembly. Moreover, Phoebe, Priscilla, Euodia and Syntyche, not to mention the four daughters of Philip who prophesied, clearly exercised important spiritual ministry in the early church.

From the account of creation onwards, the Bible makes it clear that men and women have complementary roles. 'In the Lord woman is not independent of man nor man of woman.'[16] They are different, not only biologically (virtually the only difference that many in modern society are prepared to admit), but also emotionally and temperamentally. However in no sense can either sex claim to be better than the other. They are simply different. Although it is true that man is the head of a woman, there is no thought of superiority and inferiority in this headship. Paul explains that 'the head of every man is Christ..., and the head of Christ is God.'[17] Just

[16] 1 Corinthians 11:11.   [17] 1 Corinthians 11:3.

as the Persons of the Godhead are equal but distinct, so with man and woman. 'All are one in Christ Jesus.' We should therefore learn to work together and share together, bringing to each other the mutually complementary gifts that will help to edify the whole body of Christ.

There is no question, then, about the *ministry* of women in the church. There are many invaluable spiritual gifts and ministries that God undoubtedly gives to women, making them indispensable to the healthy working of the body of Christ. The church that restricts women to cleaning and cooking greatly impoverishes its own spiritual life, and will often lack the warmth and love that women especially can contribute. General Booth used to say that all his best men were women! His own daughter was a most outstanding evangelist, whose gifts of preaching were beyond question.

If this biblical truth about the complementary role of women within the church could be clearly grasped by men as well as women, it would save some women from the feeling that they must 'compete' with men and fight to be 'equal' with men. In God's eyes we are all equal. Even though men and women may have different functions, we are all mutually interdependent.

What is meant, then, by the headship of a man over a woman; and in what sense should a woman submit to a man?
Paul writes that 'the husband is the head of the wife as Christ is the head of the church... As the church is subject to Christ, so let wives also be subject in everything to their husbands.'[18] Although Paul makes it clear in this passage that marriage is a partnership that should be marked by a deep and sacrificial love, the ultimate responsibility and final authority in decision-making should rest with the man. This authority is given to him not for dominating his wife, nor for restricting her from exercising her gifts within the family; rather just the reverse.

Paul goes on to say, 'Husbands, love your wives, as Christ loved the church and gave himself up for her...' This headship, therefore, is for protection and support. The man gives his wife the authority to act within the family (caring

[18]Ephesians 5:23f.

for the children, handling the household money, etc.), while taking the ultimate responsibility away from her shoulders and onto his. She is in this way set free to get on with her work, knowing that she has the support of her husband since he has given her authority so to act.

It means also that she can turn to someone for counsel and advice, and in practice the two of them will discuss most affairs of the house and family together. Most of the decisions will be (or should be) joint decisions; but when uncertainties or differences of opinion exist, the man should have the final say, whether or not he seems to be right in his decision. If both were to exercise equal authority in the home, inevitable tensions would arise; and this, of course, is one reason for many breakdowns in marriage.

This biblical order within Christian marriage is also true within the Christian church. Again, the headship should ideally rest with the man; but when this is rightly understood and exercised, this simply gives the woman the protection or covering that she needs in the ministry that God has given her, whatever that ministry might be. She is thereby given authority to act by the male leadership of the church, and in this way her ministry should be received by the rest of the church.

When a woman's husband is not a leader of the church, her first responsibility is to submit to her husband. Relationships understandably become tense when a woman accepts the headship of a leader of the church before the headship of her own husband; and sometimes this can be used to give a 'spiritual' justification for her own independence within the home.

When a woman is single, divorced or widowed, it is good for her to come under the headship and protection of a man, who may be one of the leaders in the church. In many instances, it may be wise for this leader to exercise a joint headship with his wife over the woman in question, so that she has the covering of a married couple. In many practical matters as well as spiritual counsel, it is the older women who are to train the younger women, 'that the word of God may not be discredited.'[19] Nevertheless, it is the mature male

[19]Titus 2:3-5.

leaders of the church who must exercise their ultimate
headship over the family of God in that church.

Although all those in Christ are part of God's new creation,
the distinctions of the old creative order are not abolished
until the 'new heavens and new earth' are revealed. In heaven
for example there is no marriage. But here on earth, although
the brother-sister relationship is a most important one to be
understood and developed within the family of God, the extra
relationship of marriage must still be carefully observed. The
old creative order is not a thing of the past.

In New Testament times, the woman's cultural and
outward signs of this order were her long hair (her 'pride')
and the veil that she would always wear on her head in
public. No respectable woman would think of appearing
without her veil, for if she did she was liable to be misjudged.
She might just as well go around with her head 'shorn or
shaven' — something 'disgraceful'. To be a member of
Christ's new created order did not mean flouting the cultural
symbols of that day and age.

William Ramsay once expressed it like this: 'In Oriental
lands the veil is the power and honour and dignity of the
woman. With the veil on her head she can go anywhere in
security and profound respect... But without the veil the
woman is a thing of nought, whom anyone may insult... A
woman's authority and dignity vanish along with the all-
covering veil that she discards.' A woman without a veil,
therefore, was a common mark of a prostitute. She was
literally a 'loose' woman, since she was not under the
authority of her husband.

Now it may have been that, because Jesus loved and
welcomed everyone including harlots into the kingdom of
God, some women felt such cultural symbols were no longer
important. However, for a woman to pray or prophesy in
public without a veil or with short hair, not least in a
notoriously immoral city like Corinth, was clearly open to
abuse and could quickly become a cause for scandal. Paul
therefore instructed the Christian woman 'to have a veil on
her head, because of the angels'.[20]

Opinions differ as to the right interpretation of this verse. It

[20] 1 Corinthians 11:10.

may be that Paul was reminding them that the good angels were always present, observing the conduct of Christian assemblies; and therefore nothing unseemly must happen in their presence. Or it may be a warning about evil angels. Elsewhere in Scripture the word 'angel' can be used for an evil messenger.[21] If that is what Paul meant, he seems to be saying that if a woman is not in submission to a man (her husband or the leader of the church — the submission symbolised by the veil), she becomes a target of the enemy; she is not in the God-given place of protection and safety.

The essential point in the passage is this matter of order, and not the external veil. In fact the word 'veil' is not in the original Greek at all; the word is *exousia*, meaning authority. The verse therefore reads: 'That is why a woman ought to have an authority on her head (i.e. come under someone else's authority), because of the angels.' In some countries there will be other external symbols that indicate the culturally accep-table order of men and women in that society, and these should not be disregarded.

It is pressing the words out of their original meaning, however, to insist on long hair and some form of head covering for women in most western lands where such a head covering is no longer of any significance at all.

In those societies where the role of men and women have changed considerably — without any sense of disorder, immodesty or indecency — it would be foolish to insist on externals which are no longer relevant.

But let not the men feel threatened by the women and thus reject the God-given ministry and authority which some of them undoubtedly have! And let not the women fight for their rights in a style more conducive to Women's Lib than to the Spirit of God! We need to discern what the Spirit of God has said in the Scriptures, and what his application of this is in the church and society today.

Should women be elders in a church?
We have seen already that it is ideally the spiritually mature man who should accept the final headship, even though men and women together will exercise joint and complementary

[21] e.g. Revelation 12: 7,9.

ministries. Where the ideal is not to be found, the spiritually mature woman may have to take the primary lead, as is the case in many homes. Deborah is an interesting example for such situations, since even in the culture of those days she took the lead in the absence of strong male leadership. Yet all the while she encouraged the men to take their full responsibility.

To accept the headship of a spiritually mature man should in no way restrict the particular ministries that God has given to women. Paul wrote that 'the head of Christ is God'; and because Jesus came fully under his Father's authority during his earthly ministry, he was able to accomplish everything that he did. In no sense was he restricted or unfulfilled, even though he stated, 'I have not spoken on my own authority; the Father who sent me has himself given me commandment what to say and what to speak... What I say, therefore, I say as the Father has bidden me.'[22] His full submission to the authority and headship of his Father was in fact the secret of his amazing wisdom, discernment and power. There is a right order in the Trinity, and there should be a right order reflected in the church.

There need be no reason, therefore, for women to feel restricted and unfulfilled in the church *when* the concept of headship is rightly understood. Rather it should give them the authority to exercise the ministries that God has already given them, but with the support and protection of the men.

If we accept those principles in general terms, it would seem possible for a woman to be an elder, although coming under the primary authority of a presiding male elder. The complementary gifts and insights of men and women could enrich the vision of the whole eldership, strengthen their pastoral oversight, stimulate their thinking, and give greater balance to their decision-making.

Where there are basic objections to a woman having authority over men, could not a woman still be accepted as an 'elder of women and children' within the congregation? As we have seen, this certainly was the pastoral pattern even in the first century, with the older women training the younger.

If that idea is still not acceptable in some churches, a

[22] John 12:49f.

strong case could be argued for a spiritually mature and gifted woman to be given ready access to the meetings of elders. She might well have a ministry of prophecy, teaching, or healing; she may bring gifts of wisdom and knowledge; she would almost certainly have a special understanding of the women within that church that the men would be unlikely to possess. After all, at least half of the congregation are likely to be women! In that case, might not such a mature Christian woman, gifted by the Spirit of God, be regularly welcomed to the elders' meeting?

In practice, considerable caution should be exercised where there is a spiritually mature wife suitable in herself for eldership (or for access to elders' meetings) when the husband is spiritually immature, or even an unbeliever. But if her husband is an elder, or if she is single, the male leaders of the church need to recognise and accept the *charisma* of leadership and any other gifts which God may well have given to her.

The familiar argument against this, namely that Jesus chose twelve *men* for his apostles, cannot be pressed. On those grounds, we could also stress that Jesus chose twelve *Jews*! The cultural pattern of his day probably explains the wisdom of giving the primary leadership to men — even though the attitude of Jesus towards women was quite revolutionary and almost shockingly 'liberated'. But each of the apostles was likely to become the 'presiding elder' in a church or group of churches (certainly true of some). And we have already seen that such a responsibility should ideally be given to the men.

What can be said, then, about the explicit instruction that women should not be permitted to speak or teach in church?
Here, as always, it is vital to try to understand the significance of what Paul was saying in its rightful context. Writing to the somewhat disorderly and noisy Corinthian church, Paul said, 'The women should keep silence in the churches. For they are not permitted to speak, but should be subordinate, as even the law says. If there is anything they desire to know, let them ask their husbands at home. For it is shameful for a woman to speak in church.'[23]

Paul had already made it clear that it was perfectly in

[23] 1 Corinthians 14:34f.

order for a woman to pray or prophesy in church, providing she came under the headship of a man (her husband or the leader of that church). What did he therefore mean by 'speak' in this passage?

Some commentators suggest that an equally possible and more helpful translation of this word would be 'chatter'. As was customary in those days (and in some parts of the world today), men and women probably sat separately in church (as in the Jewish synagogue), and some of the women were chattering to their husbands across the church about some point in worship or teaching. The result was little order or peace about the time of worship — hardly a conducive atmosphere in which the Holy Spirit could move freely. Paul had to write firmly about the need to regulate the gift of tongues. Without the necessary gift of interpretation, it would all be a meaningless babble, noisy and unedifying to the body of Christ. Unseemly chatter would be equally disturbing, and at Corinth it seems that the women were especially guilty of this. Paul understandably told them to keep quiet, and to talk to their husbands after the service if they had questions to ask or comments to make.

Other commentators suggest that, by Paul's appeal to the *law*, he was very much aware of the cultural customs of the day. Just as it would have been scandalous for a woman to appear in public with her head uncovered, so it would have been equally shocking for a woman to teach when men were present. It was the man who was to rule over the woman.[24] Therefore a woman must keep silent. Freedom in Christ did not mean flouting the cultural and religious customs of the day. As William Barclay has commented: 'In all likelihood what was uppermost in his (Paul's) mind was the lax moral state of Corinth and the feeling that nothing, absolutely nothing, must be done which would bring upon the infant church the faintest suspicion of immodesty. It would certainly be wrong to take these words of Paul out of the context for which they were written.'

In western society today, of course, it is perfectly natural for a woman to have her head uncovered in public, and also to speak to a mixed gathering of men and women. It would be a

[24]Genesis 3:16.

great mistake to make this specific instruction to the Corinthian church nearly 2,000 years ago a binding command for all situations in all ages, regardless of cultural changes.

In 1 Timothy 2, however, Paul appears to give stronger, theological reasons for his injunction: 'Let a woman learn in silence with all submissiveness. I permit no woman to teach or to have authority over men; she is to keep silent. For Adam was formed first, then Eve; and Adam was not deceived, but the woman was deceived and became a transgressor. Yet woman will be saved through bearing children, if she continues in faith and love and holiness, with modesty.'

What Paul probably had in mind here was the teaching of apostolic and therefore authoritative doctrine. The New Testament was, of course, not yet completed; and several times in the Pastoral letters Paul urged Timothy to 'follow the pattern of sound words...; guard the truth that has been entrusted to you by the Holy Spirit...'[25] He warned this young leader about the numerous dangers of false teachers, and to be especially watchful of those who would 'make their way into households and capture weak women' who listen to anybody and never arrive at the knowledge of the truth.

It is certainly a debatable point today, but *in general* (always dangerous!) women *may* not be able to grasp and hold firmly the delicate balance of Christian *doctrine* as well as men. By the very intuitiveness of their nature, women may see certain issues much more quickly and clearly than men — and by the same impulse be more strongly tempted to go off on a tangent and away from the biblical balance of the 'whole counsel of God'. That would certainly have been much more of a danger in the first century when the education of women was not encouraged. Rabbi Eliezer said: 'Whoever teaches his daughter the Law, teaches her, as it were, silly things'[26] — because of her sex!

Paul was quick to see this danger of being vulnerable to false teaching in a new situation where the Christian faith brought considerable freedom to women. He therefore drew from the story of creation the God-given headship of man over woman, and then from the story of the fall the vulnerability of woman to the dangers of deception. Although

[25] 2 Timothy 1:13f.   [26] Sotah 20a.

Adam was formed first, it was Eve who was first attracted to the forbidden fruit, perhaps because of her livelier imagination; but it was also Eve who was first led astray by the deceiver!

Some have argued that Paul's strong teaching in this passage was especially necessary when, at that time, everything depended on the careful and accurate verbal instruction of the sacred deposit of God-given truth. Since the completion of the New Testament canon we now have that deposit of apostolic doctrine in written form, and therefore the teaching role of women in the church could be seen in a different context. Whether this is the case or not, certainly it would be wrong to take a cautionary or corrective word *out of its historical context* and make it normative for subsequent generations where the context is fundamentally different.

Internationally, the role of women in society has changed beyond recognition during this century, and one would have to be a male chauvinist to try to maintain that the changes have been totally disastrous! It was only seventy years ago that Marie Curie had her furious battle (leading to bitter persecution) to be recognised as one of the outstanding physicists of her generation. Even twenty-five years ago, who could have predicted that Mrs. Margaret Thatcher could have become leader of the Conservative party in the United Kingdom? Who could have guessed that Israel would ever have elected Mrs. Golda Meir as Prime Minister?

It is not that the church should necessarily follow the lead of the world; but it is a tragic fact that the entrenched conservatism of the church, at numerous times in its history, has quenched the Holy Spirit and underlined the church's sad reputation of irrelevance. Obedience to the Spirit of God ought to result in the church setting the pace for the world — as fortunately it has done on many issues such as freedom in education, emancipation from slavery, the fight for human rights, medical and social care, and the protection of workers by trades unions.

If it is true, then, that the Pauline strictures about the teaching role of women were largely (if not entirely) governed by the cultural context and the incompletion of the Scriptures, the situation today is very different. John Stott has commented: 'Today there are no Apostles, and both men and

women teachers are under the authority of Scripture. So I see
no reason why women should not teach without usurping any
improper authority. I think women gifted for such ministry
should be ordained, but I would like to see them in a team
ministry.'[27]

Part of the church's present confusion concerning the
teaching role of women may be further complicated by the
twentieth century Protestant image of Christian teaching. We
tend to assume that this means the formal 20-30 minute
sermon (or longer) in a public act of worship on Sunday
morning or evening.

In the early church, although the public proclamation of
the gospel was snatched up in every conceivable place —
synagogues, debating chambers, courts, prisons, streets, market places, etc. — the regular teaching of the faith was
normally done in much smaller groups, usually meeting in
someone's house. The force of 1 Corinthians 14 is that
everyone had something to contribute: 'a hymn, a lesson, a
revelation, a tongue or an interpretation... You can all
prophesy one by one, so that all may learn and all be
encouraged.'

With this pattern as a rough guide, and translating it into
our contemporary church life, there seems to be no reason
why women should not be fully involved in the overall
teaching ministry of a local church (such as in Bible study
groups, confirmation classes, house fellowships and youth
organisations); and in some groups it may well be the women,
rather than the men, who have the gifts that are needed. The
crucial question is to discern and to encourage the God-given
gifts to the body of Christ, and to submit to *his* sovereign
leading in the distribution of such gifts.

I have often thanked God, to take only one example, for the
outstanding teaching gifts bestowed upon Corrie ten Boom —
gifts that have been unquestionably and outstandingly used
by God for the instruction and encouragement of Christians
throughout the world. Can we honestly say that these gifts
have been 'second-best' for the church? It may be precisely
the feminine insights, feeling, and simple beauty of her
teaching that have given her (and many others) an invaluable

[27] Quoted in the *Church of England Newspaper*, 13 August 1976.

complementary role to the more prosaic style of numerous male teachers.

In my own preaching ministry (and in my vision and leadership of the church), I have frequently had my thinking sharpened by the immensely helpful comments from certain women with prophetic insights (or possibly feminine intuitions under the control of the Spirit!). On many occasions I have praised God for extraordinary spiritual illumination — sometimes in the context of a mission — given to me by women with a profound grasp of the truth and the relevance of certain biblical passages for particular situations. In each instance there is no doubt that these have been gifts from God for the benefit of the church, or for its mission in the world.

What about the ordination of women?
This vexed question is fraught with emotional and traditional prejudices that make clear, theological reflection extraordinarily difficult. As I am writing this page I see that the Russian Orthodox Church has again declared that the ordination of women to the priesthood is an 'insurmountable obstacle' to unity with the Church of England. Other Orthodox Churches are thought to be even more rigid in their opposition. And at a time when churches have been coming closer together than for centuries throughout Christendom, many feel it unwise to override the strong and adamant feelings of numerous Christians, whatever might be the rights and wrongs of the theological thinking behind such feelings. It was to the Ephesian church that Paul, stressing the universal concept of the body of Christ, wrote urging them to be 'eager to maintain the unity of the Spirit in the bond of peace'.

Undoubtedly many of the tensions would be removed if we saw ordination in the light of New Testament teaching about shared ministry, and if we remembered that the early church thought of ordination primarily in the local church setting. It is not a question of giving or denying women equal *status* in the church, because we saw that the whole idea of status should be foreign to Christian ministry. What matters is *service*. If a woman is willing to serve within the body of Christ, in whatever capacity, there is little doubt that the Spirit will increasingly give her gifts and ministries that are necessary in that particular church; and it is perfectly

possible that these might include the *charisma* of leadership
and/or teaching. In that case, a formal recognition of such
gifts and the authority to use them within that local church
would seem to be appropriate; and this surely is what is
meant by ordination. If there is no theological objection to
the *ministry* of women, which might include prophesying and
skilled counselling (both ministries requiring a marked sensitivity to the Holy Spirit), what could be the objection to a
woman presiding at the eucharist or at a wedding? What is to
prevent her from pronouncing absolution? In the Church of
England, she can already baptise and bury, counsel and
preach, so what is the logical or theological reason for
drawing the line there?

In the mission field, where the women outnumber the men
by eight to one (a constant rebuke to the men), the 'weaker
sex' are frequently thrust into a primary leadership role. That
may not be the ideal situation; and in some churches the men
are far too willing to 'leave it to the women' when it comes to
leading in prayer, exercising spiritual gifts, evangelising and
counselling. However, what really matters is recognising,
accepting and authorising the gifts given to both men and
women by the Spirit of God. In the healthy situation we have
seen that it should be the spiritually mature man who is the
presiding elder, and a woman should be in the best position
to take her full part in the life of a church when she has that
covering and support. But that will liberate, not restrict, her
for her God-given ministry in that Church.

Having said all this — and much depends on a revised
understanding of ordination, leadership and ministry — a
real danger facing the church today is that we should imbibe
the spirit of the world in this whole area of women's work.
The New Testament has always taught the 'equality of
women' when it comes to our standing in the sight of God. As
far as salvation is concerned, the barriers of sex are broken
down in Christ. God's promised Holy Spirit is for all flesh,
and both men and women might be given prophetic and
other gifts.

God, however, never intends to eliminate the marks of our
humanity whilst we live on this earth, and it would be foolish
to pretend that there are, or should be, no differences at all
between men and women, apart from biological.

When, therefore, the cry goes up for 'equal status for women', we need to be on our guard lest a wrong and worldly ambition creeps into the church. Once again, *status-seekers keep out!* What Jesus demonstrated by his own selfless example, and what he looks for most of all in the church today, is the strong, humble, gentle and beautiful spirit of *service*. That service may involve highly trained spiritual gifts of counselling, prayer, teaching, leadership, evangelism or prophecy. It may equally involve the foot-washing, practical care of individuals in all their numerous needs. Those who would receive a special welcome into heaven, said Jesus, would be those who fed the hungry, refreshed the thirsty, welcomed the stranger, clothed the naked and visited the sick. Is preaching from a pulpit a 'bigger and better' job in the eyes of God than instructing individuals or small home groups? Is pronouncing the absolution a 'greater role' than the loving care of someone in need? Is it 'more important' to preside at the eucharist than to 'shut the door and pray'? We need to ask searching questions.

Further, questions about the ordination of women raise the more basic issue: to what are they being ordained? As Michael Harper comments, 'To ordain women will only add to the confusion; it will simply perpetuate the caste system, only include women as well as men. We shall be no better off.'[28]

What we all, both men and women, need to remember is that ambition for the *status* of ordination is never right. Admittedly, in much of the church as it stands at the moment many women would have few opportunities in the spiritual ministry of a church unless they were ordained; and until the concepts of shared ministry and leadership are more widely accepted, the question of ordination of women is much more urgent. Until there is a radical re-appraisal of the whole ministry of the church, with a clear grasp of the important distinction between 'leadership' (or headship) and 'ministry', it *may* be necessary to press for what would unfortunately be a divisive move. This would certainly give many women much wider scope in terms of a genuine spiritual contribution to the life of the church, instead of being largely confined to

[28] Op. cit., p. 30.

flower-arranging and tea-brewing. On the other hand, the
consequences of this throughout Christendom must be considered carefully. A member of staff at a theological college
once provocatively remarked: 'The problem is not when we
can start ordaining women, but when we can stop ordaining
men.'

Anyone who is ambitious *only to serve Christ*, and members
of his body on earth, will certainly find ways and means of
doing so, whether or not there is any official recognition of
this service. In God's kingdom, what brings life to others is
only the life of Jesus, not our gifts and talents; and his life
often emerges strongly in the midst of pain and frustration. If
we are primarily seeking for personal fulfilment by being
officially recognised, God may have to bring us to the point
where our personal ambitions are crucified, in order that the
life of Jesus may be manifested. Was this the reason God kept
his own Son in the carpenter's shop for some thirty years
before releasing him into his brief but devastating ministry?
Remember, too, that Jesus had no official status at all; yet in
no way was he hindered in the extent and power of his
ministry. When the Spirit of God is moving freely in our lives,
questions about 'status', 'office' and 'position' will be dwarfed
into insignificance.

In our ecclesiastical thinking, presiding at the eucharist,
preaching from the pulpit, pronouncing the absolution and
tying the marriage knot, have been blown up out of all
biblical proportion. The whole church must learn again the
profound truth that Jesus taught his enthusiastic, lovable but
sometimes status-seeking disciples: 'Whoever would be great
among you must be your servant, and whoever would be first
among you must be slave of all.'

AN EXAMPLE OF ONE LOCAL CHURCH

Having seen something of the biblical basis of ministry and
leadership, it may be helpful looking at one example of the
application of these principles. Forgive me for describing our
own Anglican situation in York. I do so, not to offer a
blueprint, but in order to show that such patterns are possible
within the given structures of existing denominations.

When I first came to York in 1965 to look after St.

Cuthbert's Church, I was the only ordained clergyman, and remained 'on my own' for eight years. However, as the congregation grew in size (we started with only a dozen or so), I was clearly unable to meet all the needs of the whole church, especially as I was frequently away from York on missions in universities, schools and churches, at home and abroad. Understandably, and with good biblical precedent, there was some murmuring within the congregation that some of their needs were not being met, and something had to be done about it.

After some teaching and encouragement about this, a growing number became involved in the ministry of the church: visiting, preaching, typing, counselling, prophesying, singing, cleaning, tape-recording, organising — 101 jobs emerged, and an increasing number within the congregation were willing to play their part, according to their gifts and abilities. So far so good, especially when I was around to co-ordinate the work.

When I was away, however, there was sometimes a measure of confusion, and pastoral needs were clearly being neglected. I looked again at my Bible, and the principle of shared leadership within the body of Christ became obvious. We needed some 'pastoral elders', which seemed at the time the best expression to use.

After further teaching, I asked the congregation to pray about the matter for a week, and then to submit to me in writing the names of up to seven men (no special significance about the number, except that it was the number suggested in Acts 6 and it seemed to be about right in our situation). These men had to be recognised as being 'full of faith and of the Holy Spirit', and it should be obvious to all that God was already using them in pastoral counselling. Naturally I prayed much as well, and by the end of the week chose six men who seemed to be most fitted for this work. It was clear confirmation for me when the nominations sent in by the congregation tallied exactly with those on my own list! In no sense was this an election. The church is not a democracy, and the elders have always been ultimately my appointment, although checked by the congregation in the way described.

To begin with, the elders were appointed for one year at a time, but this was soon changed to three years. This means that when, for various reasons, a man is no longer able to fulfil the exacting and tiring responsibilities of an elder, it is possible to ask him to stand down in favour of another man. Three have done this so far (all with grace!), and this scheme should prevent the eldership from becoming in any way a rigid and traditional block in the church.

Soon, however, even this development was not enough. With the congregation now 2-300 strong, most newcomers felt swamped by the numbers. For some, it was several months before they felt in any way that they 'belonged', and others grew discouraged and left. It was obviously important to divide up the congregation into smaller groups, although still maintaining the unity of the whole.

After a parish half-day conference about this, the elders organised the congregation into a number of 'area groups', appointing a leader, or leaders, in charge of each area group, with each elder having the oversight of two or three groups. These groups are as strictly geographical as possible, so that the members of each group should be able to care for one another, often in simple and practical ways, such as providing meals when someone is sick. Therefore, instead of the bottle picture, the church structure becomes like this:

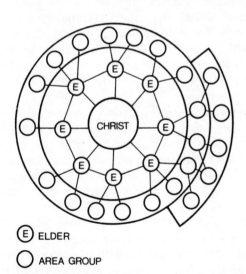

Ⓔ ELDER

◯ AREA GROUP

The responsibilities of area group leadership were spelt out as follows:

1. To have the pastoral care of the group;
2. To arrange regular house meetings once a fortnight;
3. To encourage the group to relate to each other in depth, to serve the whole body of Christ, and to think of witness, evangelism and service within that area;
4. To stimulate Bible study and prayer;
5. To be sensitive to other churches in that area, and to build up good relationships wherever possible;
6. To come to a leaders' meeting at 7 a.m. every third Saturday morning.

These groups were not to be less than eight in size, and, if possible not more than 16-20 before they split or budded. Each elder should meet regularly with his two or three leaders, so that lines of communication could be kept as good as possible. This constant link between the leaders is vital, since the harmony of a church depends on the harmony of its leaders.

With such a pattern, every person in the church should be able to belong to a small enough group, in which personal needs can be shared. Therefore, if anyone requires help (of any kind), he should see first of all his group leader, or someone else within his group. If the group leader feels unable to give the help required, he consults his respective elder; and if the elder needs further help, he discusses the matter with the rest of the elders (confidences being respected). At times those with specialist counselling gifts will be asked to assist.

Where possible, assistant-leaders are also appointed so that they can be prepared for the time when the group has to split. Training in leadership and pastoral work is a constant need; and apart from the Saturday morning meetings, when various aspects of the work can be discussed, we have a residential training weekend for all leaders once a year. This has always proved invaluable.

The elders (we now have ten) meet every Saturday at 7 a.m., usually for about two hours, but about every six weeks that time is extended to the whole morning. This has proved the minimum time necessary to pray and talk through the policies and pastoral needs of the church.

At the time of writing our ten elders consist of a curate, a retired clergyman, a doctor, a barrister, a university lecturer, four full-time church workers and myself. Five of these are Readers in the Anglican church. Five are members of the deanery synod. Eight of them are also members of the Parochial Church Council, and a strong representation would seem important to avoid any possibility of tension between the two groups. However, since the P.C.C. must inevitably deal more with administrative and financial matters, and since the elders attend more to the pastoral and disciplinary aspects of the work, it is unlikely that all the elders will be, or need to be, on the P.C.C. In practice, we have never found any tension between the two groups, and the P.C.C. anyway was responsible for the eldership scheme in the first place.

In some churches it might be right for the Churchwardens or the Standing Committee to form the first eldership. What is important is that the elders should be marked for their *spiritual* maturity and not necessarily for their official position in the church. Then every three years, after the appointment of the elders, there is a solemn commissioning service, usually taken by the Bishop (or Archibshop in our diocese of York) so that the spiritual authority of the elders is officially recognised by the congregation.

All the decisions at the elders' meetings are unanimous, and if there is a difference of opinion we wait prayerfully until we reach an agreed policy. As an illustration of our submission to one another, I submit all invitations for speaking engagements to the elders; and therefore whenever I go out from the church, say on a mission, I am 'sent out' with the full approval of the elders, who often lay hands on me and pray for me in the presence of the congregation.

Together with this structure of leadership, we are also training a number of teams for the mission of the church. At present I have the privilege of leading missions for renewal or evangelism in parishes, towns, cities, dioceses and counties. Always I go with a team, whose particular gifts are in music, singing, drama and dance, so that I can set the preaching and teaching in the context of worship, with relevant communication for the media and many different groups of people. We work very closely as a team, praying and worshipping together, trying to understand the will of the Lord together for each situation and each meeting, before we go out together for the task that is given to us. It is often here that the gifts of the Spirit are manifested, giving us a clearer sense of direction; and in our relationships together something of the reality of the body of Christ can be *seen* — which, we are often told, is perhaps the most powerful appeal that God can make through us as his ambassadors.

Other elders also go out to lead missions or speak at conferences, and sometimes other teams are taken with them. All this is a vital part in the sharing of the ministry and mission of the church. Men and women work closely together, each contributing what God has given them for the upbuilding of the whole body of Christ. Every member of the congregation is trained in some measure for effective witness and service. Discipleship courses, training courses, Christian night-schools are planned — all of which involve study and practical work — so that each Christian has a growing understanding of his or her faith in order to share Christ with others. However, we have seen time and again that the best sphere of learning and working is in the context of the small group.

It is interesting to note that much the same patterns of development and growth have been worked out by the Urban Church Project. Research into the self-limiting factors of the parish structure has shown that, with a single clergyman, the average congregation levels off at about 175 regardless of the size of the parish. Larger congregations are purely the result of more assistant clergy in those parishes.

If there is to be any appreciable growth, the development of small groups and the sharing of pastoral ministry and leadership become essential. Since 'the quality of pastoral care per member decays as the congregation expands', the dividing into small groups (ideally about twelve in size) is the only way to prevent the inevitable stalemate. In those groups, there must be a 'depth of sharing and love, mutual ministry, and exhortation, bearing, caring, teaching and working, utilising all the gifts of all the members in the service of the Kingdom.'

This is one of the 'imperatives' that the report stresses for the continuing mission of the church. 'The credibility of the church's communication depends, in large measure, upon the authenticity of its communal life. Small human groups are notorious for their tendency to fragment and fly apart, and one of the most powerful demonstrations of the effect of the Gospel is the capacity for sustaining community.'[29]

Professor Hanson once wrote[30] of the church's 'capacity for enduring and for renewal of its life.' He began, 'If I were a dedicated Marxist...' and went on to show that the organisation he would like to see in order to serve his cause would not be dissimilar to existing church structures. He would want to see 'the country dotted with small communities of people with a common ideology and purpose, contributing financial-ly, with full-time officers, engaging in voluntary activity among themselves and in the community, and attracting others by the offer of friendship, a sense of belonging, and "some sort of moral purpose".' Such a structure of small closely-knit groups, made alive by the Spirit of God, is what the church is all about.

[29] Helpful guidance about the running of these small groups, their relationships to one another and to the rest of the church, questions about their growth, lifestyle and authority — these and other points are given in a paper called *Divide and Conquer*, obtainable from 19 Bosworth Road, Dagenham, Essex, England.
[30] Article in *The Times*, 14 January 1976.

CHAPTER SEVENTEEN

The Mission of the Church

GOD IS A missionary. His redemptive work in the world is missionary work. The Latin for 'sending' is *missio*; and in his love for us God sent, or 'missioned', his Son. Likewise Jesus told his disciples, 'As the Father has sent me, even so I send you.' And he gave them the gift of the Spirit to empower them for this missionary task. Every Christian is therefore inescapably a missionary for Christ.

In view of this, it is tragic that many church members think of missionary work as something quite distinct and special compared with the life and work of the ordinary local church. This is encouraged by the special events in the church's calendar, such as a missionary Sunday, a missionary speaker, a missionary film. The overall impression is clear: missionary work belongs to an unusual body of Christian super-stars who have either exceptional gifts or a rare dedication to God that is not expected of the ordinary man in the pew. Indeed, the 'remoteness' of most missionary work, in the eyes of the average church member, keeps the whole challenge at a safe distance; and a slightly larger donation to the special missionary collection helps to ease the conscience with the feeling of 'having done my bit'.

Such a view of missionary work is doubly disastrous.

First and foremost it conceals the truth that the 'ordinary' Christian is called by God to be a missionary where he lives and works. Whether he realises it or not, and for better or for worse, he *is* a witness for Christ, and must accept the full responsibilities of this calling.

Secondly, since God's harvest-field is the world, it is up to the Lord of the harvest to place his workers where he wills. No Christian can serve his Lord on condition that he lives in, say, the comfortable surroundings and social environment that he has always enjoyed. He is to be available to Jesus for work in Godalming or Guatemala, Chicago or Chile. As far as personal preferences are concerned, the Lord of glory would hardly have chosen the cattle-shed in Bethlehem or the carpenter's bench in Nazareth; but he went where his Father sent him, and 'though he was rich, yet for your sake he became poor'.

A healthy church will always be especially concerned about its missionary work both on its own doorstep and overseas. It will try not to be insular and parochial, but develop steadily a worldwide perspective of the work of God, and encourage everyone to be directly involved in some form of missionary concern. There should be a constant flow of candidates for the harvest fields abroad; and these men and women should be strongly backed by the church in terms of finance, prayer and the personal links forged through letters and gifts at regular intervals.

A retired missionary told me recently that for over twenty years his home church in England had not only supported his family in Africa with generous financial resources and intelligent and persistent prayer, but every month they had received letters and magazines, and at regular intervals they had been sent recently published Christian books and (during the later years) tapes and cassettes. I happen to know that the same church supports a considerable number of individual missionaries and their families in a similar way, and it is not surprising that many within its congregation are constantly challenged to consider prayerfully God's calling for their life.

Certainly the church of God is not designed as a club whose activities are purely for the enjoyment of its members. As William Temple once remarked, 'it is the only society on earth which exists for the benefit of the non-members'. It is impossible to divorce the work of the church from the work of mission. 'The church exists by mission as fire exists by burning,' to quote Emil Brunner's famous remark.

Further, although we have seen so far in this book various aspects of the church's life that might call for radical spiritual or structural renewal, it would be the greatest mistake to wait until we have set our own house in order before engaging on the wider missionary tasks of the church. Lesslie Newbiggin once exposed this popular misconception in these words:

> It is taken for granted that the missionary obligation is one that has to be met *after* the needs of the home have been fully met; that existing gains have to be thoroughly consolidated before we go further afield; that the world-wide church has to be built up with the same sort of prudent calculation of resources and costs as is expected of any business enterprise. Must we not contrast this with the kind of strategy that the New Testament reveals, which seems to be a sort of determination to stake out God's claim to the whole world at once, without expecting that one area should be fully worked out before the next is claimed?[1]

Having stressed the primacy of missionary work in the agenda of the church, it is important to see that the aim of missionary work is not just to win individuals for Christ; it is to extend the kingdom of God, or to build up God's church. God aims to people this earth with his new society that centres on his Son Jesus Christ. Only in this way will 'the earth be filled with the glory of God as the waters cover the sea'. The church must be involved in mission; and mission must be concerned with the church. 'An unchurchly mission is as much a monstrosity as an unmissionary church.'[2]

THE CONTEXT OF MISSION

The Lausanne Covenant made a highly important statement that has often been neglected, especially in the evangelical section of the church (until recent years): 'Our Christian presence in the world is indispensable to evangelism.'

In every generation, and in every part of the world, the word has to become flesh before people can see the truth and reality of God. In this word-resistant age, it is not enough to throw biblical statements at the outsider. For most folk, God-words are empty words. But when the word can be demonstrated in our lives, relationships, lifestyle and love, the *presence*

---

[1] *The Household of God*, pp. 143f.   [2] L. Newbigin, op. cit., p. 148.

of the living Christ will be clearly manifested and perceived. Calling for radical discipleship, some of the church leaders from Latin America at the Lausanne Congress affirmed that

> the communication of the Evangel in its fullness to every person world-wide is a mandate of the Lord Jesus Christ to his community. There is no biblical dichotomy between the Word spoken and the Word made visible in the lives of God's people. Men will look as they listen and what they see must be one with what they hear. The Christian community must chatter, discuss and proclaim the Gospel; it must express the Gospel in its life as the new society, in its sacrificial service to others as a genuine expression of God's love, in its prophetic exposing and opposing of all demonic forces that deny the lordship of Christ and keep men less than fully human, in its pursuit of justice for all men, in its responsible and caring trusteeship of God's creation and resources. There are times when our communication may be by attitude and action only, and times when the spoken word will stand alone; but we must repudiate as demonic the attempt to drive a wedge between evangelism and social action.[3]

Although evangelism and social action are distinct, both are vitally and equally important in the total mission of the church. It is inadequate to call only for repentance from personal sins, and salvation for individuals; and it is nonsense to talk about the 'evangelising' of social structures. The Great Commission calls Christians to preach the gospel *and* to teach new converts to observe all Christ's instructions, many of which had strong social implications. Likewise the Great Commandment tells us to love our neighbour, and we cannot do this in the fullest sense unless we care about both his spiritual and social needs.

The urgent call to take social action seriously is made by a graphic illustration and comment from Clifford Christians:

> Imagine that all the population of the world were condensed to the size of one village of 100 people. In this

[3] Quoted in *The New Face of Evangelicalism*, Hodder & Stoughton, p. 77.

village, 67 of the 100 would be poor; the other 33 would be in varying degrees well off. Of the total population, only seven would be North Americans. The other 93 people would watch the seven North Americans spend one-half of all the money, eat one-seventh of all the food, and use one-half of all the bath-tubs. These seven people would have ten times more doctors than the other 93. Meanwhile the seven would continue to get more and more and the 93 less and less.'

The trouble is that the wealthy seven continually try to evangelise the other 93.

We tell them about Jesus and they watch us throw away more food than they can ever hope to eat. We are busy building beautiful church buildings, and they scrounge to find shelter for their families. We have money in the bank and they do not have enough to buy food for their children. All the while we tell them that our Master was the Servant of men, the Saviour who gave his all for us and bids us give all for him... We are the rich minority in the world. We may be able to forget about that or consider it unimportant. The question is, can the 93 forget? [4]

Fortunately there are numerous examples of costly Christian service where the love of Christ for the whole man is clearly expressed. In Chile, with a total population of only 10 million, the military coup in 1973 led, in four years, to 200,000 people being detained for political reasons and more than a quarter of a million fleeing from the country as refugees. Many of those detained have been tortured with electric shock treatment, and some mutilated bodies have been found of those who did not survive their interrogation. Others have simply 'disappeared'. By 1977 there was greater poverty in Chile than had been experienced since the turn of the century, and unemployment in the shanty towns reached 90 per cent. About 40 per cent of the children have suffered from serious malnutrition. The churches, however, have been outstanding in the defence of basic human rights. Legal

[4]Quoted by Walter Hollenweger, *Evangelism Today*, Christian Journals Ltd., p. 7.

aid has been offered to prisoners, canteens set up for children, and workshops have opened for the unemployed. The bishops and church leaders have also spoken fearlessly against the oppression and injustice, calling vigorously for a return to democratic elections. Naturally they have put themselves in danger by their courageous stand, but they are following the example of the Old Testament prophets and indeed of their Master.

It may be here, as well as in other issues, that Christians from different theological positions need to learn from one another. Evangelicals, at any rate until recently, have constantly stressed that the primary task of the church is evangelism, the personal salvation of individuals. As a result, social and political issues have all too often been neglected. Individuals are called to repent of their sins, to come to Christ, and to change their lives in the power of his Spirit; but little is done to change the oppressions and injustices in society which have such an influence on their lives. At the other end of the scale come the secular theologians, such as Harvey Cox, who stress the priority of humanisation. Evangelism is politics and salvation is social justice: 'Why are men not simply called to be human in their historical obligations, for this is man's true end and his salvation?'[5]

Any such polarisation of views is biblically unbalanced. Ronald Sider, the founder chairman of Evangelicals for Social Action, has made the point that sin is both personal and structural.[6] Unquestionably the Bible stresses that each individual must give account of himself to God; but personal sin and personal salvation stop short in the answer to the questions raised by the depressed and unjust societies in which we live. The prophets spoke strongly against the oppression of the poor, against the evil economic structures, and against the lack of concern, on the part of the rich and powerful, about the gross injustices of the day. God is clearly concerned about order, justice and righteousness within society, and not only the salvation of individuals. Certainly there is the urgent need for individuals to repent; but, says

[5]Gibson Winter, *The New Creation as Metropolis*, Macmillan, New York, p. 61.
[6]From an interview in *Third Way*, 13 January 1977. See also *Evangelism, Salvation and Social Justice*, by R.J. Sider and J.R.W. Stott, Grove Booklet No. 16.

Sider, in order to make any impact on the society in which we live, we must also change the church. 'The church should be living a new corporate lifestyle fundamentally different from that of surrounding society. It is folly to try to call on secular society to legislate what we have not been able to persuade our own members to live.'

In New Testament days, the church crashed through the class-barriers of contemporary society in an astonishing way. Gone were the distinctions between Jew and Greek, slave and free, male and female, when it came to the unity of the whole body of Christ. Moreover, the spontaneous and generous sharing of money and possessions in a massive and impressive way was a prophetic challenge to the economic injustices of the first century.

The principle of 'equality' is twice explicitly stated by Paul in his second letter to Corinth: 'As a matter of equality your abundance at the present time should supply their want, so that their abundance may supply your want, that there may be equality.'[7]

Sider comments:

> Now if the one world-wide body of believers today would dare to implement that vision so that something like economic equality existed within the universal body of Christ it would probably be the single most important thing that we could do to relieve the tension between rich and poor nations. I suspect also that it would be the single most powerful evangelistic step we could take. When the church in Jerusalem shared dramatically they found that the work of God was increased. The evangelistic impact of the first Christians' financial sharing was just outstanding. Unfortunately, the radical character of New Testament *koinonia* is largely missing from the contemporary Western church... The Christian must live out the ethics of the Kingdom in all his activities... There is a deep wrestling with what it means to be the church... The central concern is that we must have a visible new model in the midst of surrounding society's sin and evil.

[7] 2 Corinthians 8:14.

A Hindu poet, Rabindranath Tagore, said to a Christian leader in India, 'On that day when we see Jesus Christ living out his life in you, on that day we Hindus will flock to your Christ even as doves flock to their feeding ground.' This may be more poetic than prophetic, but the basic challenge is still there.

If we are to take the lordship of Christ seriously — and this is the only way of making his presence known in today's world — we must commit ourselves whole-heartedly to his lifestyle. We must live as he lived if our message is to have any credibility in the eyes of others. In a telling passage from *The New Face of Evangelicalism*[8] Jacob Loewen recounts a discussion between some missionaries and a group of teachers from a tribe in South America. One of the missionaries asked, 'What would you consider to be the axle of the missionary's way of life?' Unanimously and unhesitatingly they replied 'Money!' Astonished by this, the missionaries asked if they often talked about money. 'No,' came the reply; 'they usually talk about God and religion, but money is still the most important thing in their way of life.' They then illustrated this with numerous examples of how, in practice, money was the ultimate yardstick in both the material and spiritual areas of the missionaries' life and culture. That reflection applies not only to that tribe in South America. 'The church is always asking for money' is a very common feeling amongst unbelievers today, and it denies the God of free grace who 'gave his only Son'.

We urgently need more Christian leaders of the calibre and courage of the Brazilian Archbishop Dom Helder Camara who has refused the material and financial privileges of his office, and who has devoted his life to seeking justice for the poor and oppressed. Although the conservatives in both church and government have called him 'the red bishop', he has openly rejected Marxism, and is a strong critic of both the Soviet Union and the United States. He clearly preaches non-violence; yet he believes that the violence of the rich against the poor, and the violence of the developed countries against the under-developed, is more to be condemned than the violence that these create.

He writes: 'I used to think, when I was a child, that Christ might have been exaggerating when he warned about the

[8] pp. 184f.

dangers of wealth. Today I know better. I know how very hard it is to be rich and still keep the milk of human kindness. Money has a dangerous way of putting scales on one's eyes, a dangerous way of freezing people's hands, eyes, lips and hearts.'[9]

There is a real truth that, biblically and in every age, God is on the side of the poor. It is not that he loves the poor more than the rich; but God is essentially the God of justice and righteousness, and it is the poor who are so often oppressed by the rich. The church, therefore, must be active in its concern for justice and equality, demonstrating God's sacrificial love and concern towards those who are unlikely to receive support from other sources. If Christian mission towards the poor is to have any credibility, the church must first be willing to forego the rights, privileges and powers so long associated with it (albeit eroded in some countries today), and deliberately choose to adopt instead the lifestyle of its Master.

The integrity of the church is to be seen, of course, in many other ways apart from radical changes in its material way of life and sharing resources, although this particular area speaks especially powerfully in the west where probably the major sin is covetousness. However, the world is also marked by alienation and loneliness, bureaucracy and personal insignificance; and therefore the existence of a warm, caring, loving and accepting community, marked by unjudging friendship, speaks volumes for the validity of the good news of Jesus Christ.

This new community of the people of God, the church, is therefore a vital part of the gospel. It is, or should be, clearly distinct from the rest of society in its ethic and lifestyle which demonstrate the reality of its beliefs and Saviour. Biblical evangelism should set forth, not only the riches that God offers us freely in Christ, but the demands of radical discipleship, including the renouncing of both personal sin (dishonesty, immorality, pride, etc.) and social sin (e.g. involvement in racial conflicts and economic injustices). When an individual responds to the gospel, he commits himself both to Christ and to the new society that Christ has come to build. The very existence of that society, if it is following the instructions of its Master, will be a constant challenge to the ambitions and standards of the rest of the world; and

[9]Camara, *Revolution through Peace*, Harper: New York 1971, pp. 142f.

the reality of the love of God within that new society will be measured by the practical and sacrificial care of those in need, as the apostle John makes clear in his first Epistle.

In this way, both evangelism and social action are, or should be, inseparable partners in Christ's mission through the church to the world. Social action will often prepare the way for effective evangelism, since a clear demonstration of the love of God will give credibility to any proclamation about that love. Correspondingly, any lack of social concern, in situations where it is manifestly needed, will make the preaching of the gospel mere empty words. As Michael Cassidy has expressed it: 'Obedience to the Great Commission demands going beyond proclaiming to winning and discipling... We must not settle for decisions or pew-warmers, but for disciples... Justice, structural change, compassionate caring and practical service now become new imperatives for us. Individual Christian salvation and Christian social ethics belong together.'

In practice it is often those who are profoundly conscious of *some* need who will be most open to the truths of the gospel. Christian workers in Bangladesh have reported that thousands in that country have been open to the gospel and have responded to Jesus Christ to a degree that has never been experienced before. It is well-known, too, that the spread of the gospel in Latin America and in many African countries, where the social needs are often immense, has been simply staggering. It is still exceedingly hard for those who have riches to enter into the kingdom of God. Therefore genuine social action is not only valid in itself as an expression of God's love for the whole person and the whole world; it is not only useful as a form of 'pre-evangelism'; it will often lead to the most fruitful evangelistic work of all. Donald McGavran gives an interesting example of this in *Understanding Church Growth:*

In 1840 the American Baptists started a mission at Nellore on the eastern coast of India. For twenty-five years they laboured among the upper castes, winning less than a hundred converts.

In 1865 John Clough and his wife came out as new missionaries. As they learned the language and studied the Bible to see what God would have them to do, each independently came to the conclusion that, on the basis of

1 Corinthians 1:26-28, the policy followed rigorously by the elder missionaries of seeking to win only the upper castes was displeasing to God. The Madigas (Untouchables), known to be responsive to the Christian message, had been bypassed lest their baptism made it still more difficult for caste Hindus to become Christians. The Cloughs moved from Nellore, opened the station of Ongole, and began baptising some remarkably earnest and spiritual Madiga leaders. By 1869, hundreds were being added to the Lord.[10]

It is a simple fact that most of the great Christian movements developed, often with phenomenal growth, when Christians began seriously to preach and demonstrate the gospel to the poor.

Having said this, it is important to realise that it is not possible to do everything at the same time; nor should every Christian be expected to have the same gifts and callings. Although every Christian is called to be both a witness and a servant of Christ, *some* are called to be evangelists, and their primary ministry and responsibility will be the winning of men and women for Christ; whereas *others* may be called primarily to social work or political action. Evangelistic missions, therefore, are not invalidated if they have no specific social programme as part of their week of special meetings; and social or political involvements are not less than Christian if they do not attempt to include some evangelistic thrust. As with all other gifts and ministries within the body of Christ, they are different but complementary. John Stott rightly observes: 'Although we should resist *polarisation* between evangelism and social action, we should not resist *specialisation*. Everybody cannot do everything... Within each local church, which as the body of Christ in the locality is committed to both evangelism and social action, there is a proper place for individual specialists and for specialist groups.'[11]

THE METHODS OF MISSION

I have written more fully about this in *I Believe in Evangelism*,[12]

[20]Op. cit., Eerdmans, Grand Rapids 1970, p. 19.

[11]Op. cit., p. 22.
[12]Hodder & Stoughton.

and in this chapter there is room to sketch only a few points all too briefly.

Personal evangelism

The first Christians knew that they were all ambassadors of Christ, and wherever they went they gossiped the gospel. It was not the apostles, the 'professionals', but the ordinary, nameless Christians who first brought the gospel to Rome, Alexandria, Antioch, Cyprus, Ephesus, and along the Phoenician seaboard. In Acts 8:4 they were all scattered because of the persecution following the martyrdom of Stephen. Did they go into hiding until the troubles were over? Not a bit of it! 'Those who were scattered went about preaching the word' — and often in the most unlikely places.

For example, the Jews had always been utterly scornful about the Samaritans, whose religion was a pagan corruption of the Jewish faith. Yet we find one of the seven who had been set apart to organise 'meals on wheels' for the Greek widows, going into Samaria to proclaim Christ. The results from this 'amateur evangelist' were overwhelming: 'Multitudes with one accord gave heed to what was said by Philip, when they heard him and saw the signs that he did. For unclean spirits came out of many who were possessed, crying with a loud voice; and many who were paralysed or lame were healed. So there was much joy in that city.'

Again, Peter mentions in passing the Christians scattered in Pontus, Galatia, Cappadocia, Asia and Bithynia. Who carried the good news there? It was almost certainly the 'little people' who went about the streets and market places chattering Christ. There was a natural spontaneity about it all. Nobody was paid for it; nobody had any formal training. Even with the apostles, the Jewish leaders were astounded at their boldness, seeing that they were 'uneducated, common men'. Origen once accepted the sneer of Celsus that this movement had spread amongst 'workers in wool and leather, laundry workers and the most illiterate and bucolic yokels'. But God has often chosen 'what is foolish in the world to shame the wise, [and]...what is weak in the world to shame the strong,' as Paul once observed. Men and women, Jew and Gentile, young and old, educated and common — all, empowered by the Spirit of God, became natural and effective witnesses to Jesus.

If someone is holding a full glass and someone bumps into him, what will spill out? Answer: whatever is in the glass! If someone's heart is full of the Spirit of Jesus and someone 'bumps' into him, what will 'spill out'? Answer: whatever is in his heart — the Spirit of Jesus. Fill anyone with the love and power of God, and nothing can stop him talking about Jesus. There is no substitute for this natural, authentic, personal evangelism. It is significant that in the Gospel records we have no less than nineteen personal conversations that Jesus had with men and women.

The broadcaster and writer David Winter, an open critic of some of the massive and expensive congresses on evangelism, once said that 'eloquent speeches, visual aids, films, seminars and discussion groups are, after all, no substitute for the daily unspectacular witness of the rank and file Christian. If that witness is consistent and open, then no improvement in tactics or strategy will better it as a means of winning people for Christ. If it is not, then no evangelistic programme, no matter how ambitious or sophisticated, will make the slightest impact. That is a lesson we have been slow to learn.'

Having made that point, it is the greatest mistake to assume that the mission of the church must always be in these personal terms. The president of the Church of Christ in Zaire, I.B. Bokeleale, has stressed that in Africa people do not exist as separate entities, but as part of a family, a clan, a tribe. The same could be said of many other places on this earth. Until recently, however, Christian leaders have not given due note to the references in the New Testament to whole families or households coming to Christ and being baptised together. The western emphasis (which is often thoroughly middle-class) on personal evangelism can betray an unbalanced emphasis on the individual, and this may violate one of the most basic principles of many Africans and of those from other cultures. Other methods of evangelism and mission need to be considered.

Small groups

'A small group of eight to twelve people meeting together informally in homes is the most effective structure for the communication of the gospel in modern seculurban society... The small group offers the best hope for the discovery and use of spiritual gifts and for renewal within the church.'[13] This is the note that is currently being sounded again and again by Christian leaders in many different parts of the world. 'Sustaining small groups, and keeping them as small groups, is essential for the very life of the church... Growth must be through the multiplication of the smaller groups.'[14]

Certainly this was the unquestioned pattern of the early church for the first three centuries. They met almost exclusively in one another's homes, and were therefore well equipped for fellowship, spiritual growth and spontaneous evangelism. The spiritual momentum of the Reformation was in large measure spurred on by the emphasis on small group Bible studies. The same was true with the Wesleyan revival in the eighteenth century: John Wesley saw the absolute necessity of the 'class meeting' for effective instruction, discipline, pastoral care and growth. The astonishing spread of the Pentecostal Church, especially in Latin America, could never have happened without this same pattern of the small group. Howard Snyder has commented: 'Virtually every major movement of spiritual renewal in the Christian Church has been accompanied by a return to the small group and the proliferation of such groups in private homes for Bible study, prayer, and the discussion of the faith.'

Snyder lists some of the advantages of these small units as the basic structure of any local church.[15] They are *flexible*, so as to meet changing situations or to accomplish different objectives; they are *mobile*, going to where the people are, or to where the action is; they are *inclusive*, demonstrating a winsome openness to people of all kinds — 'when a person is drawn into a little circle...he is well aware that he is welcome for his own sake, since the group has no budget, no officers concerned with the success of their administration, and nothing to promote.'[16] They are *personal*, offering the best and most thorough form of communication; they can *grow by division*, multiplying like living cells almost indefinitely without large financial outlays; they can be an *effective means of*

[13] Howard Snyder, *The Problem of Wineskins*, I.V.P., p. 139.
[14] David Wasdell, in a paper called *Divide and Conquer*, p. 19.
[15] Op. cit., pp. 140ff.
[16] Elton Trueblood, *The Incendiary Fellowship*, New York: Harper & Row, p. 700

evangelism, offering a natural environment for proclamation and dialogue; they require a *minimum of professional leadership*, drawing in many who have never known any formal theological training but who, with growing spiritual gifts and constant encouragement, may develop into fine leaders; and they are *adaptable to the institutional church* — no massive restructuring is required, let alone a call to come out of the local church to form yet another church (and probably yet another denomination in due time). Some adjustments will have to be made, no doubt, but none that need threaten the essential life of the local church.

Some of the traditional organisations associated with many local churches will however need to be looked at critically. George Webber has expressed it like this:

> The clear demand of mission is that the multiplicity of congregational organisations be eliminated. A missionary congregation does not need a women's missionary society, but women engaged in mission. For male fellowship let the men join the Rotary or the union and in that context become salt that preserves the secular structures of community... The small groups in a congregation, along with the vestry, session, or governing board, can manage to fulfil the necessary institutional requirements of the congregation without setting up a host of organisations to fill out in full a denominational table of organisation for the local church.... Thus we conclude that congregational organisation must be functional for mission. The time in small groups must have one eye always on the worldly involvements of their members, so that the precious time the church requires will be used for equipping the saints.'[17]

Lawrence O. Richards, who has also made an extensive study on the use of small groups in the mission of the church, emphasises the importance of the group to hold three objectives in focus at the same time: they should encourage personal spiritual growth and mutual ministry amongst the members; they should aim to strengthen the unity and

[17] *The Congregation in Mission*, pp. 163f.

[18] See *A New Face for the Church* and *A Theology of Christian Education*, Zondervan.

fellowship of the church; and they should be mobilised for service and evangelism within the community. Any one of these aims pursued without the others will lead to an imbalance that could impair spiritual life and health. However, when these groups are functioning and developing along the lines suggested, they will prove one of the most fruitful means of Christian mission through a local church.

Preaching

We have already devoted Chapter eleven to this theme, and little more needs to be added here except to stress that since man, made in the image of God, is a rational being, the importance of instructing the mind before appealing for a commitment of the will must never be forgotten.

The gospel is not an invitation to an existential experience or an imposition of ethical standards. It centres on the person of Jesus Christ, whose teaching and saving acts demand careful and accurate exposition before any intelligent and rational response can be expected. The task of the preacher, as he seeks to be an effective communicator of God's self-revelation, is an all-absorbing and life-long task. He must grapple with the text, using both humble prayer and all available aids, in order to understand the original meaning of the passage for those who first heard it; then he must apply himself to see what the valid and relevant application of that text is today in a totally different cultural context.

The whole field of hermeneutics (the science of interpretation) is one that must be taken seriously by those who are called to be heralds of Christ. Just as a missionary in a foreign country must labour over the task of learning the language and culture of that country before he can ever hope to make the gospel clear, so the preacher must give much the same diligence over the word of God wherever he is called to preach. It is the good news of Christ that is God's power in the lives of people, not our own opinions or over-hasty application of what was first given in a thoroughly different setting. The church that is seriously engaged in its missionary task must give every encouragement and support to those within its fellowship who have been given, in whatever measure, the gifts of teaching and evangelism.

Dialogue

Some Christians have been distinctly cautious about the whole concept of dialogue, especially when talking to those of other faiths, for fear of giving the impression that our search for truth is entirely open-ended.

However, engaging in dialogue does not automatically mean being willing to embrace the other man's religious beliefs; rather it means a willingness to *listen*, in a spirit of genuine love and humility, and to try to *understand* what the other man's religious beliefs really are. So often Christians fail miserably at this point, and are therefore accused of being narrow and intolerant. The answer to such accusations is not to retreat from the absolute truths of the gospel, as centred in Jesus Christ, nor to waver from the uniqueness of his person, his death, and his resurrection; but to show the other man the love and respect he deserves because of the common humanity that we share. The aim of the dialogue will still ultimately be to win that person to Christ; but we cannot communicate the One who was full of grace and truth until wrong attitudes and prejudices have been cleared from our own lives. So often we hear only what we *expect* to hear, and maybe *want* to hear. Most of the tensions of life are ultimately due to a lack of communication or of understanding.

When an atheist says to me, 'I don't believe in God', I often reply, 'Tell me what sort of a god you do not believe in.' As often as not, I find that he has a strange and twisted caricature of God in his mind. So I comment, 'Well, I don't believe in that sort of a god either!' In this way, we find common ground; and, after that, communication can be much more meaningful. If we cannot listen graciously and sensitively to someone who does not share our beliefs, we have absolutely no right to try to impose those beliefs on him.

Healing

In the New Testament it is striking how often the expressions 'see and hear' or 'seen and heard' are to be found. Individuals were called to believe in Christ not only on the basis of the truth that had been preached, but often because of a visible manifestation of the power of God vindicating the truth of the gospel.

When John the Baptist, languishing in prison and perplexed by Christ's apparent lack of concern, sent two of his
disciples to express his own doubts about Christ, the answer
was anything but doctrinaire: 'Go and tell John what you
have *seen and heard*: the blind receive their sight, the lame
walk, lepers are cleansed, and the deaf hear, the dead are
raised up, the poor have good news preached to them.'[19] At
Pentecost, Peter had no trouble in convincing the crowd that
something significant had happened to the 120 disciples; he
simply explained that the manifestation 'which you *see and
hear*' was the promise of the Holy Spirit, now poured out by
Christ, following his exaltation at the right hand of God.[20]
Peter later explained to the ruling authorities the reason why
nothing could restrain their preaching of the risen Christ: 'we
cannot but speak of what we have *seen and heard*.'[21] Then, in
Samaria, 'the multitudes with one accord gave heed to what
was said by Philip, when they *heard* him and *saw* the signs
which he did' — exorcisms and healings.[22] Paul, too, was
commissioned to be 'a witness for him to all men of what you
have *seen and heard*.'[23] Later he wrote that his fruitful
evangelistic work amongst the Gentiles had been 'by word
and deed, by the power of signs and wonders, by the power of
the Holy Spirit.'[24]

Today, we have plenty of words and deeds, but not so
many obvious and visible signs of the power of God at work in
people's lives. Yet healing undoubtedly was, and still is, very
much a part of the church's mission in the name of Christ.

Simplistic teaching about healing must, of course, be
rejected. It is not true that 'if you have faith, you will be
healed'; and such a suggestion can have disastrous consequences, leading to deep depression, feelings of failure, and
perhaps utter despair. A quick look at the healing ministry of
Jesus may be instructive at this point.

In the Gospel records the healings performed by Jesus were
commonly called *signs*: they were all demonstrations of some
truth about God. For example, they spoke of the greatness of
God, of the deity of Christ, of his compassion, of the truth of

[19] Luke 7:22.
[20] Acts 2:33.
[21] Acts 4:20.
[22] Acts 8:6f.

[23] Acts 22:15, cf. John 3:32;
Philippians 4:9; 2 Peter 1:18;
1 John 1:3; Revelation 22:8.
[24] Romans 15:18f.

the gospel, of the universality of God's salvation, of the power of his kingdom, and of the authority of Christ to forgive. Yet, although Christ healed many people during his earthly ministry, and although on certain occasions we read that he healed every disease and every infirmity (no one was apparently turned away), his sovereignty can still be clearly perceived. We can see this in at least four ways.

First, Christ was sovereign in his *timing*. Why did the woman go on bleeding from a haemorrhage for twelve long years, having suffered from many physicians, having spent all she had, and having become worse? Why did the sick man pathetically hang around the Pool of Bethesda for thirty-eight years, waiting for the 'troubling of the waters'? Why did Christ seemingly step over all the other sick people in that pool, in order to heal that one man? Why was the cripple from birth laid daily at the Gate Beautiful, until the time at last came for him to be healed, as recorded in Acts 3?

Secondly, Christ was sovereign concerning the *conditions* for healing. Various books on healing suggest reasons some people are not healed in answer to prayer: lack of repentance or faith, lack of commitment to Christ, etc. But in the Gospels, there were often no conditions attached at all. With many, there was no sign of repentance or faith; they were not yet disciples of Christ; in other words, there was no spiritual reason why they should have been healed, apart from this matter of God's sovereignty.

Thirdly, Christ was sovereign in *limiting* his healing power. Although on one occasion he healed the centurion's servant with only a 'word' and at a distance, [25] and later did much the same thing with the son of an official, [26] why did he not 'say the word' for countless others all over Palestine, let alone the rest of the world? Again, although his power to heal was manifestly with the Twelve and with the seventy, and although the gift of healing was, and is, given to some within the body of Christ, why is this gift not more widely distributed, since we all know many who are sick? And even when some did experience healing, or do today, Christ did not, and does not, necessarily save them from further suffering in the future.

Fourthly, Christ was sovereign in the *nature of the sickness*

[25] Matthew 8:5-13.   [26] John 4:46-54.

that he healed. While we are told sometimes that he healed every disease, it seems that he was usually concerned with those diseases which were beyond the power of physicians to heal, for one reason or another, such as the woman with the haemorrhage. Normally he dealt with those who were blind, deaf, dumb, lame, or demon-possessed, for whom there was no known cure. There are one or two exceptions to this, but generally speaking God allows us to do for ourselves what we can do (we do not read of him healing a common cold, for example), and only intervenes in special ways when our normal resources, which are all ultimately dependent on him, dry up. That is possibly why Paul took the beloved physician Luke on his many travels, and why he told nervous Timothy (suffering from some psychosomatic disorder?) to take a little wine for his frequent ailments.

A clear recognition of the sovereignty of God, even in the healing ministry of Christ, may help us in what is often an extraordinarily puzzling aspect of the church's total mission. Michael Green helpfully comments:

God does not always choose to heal us physically, and perhaps it is as well that he does not. How people would rush to Christianity (and for all the wrong motives) if it carried with it automatic exemption from sickness! What a nonsense it would make of Christian virtues like longsuffering, patience and endurance if instant wholeness were available for all the Christian sick! What a wrong impression it would give of salvation if physical wholeness were perfectly realised on earth whilst spiritual wholeness were partly reserved for heaven! What a very curious thing it would be if God were to decree death for all his children whilst not allowing illness for any of them![27]

Having accepted the sovereignty and mystery of God in this whole realm, it is nevertheless true that God still heals, still gives gifts of healing, and still demonstrates his power and authenticates the truth of the gospel by setting people free from a whole variety of diseases and occult oppression. Since his concern is with wholeness, it may be wrong always

[27] *I Believe in the Holy Spirit*, Hodder & Stoughton, p. 176.

to look for physical healing. Often he may be more concerned with inner healing, the healing of memories, or the healing of bad relationships. Numerous people have deep psychological hurts and wounds for which the healing love of Christ is even more urgently needed than in the more obvious physical handicaps; and it is here that the healing ministry of the body of Christ comes into its own.

A consultant in the medical profession once wrote to me about the healing of a woman who suffered from constant depression, marriage failure, and occasional thoughts of suicide:

> Many of the problems stemmed from way back in child-hood. You will be pleased to hear that through the tremendously impressive ministry of [name supplied], working entirely under the power and guidance of the Holy Spirit, all these very painful and deeply buried memories stretching, as we found, right back to the conception itself, all these were completely healed. That is to say, the Holy Spirit reached right down into the years and took them all away, replacing these with real peace and the beginnings of spiritual love and joy. The effect on 'A', I need hardly say, has been very considerable, almost I might say, dramatic... I should, however, comment that the whole atmosphere of [the house], the attitude of all the members of the community and indeed the many guests whom we spoke to throughout the time boosted our flagging Christian morale and filled the dry arid areas with real spiritual hope and enlighten-ment.

Further, although a cautionary word has been given about the 'only-have-faith' attitude towards healing, there is no doubt that the presence of a strong, positive faith in the love of God and in the power of Christ can make an immense difference when it comes to any real healing ministry.

In *The New Face of Evangelicalism* an account is given of an Indian woman in South America who was dying of pneumon-ia. The believers decided to try to save her life by prayer. Two missionaries were asked to join the prayer group. There was some slight improvement in the woman's health, but she soon relapsed and was again on the point of dying. The Indian Christians held another prayer meeting, but this time exclud-ed the two missionaries. 'Isn't it wonderful!' said one of the Indian Christians to the two missionaries later. 'This morning Nata was dying, and here she is — well and making supper!' 'Yes,' said another Indian, 'God is good! God is great! His Spirit is powerful and he has healed her.' One of the missionaries mentioned that they had not been invited to join the believers for this second time of prayer. 'I'm sorry,' came the reply, 'but we couldn't invite you. You two don't really believe, and you cannot heal by God's power when you have unbelievers in the circle.'[28]

That humbling lesson learnt by the 'professionals', about the necessity of true and united faith, may not be so in every case (I know of one or two healings where no one was more surprised at the startling results than the person who had prayed for a healing!); but it may often be the prevailing atmosphere of unbelief that hinders the Spirit of God from working. On three or four occasions (over several years), having meditated on the promises of healing in the Scrip-tures, God has *given* me the gift of faith (I use the words deliberately) to know that he was about to heal — and he did. On many other occasions I have prayed in response to the love of God for that sick person. Occasionally healing has occurred; often not. But in every case there has, I believe, been definite blessing of one form or another. I disclaim any personal gift or ministry along these lines, but I still very much believe that God by his Spirit gives gifts of healing within his body 'as he wills'.

What is needed, as an essential prerequisite, is a strong atmosphere of prayer, preferably with the support of a healing group, even if it is only two or three. It is the Lord who heals, and our dependence upon him in prayer is essential. It is helpful, too, to read out a passage such as Psalm 103 or James 5:14-16, leading in to the laying-on of hands: this can encourage the sufferer to relax in the knowledge of the love of God who is present through faith. In any healing ministry we need to pray for discernment, too, for surface problems may often conceal much deeper hurts or

[28]Op. cit., p. 182f.

resentments that first need to be dealt with. We may even be
coming against evil powers which are holding the sufferer in
some satanic bondage, and which need to be broken first with
the power and authority of Christ.

Generally speaking it is helpful to pray with a small group
of true believers present; and, wherever possible, in close
consultation with the medical profession. We should thank
God for *his* healing powers through listening to medical
opinions. Our own personal preparation is also of considerable importance, as we seek to place ourselves completely in
God's hands, asking for his cleansing from our sins, and his
empowering with his Spirit. I have also found that anointing
with oil can help to encourage and maintain faith, while
resting in the sovereignty of God's will and mercy.

Literature
All revolutionary movements know the astonishing power of
the printed word. In the developing countries, in particular,
with millions of men and women learning to read for the first
time in the history of those nations, hungry minds consume
almost anything that is going. Often the literature most
readily available comes from communist sources or from the
proliferation of religious sects that abound everywhere.
However, the Bible Society and many Christian publishers
have also been increasingly alert to this vital aspect of
Christian mission; and even in western 'Christianised' society
the almost total ignorance of the facts of Jesus Christ and the
truth of the gospel is astonishing amongst the vast majority of
the population. Many have a twisted Sunday School caricature of the Christian faith, with a mixture of the religious
eccentricities and travesties that so often reach the press and
television. Therefore the value of straightforward translations
of the Scriptures, such as the *Good News Bible*, and non-
technical books which spell out the heart of the gospel,
cannot be overestimated.

Frequently I meet with men and women (of all ages) who
are looking for some basis to their life. They are aware that
they have no sense of direction and no meaning to their
existence. One way or another they are conscious of a
gnawing spiritual hunger which cannot be satisfied by the
materialistic and affluent world around them. Although a

living demonstration of the reality of God within his church is probably the most helpful and convincing evidence for anyone in such a position, many want to read and think through the bewildering variety of philosophies and religions that face the honest seeker today. Having written one or two Christian books for such people myself, I am often humbled by letters I have received from people I have never met who have been brought into a personal experience of Christ through something they have read.

The church should not only write and publish suitable books, but of course make them available as widely as possible to the huge cross-sections of society that would never enter church buildings. Many shops and multiple stores, railway stations and airports, have a great variety of books for sale. In different parts of the world I have come across local churches which have obtained permission from various shops to erect simple revolving wire-framed bookstalls with attractive Bibles and Christian paperbacks for the shopper or traveller. Christian bookshops in towns and cities can also be excellent centres for missionary work. Imaginative uses of literature such as this will almost certainly prove fruitful in the overall mission of the church.

Radio and television

Opportunities for mass communication through radio or television will vary considerably from place to place; but the church should examine carefully what *could* be done in any situation, and use such means to the full. I have frequently been impressed by the imagination shown by Christians who have given their time and energies to local radio, helping in some measure to make the church relevant to the community at large.

'Results' of such things as the epilogue are hard to gauge, but many stations are open to far more than the two or three minute epilogue. I have sometimes been involved in valuable phone-in's, where it is possible to discuss the heart of the Christian faith with people in their homes, while thousands are listening in. Drama, discussion, open debate, news items, Christian music, dial-a-hymn — these are some of the ways in which I have seen local radio, especially, being well used in the mission of the church.

In other countries and cities the opportunities are endless.

Some churches in North America have their regular weekly, or even daily, television programmes. If that is beyond the scope of most, I know of another church that broadcasts the first hour of its main morning service every Sunday, and a team of church workers are sitting by the telephone to receive calls from sick and needy people during the programme. Further teams go off immediately by car to answer the 'distressed calls'. In this city, where the problems of drugs and suicide have been staggering, such a service has literally been a life-saver for many a person over the course of years.

At the very least, each church needs to explore prayerfully what can be done, and then encourage some of its members to be trained and ready for opportunities that arise. To begin with, it may seem a slow and unprofitable business; but it would be tragic if the church neglected the most influential means of communication for our present generation.

The arts
Although the church, in past centuries, has often been a strong and generous patron of the arts, there are some Christians today who stress that this was particularly true of the medieval church when at the height of its corruption and carnality; and therefore a vital part of the Reformation was to sweep all this on one side in order to get back to the purity of the preaching and studying of the written word of God in the Scriptures.

One critic has linked drama and dance with 'images, vestments, ceremonial, and other devices known to human artistry', but points out that there is no support to be found for any of these within the New Testament. Another Christian leader, whose friendship and teaching gifts I greatly respect, wrote to me to say that in the New Testament 'there is not the slightest hint that the Christian should employ the means available from the world for trying to communicate the gospel. It was not as if the Greek world was devoid of the very things which today are being advocated,' he went on to say. 'The theatre was very much a factor of Greek life, and Greek drama and Greek dancing were there for imitation. But search the New Testament from end to end and there is never a hint that such means should be employed.'

At first sight, the Scriptures as a whole seem to confirm this viewpoint. The writer of Ecclesiastes admits that cultural and artistic pursuits were, after all, nothing but emptiness and a striving after wind. The first mention of music and craftsmanship comes from the dubious pedigree of Cain;[29] and the downfall of Babylon, resplendent in its artistic wealth, is a cause for triumphant rejoicing in heaven.

As I have often heard from those who criticise the use of various artistic forms in the communication of the gospel: 'God is pleased by the foolishness of preaching to save them that believe.' A writer went on to say,

> It is plain that the introduction of drama and dance as supplements to the preaching of the Word indirectly expresses a diminishing confidence in preaching as the great and sufficient means for the spread of the gospel... It may be that people can derive new thoughts about a biblical narrative from absorbing it in dramatic presentation. But it is perhaps dangerously easy to miss the significance of this. May it not be simply a commentary on the fact that people are not spending very much time reading the Bible?[30]

However, a better translation of Paul's words is given in the R.S.V.: 'It pleased God through the folly of *what* we preach (i.e. the message of Christ crucified) to save those who believe.'[31] Paul was talking about the God-given changeless message of Christ dying for our sins and rising again from the dead; he was not in any way discussing the means or methods of communication. Further, in a generation which is certainly *not* spending very much time reading the Bible, the whole question of communication becomes urgent.

A closer look at the Scriptures will, however, reveal that God is far from 'Philistine' when it comes to the arts; and man, made in the image of God, has much to learn from his Maker. God is not only Redeemer; he is Creator and Sustainer, whose unsurpassed artistic and creative beauty is a perpetual expression of his majesty and glory: 'The heavens are telling the glory of God; and the firmament proclaims his

[29] Genesis 4:21f.
[30] David Marshall, *Christian*
Graduate, September 1974.
[31] 1 Corinthians 1:21.

handiwork...'[32] He has given us all things richly to enjoy; and Paul rejoins us to think about those things that are honourable, just, pure, lovely, gracious and worthy of praise.[33]

To speak therefore of any conflict between 'the word' and 'art' is to misunderstand the very nature of God's self-revelation. If we believe in God we must view the world sacramentally: 'Ever since the creation of the world his invisible nature, namely, his eternal power and deity, has been clearly perceived in the things that have been made.'[34] Without 'the word' there could be no art, since it was by the word of God that the world was created;[35] and without art there could be no words, no communication, no Scripture. We cannot separate the truth from the means by which that truth is made known to us. In Christ, to take the supreme example, we have both the medium and the message. We should not be surprised to find much beauty and poetry within Scripture itself. Even the artless simplicity of the Gospel records, for example, has an artistic beauty of its own. From the creation of the world to the word made flesh in Jesus Christ, and then to the written word in the Scriptures, God has always clothed the bare propositional truth about himself with his own creativity and glory. The bare word is never enough; it always needs to become flesh. Christ sadly had to rebuke many times those who knew God's word in their heads, but failed to let it become true in their lives and actions.

God is concerned with what we are and with the ways in which we express ourselves. The words we speak or write, the clothes we wear, the music we play, the songs we sing, the movements of our bodies, the expressions on our faces, the work done with our hands, the relationships we make with other people – all these are extensions of our personalities. And it is these personalities that, with all their variety, God wants to transform increasingly into the likeness of his Son. Art, therefore, is intrinsically a part of the life that God has made: it is to be appreciated, enjoyed, and, for the Christian, offered back to God as part of the worship of our glorious Creator. For the church to be afraid of art, or even worse to oppose art, is a tragic sign of a church that misunderstands its

[32] Psalm 19.
[33] Philippians 4:8.
[34] Romans 1:20.
[35] Hebrews 11:3.

Creator, denies the humanity of its members, and has become irrelevant to the world which it has been called to redeem.

What, then, are some of the areas of artistic expression that, when redeemed for the glory of Christ, can become valid and beautiful expressions of worship and also relevant and powerful forms of communication?

Dance for centuries was a natural and joyful form of worship for the people of God. Since it was an integral part of the great Jewish festivals, it is almost certain that Jesus himself danced, no doubt on many occasions, and so did most of his disciples. Further,when Paul tells Christians to 'sing psalms and hymns' some commentators suggest that Paul would have included the *style* in which the psalms were sung, not just the words themselves. We know from the psalms themselves that often this included praising God's name with dancing.[36]

The Bible, too, is full of *drama*, as seen once again in the great feasts. Some of the prophets, such as Ezekiel and Agabus, communicated their message in highly dramatic form, which no doubt made a much more vivid impression on the onlookers than the bare words. Jesus himself was the supreme master of communication, and there is little doubt that some of his teaching and parables had considerable dramatic and visual content as well as matchless words. At times he would pick up a coin, or set a child in the midst of his disciples, or point to a sower scattering seed. Think of the perfect dramatic timing on the last day of the Feast of Tabernacles, during which there was no water-pouring ceremony which had been the climax of the seven previous days. Jesus stood up in the middle of the Temple, where everyone could see and hear him, and said in a loud voice: 'If anyone thirst, let him come to me and drink. He who believes in me, as the scripture has said, "Out of his heart shall flow rivers of living water." '[37] The atmosphere must have been electric, deliberately so, because of the sheer timing and drama of his action.

Further, the washing of the disciples' feet, and the taking of the bread and wine at the Last Supper were all superb drama. If the critic tries to say that these things were natural and spontaneous, far removed from the rehearsals that precede drama within the church today, it could well be

[36] Psalm 149:3; 150:4.   [37] John 7:37f.

argued that Jesus had 'rehearsed', at least in his mind, every tiny detail of the Last Supper, with its highly symbolic links with the Passover Feast.

Most dramatic of all was the incarnation. Apparently, it was insufficient for the prophets and apostles to preach the word of God by mouth or to write it in the Scriptures. The word had to become flesh, so that all could *see* the glory of God in the face of Jesus Christ. If we see that 'all the world's a stage', Jesus became the principal actor in the most powerful drama the world has ever seen. Even today's films based upon his life, such as *Jesus of Nazareth* directed by Franco Zeffirelli, have made a most profound impact on countless millions of people who would never listen to a conventional sermon preached within the safe precincts of an austere religious building. God surely is the God of drama.

The *visual arts,* such as painting, architecture, sculpture, tapestry, banners — all these and many more can be expressions of worship and effective means of communication. We have seen that our clothes, houses and possessions are all expressions of our personalities; similarly our church buildings and music, our pictures and glass, are all extensions of the faith and life of the body of Christ who gather together to worship their Creator and Redeemer. Look at the astonishing and beautiful details designed by God himself for the tabernacle and the temple. So important was it that this artistic work should be worthy of his name that God filled Bezalel with his Spirit, 'with ability and intelligence, with knowledge and all craftsmanship, to devise artistic designs, to work in gold, silver and bronze, in cutting stones for setting, and in carving wood, for work in every craft.'[38] Many of these details had no pragmatic or doctrinal function at all; they were designed simply for beauty since God is the God of beauty.

In spite of the misgivings expressed earlier in this book about our numerous church buildings, it is surely true that, of the millions of tourist who flock round the great cathedrals of the church, some, at least, must gain a deep sense of awe and wonder of the God in whose honour they were designed and built. I know of one leading architect, a self-confessed agnostic, who became a believer when he was working on the

[38] Exodus 31:1-5.

restoration of such a cathedral. If God's children are silent, the very stones will cry out.

See, too, how the world has been enriched by the *poetry* and *literature* of the Bible. Here, as with many other art forms, God can touch the heart and spirit of man, which is just as important as our minds and intellects. Salvation means 'wholeness'. God wants us in Christ to be whole people, not just sanctified intellectuals. Mind, heart, spirit, emotions, body and will — all are called to respond to the God of love and truth. Look at the glorious love-poem, the Song of Solomon. Most Christians interpret this as a beautiful picture of the love relationship that Christ has with the individual believer, or with his bride, the church. That may be good hermeneutics! But the Song of Solomon is also a profoundly moving description of human love, with its joys and pains, fulfilments and frustrations. It also states that human love, in its most intimate form and within the limits set by God, is a beautiful and sacred part of our created life.

Music, of course, has always been the most natural expression of praise and worship; and here every instrument and everything that has breath is called into the praise of the Lord. What could have been more moving than hundreds of thousands of Israelites singing antiphonally the song of Moses after the crossing of the Red Sea? And how natural it must have been for the climax of praise to have come when Miriam the prophetess took her timbrel and danced with the other women to the same song: 'Sing to the Lord, for he has triumphed gloriously...'[39] So powerful was music in worship that at times, 'when the song was raised, with trumpets and cymbals and other musical instruments, in praise to the Lord, "For he is good, for his steadfast love endures for ever," the house, the house of the Lord, was filled with a cloud, so that the priests could not stand to minister because of the cloud; for the glory of the Lord filled the house of God.'[40] I have on many occasions witnessed at least something of this phenomenon when, in response to the worship of God's people in the Spirit, there has been an overwhelming sense of the power and reality and presence of God. I have seen men and women, of different ages and from different backgrounds,

[39] Exodus 15.   [40] 2 Chronicles 5:13f.

reduced to tears, wanting to be counselled, and seriously searching for the God who is there.

Once we see something of the value of art in Christian worship and mission, there are still many questions to be thought through. What is good and what is bad? What is moral and what is immoral? How far must the artist's integrity and freedom of expression be preserved at all costs? Is it ever right to think of art as a useful tool for evangelism? Can we make any valid distinction between the 'spiritual' and 'secular'? What is wholesome and fitting within church buildings? What is acceptable as a form of valid communication on the streets (such as fast-moving and often humorous street-theatre), and do different principles apply when that communication takes place within a worship service? Since certain art forms seek to express the reality of life as it is, what restrictions should be placed on the ugly and profane realities of life when that art is set in a Christian context? These and other questions are beyond the scope of this one section of this present book, but they need to be taken seriously if this whole area is not to fall into the abuses that have brought art under such suspicion for years in the minds of many Christians.

Questions need to be raised, too, about the quality of art that is expressed in a Christian context. Derek Kidner has put the point well:

> Whatever we produce should be, it would seem, not only morally but aesthetically above reproach. From this it is a short step to the conclusion that for the service of God nothing but the highest in music, art and literature is fit to be considered. Yet this too is facile. It makes the mistake of prescribing for God what he should have, instead of discovering what he prefers — as a child might prescribe for a king nothing but crowns and state robes, and be shocked to discover him in tweeds. For there is no doubt that, however we account for it, God has often used the poorest of equipment; not only obscure and weak men, but often their equally unprepossessing products — ugly mission halls, second-rate pictures, bad tunes, illiterate tracts. All these he has so often made to be the gate of heaven to people of all kinds... We find then, not that God insists on good art or on bad, but that he does not restrict himself to

either. The connoisseur and the 'Philistine' both need to
weigh this fact well. The former needs to be reminded by
it, first, that art is not all-important; secondly, that our
most beautiful offerings cannot enrich God; thirdly, that
worship is not the preserve of an aesthetic élite, but should
call forth the 'Amen' of him 'that occupieth the room of
the unlearned'; fourthly, that the very excellence of some
art is a disqualification, when it makes it a better master
than servant... The 'Philistine', for his part, has to beware
of drawing the wrong conclusions from God's use of bad
material. Because Sankey or Alexander used a certain
idiom and God accepted their work, it does not follow that
they had stumbled on a formula worth copying... There
is a right and a wrong way of meeting people at their own
level. [41]

And the right way is that it should be in the Spirit,
glorifying to God, serving and edifying the people of God, or
communicating effectively to those who are not yet his
people.

Bearing this last point in mind, it would be the greatest
mistake, in the fresh discovery of certain art forms such as
dance and drama, if the preaching and teaching of the
gospel were in any way neglected, worse still ignored.
Art is no substitute for clear, biblical proclamation. It is still
the gospel of Christ that changes the lives of men and
women; it is still the word of God that vitally nourishes
our struggling faith. The church that replaces the thorough,
prayerful and consistent teaching of the Scriptures with
music, dance, drama, discussion, or anything else, has
signed its own spiritual death-warrant. Michael Green has
rightly commented:

God loves partnership... The message of redemption goes
alongside the fact of creation. The creative Christian artist,
and the imaginative Christian preacher go hand in hand in
the purposes of the God who joined them together. What a
pity it is when either side initiates divorce proceedings.
The most effective evangelism takes place when preaching

[41]*The Christian and the Arts*, I.V.P., p. 19f.

and dramatic presentation not only 'come together' but 'stay together'.[42]

There is therefore today a great need for churches to encourage and, as far as possible, to support Christian artists as they bring their gifts to the service of Christ and his church. The Nottingham Statement, stemming from the Congress for Evangelical Anglicans in 1977, affirmed that 'we believe it to be important for local churches to encourage the maturing of artistic skills among their members... In times past, evangelicals provided for missionaries to enter foreign cultures; for the future, it may be important to employ the same principle in dealing with our commitment to training for involvement, in the mass media.' Such Christian artists may well play a major part in the church's mission of tomorrow, and the church as a whole must have the vision and courage to bring this to fruition.

Effective Christian mission, then, has great variety. It is God communicating with the people whom he has made and loved — a communication which, if it is truly from God, will always be relevant, fresh, meaningful, bringing both his life and his love to those who need him, whether they realise their need or not. The church must therefore constantly re-examine its methods of communication and refuse to be tied to the cultural traditions of the past. The essential gospel, like the God who gave it, never changes.

Christians need to learn again from probably the greatest missionary the church has ever known, the apostle Paul. He was utterly determined, however personally painful or humbling it might be, to be relevant to the Jew, to the Gentile, to the weak — to everyone: 'I have become all things to all men, that I might by all means save some. I do it all for the sake of the gospel'.[43]

---

[42]*Gallery*, Christian Arts Project,   [43] 1 Corinthians 9:22f.
Vol. 1, No. 1.

CHAPTER EIGHTEEN

The Unity of the Church

'OF ALL THE items on Congress, Council and local church agendas, unity is the one which consistently wins top prize for the highest ratio of input of paper to output of action.'[1] Because of this, the whole theme of the church's unity is viewed by many with boredom, and by others with suspicion.

Yet from the New Testament onwards, Christians have been unquestionably committed to the principle of a united church. At the Council of Constantinople in 381 the confessional Creed of Nicaea-Constantinople was drawn up stating a firm belief in the 'one, holy, catholic and apostolic Church'. There has never been any question about the church of God being one church, when viewed from a biblical or theological perspective. The practical difficulty arises, however, when the questions are asked: What sort of unity? How can that unity be expressed? What *is* the universal church? Where is it to be found? Can this church or that church, this group or that group, be regarded as part of the one true church? What is the minimal requirement for membership in the universal church of God? Can divisions be justified on *any* basis? If so, what? Should not the wheat and the tares be allowed to grow together until the harvest? Will there not always be good and bad fish in the same net? What are the criteria for Christian unity? In the great divides of Christendom, will it not always be true that 'East is East, West is West, and never the twain shall meet'? On what basis could Protestants and Catholics unite?

[1] 'The Unity of the Church', a chapter by C.O. Buchanan in *Obeying Christ in a Changing World*, Fountain Books, Vol. 2, p. 144.

What is a true church?

Let us consider first what is meant by a true church.

Not every claim to be a church is necessarily valid. In the letter to the seven churches in Revelation 2 and 3, Christ twice refers to a 'synagogue of Satan',[2] and he warned the church at Sardis that they had a name of being alive but in fact were dead. What, then, are the essential ingredients of a true church?

We are concerned here not with elements that are desirable for the well-being of the church, but with the basic essentials before the church can have any being at all. This has always been a matter of the utmost importance from the first century to the present day, especially when it comes to any division within the church. At the time of the Reformation, Calvin and Luther, Cranmer, Jewel, Hooker and Hall naturally pursued this question in order to justify their monumental break with Rome.

The Reformers first of all pressed the distinction between the church visible and the church invisible. 'I have observed that the Scriptures speak of the Church in two ways,' wrote Calvin in his *Institutes*. There is 'the Church as it really is before God — the Church into which none are admitted but those who by the gift of adoption are sons of God, and by the sanctification of the Spirit true members of Christ'. Then there is also 'designated the whole body of mankind scattered throughout the world who profess to worship one God and Christ.' This visible church included 'a very large mixture of hypocrites, who have nothing of Christ but the name and outward appearance.' Even so, not only is it 'necessary to believe the invisible Church, which is manifest to the eye of God only', but 'we are also enjoined to regard this [visible] Church...and to cultivate its communion.'

The distinction made by Calvin and others was intended not in order to separate from the visible church, but to reform it. As the real church consists of real people, it can never be solely invisible. God alone knows who are truly the elect, and therefore it is inescapable that the real church will always consist of both wheat and tares, genuine and counterfeit,

[2] Revelation 2:9 and 3:9.

growing up together until their separation on the Day of Judgment. The leading Reformers were always against the constant tendency to cream off from the visible church a spiritual élite to form a 'pure' fellowship consisting only of members of the invisible church. Although the hidden and spiritual aspects of the church are of prime importance, its visible form, complete with inevitable mixture and impurities, is part of its essential nature. 'If we say with the creed *credo ecclesiam* (I believe in the church), we do not proudly overlook its concrete form... Nor do we look penetratingly through this form, as though it was only something transparent and the real church had to be sought behind it... Hence we cannot rid ourselves in this way of the generally visible side of the church. We cannot take refuge from it in a kind of wonderland...'[3]

Yet that is precisely what some Christians have done throughout the centuries. Impatient with the mixture of impurities in terms of faith, life or doctrine (often minor doctrine of secondary importance), some pull out of existing denominations to form another fellowship of like-minded Christians who, for the time being at least, enjoy greater freedom in worship or flexibility in structure. Soon, however, another denomination is born; and a little later another visible church, with the same impurities as before, will have come into being. Although the distinction between the visible and the invisible church is a valid one, a separation between the two is impossible.

Nowhere better is this expressed than in these words by Hans Küng:

There are not two Churches, one visible and one invisible. Nor must we think, with Platonic dualism and spiritualism, of the visible Church (being earthly and 'material') as the reflection of the real invisible Church (being spiritual and heavenly). Nor is the invisible part of the Church its essential nature, and the visible part the external form of the Church. The one Church, in its essential nature and in its external forms alike, is always at once visible and invisible. The Church which we believe is *one* Church: visible and invisible, or perhaps rather hidden,

[3] Karl Barth, *Church Dogmatics* IV/1 Edinburgh 1965, pp. 653-654.

at once. This is the Church which believes and is believed.[4]

Marks of a true church

With this distinction (but not division) in mind, what are the marks of a true church? One outstanding and essential mark is *faithfulness to the gospel of Jesus Christ*.[5] 'The church of the living God,' wrote Paul to Timothy, '[is] a pillar and bulwark of the truth.'[6] Paul further mentioned 'the glorious gospel of the blessed God with which I have been entrusted'[7], and exhorted Timothy to 'follow the pattern of the sound words which you have heard from me, in the faith and love which are in Christ Jesus; guard the truth that has been entrusted to you by the Holy Spirit who dwells within us.'[8] The church is to believe, guard, live by, and proclaim the gospel of Christ. Without this, there is no salvation, no knowledge of God, and no church.

The Reformers emphasised the purity of the gospel and the rightness of the sacraments as being basic marks of a true church. 'Wherever we see the Word of God sincerely preached and heard,' wrote Calvin, 'wherever we see the sacraments administered according to the institution of Christ, there we cannot have any doubt that the Church of God has some existence.' Or again, 'when the preaching of the gospel is reverently heard, and the sacraments not neglected, there for the time the face of the church appears...' Article VII of the Augsburg Confession of 1530 said: 'The Church is...the community of saints, in which the pure Gospel is preached and the sacraments properly administered.' Article 19 of the Church of England says much the same: 'The visible Church of Christ is a congregation of faithful men, in which the pure word of God is preached, and the Sacraments be duly administered according to Christ's ordinance in all those things that of necessity are requisite to the same.' It is worth noting that no mention is made here of church order as a mark of the church. It is not until the nineteenth century and the Tractarians that we find any strong view among Protestants about episcopacy as essential to the being of the church.

---

[4] *The Church*, Search Press 1968, p. 38.
[5] However, see also Chapter 17 of this book.
[6] 1 Timothy 3:15.
[7] 1 Timothy 1:11.
[8] 2 Timothy 1:13f.

Moreover, the Roman Catholic theologian Hans Küng holds the same position:

> How do we know when the Church is on the right path? Where is the golden thread? The short answer to the question is that the Church is headed in the right direction when, whatever the age in which it lives, the Gospel of Jesus Christ is its criterion, the Gospel which Christ proclaimed and to which the Church of the apostles witnessed... The Church must ever and again wander through the desert, through the darkness of sin and error... There is, however, one guiding light it is never without, just as God's people in the desert always had a guide: God's word is always there to lead the Church. Through Jesus, the Christ, it has been definitively revealed to us. The word of Jesus Christ, as testified by the apostles, is the Church's guide. It is the word to which the Church appeals and according to which it must examine its activities in the confusion of this world. With the message of Jesus Christ behind it, the Church is headed in the right direction. [9]

Certainly there are many other ingredients which are beneficial to the church, but the only absolute requirement is to hold fast and to proclaim the gospel of Jesus Christ as revealed in the written word of God, the Scriptures. 'As soon as falsehood has forced its way into the citadel of religion,' warned Calvin, 'as soon as the sum of necessary doctrine is inverted, and the use of the sacraments is destroyed, the death of the Church undoubtedly ensues.' Nevertheless, although much is to be said for the basic simplicity of these hallmarks, sadly they have been tragically insufficient to protect the church from the numerous splits and divisions that followed the Reformation.

The Roman Catholics, on the other hand, have largely stressed the four-fold marks of unity, holiness, catholicity and apostolicity, in accordance with the confessional statement of 381. In general terms there is again no quibble. But how are the marks recognised? Is it sufficient to appeal to legal and ecclesiastical conformity? What about the final and authoritative court of appeal in the New Testament?

[9] Op. cit., pp. x, xi.

The difficulty with credal formulae and propositional definitions is that it is possible to have all the necessary requirements yet be totally without the signs of life. It is not enough to adhere to the Scriptures, or to administer faithfully the sacraments, or to belong to the universal institution of the church, unless there is true spiritual life. It was the Holy Spirit who brought about the birth of the church. Without his indwelling power there could never have been a church, no matter how loyal or doctrinally correct the first disciples might have been. Indeed it was the marked demonstration of the activity of the Spirit that convinced Simon Peter, and later the council at Jerusalem, that the Gentiles rightly had a place within the Church of Jesus Christ. The plain fact was that Cornelius and his household had come alive spiritually.

Certainly the early church soon realised that part of the objective evidence of the Spirit's work lay in a right belief in one or two crucial doctrines, such as the divinity and humanity of Jesus Christ;[10] but one of the first requirements for the unity of the church in the first century was the manifest presence of the Holy Spirit. Through the cross of Christ, such unity was possible; and through the life of the Spirit, such unity was real. This is a point that seems often to be overlooked when the church is looking for the theological basis on which its unity today can be found.

I doubt if any amount of religious reasoning could have persuaded Simon Peter about the inclusion of the Gentiles within God's plan of salvation. For him, it was quite unthinkable. But when he experienced for himself a vision from God, and later the Spirit's sovereign action in the house of a Gentile, he could only declare, 'Can anyone forbid water for baptising these people who have received the Holy Spirit just as we have?'[11]

In the same way I very much doubt if any amount of reasoning can persuade some people about the possible future unity between, say, Catholics and Protestants. However, the current renewal of the Holy Spirit in both traditions, bringing authentic and unmistakable spiritual life, has given at least a taste of this unity, and has astonished many Catholics and Protestants who were just as intransigent

[10] 1 John 4:1-3.   [11] Acts 10:44ff.

in their position as the apostle Peter. This is a point that we shall return to again.

Why unity?
Many Christians have deplored the wearisome ecumenical discussions that have shuffled from conference to conference throughout this century, on the grounds that we are already one in Christ Jesus — a oneness that is triumphantly proclaimed at the great Christian Conventions and Conferences throughout the world, and that can fairly easily be seen amongst Christians who share much the same doctrinal convictions overriding their denominational labels. Nevertheless, the plethora of churches in almost every place presents a continuing and conflicting headache which cannot be brushed under the carpet of special conventions and united services.

What are the consequences of the numerous divisions that exist within the church of God?

(a)   It is undeniable that these divisions seriously weaken the worldwide mission of the church. More than 200 separated churches belong to the World Council of Churches, and there are other churches, such as the Roman Catholics, who do not belong to this Council. When Jesus said that the mark of true Christian discipleship should be love for one another, is it surprising that the world, by and large, is unconvinced about the gospel that we proclaim? Four times in John 17 Jesus prayed that his disciples should be one, with a unity and love that reflects the perfect relationship that exists within the Trinity. His urgency was because he knew that only in this way would the world believe and know the truth about him. Why should those of other religions be persuaded about the uniqueness of Jesus Christ when faced with such a torn and divided church? How can the agnostic or atheist believe in the reality of God? It is only when we love one another that 'God abides in us'.[12]

The missiologist A.F. Glasser has written with sadness, 'One cannot believe that the more than 125 separate societies serving in Japan alone can be viewed as an answer to our Lord's prayer "that they may all be one".' Bishop Festo Kivengere of Uganda has said, 'By our denominationalism

---

[12] 1 John 4:12.

we tell the world how much we hate each other.' He considers this problem second only to apartheid as a hindrance to the gospel in South Africa. There is an uncomfortable truth in the parody of the famous hymn:

> Like a mighty tortoise
> Moves the Church of God;
> Brothers we are treading
> Where we've always trod;
> We are all divided,
> Many bodies we,
> Very strong on doctrine,
> Weak on charity.

(b)   The urgent and obvious need for spiritual renewal and structural reform within most churches (urgent and obvious if we are to be relevant at all in the last quarter of the twentieth century) is frustrated repeatedly by entrenched positions held by majority or minority groups within those churches. We tend to cling to our traditions, and in particular to those distinctive traditions that have separated us from the other churches. We therefore magnify out of all proportion the secondary issues which have become the *raison d'être* of our particular group. No doubt we justify these positions by a strong appeal to Scripture or tradition; but often it is more a crisis of group identity. We fear lest we change the boundaries within which we feel safe. The barriers may separate us from other brethren, but at least we know where we belong; it would be too risky, too vulnerable, trying to live without those barriers. Moreover, some of those barriers were erected by the Reformers at the cost of their own lives. They are rooted deep into history and cemented with the blood of martyrs. Can we pull down those divisions for which they gave the ultimate sacrifice? Can we betray the past and deny our heritage? So the argument goes.

Certainly, as we shall see later, we must not ignore the lessons of history in our search for reunion. But neither should we be trapped by the past. Nor should we fight yesterday's battles in today's world. What helpful contribution to the tragic situation in Ulster today are the annual celebrations (for the Protestants) of the Battle of the Boyne in 1690? Does that help to defuse the explosive situation in that Province? Does it convince anyone of the love of God and the relevance of Jesus Christ to meet the needs of today? Yet many dedicated Christians are living in, and perpetuating, the conflicts of yesterday (which may be several centuries ago). Yes, our godly ancestors may have died for certain issues which led to the division of churches. But our Lord and Master died on the cross to break down all those barriers, and to make us all one. If we look back in history (as we should), we must look back, most of all, to the cross and resurrection of Christ and to the significance of these — not least in the context of the church's unity.

(c) Although some of the reasons for our divisions *may* be defensible — though probably nothing like so defensible as we may think — our *attitudes* towards others as we maintain and perpetuate those divisions are nearly always quite inexcusable. Christian groups and churches are notoriously negative and suspicious towards one another, fearing the worst instead of believing the best. We are often ignorant of one another; we do not listen to one another; we are quick to attack and criticise, pre-judging each other's position. A friend of mine once said that most Christians are members of the Royal Artillery: we fire at one another at a safe distance but rarely come to grips with the real issues that may still divide us.

In a very helpful chapter[13] on the Roman Catholic Church, Julian Charley, at one time Vice-Principal of St. John's Theological College and a member of the Anglican-Roman Catholic International Commission, talks about some of the remarkable changes within that church since 1960, and makes the following comment:

The situation can produce three quite distinct reactions. The first is the conviction that 'Rome has not changed': the leopard has retained its spots. Many Protestants would go further and say that 'Rome will not change'. Because they understand Roman Catholicism to be a cast-iron system, some would go so far as to say, 'It cannot change'. Others would even add under their breath, 'It *must* not change— it would make life far too complicated'. Such an

[13]*Obeying Christ in a Changing World*, Fountain Books, Vol. 2, p. 155f.

attitude needs to be faced with several pertinent questions:

1. Have you considered carefully the remarkable changes and developments that have taken place since 1960...?
2. If that is not enough at least to modify your attitude, what do you require to convince you that the change is real?
3. Do you really *want* the Roman Catholic Church to be reformed, or would you rather it was not?

... It would be a very sad thing if evangelicals were to remain stubbornly inflexible at a time when the Catholic Church is constantly summoning its members to seek repentance, reconciliation and intensified dialogue with other churches.

Even if some Protestants were wholly right in their doctrines, such negative and suspicious attitudes are inexcusable. Perhaps we need the humility of Paul when he wrote, 'If I understand all mysteries and all knowledge..., but have not love, I am nothing.'

(d)   The divisions within the church destroy much of the fellowship, love, prayer, evangelism, strength and support that Christians in a given locality ought to enjoy together. It is when God's people dwell together in unity that he commands his blessing amongst them.[14] In many parts of the world we find tiny and struggling congregations. In the same village or small town we find a few Anglicans trying to maintain and heat a large Gothic or Victorian structure; down the road a few Methodists are doing the same in their less pretentious building; round the corner the Baptists are likewise having a battle with inflation and waning interest; and within a stone's throw a similar story holds for the United Reformed, the Roman Catholics (apart from reasonable attendance at mass), the Brethren of the Elim Church. Each little group could benefit immeasurably from the others; yet still the separations persist. No wonder God is hesitant about blessing their individual efforts. No wonder the impact on the rest of the town is negligible.

(e)   Most of all, the disunity within the church is a constant offence to God, who, in his love, naturally longs to

[14]Psalm 133.

see his family united; it is an affront to Christ who, by his death, broke down all those walls of hostility that divide us, so as to reconcile us all to God in one body; and it constantly grieves the Holy Spirit who has come to dwell within us to produce the fruit and gifts that are necessary for a truly united church. On what biblical or theological grounds can we justify the break-up of the privileged family of God, or the tearing apart of the body of Christ, or the demolition of the temple of the Holy Spirit? The demonstration of our love and oneness in Christ should be one of the most beautiful and attractive aspects of the gospel of Christ, and we have made the church into an object of constant mockery and scorn.

Since the heart of man is inherently sinful, we should not be surprised by the conflicts that exist at all levels in society, from the home to international affairs. Our natural self-life inevitably produces '...hatred and fighting, jealousy and anger, constant effort to get the best for yourself, complaints and criticisms, the feeling that everyone else is wrong except those in your own little group...'[15] However, the promise of God to his people is a new heart and a new Spirit; and if the Holy Spirit is active at all, the hallmarks of his presence must be seen, namely 'love, joy, peace...' Therefore loving, joyful and peaceful relationships between all true Christians should be one of the most powerful witnesses to the truth of the gospel.

For this reason, the New Testament is emphatic about the urgent necessity of our unity in Christ. The strength of the early church lay partly in the fact that they were standing firm 'in one spirit, with one mind striving side by side for the faith of the gospel'.[16] Paul urged the Corinthians to be 'united in the same mind and the same judgment', for their divisions were scandalous: was Christ himself divided? While strife existed among themselves, they were behaving like ordinary men; there was nothing spiritual about them. He warned them that if, by their divisions, they destroyed God's temple (for they were no less than that), God would destroy them.[17] Elsewhere he taught that they were all members of the one body, and that all natural distinctions had gone in Christ: 'There is neither Jew nor Greek, there is neither slave nor

[15]Galatians 5:20 (Living Bible).   [17]1 Corinthians 1:10ff; 3:1-17.
[16]Philippians 1:27.

free, there is neither male nor female; [and he might have
added today, there is neither Protestant nor Catholic, neither
Anglican nor Baptist] for you are all one in Christ Jesus.'[18]

Most impressive of all, he appeals to the churches in the
region of Ephesus to be 'eager to maintain the unity of the
Spirit in the bond of peace. There is one body and one Spirit,
just as you were called to the one hope that belongs to your
call, one Lord, one faith, one baptism, one God and Father of
us all, who is above all and in all.' Different gifts might be
given to different members of the body of Christ; but these
were in order that the whole body, 'joined and knit together',
might grow up in every way into Christ. [19] No appeal could be
more emphatic than this. He names each Person of the
Trinity in order to urge them to maintain their unity as
Christians. He reminds them of their faith and hope and call
and baptism. He emphasises that they are one body in Christ.
Nothing, absolutely nothing, can be allowed to come between
them. What would he have made of the present host of tragic
divisions?

What unity?
The unity of the church is essentially a spiritual unity, which
depends entirely on the unity of the Godhead, the cross of
Jesus Christ, and the fellowship of the Holy Spirit. As soon as
we look for the basis of unity in any other direction we shall
inevitably fail.

When we come to the cross of Christ, we come not as
Protestants or Catholics or anything else; we come as sinners,
who urgently need the mercy and forgiveness of God. At the
cross there is no distinction whatsoever. And providing we
put our trust in Christ, God accepts us in the Beloved, and
treats us as his sons. Once again, there is no distinction. 'For
all who are led by the Spirit of God are sons of God.' We are
all children of the one Father; we *all* belong to the one
body; we are *all* indwelt by the one Spirit; we are *all*
members of the one true church. The universal church of God
is already one. We still readily affirm our belief in the 'one,
holy, catholic and apostolic church'. Further, since this is
fundamentally a spiritual unity, every true and fresh work of

[18]Galatians 3:28.   [19]Ephesians 4:1-16.

the Spirit of God will enhance that sense of unity that Christians ought to be experiencing as part of their inheritance in Christ.

Morgan Derham once wrote: 'Christian unity will not be "inaugurated" in 1980 or any other year; it was inaugurated on the cross, is given by God, and wrought by the Holy Spirit in the hearts of his people. And history teaches us that when revival comes, the Spirit takes virtually no notice of denominational labels, and, what is more, those who experience revival do not worry about them either.'[20]

Given the spiritual unity of the church that already exists, it clearly must be *seen* to exist if words like 'love' and 'unity' are not to be totally devalued. We cannot fool anyone by pious statements that we are already united. Where is the evidence? What visible demonstration is there of our oneness in Christ? These are the pertinent questions, at least in the eyes of the world. The 'Ten Propositions' of the Churches' Unity Commission are therefore quite right in stressing that 'We reaffirm our belief that the visible unity in life and mission of all Christ's people is the will of God... We agree to explore such further steps as will be necessary to make more clearly visible the unity of all Christ's people. The trouble is that we have heard it all before. Look at the volumes of words surrounding the Anglican-Methodist Reunion Scheme — all to what end?

The first step is surely mutual trust and recognition. Christ's church is not to be seen as a vast, totalitarian, monolithic structure, based on the principle of organisations, structural and liturgical uniformity. Christian unity, envisaged by the New Testament, is surely something quite different.

In the first century we see a multiplicity of churches, according to the geographical locality (the church at Ephesus, Philippi, Thessalonica, etc.), all of which were expressions of the one true church of Christ. We also find regional churches in Judaea, Galatia, Samaria, Macedonia and Asia, which were still manifestations of the one true church. We find further differences in churches according to culture or language: some were Hellenistic churches, other Judaeo-Christian. We find a 'high' church in Jerusalem and a 'pentecostal' church in Corinth. The style of worship no

[20] *The Christian,* January 1968.

doubt varied from place to place. Yet this variety never conflicted with the unity which was still apparent within the whole church of God. It is true that there were false teachers and false groups springing up at an alarming rate; but the churches that existed in various places and that expressed themselves in various styles were still clearly one in Christ Jesus, as they held firmly to the foundation of apostolic doctrine.

Moreover, since no single Christian, nor even a single group of Christians, has a monopoly of the whole counsel of God, is it not likely that different churches may see very clearly certain aspects of God's truth while apparently being blind in other areas?

For myself, I welcome the strong emphasis on the sovereignty and holiness of God stressed by some of my Calvinist brethren; I am profoundly thankful for the joyful enthusiasm of the Pentecostal churches that has made many of us look again at our doctrine and experience of the Holy Spirit; I shall always be grateful for the thorough biblical foundations given to me by evangelicals from the time of my conversion onwards; I thank God for the disturbing challenge that radical Christians give towards the church's involvement in politics and social reform; I have been enriched by the deep devotion and disciplined prayer life of many of my high church friends; and I have benefited enormously from Roman Catholics in my whole understanding of community and the corporate nature of the church. So the list of acknowledgements could continue almost indefinitely.

Although Paul used the body-metaphor in 1 Corinthians 12 to describe the healthy functioning of a *local* church, the basic principle of unity in diversity could well be extended to the many member churches within the one universal body of Christ. 'The body does not consist of one member but of many.' However, this should in no way destroy the unity of the body, but rather enrich it. Each member is different, yet each is indispensable. In this way there should be 'no discord in the body', providing that the members have the same care for one another. The important factor is that each member should trust and recognise the other members, having no time for the exclusive arrogance which says, 'I have no need of you.' The member churches of the one body of Christ *ought* to be different. The patterns of ministry and the expressions of worship would surely need to vary from place to place. The cultural variations alone between rural and inner-city areas, between England and Rwanda, between the United States and Germany, are simply enormous. Although we are one in Christ, God does not obliterate our personalities, our individualities, or the cultural settings in which we live and work. What God is concerned about is that the one gospel of Christ should be utterly relevant in every place where the church exists; and for that to happen, the gospel must be proclaimed within the culture of the community surrounding any existing local church.

If we fail to do this we are like missionaries travelling to a foreign land but refusing to learn the language of the people. Communication becomes impossible. In fact the cultural presentation of our message may often make a much greater impact, for better or for worse, than the message itself. Our lifestyle, our services of worship, our efforts of evangelism, our involvement in society — all these, and many other factors, *must* vary from place to place if the church is to speak in meaningful ways to the people living in that place; but this should in no way destroy the unity of the whole church of God. Variety is not harmful to Christian unity. What is damaging is the exclusive and excluding attitudes which insist that '*we* are right and others are wrong.'

It is, after all, 'with all the saints' that we are able to comprehend the breadth and length and height and depth of God's immeasurable grace and inscrutable wisdom. The fact that different groups may see clearly one facet of the diamond need not destroy the unity of the diamond. If we were more ready to recognise the best in each other, instead of focussing on the worst, Christian unity would be much more of an existing reality, even in our present multiplicity of denominations. As Hans Küng writes:

It is not part of the nature of the Church to have a uniform form of worship, nor uniform hierarchies, nor even a uniform theology. In the light of Ephesians 4:4-6, the opposite would seem to be true. Diversity in worship: one God, one baptism and one Lord's Supper — but different peoples, different communities, different languages, different rites and forms of devotion, different prayers, hymns and vestments, different styles of art and in this sense different Churches.

Diversity in theology too: one God, one Lord, one hope and one faith — but different theologies, different systems, different styles of thought, different conceptual apparatus and terminology, different schools, traditions and areas of research, different universities and theologians, and in this sense again different Churches. Diversity finally in Church order: one God, one Lord, one Spirit and one body — but a different order of life, different laws, different nations and traditions, different customs, usages and administrative systems, and so in this sense too different Churches.

In all these spheres the 'unity of the Spirit in the bond of peace' can be preserved 'with all lowliness and meekness, with patience, forbearing one another in love' (Eph. 4:2f). It is not necessary for this diversity and variety to breed dissensions, enmity and strife. In certain cases, some characteristics or individual peculiarity can be sacrificed for the sake of peace and love, and mutual concessions made. As long as all have the one God, Lord, Spirit, and faith and not their own private God, Lord, Spirit and faith, all is in order.[21]

Mavumilusa Makanzu, an evangelist from Zaire, has said that the African church needs 'liberation' from the theological questions of the West: 'They're not our questions.' René Padilla, from Latin America, has made a similar comment: 'Many of the divisions that separate Christians today can hardly be said to be related to the question of truth. Cultural background, social class, historical origin, psychological make-up and tradition often play a far more important part.'

Towards Reunion
Although many misgivings have been expressed, there is little doubt that the contributions of the Ecumenical Movement, the World Council of Churches, Vatican II and the Charismatic Movement, have all helped towards a far healthier and more positive approach to reunion than might have seemed possible twenty years ago. Among many Christian leaders there is the deep conviction that it is only by concentrating on the fundamentals of our faith, supremely the cross of Christ and the renewal of the Holy Spirit, that any real experience of unity will be a serious possibility.

[21]Op. cit., p. 275.

Cardinal Suenens once said, in answer to a question about this, 'I believe that the solution of ecumenical disunity will not finally be the result of a dialogue between the Church of Rome and the Church of Canterbury or the Church of Moscow. It will not be a dialogue between the Churches as such, but a dialogue between Rome and Jesus, Canterbury and Jesus, Moscow and Jesus, so that we can become more and more united in him.'

When you travel by air and the plane lifts off the ground, the walls and hedges which may seem large and impressive at ground level at once lose their significance. In the same way, when the power of the Holy Spirit lifts us up together into the conscious realisation of the presence of Jesus, the barriers between us become unimportant. Seated with Christ in the heavenly places, the differences between Christians can often seem petty and marginal.

It is by the renewing work of the Holy Spirit that Christians, from many different persuasions and traditions, can experience an altogether new love for Jesus and a new love for one another. It is true that, in the first instance, this is more at the level of feelings and experiences, and the theological differences will have to be tackled later. But it is far better looking at the theological issues from the basic positions of love and openness than from the standpoint of suspicion and hostility. It is often our attitudes that have to be dealt with first before we can begin to listen to one another and hear what each is saying. Otherwise we tend to hear only what we want to hear, in order to confirm our worst suspicions.

To begin with, some understanding of the historical background to our divisions is very important. Sometimes it will be seen that the splits were remarkably small initially, and were often caused by a complex mixture of politics, culture, theology, economics and philosophy. Some of those factors responsible for the splits have changed entirely, yet still the divisions perpetuate.

The Reformation in Europe was a classic example of the way in which many very different factors contributed to the break away from the Catholic Church. Nevertheless, doctrinal issues and ecclesiastical corruption were certainly foremost in the mind of Martin Luther; and it was through the re-discovery of the Bible that he and others came to see how far the institutional, medieval church had departed from the truths of Scripture. The central issue was, of course, the main theme of Paul's epistle to the Romans, justification by faith.

It is important to stress, however, that Luther was concerned primarily with the doctrine of salvation, not the doctrine of the church. It is true that he exposed the gross corruptions of the secularised and bureaucratic institution, but he certainly had *no intention of leaving the Catholic Church* when he nailed his Ninety-Five Theses on the door of the castle church in Wittenberg on the 31st October 1517. His protest was primarily the result of his own spiritual crisis as he wrestled with the problem of his own salvation, and it was intended primarily to denounce the appalling deceptions practised on the common people by Tetzel's sale of indulgences. *In no way* did Luther intend to force a breach with the papacy. He was simply hoping for reform *within* the church, and it was only some years later that the split between Luther and the hierarchy in Rome became inevitable. Although Protestants often glory in the history of the Reformation, and in the re-discovery of biblical truths, in many respects this was a tragic chapter in the history of the whole church. It led to the breaking up of the unity of the body of Christ into the multiplicity of denominations that have proliferated ever since.

It is interesting to read Hans Küng, the Roman Catholic theologian, on this point:

> It is unthinkable to deny, and would today be admitted by Catholic historians and theologians too, that Luther (and accordingly the other Reformers as well) aroused a new awareness in the Church of the norm of the Gospel, of faith in the work of Christ, as the only mediator; that in his total theology he helped to revive original New Testament perspectives (the primacy of grace, the priesthood of all believers, ecclesiastical office as ministry, the importance of the word, the opposition between the law and the Gospel, the ethos of everyday life and work, etc.), and that in this way he made an important contribution to the reform of the Church — indirectly to the reform of the Catholic Church too. But the unity of the Church which Luther hoped to reform had been destroyed, and on the Protestant side further divisions followed this first great schism. It was

a terrible price to pay... Was it only Luther's violent and reckless temperament which made the break inevitable? Were not the Reformers in general often blind to what was genuinely Catholic? Were not certain aspects of the New Testament over-emphasised and others neglected?...'[22]

Luther's explosive outbursts quickly polarised the situation, and led to the feelings of bitterness and animosity that have characterised this schism for nearly half a millennium. The Colloquy of Ratisbon in 1541 nearly succeeded in reconciling Roman Catholics and Lutherans, particularly on the highly controversial issue of justification, indicating that the doctrinal divergences were not so great as had been feared. But this was rejected as 'betrayal' by both Rome and Wittenberg, and the newly-formed entrenched positions on both sides were finally cemented by the Council of Trent (1545-63). Until 1960, four hundred years later, there was little change in the situation, with Roman Catholics and Protestants locked in open hostility. Dialogue was virtually impossible.

The Second Vatican Council, however, paved the way for such dialogue. The Roman Catholics had previously referred to other churches only as heretics and schismatics, but now it called other Christians 'separated brethren'. Further, whereas previously it had recognised only individual Christians outside its own ranks, it now referred to 'churches and ecclesial communities separate from the Roman apostolic see'. Thus the Roman Catholic Church no longer identifies itself exclusively with the Church of Christ.

Moreover, Vatican II has revealed a remarkable divergence of views within its communion. No longer is it possible to say precisely what a Roman Catholic believes. In many ways this church now displays something of the 'comprehensiveness' which has long characterised the Anglican Church. Some of the new services in the Church of Rome are strikingly similar to the new services in the Church of England. Church buildings are being shared. Bible reading is increasingly encouraged. Prayer groups are mushrooming in many places. The laity are coming into their own in terms of a real

[22]Op. cit., p. 280.

spiritual ministry. The charismatic renewal has developed within Roman Catholic circles in many parts of the world at an astonishing rate, making possible joint prayer and praise and fellowship with Protestants in a way that would have been totally impossible before the 1960s.

I had the privilege of being one of the main speakers at the Third National Charismatic Conference in Dublin (1976), when some 5,000 Roman Catholics and about 1,000 Protestants were gathered together from all over Ireland. The whole Conference was thoroughly Christ-centred and cross-centred. There was a glorious atmosphere of praise and joy, and an overwhelming sense of the love of God. All the teaching and exhortation I heard was thoroughly biblical, and there was nothing which offended my Protestant and evangelical susceptibilities! Indeed, I wished that the same spirit of worship and love could have been manifest in the numerous conferences and conventions that I had attended from my own particular tradition over the years.

All this is not to suggest that there are now no problems in the move towards reunion with Rome. Of course there are; and some of them are important doctrinal difficulties which need to be tackled seriously and honestly. In an *Open Letter* on relations between the Anglican Churches and the Roman Catholic, Eastern Orthodox, Old Catholic and Ancient Oriental Churches,[23] the tone of which welcomed warmly the much better attitudes and understanding that have recently existed, there was a warning that 'acute problems seem to us to arise regarding the status and effect of traditions like the sinless conception and bodily assumption of our Lord's mother, the addressing of prayer to her and others of the faithful departed, the universal primacy of the Pope, and the infallible teaching authority of Popes and General Councils...'

This is not the time to paper over the cracks. But there is now a far better climate in which to talk openly and freely. For Protestants who feel that nothing could ever change in the Roman Catholic Church, read Hans Küng, Nicholas Lash, David Power or Jean Teillard. These and other men are deeply concerned for reform and renewal within the

[23] Published in June 1977, under the auspices of Latimer House, 13 Banbury Road, Oxford, England.

church, just as many of us are in other traditions.

It is remarkable that theologians on the Anglican-Roman Catholic International Commission have reached substantial agreement on crucial issues such as the eucharist, ministry and authority. There is much greater common ground than has hitherto been supposed. Julian Charley, in a most helpful chapter on the present position, emphasises the need for further clarification, but says,

> We should affirm our acceptance of Roman Catholics in principle as our fellow-Christians... We must be willing to make time for much honest, loving dialogue — there are no short cuts. In this dialogue we must be open to the Word of God and the Spirit of God, realising that we too have much to learn as well as to teach, to receive as well as to give... Let us for our part be sure that there is nothing in us which holds back the outworking of the one body of Christ in the world.[24]

Reunion, of course, is not confined to the healing of the great schisms of Catholic and Protestant, and of East and West. There is a great need for the healing of bad or broken relationships within the Protestant churches, too. But the principles and attitudes are highlighted in this much greater and more difficult issue; and if we can see some daylight there, the search for unity in other directions should have some helpful guidelines. The time has come when we can no longer excuse our disunity by appealing to the invisible unity of all true Christians. What matters is the credibility of the church and its message in the eyes of the world.

Nor can we evade the issue by talking about our ultimate unity in the next world. The New Testament church was ceaselessly exhorted by the apostles to be a united church, and we have seen that this was plainly the deep concern of Jesus Christ. Therefore any concern for fresh spiritual life that is in accordance with the teaching of the New Testament must also lead to a concern for the unity of the church. Our search is not for uniformity. But it is only when we can pray together, work together, worship together, break bread

[24] Op. cit., p. 158.

together, and truly love and trust one another, that we can begin to speak of a united church, however varied its form of expression and worship may continue to be.

The Way Forward

We have already discussed the way forward in some measure.

First, there is the need for *deep repentance for wrong attitudes*, for lack of love, for failure to listen to one another, for hasty words and for entrenched positions — for everything, that is, that caused or perpetuated the divisions all down the years. Above all, we must repent of the fact that our disunity has hurt not only each other, but most of all God himself.

Secondly, we need *to come humbly to the cross of Christ*, to see the pain that he bore both to bring us back to God and to break down the walls of hostility between us. At the cross we are all wrong; it is not 'him' or 'them'; it is 'us' and 'me'. Moreover, at that cross there is always forgiveness and healing. If God could unite Jews and Gentiles at the cross, the potential unity of all professing Christians, however deeply divided they may be, is guaranteed.

Thirdly, we must *pray together and work together for genuine spiritual renewal*. Until we have a fresh love for Jesus, we are not likely to find fresh love for one another. But the renewing work of God's Spirit in our hearts will certainly lead to the renewing of hearts and minds and attitudes, without which unity will be impossible.

Fourthly, we need *to establish healthier relationships within our own locality*. Annual united services are not enough. Personal friendships need to be formed at the leadership level, since it is often here that the barriers are strongest, perhaps because of professional jealousy or the feeling of being threatened. However, fellowship is usually best encouraged by working together for some common project other than unity, such as a town or city mission, or some social or political action, or some meetings concerning spiritual renewal. The spirit of competition, with the associate evils of pride or envy, must go. Instead there must be a serious commitment, at all levels, to work together instead of duplicating and thus competing with each other's work.

Colin Buchanan has suggested an 'ecumenical map' of a country, instead of each denomination assuming responsibility for every person in that country. 'It might mean some areas were not really "worked" by the Church of England at all... It might mean a slow phasing out of any special place in the country for the Church of England, as the other Churches were slowly phased into sharing that particular trusteeship for every person in the country, every square inch of the territory, which we have traditionally held. Would we mind? Should we mind?'[25]

Fifthly, we must press for *mutual recognition and acceptance of church membership and ministries*. Personal allegiance to Jesus Christ as Lord and Saviour, with probably the outward seal of baptism (of whatever mode), should be sufficient for us to accept one another as brethren in Christ. It is only God who knows the heart of man; and although we need to be discerning about the spiritual health of church members, we are not called to be any man's judge. If the Judge of all the earth has decreed that wheat and tares should grow together until the harvest, we are not called to make a separation before that day.

Likewise, we need to recognise the God-given ministries that undoubtedly do exist within the various strands of the Christian church. Whether or not there has been episcopal ordination, we should accept those in whom there is the *charisma* of leadership, service and teaching. If the first apostles had the generosity and wisdom to accept Paul's mission and ministry to the Gentiles on the grounds that God was manifestly with him, who are we to reject the ministries of others who are not of our communion? It is hard to see how there can be any real moves towards unity until such mutual recognition is accepted.

It is a sad omission, therefore, that the Anglican/Roman Catholic *Agreed Statement on Ministry* makes no reference to the encyclical letter *Apostolicae Curae* by Pope Leo XIII in 1896, when he condemned Anglican Orders as null and void. Silence on this official viewpoint, which has not been openly changed, would seem to present a major obstacle to mutual acceptance of such ministries. However, the Statement covers a lot of excellent ground on the *nature* of ministry, and declares that 'agreement on the nature of ministry is prior to consideration of the mutual recognition of ministries'. It is to be hoped that this will soon follow if serious hopes for reunion are to be strengthened. At the same time undue speed in this direction could easily lead to a worsening of

[25]Op. cit., p. 135.

relationships with other Protestant denominations not engaged in this dialogue. Although many Christians are understandably impatient at the slowness of developments, the
deeply entrenched positions which have been attacked and
defended with so much blood over 450 years are not going to
disappear quickly. Most healing takes time, and we must
trust in the Lord who is sovereign in his timing as he brings us
all back humbly to the cross of Jesus Christ.

Sixthly, we must see that *truth is not to be sacrificed but
rediscovered*. Diplomatic compromises and ambiguous formulae are no solution for a united church. 'We must reject
"unity at any price". A church which abandons the truth
abandons itself.' [26] However, it will be disastrous if we try to
fight again the battles of the past. The mere repetition of
polarised positions which caused the divisions of the past will
never lead to unity. We need instead to look together at the
biblical truths that are relevant to the tensions of today, and
re-state them in words and phrases that are true to God's
revelation in Scripture but which are free from the polemical
and historical overtones that would distort our vision.

For example, concerning our understanding of the doctrine
of Christ, John Stott states clearly the necessity we have to
change our apprehension of him:

> For though in himself he does not and could not change,
> *we* change and *the world* changes; and therefore the Christ
> whom we perceive and whom the world needs is bound to
> change also... For instance,...the Chalcedonian Defini-
> tion [27] has been immensely significant in the subsequent
> history of the Church. And yet, along with all the creeds
> and confessions of Christendom, it belongs rather to
> tradition than to Scripture...and is not therefore to be
> regarded as infallible or irreformable. [28]

Hans Küng says much the same:

> Every truth needs translating. There are irreformable

---

[26] Hans Küng, op. cit., p. 289.　　remaining in one 'person'.
[27] Agreed in AD 451 about the two　　[28] *Obeying Christ in a Changing World*,
distinct 'natures' of Christ, whilst　Vol. I, Fountain Books p. 17.

constants of truth, given to us by the revelation of God himself; but we must be able to recognise them as such in every age, and for this very reason it is essential that the human, ecclesiastical formulations of them reflecting the thoughts and language and outlook of a particular age, are not regarded as irreformable areas. If the *truth* of faith is to be recognisable to men of any age, the *temporal guise* of faith must change with the times. A Church which truly desires to find unity with other Churches must be a lover and follower of truth, completely devoted to truth; it must be a Church which knows in all humility that it is not the manifestation of the whole truth, that it has not fulfilled the whole truth, a Church which knows that it must be led anew by the spirit of truth into all truth.[29]

This will certainly involve painful sacrifices, and in particular the willingness to move away from some of the historical and doctrinal battlegrounds of the past to the issues of the present.

Seventhly, the *doctrinal basis for unity must the unchangeable gospel of Jesus Christ, as given in the Scriptures as a whole.* If the basis is 'the church', the immediate question will be 'Which Church?' If we attempt to come together on an aggregate of beliefs or on some lower common denominator, we shall be either more than, or less than, the church that Christ founded upon the rock, against which even the gates of hell could not prevail. The church of Jesus Christ is built on the apostles and prophets, Jesus Christ himself being the chief cornerstone. In other words, its basis must be the original message of Christ, as revealed in its original, unique, irreplaceable and irreformable truth as given in the Scriptures. Every denomination and tradition must bend to this God-given revelation. Every viewpoint and structure must bow to the word of God and to the Lordship of Christ. The right interpretation of Scripture calls for much prayer and study, with the humble acknowledgment that no one person or denomination has a monopoly of the whole truth of God. The dictum of Rupertus Meldenius still contains much wisdom: 'On the necessary points, unity; on the questionable points, liberty; in everything, love.'

[29]Op. cit., p. 290.

CHAPTER NINETEEN

The Mark of the Church

VIRTUALLY EVERY SPECIFIC grouping of men and women throughout the world is marked by some badge or symbol. Societies, clubs, associations, unions, companies, guilds, institutions, colleges, universities, schools, regiments, squadrons, fleets — all, almost without exception, have their distinguishing mark.

So it is with the Christian church. From earliest days, as seen by paintings made inside the catacombs in Rome, one sign was the fish, since *ichthus* (Greek for 'fish') formed a simple acrostic for the Greek words 'Jesus Christ, Son of God, Saviour'. The cross was another obvious sign — indeed it has generally been regarded as *the* sign of the church all down the centuries since the days of the New Testament.

However, Jesus gave another distinguishing mark which should be the outstanding feature of his disciples in every generation and in every place: 'A new commandment I give to you, that you love one another; even as I have loved you, that you also love one another. *By this* all men will know that you are my disciples, if you have love for one another.'[1]

Francis Schaeffer has written a booklet where he calls this love *The Mark of the Christian*.[2] I believe he is right; and it follows that love should also be the hallmark of the church. However, as with many of the sayings of Jesus, there is a deceptive simplicity about this one, and it is important to understand what sort of love he was talking about, and how it should be expressed.

[1] John 13:34f. [2] Pub. by I.V.P.

Spiritual

Love has always been one of the most powerful factors in the lives of human beings, and the Greeks differentiated between the various forms of love. They knew all about the strong, passionate, sexual desires, which could sometimes be over-powering in their intensity, and they called this *eros*. They knew about family affection, too, the bond between parents and children, brothers and sisters — a quality of love which has virtually nothing to do with sex — and they called this *storgé*. They knew, too, of the special relationship between husband and wife, or between two very close friends — a strong, warm and beautiful attachment between those who share their lives together, their joys and their pains. And this deep and powerful love they called *philia*.

Christian love, however, is distinct. The word which is used for God's love to us in his Son Jesus Christ, and which is also the love that should be the mark of the church, is *agapé*. This word and its verb come no less than 250 times in the New Testament. It is not the natural and instinctive quality of love that is to be found in every human being. It is essentially spiritual, in the sense that it is imparted to us by the Spirit of God: 'God's love has been poured into our hearts through the Holy Spirit which has been given to us.'[3] 'The fruit of the Spirit is love…'[4] No man can experience or express this quality of love unless he is a Christian, with the Spirit of Christ living within him. He may admire the characteristics of this love; he may agree with its purity and selflessness; but his life cannot exhibit it without the help of the Holy Spirit.

Further, this love springs from a personal response in the heart of a believer to the love that God has given us in Christ: 'We love, because he first loved us.'[5] It follows, then, that we cannot love others, in the way that Jesus commanded, until we first love God and experience his love in our hearts. Nothing is more vital than this: it is the first and great commandment, and it is the essential proof of the reality of our Christian profession of faith. A.W. Tozer once wrote:

It is rarely that we find anyone aglow with personal love

---

[3] Romans 5:5.   [5] 1 John 4:19.
[4] Galatians 5:22.

for Christ. This love, as a kind of moral fragrance, is ever detected upon the garments of the saints. The list of fragrant saints is long. It includes men and women of every shade of theological thought within the bounds of the orthodox Christian faith. This radiant love for Christ is to my mind the true test of catholicity, the one sure proof of membership in the church universal.

It was for this reason that the ascended Christ spoke so sharply to the church at Ephesus. In many ways it seemed to be the model church of the first century: 'I know your works, your toil and your patient endurance, and how you cannot bear evil men but have tested those who call themselves apostles but are not, and found them to be false; I know you are enduring patiently and bearing up for my name's sake, and you have not grown weary.' What more could you ask from any church? Surely here was the ideal: sound in doctrine, hard working in practice. However, the one all-important distinguishing mark was lacking: 'But I have this against you, that you have abandoned the love you had at first.' Christ therefore commanded them to repent: 'If not, I will come to you and remove your lampstand from its place, unless you repent.'[6] This was no empty threat. A church which lacks this essential hallmark ceases to be a church of Jesus Christ. It has grieved and quenched the Spirit. It has snuffed out the life and light of Christ, and thus is no longer recognisable as a church, no matter how correct in doctrine or diligent in good works it may continue to be. In fact, the church at Ephesus experienced a short revival after this warning of Christ; but before long it became once again loveless and lifeless, and Christ removed the lampstand from its place. It became extinct, and there has never been a Christian witness there since. Today the population is entirely Muslim.

There is no substitute for this love; and it is impossible for us to love one another as Christ has loved us unless we maintain, and deepen, our first love for him. This theme can be traced through the Scriptures. Jeremiah was sent to plead with apostate Israel: 'Thus says the Lord, I remember the devotion of your youth, your love as a bride...'[7] Hosea,

---

[6] Revelation 2:1-7.   [7] Jeremiah 2:2.

through his own painful domestic crises, had the same prophetic burden: 'What shall I do with you, O Ephraim? What shall I do with you, O Judah? Your love is like a morning cloud, like the dew that goes early away... I desire steadfast love and not sacrifice...'[8] After Peter's tragic denial, Jesus did not question him about his understanding of the atonement, nor rebuke him for his failure to believe in the resurrection. Of course such doctrines are of immense importance, and for forty days Jesus taught his disciples in great detail all the truths concerning the kingdom of God. Still, the immediate question that the risen Christ pressed home to Peter was much more basic and personal. Three times he asked him, 'Do you love me? Do you love me? Do you love me?' Peter was terribly confused about the whole significance of Christ's death and resurrection, the twin focal points of the Christian faith. Yet, first things first; and nothing, absolutely nothing, is more important than our personal love for Jesus, resulting, through the gift of the Holy Spirit, in this godly quality of love amongst his disciples.

Practical
Virtually all other forms of love inevitably involve the feelings and emotions. When a man or a woman *falls in love*, it is something which happens to them. They have little or no control over the matter, although the intensity of the emotion can be encouraged or discouraged depending on the degree of contact the two of them have.

Agapé, however, is much more an attitude of our *mind* which depends largely on the direction in which we set our *will*. It has almost nothing to do with the emotions, at least in the first instance. Michael Harper has described it in this way: 'Love is not feeling sentimental towards others. Nor is it primarily saying the right things. Nor is it to be found in giving, for, according to Paul, you can give your life and all that you possess to others, and still be bankrupt of true love. It is an *attitude*, which is never superior, and which is devoid of criticism, but which is deeply concerned and committed to the good of the other person.'[9]

This explains how it is that Jesus can tell us to love our enemies. Humanly speaking that is impossible — but not

[8] Hosea 6:4, 6.

[9] *None Can Guess*, Hodder & Stoughton, p. 28f.

with God. Jesus said: 'Love your enemies and pray for those who persecute you, so that you may be sons of your Father who is in heaven: for he makes his sun rise on the evil and on the good, and sends rain on the just and on the unjust.'[10]

> *No matter what a man is like, God seeks nothing but his highest good.* Let a man be a saint or let a man be a sinner, God's only desire is for that man's highest good. Now that is what *agapé* is. *Agapé* is the spirit which says: 'No matter what any man does to me, I will never seek to do harm to him; I will never set out for revenge; I will always seek nothing but his highest good.' That is to say, Christian love, *agapé*, is *unconquerable benevolence, invincible good will.*[11]

Drawing from various translations and from my Greek lexicon, I once paraphrased 1 Corinthians 13:4-7 to show the extremely practical and challenging nature of Christian love:

Love is *patient* or inexhaustible. It never runs out; it never gives up.

It patiently goes on loving, regardless of the response from the other person.

Love is *kind* or constructive. It is always looking out for ways in which it can offer practical help. It anticipates a person's need in advance.

Love is *not jealous*. It does not mind when someone else has the limelight and popularity, or is given responsibilities and privileges. It will continue to serve that person.

Love is *not boastful*. It is not anxious to impress. It will not talk too quickly about personal successes or spiritual experiences. It is much more concerned about the Lord and about other people.

Love is *not arrogant*. It does not cherish inflated ideas of its own importance. It will not exaggerate or blow its own trumpet.

Love is *not rude*. It is not vulgar or indecent. It is not flippant or foolish towards other people.

Love is *not selfish*. It does not insist on its own way. It

---

[10]Matthew 5:44f. [11]*More New Testament Words*, S.C.M., pp. 15f.

accepts the situation for what it is, and works within those limitations.

Love is *not irritable* or touchy. It is not easily rubbed up the wrong way.

Love is *not resentful*. It does not secretly list the faults and failings of another person — not even those that have hurt. It forgives and forgets.

Love *does not rejoice at wrong*. It does not gloat over the mistakes and sins of another person, in order to stand out in better light itself.

Love *rejoices in the right*. It always sees the best in people, not the blemishes. It is always positive in thought, word and deed towards others.

Love *bears all things*, throwing a cloak of silence over what is displeasing in others, and accepting without grumbling some of the trials and difficulties in life.

Love *believes all things*, trusting in God's love, that in everything God works for good with those who love him — even when there is nothing but darkness all around.

Love *hopes all things*, looking forward to the future glory which God has promised to those who love him.

Love *endures all things*, and is not shaken even in the worst of storms. It is steady and stable to the end.

Since our ideas of love are so easily coloured by worldly concepts, it is necessary to check the quality of love in our own lives and churches with this beautiful portrait of love given to us in the Scriptures. We can never be complacent. We have never arrived. Paul once prayed for the Christians at Philippi 'that your love may abound more and more, with knowledge and all discernment so that you may approve what is excellent, and may be pure and blameless for the day of Christ...'[12]

Christian love should always be marked by humble, practical service. This was the lesson that Jesus had to repeat so frequently to his disciples who were often ambitious for their position and reputation within the kingdom of God. On more than one occasion they were arguing amongst themselves as to who was the greatest.[13] Jesus therefore had to

[12]Philippians 1:9f.   [13]Mark 9:33-37; 10:35-45;
                               Luke 22:24-27.

humble them and break their pride, notably when he washed their feet at the Last Supper, otherwise they would have been of no use in his kingdom. It is only the life of Jesus, not our own gifts and talents, that will bring true life to others. For this reason, he may often have to break us, especially in those areas of natural strength, in order that *his* life and love may be released.

Simon Peter was convinced of his own faithfulness and courage, boasting that, even if others fell away from Christ, he would never deny his Master. He had to learn, the hard way, that he was as weak as anyone else, apart from the grace of God. Paul, a brilliant intellectual with many natural resources to draw from, was often afflicted and perplexed, sometimes despairing of life itself. This, he said, was to make him rely upon God and not upon himself; only in this way could the life of Jesus be manifested.[14]

True greatness, in God's eyes, is seen in a life of service, expressed in a loving, humble, gentle, serving spirit. Whatever outward 'success' or recognition we may or may not have, is quite immaterial. That is entirely up to God to give or withhold. What he wants to see (and he will work in our lives in various ways to bring this to pass) is his love flowing out freely to other people, however costly and sacrificial this may be to ourselves. Nothing less than this can bring true life, his life, to those around us.

Christian love should also be expressed in ever-widening circles.

It begins, as we have seen, with our personal love for *God and for his Son Jesus Christ*. In no sense will it be Christian love unless it is rooted and grounded here.

Next, there will be a special bond of love between *fellow-Christians*. We are to 'honour all men. Love the brotherhood.'[15] The apostle John stated that this was one of the tests of true spiritual life: 'We know that we have passed out of death into life, because we love the brethren... If anyone says, "I love God," and hates his brother, he is a liar; for he who does not love his brother whom he has seen, cannot love God whom he has not seen.'[16] By the term 'brother' John is referring to a Christian brother. There should be an especially deep

[14] 2 Corinthians 1:8f; 4:7-12.   [16] 1 John 3:14; 4:20.
[15] 1 Peter 2:17.

commitment to one another within the family of God. 'Let us do good to all men,' wrote Paul, 'and especially to those who are of the household of faith.' [17]

There should then be a particular quality of love within our *natural families*, whether or not the members are all 'of the household of faith'. Husbands are to love their wives, [18] and wives are to be submissive to their husbands, even if they're not believers. Our homes are often the hardest place in which to be consistent in this matter of Christian love, since it is here that the masks are all down. Yet it is precisely in our homes, and among our closest friends and relations, that we need to work out the true meaning of practical Christian love.

Extending the circle still wider, we are to 'love our *neighbours* as ourselves'. That will, of course, literally include our next-door neighbour, although the sheer proximity of this has its own problems. This little couplet holds more than a grain of truth:

> To love the world to me's no chore,
> My big trouble's the man next door.

However, we cannot stop there; for when the lawyer, 'desiring to justify himself' asked Jesus, 'And who is my neighbour?' Jesus replied with the story of the good Samaritan. [19] The whole punch of this story may miss us entirely unless we appreciate something of the almost total hatred the Jews had for the Samaritans. Tony Thistleton recounted how a clergyman tried to make the point of this well-known parable clear to his Protestant congregation in Liverpool by describing how an Orangeman passed by on the other side, but a Roman Catholic priest ministered to the man in need. [20] In other words, Christian love must go out to everyone, regardless of creed, colour, culture, or anything else. It will extend to our *enemies*, as we have seen. Lincoln was once accused of being too kind and courteous towards his opponents; it was his duty, he was told, to destroy them. He replied, 'Do I not destroy my enemies when I make them my friends?' Paul, quoting from Proverbs, wrote: 'If your enemy is hungry, feed him; if he is thirsty, give him a drink; for by doing this you will make him burn with shame.' In this way we 'conquer evil with good'. [21]

[17] Galatians 6:10.
[18] Ephesians 5:25ff.
[19] Luke 10:29ff.

[20] *Obeying Christ in a Changing World*, Fountain Books, Vol. I, p. 107.
[21] Romans 12:20f, Good News Bible.

Crucial

When Jesus said, 'By this all men will know that you are my disciples, if you have love for one another', he was making a devastating statement. Love is the one crucial mark of the Christian and of the church in the eyes of the world. The man in the street frankly could not care less about our doctrinal differences, our religious squabbles or our churchy debates. Most of these, he feels, are no more than verbal or theological hair-splitting. When I arrived at one church, the churchwarden told me: 'We don't mind if you stand at the north, south, east or west of the communion table; we don't worry if you wear a stole or a scarf or a lounge suit — *as long as you get on with the job!*'

The one feature that will always make its impact on every section of society, regardless of age or class, is the distinguishing feature of true Christian love. The world cannot imitate this. It is entirely from God. The world can imitate the church's statements of faith, programmes, publicity, methods of government, social concern — everything, except true *agapé* love. This love is the Christian's ultimate apologetic. It is the one fact, more than anything else, that will convince an unbeliever about the reality of the Christian's faith.

Moreover, in John 17 Jesus said something even more startling. Four times he prayed fervently that his disciples might be one, experiencing amongst themselves, as far as possible, the perfect love and harmony that exists within the Godhead. Why? 'That the world may *believe* that thou hast sent me..., so that the world may *know* that thou hast sent me.' In other words, the credentials of Christ himself would be tested in the eyes of the world by the love and unity that exists amongst those who are his disciples. Nothing could be more searching for the church than that. The love that we have for one another is the evidence, not just of our own discipleship, but of the divinity and authenticity of Christ himself.

Krishna once said, having examined the lives of Christians for many years: 'Christians claim that Jesus Christ is the Saviour of sinners, but they show no more signs of being saved than anyone else.' There was once a period when Gandhi was spiritually restless, and he began to attend a church regularly. He found the sermons boring, the congregation not very devout; sometimes he slept, and woke up feeling guilty. But then he noticed that several of the Christians were sleeping too, which eased his conscience. Worst of all, he was snubbed by the Europeans because of the colour of his skin. He left that church, and abandoned his enquiry into the Christian faith for good.

Fortunately, numerous examples can be given when the clear evidence of Christian love has been the crucial factor in someone's conversion. A Christian who has worked extensively amongst communists once remarked that their conversion to Christ came nearly always as a result of the love of God manifested in the lives of his people; hardly ever were they won for Christ by being out-argued.

One of the most powerful features of the early church was the way in which Christ broke down all the natural human barriers which separated people. The astonished cry of the heathen in those days was 'See how these Christians love one another!' When they saw the costly sharing of lives and possessions amongst those who would normally have been at each other's throats, this, to the outsider, was the plainest proof that here was something or someone at work apart from mere human beings. This was the authentic mark of the church which rang true. False prophets and teachers abounded; there was no shortage of religion for those who wanted it. But Christian love is unique.

The same applies today. Many of the British troops in Northern Ireland have been sickened by religion because of the endless conflicts and continual strife. Even where there are no bombs and bullets, the verbal violence is considerable. What the world has always looked for, if it is to be convinced, is this one crucial mark of love.

We should note carefully that this is the way in which the *world* will judge the reality of a person's professed faith in Christ; *Christians*, however, have other tests as well. John, in his first letter, gives some of the evidences of true spiritual life. There should be some experience of a *new family*, as we enjoy fellowship with the Father and with one another through Jesus Christ; there should be a *new obedience*, for 'by this we may be sure that we know him, if we keep his commandments'; there will be a *new love for God* replacing our old love for the world, the 'world' being everything that does not come under the lordship of Christ; there will be a *new hatred for sin*, and we shall not be able to continue in sin if God's nature is truly within us; there should be a *new peace* in our hearts and consciences, a sense of relief and the joy of being forgiven; there will be a *new enemy*, since the whole world is in the power of the evil one; but there will also be a *new power over evil*, for if we really believe that Jesus is the Son of God, we shall overcome the world.

Our doctrinal beliefs will also be important tests as to the reality of our Christian discipleship. John warns his readers about the 'many false prophets' that have gone out into the world. Since the earliest days there have been those who have denied either the divinity or the humanity of Christ. However, if Jesus was not both perfect Man and perfect God he could not have been the one mediator between man and God, and the whole Christian gospel falls to bits. John therefore writes: 'By this you know the Spirit of God; every spirit which confesses that Jesus Christ has come in the flesh is of God, and every spirit which does not confess Jesus is not of God;' Paul also gives, as a spiritual test, the acknowledgment that 'Jesus is Lord!'[22] And writing to the Galatians, to whom he spells out the absolute importance of the doctrine of justification by faith — otherwise 'Christ died to no purpose' — he says that if anyone preaches a gospel contrary to this, 'let him be accursed'.[23]

As Christians, therefore, we have a variety of tests by which we can discern whether or not the Spirit of God is really at work in the life of an individual or in some religious movement. However, such tests require careful spiritual handling, whereas the world is still looking for the one outstanding credential — *love*.

Painful

From what we have seen so far, Christian love will often be painful. The Prior of Taizé once wrote: 'To have opted for love: that choice opens in a man a wound from which he never recovers'.[24] If we open our hearts to others we make ourselves at once vulnerable; it may be that we shall be crucified in the process.'

C.S. Lewis once described the dangers of love:

[22] 1 Corinthians 12:3.   [24] *Struggle and Contemplation*, p. 28.
[23] Galatians 1:6-9.

To love all is to be vulnerable. Love anything, and your heart will certainly be wrung and possibly broken. If you want to make sure of keeping it intact, you must give your heart to no one... Wrap it carefully round with hobbies and little luxuries; avoid all entanglements; lock it safe in a casket or coffin of your selfishness. But in that casket — safe, dark, motionless, airless — it will change. It will not be broken; it will become unbreakable, impenetrable, irredeemable... The only place outside Heaven where you can be perfectly safe from all the dangers of love is — Hell.

Since we so easily hurt one another, due to the selfish impurities in our lives, we shall need constantly to forgive and to be forgiven if this quality of love is to be maintained and manifested within a Christian fellowship. This is surely why Jesus talked so frequently about the absolute necessity of forgiveness — 'seventy times seven'. If the fellowship of a local church is superficial and distant, there will be no great need for forgiveness and no great experience of love. However, as soon as we are drawn closer together by the love of Christ and begin to commit our lives to one another as well as to him, the urgent need for forgiveness will soon become apparent.

The German philosopher Schopenhauer once said that people are rather like a pack of porcupines on a freezing winter night. The sub-zero temperature forces them together for warmth. But as soon as they press very close, they jab and hurt one another. So they separate, only to attempt, in vain, over and over again, to huddle together. Love is painful. For Jesus it meant the crown of thorns and the agony of the nails. It meant becoming sin for us, bearing in his own body the punishment for sin that all of us deserved. But this is the price that must be paid before others will be drawn to God through Jesus Christ: 'I, when I am lifted up from the earth [i.e. crucified], will draw all men to myself.'[25] Today, the church, as the body of Christ on earth, must also know something of this same crucifixion, together with its pain, before men will be drawn by the love of God to himself.

Naturally we shrink back from having to drink this cup

[25] John 12:32.

of suffering. 'I have observed one thing *among true Christians* in
their differences in many countries,' writes Francis Schaeffer.
'What divides and severs true Christian groups and Christians — what leaves a bitterness that can last for 20, 30 or 40
years (or for 50 or 60 years in a son's memory) — is not the
issues in doctrine or belief which caused the differences in the
first place. Invariably it is lack of love — and the bitter things
that are said by true Christians in the midst of differences.
These stick in the mind like glue. And after time passes and
the differences between the Christians or the groups appear
less than they did, there are still those bitter, bitter things we
said in the midst of what we thought was a good and
sufficient objective discussion. It is these things — these
unloving attitudes and words — that cause the stench that
the world can smell in the Church of Jesus Christ among
those who are really true Christians.'[26]

We must learn to say sorry. We must learn to humble
ourselves under God's mighty hand, and before one another.
We must learn that we all need to come, and to come
together, to the cross of Jesus Christ, in order to repent deeply
of the attitudes and resentments that so often divide us and
that destroy the quality of love that the world urgently needs
to see. It is only at the cross that we find peace with God and
peace with one another. It is there that all the barriers of
hostility have once for all been broken down, and we have to
repent for building them up again by our wrong and sinful
attitudes.

It is when we come to the cross humbly experiencing God's
forgiveness, that we are able to go out in love to others, both
to forgive and to be forgiven. And it is when we open our
hearts to the Holy Spirit, and keep them open, that God can
continuously pour in his love. This must be the church's first
and foremost aim; and insofar as that aim is achieved, men
and women from all cultures and creeds will come to believe
in the God of the one true church, the church that is built
with living stones upon the rock of Jesus Christ.

---

[26] *The Mark of the Christian*, I.V.P., p. 21f.